Also by Ramani S. Durvasula, Ph.D.

You Are WHY You Eat:
Change Your Food Attitude, Change Your Life

Should I Stay or Should I Go?:
Surviving a Relationship with a Narcissist

"Don't You Know Who I Am?"

How to Stay Sane in an Era of Narcissism, Entitlement, and Incivility

RAMANI S. DURVASULA, PH.D.

Post Hill
PRESS

A POST HILL PRESS BOOK

"Don't You Know Who I Am?"
How to Stay Sane in an Era of Narcissism, Entitlement, and Incivility
© 2021 by Ramani S. Durvasula, Ph.D.
All Rights Reserved
First Post Hill Press Hardcover Edition: October 2019

ISBN: 978-1-64293-357-4

Interior design and composition, Greg Johnson, Textbook Perfect

Post Hill Press
New York • Nashville
posthillpress.com

Published in the United States of America

To Maya and Shanti—
My muses and my heart

To Padma—
My truth and my guardian angel

To Mom—
My inspiration

CONTENTS

Introduction xi

    What Does "Toxic" Mean? xv
    Why You Should Care xviii
    The Genie Is Out of the Bottle xx
    Who Was Your First Narcissist? xxii
    How This Book Can Help You Navigate Toxic People and Relationships xxiii
    Why I Wrote This Book xxvii

Part One
**THE NARCISSISTIC ROADMAP: NAVIGATING
THE TOXIC POTHOLES** 1

**CHAPTER 1: Narcissists, Jerks, and Tyrants: Is Being
an "Asshole" a Diagnosis?** 3

    The Narcissist: The Insecure Tyrant 5
    The Toxicity Paradox 6
    Are Toxic People Happy? 8
    What Is Narcissism? 9
    Can a Narcissistic Personality Be Treated? 19

CHAPTER 2: The Anatomy of Narcissism and Interpersonal Toxicity 25

    The Five Clusters of Narcissism 26

CHAPTER 3: What Flavor Is Your Narcissist? 86

    The Grandiose "Classic" Narcissist 87
    The Malignant Narcissist 88
    The Covert/Vulnerable Narcissist 89
    The Communal Narcissist 93
    The Benign Narcissist 95
    Entitled People 96
    Which Subtype Is Your Narcissist? (Hint: The Thirty-One Traits Can Help) 100
    Psychopath vs. Sociopath vs. Narcissist: A Toxic Continuum 101
    Narcissistic Patterns in Other Disorders 106

CHAPTER 4: Toxic Universe: The Narcissistic World Order **108**

Why Do We Fall for Toxic People? 110
The In*toxic*ation of Fame 114
The Toxic Playground: Social Media 115
Follow the Money 121
The Measure of Success 124
Toxic Masculinity 128
Education 130
Consumerism and Materialism 132
New Age Narcissism 134
What's Your Brand? 137

CHAPTER 5: How (Not) to Raise a Narcissist **139**

A Framework for Understanding the *Why* of Narcissism 140
The Paradoxical Issue of Indulgence 151
Are We Stuck in a Generation of Parental Overcorrection? 154
The Child as Hyperconsumer 155
A Formula for Raising a Narcissist 157

Part Two
THE TOXIC NARCISSISTS IN YOUR LIFE   **164**

CHAPTER 6: The Narcissist in Your Bed **166**

The Cautionary Tale 168
Transactional Narcissistic Relationships 171
Love Bombing: The Gateway to a Toxic Love Affair 172
Why Do We Stay? 174
We Know Better 175
The Toxic Toll on Your Health 177
The False Hopes That Keep Toxic Relationships Afloat 179
What Is Love? 182
The Mantra of the Narcissistic Relationship 185
Infidelity 187
Coparenting With a Narcissist 188
Domestic Violence 193
Takeaways: Toxic Partners 196

CHAPTER 7: The Narcissist Who Raised You **202**

The Key Characteristics of a Narcissistic Parent 203
The Impacts a Narcissistic Parent Can Have on a Child 206
The Unstable Foundation Laid by a Narcissistic Parent 209
Can—or Should—You Maintain Contact as an Adult? 219
Does Having a Toxic Parent Affect Your Own Parenting? 221
The Other Parent 222

The Aftermath of Having a Narcissistic Parent   224
A Chip Off the Old Block   224
Takeaways: Toxic Parents   225

CHAPTER 8: The Narcissist at Work **229**

The Tyrant's Appeal   231
#Everyonegetshurt by Toxic Leaders   234
Which Came First, the Narcissism or the Leader?   239
Moral Cleansing Theory: Why It Fails With Narcissistic Bosses   241
Your Narcissistic Coworkers   242
Why Did You Take the Job in the First Place?   244
It's Not Fair   246
Takeaways: Toxic Bosses and Colleagues   247

CHAPTER 9: The Other Narcissists in Your Life
(Siblings, Friends, In-Laws) **254**

Siblings   257
Takeaways: Toxic Siblings   260
Friends   261
Takeaways: Toxic Friends   265
In-Laws   266
Takeaways: Toxic In-Laws   268
The Toxic Person You Don't Know   268

CHAPTER 10: The Narcissist You Raised **271**

Letting Go of Your Own Child: The Painful Journey   273
Protecting Your Health and Your Wealth   274
Guilt and Grief   275
Toxic Adolescence—It May Be Temporary   276
Takeaways: Toxic Children   278

Part Three
STAYING SANE IN A NARCISSISTIC WORLD   **282**

CHAPTER 11: A Simple Survival Guide **284**

The Charlie Brown of It All   285
Closing the Gate   286

CHAPTER 12: The Big Picture **310**

Our Habituation to Narcissism   311
The Well-Being Vortex   313
The Era of Incivility   316
Global Narcissism   323

CHAPTER 13: The Aftermath 326

"Narcissists' Rights"   327
The Danger Is Real   329
Can We Prevent It?   331
That's Just How They Are   333
"The Line"   334
Close the Floodgates   336
Pink Flags   337
Family Patterns   338
You Are Enough   339
Don't Expect Justice   340
The Crystal Ball   343

CHAPTER 14: The Modern Happily Ever After 346

Open the Gate for Good People   347
Celebrate Your Scars   348
A Global Neighborhood of Goodness and Love   349
Transitioning from Survival to Growth   349
New Beginnings   351

Bibliography   353
Acknowledgments   362
About the Author   367

There may be more beautiful times,
but this one is ours.

—SARTRE

INTRODUCTION

When someone shows you who they are, believe them the first time.

—MAYA ANGELOU

In July of 2017, a twenty-three-year-old man flying in a first-class seat from Seattle to Beijing rushed to an emergency exit door forty-five minutes into the flight. He then attempted to open the door while the flight was in midair and was overpowered by the flight attendants. When they tried to stop him, he became combative, and, when the flight attendants tried to subdue him, he screamed at them, "*Do you know who I am...?*" (Apparently no one did—it turns out the young man had scored his seat through a family member who was employed by the airline.)

In July of 2014, Conrad Hilton III was seated in the first-class section of a flight to London. His antics began immediately after boarding and included berating his fellow passengers and calling them "peasants," the attempted assault of a flight attendant, and a litany of obscenities on the ten-hour flight. He claimed that this had happened to him before, and his father would tidily bail him out. He was quoted as saying, "I could get you all fired in five minutes. I know your boss! My father will pay this out; he has done it before. Dad paid three hundred thousand dollars last time." He was freed on a $100,000 bond and agreed to a plea deal that had him plead guilty to misdemeanor assault so that federal charges would be dropped against him.

The allegations regarding entitled tantrums span far and wide. In 2009, it was Miley Cyrus at a burger stand: "Are you *serious*? You don't recognize me? I'm Miley Cyrus." Also in 2009, Dina Lohan (mother of actress Lindsay Lohan) was quoted as saying at a nightclub, "Do you know who I am? You're making a huge mistake…huge." (Double points for quoting *Pretty Woman.*) In 2006, it was David Hasselhoff slurring at Wimbledon, "All I want is a drink. Do you know who I am?" In 2012, Rihanna, dancing on and subsequently shattering a nightclub table, shouted, "Don't you know who I am?" while being carried out of the club. In 2014, Shia LaBeouf, being disruptive during intermission at a Broadway performance of *Cabaret,* yelled, "Don't you know who the *fuck* I am?" In 2014, Alec Baldwin, cited for riding his bicycle the wrong way in Union Square in New York City, said, "Fuck this…this is horseshit. Don't you know who I am?" In 2007, when her credit card was declined at Banana Republic, Faye Dunaway roared, "Don't you know who I am? I'm Faye Dunaway!" In 2013, in a Korean spa, where her tattoos received disapproval from the spa staff, Margaret Cho spat angrily, "Do you know who I am? I am Margaret Cho."

It's not just our beloved celebrities engaging in this modern-day mantra—it's first-class flyers like the unknown chap flying from Seattle to Beijing. It's restaurant guests in eateries, ranging from Michelin-starred bistros all the way down to your local hot dog stand. It's the elite travelers who toss "Don't you know who I am?" (DYKWIA) tantrums when they are not upgraded (*Don't you know who I am? I am a platinum/diamond/ global elite flyer*). For some reason, travel tends to magnify this dynamic, and it's a fascinating paradox. These people do not want to be subject to the rules, but they want the rules to be obsessively applied to others. (For example, a TripAdvisor review by an angry traveler stated that too many people were being allowed into the premium airport lounge, and he was furious that his family—who had not paid the fee to enter—did not have the rules bent for them.)

It doesn't just happen in the air. It can be the man in the small town who has to wait in a long line at a local business (*Don't you know who I am? I have the biggest plumbing business in town!*) or the woman in church who takes umbrage at not getting the best seat in the house during a holiday service (*Don't you know who I am? I have been coming to this church and making donations for years*). I saw it play out at a local Trader Joe's parking lot in my town recently. An elderly man driving a souped-up Mustang screamed at an elderly woman pushing a dog in a stroller, *"Don't you know who I am? I could buy and sell you and your stupid dog!"* He then noisily pulled into a disabled parking spot without the proper placard.

"Don't you know who I am?" is the buzz phrase of our time—and, clearly, the mantra of the entitled and narcissistic. The Urban Dictionary has given a name to this phenomenon, often referred to in internet circles as DYKWIA. The Urban Dictionary does not offer definitions, per se, but instead gives a list of synonyms, including "pompous," "self-important," "stuffed shirt," "douchebag," and "prick." We can use this as a jumping-off point to set a tone, because this is often where many of us just chuckle to ourselves and view this as "someone else's problem." But we can learn from the DYKWIAers in our world.

The phrase itself reflects an utter lack of self-awareness and a grandiose entitlement. Why would or should anyone know who anyone is, unless the person is in regular contact with the DYKWIAer? For example, I could use the phrase with my children if I picked them up at school and they looked in the car window and said, "Who are you?" I might then reply, "Don't you know who I am? I am your mother." The presumption of the DYKWIAers is that they are so special that they should be familiar to others, or that their status entitles them to special privileges, even if that means others go without. That status can be conferred by celebrity, wealth, royalty, or, most often, grandiose delusion. It is also important to remember that status is relative. You can be the most important man or woman in your small town or neighborhood or workplace but, most likely, no one outside of that sphere has any sense of who you are. Celebrity and status can be local or global (or solely in someone's own head).

In some cases, the primary reason for the "Don't you know who I am?" conduct is being intoxicated and impaired—this can include prescription and nonprescription drugs as well as alcohol. Drugs and alcohol diminish self-awareness, impair judgment, result in disinhibited and, at times, combative behavior, and can fuel paranoia, anger, hostility, and confusion. Thus, the lethal combination of being in an intoxicated state and having to interact with others who will maintain normal social or legal expectations (for example, waiting in line, driving sober, speaking at a normal volume without issuing numerous expletives, paying a bill) can result in a rapid ramp-up of bad behavior, culminating in an entitled tantrum once there is any form of behavioral accountability.

Other people who utter this phrase may actually be mentally ill and experiencing breaks in reality (for example, they may be psychotic or delusional). They actually believe they are special, not due to ostensible societal markers of status, such as celebrity, community status, or wealth, but rather because they maintain delusional beliefs that perhaps they have been chosen by some holy leader or anointed by the third moon of Saturn. This type of delusional entitled behavior may also be embedded within a manic episode as observed in bipolar disorder and, with the treatment of mania or other mental illness, these kinds of entitled diatribes should dissipate. Other elements of the person's appearance and behavior at the time of an entitled rant will often be a giveaway that he or she may fall under the rubric of mental illness (for example, inappropriate or disheveled clothing, odd appearance, other strange utterances that do not make sense, unusual physical gestures). Such individuals require treatment and follow-up, and the entitled behavior is part of a larger context of mental illness.

The focus of this book will be the toxic, narcissistic, difficult, entitled DYKWIAer. These are our psychological problem children. These folks believe their own grandiose hype. In the pages to follow, we will break down the phenomena of narcissism and entitlement, which represent a new normal in America and increasingly around the world. These people truly believe they are special and that the rules do not apply to them, and often hold strong to the childlike conviction that results in genuine surprise and then anger and rage when they are not given the special treatment to which they feel they are *entitled*.

Pay attention to the DYKWIAers in your environment. They may not always utter the full phrase, but it will come out in other ways. They will sigh noisily, roll their eyes, express the fact that they feel put-upon by the world, by delays, and by what they perceive to be demands on their time and on themselves. You will look at them quizzically or perhaps at others in the room with the same silent question, "Are they really behaving like this?" Wisely, we often do not call them out, because there is no point. It may simply invite unhealthy conflict into your life and into your day that is not worth the bother. "Don't you know who I am?" is the choir of narcissism that is sounding out from boardrooms and courtrooms and classrooms and any number of other rooms all over the world.

Are Americans more narcissistic? A 2015 research study by Joshua Miller and Jessica Maples, researchers at the University of Georgia, and their colleagues from universities around the world, suggests that Americans themselves certainly think so. Research reveals that Americans rate

American citizens as a whole as being more narcissistic than their close friends and family, and that Americans view Americans as a group as being more disagreeable and antisocial. In addition, respondents from around the world rated Americans as more narcissistic and antagonistic than their own countrymen and women. Whether this is the American valuation of individualism, our adherence to capitalism, our cultural ethos regarding the pioneer spirit and Calvinist work ethic, our adoration of celebrity, and our penchant for competition, it appears narcissism may be as American as apple pie.

At the time the contracts for this book were signed, a series of scandals blew up in Hollywood and then nationally. It started with allegations against Harvey Weinstein, but before long the list grew to include media and entertainment stalwarts including Matt Lauer, Bill O'Reilly, Kevin Spacey, Mario Batali, and numerous businessmen, politicians, celebrity chefs, and tech gurus. On December 29, 2017, a *Los Angeles Times* headline read, A POWERFUL PERSON HAS BEEN ACCUSED OF MISCONDUCT AT A RATE OF NEARLY ONCE EVERY 20 HOURS SINCE WEINSTEIN. In this case, people knew *precisely* who they were. Their bad behavior was evidenced by allegations of sexual abuse, assault, harassment, and incivility, and, in most cases, their behavior was also characterized by tremendous rage, angry outbursts, entitlement, bullying, control, vindictiveness, and ruling through fear and intimidation—and all of it occurred under a banner of impunity. Few people had the courage to blow the whistle, due to realistic fears of retribution. The institutions that these men worked for also protected them and were more willing to sacrifice the women or other lower-rung employees who brought forth the accusations, than to kill their golden geese. Entitlement ruled the roost, and, until the potential fall and public humiliation of the mighty, as well as movements like #metoo, most of these guys ruled with invulnerability, and many, if not most, still do.

What Does "Toxic" Mean?

In 2018, Oxford Dictionaries chose "toxic" to be their word of the year. And that's not because the world got interested in chemicals. People looked up "toxic masculinity," "toxic relationships," "toxic people," and "toxic culture." Oxford provides multiple definitions of "toxic," with definition 1.2 being "Very bad, unpleasant, or harmful." That's a bit broad for our purposes. We also know that "toxic" can mean "poisonous," and, by extension, something that causes death or illness.

A struggle in this book and in this work and conversation is terminology—finding that right word that captures that triangle of narcissism, entitlement, and toxicity. They are not distinct entities; there is a lot of overlap, but there is also some independence. To term someone a "toxic person" or label a relationship as a "toxic relationship" or "toxic situation" or to describe a person's actions as "toxic behavior" generally implies that he, she, or it is not good for us. These personality styles are typically antagonistic and high conflict—characterized by criticism, pettiness, contempt, incivility, argumentativeness, or all of the above. Whether that is because the individual lacks empathy or is entitled, superficial, full of rage, passive-aggressive, or contemptuous, the concept of toxicity is subjective, but most people understand it when they experience it. There are some universals (lack of empathy rarely feels good), but one person's "toxic" boss is, at times, another's "hard-driving" mentor.

Toxic people are not necessarily uniformly toxic, which also makes it complicated. There are some people who are equal-opportunity tyrants— they treat everyone badly—but most are too smart for that. They have some folks they target and others whom they keep close at hand, because, if everyone thinks they are awful, it can make it difficult to sidle up to the bar. They may treat their employees horribly, and yet their families view them as loyal father figures or devoted mothers (or vice versa). They may cheat on their spouses, and yet have numerous fans who idolize them. They may sexually harass and assault women, and yet people are lined up to work with them because they think they will fast-track their own careers. They may be absolutely charming to their wealthy neighbors, private-club friends, or the person in the yacht next to them but humiliate employees, household staff, and anyone they perceive as in their service. It may be the mother who cheers on her kids who are "making the family look good" but who scapegoats or dismisses her children who may not shine on a public stage or who aren't "well put-together."

The difficulty raised by this is that different people may have very different experiences of a toxic person. One of the most galling things I hear when the story of the abuse perpetrated by a particular narcissist is shared is, "He was always nice to me, so I really don't get it." The inconsistency of narcissists can result in survivors of these situations hearing invalidating statements like this, which can only add to the hurt. Narcissists view people as conveniences, opportunities, and tools—and they treat them accordingly. When you are useful to a narcissist, he or she will leave you feeling as though the sun shines only on you. When they no longer need you, that sun will quickly move behind a cloud. It's amazing how so many people are putty in the narcissist's hands.

From that subjective perspective, a toxic person, toxic relationship, or toxic situation is one that makes the other person sick or uncomfortable. That said, these patterns can be slow. Like asbestos or some other toxin in the environment, a toxic person or situation can make you sick over time—it might not happen overnight. While the difficult, narcissistic, and entitled patterns we are about to explore often result in toxic relationships, it is not presumptive, and these terms will be used variously throughout the book. Not all entitled people are narcissistic, but nearly all narcissistic people are entitled—and we will break that down as well.

Interestingly, I have been the target of criticism by folks within the discipline of mental health for being "unkind" to people by using the term "toxic" to describe them. In being circumspect, I can understand their criticism. It's dismissive to label a person in such a scornful and stigmatizing manner. I struggled with finding a word for people who, through their words, behaviors, conduct, attitude, and emotional expression, consistently devalue, dehumanize, invalidate, and abuse other people. However, I acknowledge that many roads lead to the "reasons" why people are antagonistic, narcissistic, difficult, and abusive and that they have backstories too. But the bottom line is that, when someone abuses you, it hurts, and, over time, it takes a permanent toll. No, "toxic" is not a nice word. But these are not nice patterns. Nobody should be relegated to the status of a human punching bag. Nobody.

Toxic behavior tends to be associated with traits congruent with narcissistic, antagonistic, psychopathic, dysregulated, and passive-aggressive personality styles. These are personality styles that often cause more harm to the people around them than any other personality or mental health/illness patterns we observe. The people with these personality patterns may not be experiencing discomfort, but the people around them likely are. This is not a "moral" judgment. Nor is this an indictment of people who engage in these patterns; this is an indictment *of these patterns*. They are invalidating, they are deceptive, and they are damaging.

Why You Should Care

So, who cares? Ruthless leaders have always been a part of the story. Entitled people, whether on airplanes or in restaurants or in schools or churches or just walking down the street, have always been an issue. Celebrity worship and entitled behavior have been around since there were celebrities and tycoons. Is this not simply an old story?

Yes and no. These patterns of entitlement, narcissism, public tantrums, and toxic behavior are on the increase. The buzzword of the past few years has been "narcissism," a topic I started to tackle in my book *Should I Stay or Should I Go? Surviving a Relationship with a Narcissist*. The almighty N-word has been used to describe the president of the United States as well as more than a few other world leaders, CEOs, senators, celebrities, politicians, and institutional leaders, athletes, oligarchs, fallen studio heads, actors, and a whole host of other folks.

But who really cares about the toxicity and narcissism of people who may be in our headlines but don't really have much to do with us personally? Does their behavior really have an effect on our day-to-day lives? Does it matter to me as an individual if the occupant of the White House sends an angry tweet? Should I react if a stand-up comedian, sitcom star, or B-list musician posts a racial slur? Does it really affect my health if a studio head sexually abuses his employees and I do not know those people? What do the grandiose and angry ramblings of a company head on the other side of the country really have to do with me? If I'm not in a relationship with the person, who really cares?

All of us should.

It appears that the fish does stink from the head down. This proliferation of human toxicity and narcissism in political and corporate leaders, celebrities, and other buzzworthy folks is a bellwether for the rest of society. The bad behavior is being observed everywhere, on airplanes and in hotels, in restaurants and fast-food joints, on freeways and bicycle paths, at your kid's soccer game, and in college classrooms. You are witnessing it, as are your children, and so is everyone else around you. Entitlement, narcissism, incivility, and toxic and abusive human behavior and interactions are becoming the new normal. We devalue kindness, especially in men, and we characterize compassion and vulnerability as weakness. Having empathy in the current epoch becomes a setup to be manipulated or exploited. We admire the "strong," and, increasingly the "strong" are those who are brash, controversial, unrepentant, and anything but kind, respectful, or circumspect. The bad behavior from the folks at the top of the food chain or those who are the most influential in our society poisons the well for everyone. The tone gets set. People are propelled by a belief that they are entitled to special treatment, that the rules do not apply to them, and that can get messy rather quickly. A devil-may-care attitude has overtaken the world. Many wealthy or powerful people say, "I'm going to say what I want to say, and I don't care who I hurt," and they use money to clean up their messes. *We are living in a time of trickle-down narcissism, incivility, and toxicity.* The rest of us are impacted by this, whether by simply witnessing it, its impact on our own behavior, or how we are hurt by others. People do what they see: The more we see, the more likely we all are to be sucked into this toxic tornado.

Then there is the accelerant for the modern toxic and narcissistic world: social media. It's here to stay, and it is a key means of communication, of learning about the world, and, increasingly, a tool for constructing identity. A world of people broadcasting their every moment via Facebook Live or Instagram or as an influencer—all of this provides fertile ground for the "Don't you know who I am?" of it all, and it appears to be underscoring a deeper insecurity that is cutting across the culture and the individuals who occupy it.

This book will take you on an ugly tour of the underbelly of this new world of toxic, difficult, and antagonistic behavior and relationships that stem from entitlement and narcissism. For the sake of your health, you need to understand this, because it *is* affecting you. If you are reading this book, then you likely have at least one toxic, narcissistic, entitled, difficult person in your life, be it a spouse or partner, parent, coworker, boss, sibling, friend, or neighbor. Or you are witnessing this kind of behavior on a regular basis—being yelled at by disgruntled customers, witnessing road-rage moments during your commute, seeing angry confrontations on the subway, overhearing temper tantrums at a restaurant, or simply reading the news or looking at your social media feed. Or you have witnessed enough "Don't you know who I am?" tantrums and want to figure this out and what it means for you.

I didn't think I would come back to this topic; it was difficult enough to write about narcissism and intimate relationships in my prior book.

The thought of expanding this to help us understand what the world has become very quickly—a world of DYKWIAers, of entitlement, of narcissism, of interpersonal toxicity, of incivility—was a bit overwhelming (and depressing). However, I was seeing a sadness in the world, in my therapy practice, in my students, in my colleagues, in my friends, and in my loved ones. A heaviness in the air. People were retreating, becoming anxious, apathetic, socially withdrawn, physically ill, and, most troubling, they were feeling helpless and increasingly hopeless. My clients who bring in a range of different issues and stories were simultaneously struggling with a similar ennui due to insecurity, discomfort, and uncertainty. In addition, I live in Los Angeles, probably one of the best-preserved natural habitats for studying narcissism and entitlement. If you want to study tortoises, go to the Galapagos; if you want to study penguins, move to Antarctica. But if you want to study toxic people and narcissism, Los Angeles may be ground zero. It's a company town, and the company is show business—superficial, celebrity soaked, validation seeking, covetous, manipulative, and grandiose. Millions of people are saying, "Look at me. No, look at me." (I have lived in Los Angeles for more than twenty-five years and have a complicated fondness for the city, but I could not have become a narcissism researcher or critic had I lived anywhere else; everyone here either manifests it or has been painfully affected by it.) This book is, at times, a polemic, a survival manual, a guidebook, a recipe book, a taxonomy, a roadmap, and a manifesto of hope. Not the hope that the narcissism will abate or that the narcissists will improve. But hope that individuals can start to recognize the goodness in themselves and engage in the fine art of self-preservation. *It is never too late to take back your life from the scourges of individual and societal narcissism.*

The Genie Is Out of the Bottle

In 1979, Christopher Lasch, a writer, a historian and an academic, wrote one of the most prescient books on narcissism: *The Culture of Narcissism: American Life in an Age of Diminishing Expectations,* making him a sort of narcissism Nostradamus. In the late 1970s, Lasch was already pointing out that the US was veering into a direction of more pathological narcissism. He pointed fingers at the burgeoning "self-growth and self-enhancement movements" and that these were supplanting the importance of building communities and collective social structures and causing the loss of conviction in both our leaders and in people as individuals. Lasch also made the interesting observation that narcissism, as a pathological pattern per se, may not be on the rise, but rather psychiatrists and psychologists may be noticing it more quickly. He was already turning a lens on the societal shifts toward "all-or-nothing success" and work ethics that drew people away from community and family and only enhanced a pathological focus on the self. He pulled no punches and went after the holy grails, including education (which he also maintained had become a means of self-enhancement and a tool for maintaining increasingly authoritarian structures), and even reflected on what he termed the "commodification" of education—an issue that plagues us even more today. He foresaw the industry of external self-enhancement and the obsolescence of old age—a battle we fight via Botox and cosmetic surgery, as we fight our body's natural process, try to deny the years that pass, and view aging as a deep inconvenience, with the grandiosity of narcissism unable to reconcile the body and mind's natural tendency to give out over time.

Most notable about Lasch's observations and his thesis is that he was already warning, in very clear terms, about a dangerous genie floating out of the bottle. But, at that point, it was too late. The genie was out—the economy, both globally and domestically, took a permanent turn in the 1980s. The Self became vaunted above all else, and insecurity became fostered by materialism, consumerism, political structures, and governments. Lasch courageously opined that all structures—families, schools, governments, corporations—were part of this inside job of narcissism's being supported from the outside in and the inside out. In some of the wisest words written about narcissism, he states: "Narcissism appears realistically to represent the best way of coping with the tensions and anxieties of modern life, and the prevailing social conditions therefore tend to bring out narcissist traits that are present, in varying degrees, in everyone. These conditions have also transformed the family, which in turn shapes the underlying structure of personality. A society that fears it has no future, is not likely to give much attention to the needs of the next generation...."

We knew this was coming, and we allowed it to happen. Lasch's thesis is spot-on and even more relevant forty years later. But we didn't listen, learn, or pay attention, and here we are. The genie *is* out of the bottle, and I don't believe we can put it back. How do we save ourselves, our children, our families, and our communities?

Who Was Your First Narcissist?

Everyone remembers their first narcissist. Who was yours? If it was your parent, then you have had one since the beginning. Or maybe you recollect a family member's invalidating behavior during your childhood or the taunts of a mean-spirited girl from high school. Maybe it was even your first real boyfriend or girlfriend.

Because children cannot make sense of this phenomenon, they will not only not label it as narcissistic or toxic, but also will take responsibility for it—blaming themselves for not being a good-enough child, because, if they were, then maybe their mother or father would be happy. Even when a first major narcissistic encounter does not occur until adulthood, many people still do not know what they are dealing with. I have received countless emails and worked with numerous clients who endured invalidating, cruel, lying, cheating, selfish, cold, calculating, vindictive, distant, entitled partners for decades without understanding what was happening.

But, even if you look back and reflect on it in hindsight, you will always remember your first narcissist. That relationship impacted you in significant ways, and it may still be affecting you in ways that you may not be aware. That first (or second, or third) relationship with a narcissist may still affect your decisions, your sense of self-worth, and your aspirations—until you figure it out, and then you can slowly put the brakes on this soul-sapping situation. From a standpoint of terminology, the term "narcissistic relationship" will be used interchangeably with, and to imply, a relationship with a narcissist. While it is not the relationship per se that is narcissistic, the suffocating dynamics of a relationship with a narcissist can characterize the entire relationship. As such, the term narcissistic relationship will serve as a sort of shorthand for any kind of relationship with a narcissistic individual or entity.

The fact is you have one (otherwise you would not be reading this book). Perhaps the only ones who do not have any narcissists or other toxic people in their lives are the narcissists themselves (but I am not betting on that, as narcissists tend to be pack animals and attract other narcissists into their midst).

How This Book Can Help You Navigate Toxic People and Relationships

This book will lay out the who, what, and why of our narcissistic and entitled world, spell out the dynamics of narcissism, and clearly illustrate how narcissism is hurting your health and sense of well-being. You will be better able to identify and manage the toxic, entitled, and narcissistic people in your life, and we will explore if (and, if so, why) these patterns are on the rise.

In Part I, we'll travel the narcissistic roadmap, uncovering what exactly narcissism really is and the five sets of patterns underlying narcissism. We'll examine the primary patterns or behaviors within these traits, such as lack of empathy, lying, envy, insecurity, anger, grandiosity, paranoia, and much more. We'll also look at the different "flavors" of narcissists and why it can be so tough to walk away from them. (Hint: Narcissists are charming, controlling, and manipulative, and, even once you identify them, it can be difficult to extricate yourself from them.) I'll explain the new narcissistic world order and why social media exacerbates it. I'll also share the three Cs of narcissism and why we fall for toxic people. We'll consider the ways in which our economy, consumerism, and how we measure success all impact the rise of narcissism. Finally, this book will also serve as a recipe book for how to create a narcissist (or hopefully avoid doing it), with an overview of the theories on the origins of narcissism.

In Part II, we'll take a look at the toxic, entitled, and difficult people in your life, whether that's your significant other, parent or parents, sibling, boss or coworker, friend, in-laws, or even your own child. When I wrote *Should I Stay or Should I Go? Surviving a Relationship with a Narcissist,* I focused specifically on the intimate relationship: husband, wife, fiancé, fiancée, boyfriend, girlfriend. This was compelled by the fact that I wrote the book in response to what I had observed in my clinical practice and the need for a "manual" of sorts to help people in these relationships, because it was causing so much grief for them. As I worked and talked with people about that book, one of the main issues I heard was, "This is all very interesting, but the narcissist in my life is [fill in the blank]." Often, it was a parent, sister, boss, daughter, or son-in-law. I encountered this time and again with my own clients, students, and people who attended lectures, and I realized that narcissism, entitlement, and just generally toxic personhood can result in very different repercussions, depending on the nature of the relationship. The impact of a toxic mother is quite different than the impact of a toxic best friend. Both hurt, but both also affect us in different ways—and require different solutions.

It made sense. It can be difficult to "divorce" a parent. Enduring a boss or a toxic supervisor may be necessary to keep a roof over your head. So, while some of the core principles remain the same—the lack of empathy, entitlement, validation seeking, superficiality, arrogance, and coldness, as well as the fact that these patterns are very resistant to change and are all pretty consistent—the impacts of each type of person on your life may be quite different. In addition, your feelings about how you are treated by a toxic or narcissistic person may also be different. A narcissistic parent may bring forth different feelings than a narcissistic boss, a toxic partner, or a narcissistic child.

Interestingly, *most people who have one narcissist or toxic person in their lives have multiple narcissists in their lives.* There are several possible reasons for this, but, most likely, it is a riff on a phenomenon called "habituation." In the simplest example of habituation, if we get accustomed to something in our environment—a reward, or even something more noxious, such as noise—over time, we basically adjust to it, and it doesn't capture our attention, nor do we question it. Human beings can be incredibly adaptive and adjust to varying climates and living conditions. In the same way, we can adjust to toxic relationships. However, just as a very cold or very hot room may make us uncomfortable, so too does a toxic relationship. As a result, once we get used to a person who is deeply entitled, toxic, or narcissistic, it can become a new normal. In this way, once we adjust to one narcissist, it becomes quite simple to adjust to numerous narcissists. Sadly, we humans are also able to habituate to unhealthy circumstances, and just because we adjust doesn't mean it becomes healthy. We simply adjust to something unhealthy.

People with narcissistic parents tend to gravitate toward other relationships with narcissists. Work on "co-narcissism" suggests that people who are raised with narcissistic parents become wired to be "pleasers," to take on a role of providing validation to the people around them to the point of exhaustion. Without even thinking about it, people who were raised by one or more narcissists often gravitate toward narcissistic partners, friends, and work situations, because it is what they know. Overall, this suggests that a person with a narcissistic parent, who struggles lifelong with the feeling of being "not good enough," becomes easy prey for other narcissists. In addition, people with narcissistic parents become skilled at being the delivery people of narcissistic supply (which is the validation, praise, and fluffing that narcissists chronically require from everyone in their world); after a childhood of trying to soothe, please, impress, and compliment a difficult parent, they become masterful as adults at doing that for other people too. They are often drawn to people who pull for appeasing and "handling" (grandiose bosses; charming, demanding, and charismatic partners; validation-seeking friends; entitled people), often writing off people who are not like this as "boring," because the primitive drive to be with and please these types of people is so intense. Narcissism simply becomes your normal.

Another possible reason is that you actually think you deserve this treatment. Whether it is secondary to childhood messages, early abuse, trauma, societal messages, bullying, or other unnamed factors, you may have received the message that you are *not enough,* you do not deserve to be treated better than this, and, in some ways, being treated without empathy, coldly, and dismissively feels "right," or you do believe that you truly do not deserve better. *Everyone* deserves respect, empathy, dignity, kindness, and compassion. *Everyone.* But, if you do not know that, or believe that, it is easy to accept that the narcissistic abuse and patterns are what you deserve. It's a shame that we can't give noise-canceling headphones to everyone who has to spend time with a narcissist to silence their invalidating voice. Until we invent those, we need to do the silencing for ourselves.

Ultimately, relationships with narcissists are kept in place by two mechanisms: *hope* and *fear*. Hope that it will someday get better and that the second chances will pay off. Hope that things will change. Hope that the narcissist will finally get it. Hope that he or she will finally apologize, and you can forgive this person, and everything will be fine. And then there is fear. Fear that you will always be alone. Fear that you will never be loved. Fear that you are wrong, and the next person will get the nice version of the narcissist. Fear that you are being too judgmental. Fear that you actually do deserve the abuse. Fear that this is as good as it gets, so asking for more is hubris at best.

Overall, narcissism is becoming more common. As such, it can be more difficult to avoid, simply because more narcissists are around. Multiple roads get people to their narcissistic and toxic relationships and situations. And these relationships are different and have to be handled differently. There have been many good books written about each of these kinds of relationships individually and in far greater detail. Part II of the book is meant to serve as a compendium, and a brief survival guide to what each of these relationships does to you and how to handle them individually, while also understanding the larger context in which they are happening. Each chapter will have its own set of takeaways to help you manage the challenges of that particular narcissistic relationship.

In Part III, we will get down to the brass tacks of how to stay sane in a narcissistic world and survive it—to reflect on how these toxic narcissistic relationships and toxic situations are affecting you. I hope to teach you how to avoid narcissists when you can and recognize them early when you can't. Most important, this book is a primer for how to stay sane in an interpersonally toxic and narcissistic world. It will offer a step-by-step guide on how to navigate this terrain. There are ways to overcome this, retain your sanity, preserve your sense of humanity, and even thrive. But first, that means understanding the new world order. None of us is immune to these trends.

The world is a deeply narcissistic, entitled, and unkind place. Read the news. Scroll through social media. Watch reality TV. Even if you are so blessed that every single person in your life is a sweetheart and you manage to dodge the narcissism bullet in your family, workplace, and friendships, you are still surrounded by it. It goes beyond the public narcissistic figures that populate our world, it goes beyond social media and chronically pinging and ringing devices, and it goes beyond the "Don't you know who I am"-ing that defines the modern age. I have yet to meet a person who is immune to it (other than the people who are narcissistic).

Think of it this way: To the degree that narcissism, entitlement, psychopathy, and all the rest of it contribute to a toxic river, is that something you want to be swimming in? If you knew a swimming pool was full of poisonous water, you would avoid it. How do you navigate a toxic world? How do you manage narcissism, and all the rest of it, when it is lurking around every corner?

Part One

THE NARCISSISTIC ROADMAP: NAVIGATING THE TOXIC POTHOLES

*You have power over your mind—not outside events.
Realize this, and you will find strength.*

—MARCUS AURELIUS

Chapter 1

Narcissists, Jerks, and Tyrants:
Is Being an "Asshole" a Diagnosis?

As individuals and as a nation, we now suffer from social narcissism.
We have now fallen in love with our own image, with images of
our making, which turn out to be images of ourselves.

—DANIEL J. BOORSTIN

An article in *Vanity Fair* by Adam Ciralsky on January 17, 2018 (*"Harvey's Concern Was Who Did Him In:" Inside Harvey Weinstein's Frantic Final Days*) indicated that, when Harvey Weinstein finally got called out on years of sexual abuse, harassment, and the assault of women in Hollywood, he was less concerned about the harm he caused his victims and the heinous nature of his conduct than about who turned him in. When Bernie Madoff bilked investors of $50 billion and the wagons finally began to circle, he called his family and came clean but asked for a few days to ensure he got his affairs in order before he turned himself in—with no mention of the damage his actions had wrought on investors, charitable organizations, and older adults who lost everything.

The millennials are taking a lot of flak for being the "entitled generation." It's tempting to call out young people for behaving more selfishly than we did, and the millennials will likely do it to their children too. In fact, the so-called entitled millennials are the product of the baby boomers, who were members of the generation once labeled the "Me Generation." Joel Stein, in *Time* magazine (May 2013), opines that the seed of entitlement observed in the millennials was planted back in the 1970s before the millennials were even a spark in someone's glazed eyes. The belief is that the entitlement epidemic may be fueled by a focus on instilling self-esteem—in essence, telling someone that he or she is great and special but not linking that to meaningful behaviors. It set up a precedent whereby six-year-olds were told they were superheroes and, at sixteen, and twenty-six, and thirty-six, they are still walking around the world believing that to be true and wondering why the world is not acknowledging their superhero greatness. The enhancement of self-esteem has set up a world in which very few people are able to endure frustration or disappointment ("If I am so special, why isn't everything going my way?"). Life is not delivering, and members of multiple genera-tions—baby boomers, Gen Xers, Gen Yers, millennials, Gen Zers, and those of other generations yet to come—are lost in their anguish over unmet expectations. Entitlement, at this point in history, is not solely the province of millennials or Gen Xers or baby boomers; all generations are equally complicit and may simply be manifesting it in different ways. We can't just throw the millennials under the bus—entitlement knows no generational restrictions.

As noted before, a toxic, high-conflict, difficult person is simply one who makes us psychologically sick through his or her behavior. This can be quite obvious (being in the presence of a cruel, insulting, tantrum-throwing bully) or subtler (a person who covertly insults you but is sometimes helpful or is passive-aggressive but sometimes praises you). Our tendency to forgive and give people second chances is often what keeps these toxic patterns in place. Toxic people and their behaviors leave us doubting ourselves and questioning ourselves, and they are given a lifetime of second chances, because many people lack the confidence to call them out or walk away from them. In addition, because they are often successful or wealthy, they have more power and privilege, and call-ing them out can be even riskier or more difficult. Now that the cultural conditions are a perfect breeding ground for toxic behaviors, this is not likely to go away anytime soon.

The kingpin of the toxic-people world is the narcissist. So let's start there.

The Narcissist: The Insecure Tyrant

Narcissism is a pattern characterized by entitlement, grandiosity, lack of empathy, validation seeking, superficiality, interpersonal antagonism, insecurity, hypersensitivity, contempt, arrogance, and poor emotional regulation (especially rage). Narcissism is an interpersonally toxic pattern; if it is a person's predominant way of relating with the world, then it is not healthy for the people around the narcissistic person (it is also not healthy for the narcissist, but narcissists typically lack enough insight to recognize it).

In 2019, you cannot talk about narcissism without conjuring the Trump presidency. His election and leadership have raised lots of hackles and red flags about the concept of narcissism. His supporters and diagnostic purists get hot under the collar when mental health professionals attempt to apply diagnostic terms to him without evaluating him (this falls under the rubric of something called the "Goldwater Rule," which stipulates that a psychiatrist who has not seen a patient cannot offer a diagnostic impression). However, calling someone a narcissist is not a clinical diagnosis; it is descriptive and no different than identifying someone as friendly, or kind, or insensitive, or risk taking, or rude, or neurotic, or agreeable. However, the word carries lots of surplus meaning, and most of us believe it has a negative connotation—no one likes to be called a narcissist. And, frankly, most people don't really understand what it means. It underlies a pattern that can be termed "toxic," a word that allows us to take in more territory and bring in characteristics that do not fall under traditional diagnostic, theoretical, and clinical terminology. I don't disagree with people who state that we have no place diagnosing people we have not met. I am a bigger fan of reflecting on their actual behaviors, and if they leave you feeling bad or sick or invalidated, or just generally uncomfortable, then we can use the label of "difficult" or "toxic" (whether or not they are narcissistic). Agreeing or disagreeing with Trump's politics is beside the point. His pattern of behavior, which is often grandstanding, antagonistic, bombastic, accusatory, dismissive, divisive, dehumanizing, deceitful, and, ultimately, reflects his desperate need for validation, is all congruent with a pattern of narcissism. He isn't the first narcissistic president, and he won't be the last, but his is a more bombastic narcissism, which is why we are noticing it and why it is shaping the behavior of our culture at large.

What Do They Look Like?

Alas, there are no easily identifiable markings that would allow us to identify narcissists—though that would certainly make life easier. They don't have horns or fangs or wear a dark cloak. They can be any gender, any race, any age, any sexual orientation, any height, any weight, any nationality, any religion. Where it gets interesting is that we sometimes get tricked by making faulty assumptions. One incorrect assumption that gets all of us in trouble is to assume that someone who is "fancy" or sophisticated or highly educated or from a prominent family or holds an important position or belongs to an exclusive and elite organization or club couldn't be capable of being a toxic, narcissistic, psychopathic, or difficult person (that is, to assume that toxic people are somehow low-brow or lacking a certain sophistication, patina, or panache). Quite the contrary—the privilege that accompanies the fancier folks amongst us fosters toxic behavior, and their legitimacy may mean that people have their narcissism radar down when they are with them. I am astonished at how often writers, journalists, pundits, and media types will gasp and be shocked at the hyper-unethical, illegal, or grossly uncivil behavior of a member of the privileged elite. It's actually laughable, because having a degree from an Ivy League school or being a debutante does not imply virtue, so you need to be at the ready whether you are dealing with a rich man, poor man, beggar man, or thief. A person with five cents in the bank can be narcissistic, and a captain of industry can be narcissistic. Pay attention to the signs, patterns, and behaviors laid out in this book. If anything, narcissists and many toxic people appear better put together than the rest of us—the right clothes, the right address, the right credentials. Beware a wolf in sheep's clothing. You can protect yourself from these highly camouflaged dangers and poisoned apples amongst us. You just need to know what to look for.

The Toxicity Paradox

According to James House, Karl Landis, and Debra Umberson, researchers at the University of Michigan and the University of Texas, "*Social relationships, or the relative lack thereof, constitute a major risk factor for health—rivaling the effect of well-established health-risk factors such as cigarette smoking, blood pressure, blood lipids, obesity, and physical activity."* We can take this a step further: The lack of social relationships may constitute a risk factor for poor health but, by extension, the researchers' findings also imply that toxic relationships can be risk factors as well. It's actually an interesting toxicity paradox. For the amount of time, effort, and money people spend on healthy diets, getting enough sleep, special vitamins, exercising, healthcare, detoxes, and the avoidance of drugs, alcohol, and tobacco—all in the name of promoting health—something is being missed. All of these behaviors are integral to good health; that is true. However, when you take a longer lens and reflect on the amount of money spent on organic food to avoid the toxins of pesticides, or air filters to avoid toxins in the air, or purified water to avoid the toxins in water, or specialized household cleaners to avoid environmental toxins, or lower-emission or electric cars to avoid toxic exhaust emissions, or high-end cosmetics made from carefully sourced ingredients to avoid toxins on the skin, then why do most people keep toxic people in their lives? If people spent even a fraction of the time on removing high-conflict people and situations from their lives as they do on eliminating all of these other sources of toxins, their health would improve significantly and immediately. Think about it. Think about the last time a toxic person was removed from your life, either because of your efforts or not. After the initial shock wore off, reflect on how good you felt to no longer be invalidated.

Conversationally, people call toxic, difficult, and antagonistic people lots of things, including narcissists, sociopaths, assholes, pricks, douchebags, arrogant bastards, jerks, psychopaths, evil, psycho, mean, and bad guys. Those words are often an alarm that a toxic and likely narcissistic person is lurking, and they are more colorful than the far more clinical "narcissist." Aaron James philosophically reflects on the concept of the "asshole" in his book by the same name and defines the phenomenon as a person who "allows himself to enjoy special advantages in social relations out of an entrenched sense of entitlement that immunizes him against the complaints of other people." He also goes on to suggest that this is simply who the person is. A philosopher calls them assholes; a psychiatrist may call them narcissists. I, a psychologist, simply view them as toxic.

Are Toxic People Happy?

The big questions that often arise around narcissism and entitlement are "Do they feel good?" or "Are they happy people?" The short answer is "Not really." Most of the time, they do not think about it and typically only think about it when things are not going their way. At the core of it, difficult people and narcissists are insecure. And they manage their discomfort in a way that leaves everyone else feeling insecure. Feeling chronically insecure does not feel good.

Their inability to tolerate frustration and their subsequent lack of resilience are deeply uncomfortable. They tend to use the world and the people in it as a tool for their own gain, and, because many narcissistic people (though definitely not most!) are financially successful, they tend to have eminently enviable "Instagrammable" lifestyles. While a recent study indicates that having enough money to buy time (someone to clean your house or being able to get take-in from time to time) can increase happiness (Kahneman and Deaton, 2010), much more money beyond that does not make a difference. This lends credence to the idea that pursuing more and more and more makes no sense, because we do not need more, and "happiness" for toxic and narcissistic individuals becomes an elusive target.

When you witness toxic people on a good day, they will seem happy and as though they are on top of the world, grandiose, and full of dreams. Catch them on a day when things did not go their way, and there will be a cold, almost frightening darkness to them. Ultimately, the issue that does narcissists in is that it is never enough. Nothing is enough. You are not enough, I am not enough, their house is not big enough, their car is not fast enough, their job is not important enough, their vacation was not luxurious enough, their boyfriend is not rich enough, their girlfriend is not hot enough. Their parents weren't supportive enough. Nothing is enough and so they are always on a quest. Hang around them long enough, and you yourself will start to believe you are not enough. The short answer? Any "happiness" they experience is transitory at best and linked to how things are going in their external worlds, rather than to an inner sense of identity, serenity, or well-being. In fact, we can and should regard narcissistic people with circumspect compassion (from a distance), because they are actually very insecure and malcontented and empty. That cannot be an easy way to live, and it is deeply uncomfortable. Unfortunately, they spend most of their lives taking that discomfort out on other people.

What Is Narcissism?

There is nothing but disagreement about the word "narcissism." Clinicians who encounter it often consider it a manifestation of insecurity—a sort of malignant overcompensation. Researchers who attempt to measure it focus on individualism, self-expression, and assertiveness, and, when they measure it that way, they find that narcissism is associated with high self-esteem (for example, in the work of Jean Twenge, a professor of psychology at San Diego State University). The Narcissistic Personality Inventory is a questionnaire that measures narcissistic personality (but not narcissistic personality *disorder*) (Raskin and Hall, 1979). Once again, this scale still doesn't get at the difficult and antagonistic underbelly of narcissism (it tends to focus on more superficial grandiose "normal" narcissism or, at least, the less toxic elements of it). Some researchers have found that it yields three sorts of "subareas" of narcissism on the basis of this scale (leadership/authority, grandiose exhibitionism, and entitlement/exploitativeness) (Ackerman et al., 2011), while others think there are seven areas: authority, self-sufficiency, superiority, exhibitionism, exploitativeness, vanity, and entitlement (Raskin and Terry, 1988).

Another theoretical model that attempts to take on the measurement and conceptualization of narcissism is called the Five Factor Model of Personality (McCrae & John, 1992). This model considers personality as a hierarchical structure and breaks it down according to five dimensions: Neuroticism, Extraversion, Agreeableness, Conscientiousness, and Openness to Experience. All people have varying degrees of each of these dimensions present in their personalities, and a holistic and interactional consideration of the qualities that are most pronounced and least pronounced provide a sort of "personality snapshot" that can give psychologists a pretty accurate view of interpersonal functioning, coping, and behavioral responsivity, and can even highlight risks for mental illness. Work using this model characterizes narcissists as being high in extraversion and low in agreeableness. More specifically, this model describes narcissism as reflecting higher-than-average levels of angry hostility, assertiveness, activity, and excitement seeking, and lower-than-average levels of self-consciousness, warmth, trust, straightforwardness, altruism, compliance, modesty, and tender-mindedness (e.g. empathy) (Campbell and Miller, 2013). University of British Columbia psychology professor Delroy Paulhus used this model to simply describe narcissists as "disagreeable extraverts." The Five Factor framework highlights the narcissists' propensity to react angrily, get their own needs met, remain relatively self-unaware, be mistrustful, have difficulty following rules, and lack modesty. Paulhus' simplification is spot on.

Taken together, this literature has definitely supported the sort of "layperson's" take on narcissism that it is egoistic, grandiose, self-confident, assertive, and vain. It may not always be that pleasant, but how harmful can it be? In fact, some of these are qualities (e.g. self-confidence, assertiveness) that we actually attempt to cultivate in people. While "disagreeable extraversion" is not likely to be entirely pleasant, most people do find extraverts to be compelling and interesting. This sort of softened take on narcissism has led to a fair amount of confusion about the term and its real ramifications.

Despite the dispassionate deconstruction of personality that is required of personality research and science, it may miss some of the picture. I am committed in my belief through clinical observation and other theoretical literature that, *in its clinical manifestations, narcissism implies pathological insecurity.* That is the core of the main paradox of narcissism—most armchair users of the word conflate it with self-love or hyper-self-confidence, when it is really a deep-seated insecurity. It is this insecurity that makes the narcissist so difficult and toxic, because he or she feels chronically vulnerable. Narcissists' self-esteem is continually under threat, they constantly need validation to offset that insecurity, and they become rageful under conditions of frustration, disappointment, or stress, because these conditions threaten their self-esteem and fragile egos. This is why superficial successes are *so* important to them. For many of us, a bonus or a new car is fun, but we would be fine without either. For the narcissist, things like that are *essential*, because they help protect his or her fragile ego. The issue of insecurity is often missed by our measurements and our theories and, as a result, we may know what narcissists look like, but we still struggle to fully understand what motivates them and what makes them tick.

The pathological insecurity of the narcissist becomes no match for the normal insecurity most of us have. Most of us can soothe ourselves and balance out our day-to-day insecurities. Narcissists act as magnifying glasses for the insecurity of other people and, upon entering the worlds of other people, it's as if they infuse other people with their pathological levels of insecurity, leaving everyone destabilized. Because of this, narcissistic people are labeled "emotional vampires"—they actually suck out whatever security or sense of self another person has, leaving their victim completely insecure and the narcissist on the search for more validation.

Here's the rub: Researchers who are focused on the *trait* of narcissism, and not so much on the clinical patterns, treatment, or relational impacts, do not believe it reflects insecurity. They argue that, by labeling it as such, we can use compassionate means to "rescue" the narcissist (for example, as in the age-old myth that love conquers all—and if someone is insecure, then love should rescue them). I do not agree with that. Insecurity makes people dangerous—very dangerous. It gives them an itchy trigger finger, and it renders them selfishly infantile. High self-esteem is not a virtue; it may just be a shell or an inaccurate assessment of self. In that way, narcissists are, in fact, very poor judges of everything—of themselves, of their impact on others, of their own abilities, of other people. Their "high self-esteem" is then a by-product of their miscalculations. Narcissism and individualism are not the same thing. Narcissists are almost always individualistic, but not all individualists are narcissistic.

One of the key building blocks of the definition of "narcissism" is entitlement. "Entitlement" can be defined as "the belief that one is deserving of or entitled to certain privileges" (Merriam-Webster, 2018). Entitlement is not always a bad thing. In some cases, an "entitlement" is earned or is a tool for creating equitable access. People with physical disabilities or limitations are "entitled" to a parking spot that provides optimal or easier access to a property. People who pay a fee are "entitled" to use an exercise facility. People who successfully complete degree requirements are "entitled" to a diploma. Entitlement can become problematic when it reflects an unqualified expectation of special treatment. The *Diagnostic and Statistical Manual of Mental Disorders* (American Psychiatric Association, 2013) defines "entitlement" as "unreasonable expectations of especially favorable treatment or automatic compliance with his or her expectations." This is a more pathological definition of "entitlement," by dint of the expectations' being unreasonable and the compliance being automatic.

Does entitlement automatically imply interpersonal toxicity or narcissism? Not necessarily. Some entitlement appears to derive from a position of privilege, which can be conferred through personal attributes (such as race, social class, or gender), wealth, celebrity, or power. These statuses can often result in people being regarded with especially favorable treatment and automatic compliance with their expectations because of their position. This may result in expectations for this kind of treatment in all situations. For example, if a person is a high-flying executive or celebrity, he or she will grow accustomed to having a coterie of assistants, personal chefs, drivers, personal trainers, personal manicurists, and other personal helpers. High flyers like this can then become rather dismissive or curt with just about anyone and can quietly fall into the perception that other people exist to serve their needs. This shorthand can also trickle into other relationships they have with colleagues, employees, and even friends and family—and it can be deeply uncomfortable. However, if they are truly not toxic and simply a bit too comfortable with being "served" at all times, and they are in possession of human qualities such as empathy and respect, then they can often be snapped back into normalcy. That said, being around and witnessing entitlement in any of its forms is uncomfortable and unpleasant. Especially as the mantra of DYKWIA echoes around the world.

Is Narcissism a Mental Illness?

The *Diagnostic and Statistical Manual* is published by the American Psychiatric Association (APA) every few years and is a sort of guidebook to mental illness. It systematically lists the symptoms of all mental illnesses, ranging from schizophrenia to bipolar disorder to anorexia nervosa to Alzheimer's disease to narcissistic personality disorder.

The diagnostic criteria for narcissistic personality disorder in an earlier version of the DSM (DSM-IV-TR) are as follows (APA, 2000):

A pervasive pattern of grandiosity (in fantasy or behavior), need for admiration, and lack of empathy, beginning by early adulthood and present in a variety of contexts, as indicated by five (or more) of the following:

- *Has a grandiose sense of self-importance* (*exaggerates achievements and talents, expects to be recognized as superior without commensurate achievements*)
- *Is preoccupied with fantasies of* *unlimited success, power, brilliance, beauty, or ideal love*
- *Believes that he or she is "special"* *and unique and can only be understood by, or should associate with, other special or high-status people (or institutions)*
- *Requires excessive admiration*
- *Has a sense of entitlement* (*unreasonable expectations of especially favorable treatment or automatic compliance with his or her expectations*)
- *Is interpersonally exploitative* (*takes advantage of others to achieve his or her own ends*)
- *Lacks empathy* (*is unwilling to recognize or identify with the feelings and needs of others*)
- *Is often envious* *of others or believes that others are envious of him or her*
- *Shows arrogant, haughty behaviors* *or attitudes*

The DSM-5 (APA, 2013) takes the definition in a different direction and requires the following criteria to be met:

Significant impairments in personality functioning manifest by:

1. **Impairments in self-functioning** (and you need only **a** or **b**)

   a. *Identity: Excessive reference to others for self-definition and self-esteem regulation; exaggerated self-appraisal may be inflated or deflated or vacillate between extremes; emotional regulation mirrors fluctuations in self-esteem.* (Translation: They have problems with maintaining a consistent identity because they are deeply insecure and lack self-esteem. They need lots of validation to even know who they are. If other people are not telling them how good they are, their self-esteem suffers, and it becomes difficult to maintain their identity. They are not good at understanding and describing themselves in a realistic manner to other people, and may waver between either, saying that they are absolutely wonderful or saying that they are the worst person or a failure or that they really are great but that the reason they never "made it big" is because the world was not smart enough to take note of how great they are. They can manage their emotions well when things are going their way and they are feeling good about themselves, but, when they aren't, then they will have difficulty regulating their feelings and may react with extreme shows of emotion, most often anger and rage.)

b. *Self-direction: Goal setting is based on gaining approval from others; personal standards are unreasonably high in order to see oneself as exceptional or too low based on a sense of entitlement, often unaware of own motivations.* (Translation: They set goals based on what other people want and value, and that's why social media is such a satisfying space. They shape their goals to what will achieve "likes" and approval in public spaces. When they set goals, they will set them unrealistically high—for example, "I am going to play for the NBA," or "I am going to get a mansion or doctorate or build 50 clinics in Africa"—and will talk about these goals as though they are already happening. Or they set goals very low, because they think they are "better" than the circumstance in which they find themselves. For example, a student thumbing his or her nose at a class because he or she feels smarter than the professor and isn't going to waste time studying. However, students may say those things because they know they may not succeed in the class and they frame their unwillingness to engage in the process and their indifference as their being better than the process and the professor. The low goal setting and accompanying arrogance are ways to protect their ego.)

2. **Significant impairments in interpersonal functioning** (you need only **a** or **b**)

a. *Empathy: Impaired ability to recognize or identify with the feelings and needs of others; excessively attuned to reactions of others, but only if perceived as relevant to self; over- or underestimate own effect on others.* (Translation: They don't care what others feel, think, or need, so, even though they want the validation

14

of others, they really don't care about the other people themselves. They will pay attention to other people or attempt to understand them only if it will advance their own needs. They also tend to overvalue and overemphasize the evaluations of people whom they perceive as more powerful or important. They will be very attuned to the opinions and words of their boss or a wealthy or powerful acquaintance, because they want the status that person possesses, or they want their validation. Because of this, people with narcissistic personality disorder either do not see how their insensitive and unempathic behavior is affecting others—and they do not care—or they think that they are more impactful than they really are and overestimate their power on others, especially when those people are relevant or important to their image or their goals.)

b. *Intimacy: Relationships largely superficial and exist to serve self-esteem regulation; mutually constrained by little genuine interest in others' experiences and predominance of a need for personal gain.* (Translation: They hate to be alone and need relationships for validation. They really don't have any genuine interest in their partners' worlds or the worlds or lives of anyone close to them. When they do get into close, intimate relationships, it is often because they are playing an angle, choosing someone for money, image, youth, power, or beauty. As such, they are more likely to choose a "trophy spouse" or a wealthy partner, or someone else who can enhance their image to the world.)

Finally, the diagnosis of narcissistic personality disorder requires that the person have pathological personality traits, including antagonism, which is characterized by grandiosity, entitlement, self-centeredness, firmly holding to the belief that one is better than others, being condescending toward others, as well as attention seeking—excessive attempts to attract and be the focus of the attention of others, including admiration, and validation seeking.

These personality patterns need to be stable across time and consistent across situations (for example, at work, at home, in public, with family), and they cannot be directly due to drugs (for example, the grandiosity we may observe in someone who has used a stimulant such as cocaine or is intoxicated after drinking alcohol), another psychiatric condition (for example, the grandiosity observed during a manic phase), or a general medical condition (for example, the person's personality changes after a head injury).

In addition, the DSM notes that these impairments in personality functioning *are not better understood as normative for the individual's developmental stage or sociocultural environment.* That's where things get tricky.

For most mental disorders in the DSM, we consider the level of personal distress, dysfunction, behavioral deviance, and even dangerousness a person experiences or manifests before we slap a diagnosis on a person. In the case of most mental disorders, the people experiencing them are not comfortable (for example, they are uncomfortably anxious, they are very sad, they are using drugs in a manner that risks their health, and so on), or they are highly impaired (for example, so demented that they cannot take care of themselves or so depressed that they cannot get out of bed). In addition, we consider how much their symptoms are disrupting their lives; a person with an anxiety disorder will be so paralyzed by worry that he or she may not be able to work, or a person with a substance use disorder will spend so much time using drugs or recovering from the effect of drugs that he or she loses significant relationships. Behavioral deviance would account for things like staying up for seventy-two hours straight (like we might observe in mania) or hearing voices and seeing things that aren't really there (like we might witness in schizophrenia). Finally, dangerousness could be observed via suicidal thoughts, self-harming behaviors, or driving while intoxicated. In general, mental illness does not feel good. Above and beyond sociocultural norms, most people with mental disorders do not enjoy the way they feel, and their disorders cause disruption in their lives. However, as you'll see, we rarely witness the same type of personal distress with narcissistic personality disorder. And, maybe for that reason, in many cases, it should not qualify as a disorder.

Is Narcissism an Epidemic?

It depends on whom you ask. By definition, an epidemic is a widespread occurrence. It's difficult to get real population estimates on narcissism per se, because the survey research has not been conducted in a comprehensive manner. Depending on whom you ask, the research is inconclusive—at least involving teenagers. Some researchers suggest it is on the rise (for example, researchers such as Jean Twenge); others suggest that the rates have not increased (for example, Roberts et al., 2010). The scales we use to measure narcissism (most notably, a scale called the Narcissistic Personality Inventory) require a person to be honest, and, in some ways, these measurement scales tend to measure inaccurate perceptions of self, exaggerated self-confidence, and skewed self-confidence, rather than the more toxic narcissistic patterns that are more difficult to reliably measure, such as lack of empathy, defensiveness, and gaslighting, and do not get at the more vulnerable patterns of narcissism, such as resentment. Most people won't cop to being a jerk on a questionnaire.

The rates of narcissistic personality disorder tend to be variable across the research. Studies examining the prevalence of narcissistic personality disorder across studies have found prevalence rates of about 1 percent (Dhawan et al., 2010). Other researchers have obtained higher rates (for example, 6.2 percent), with higher rates in men (7.7 percent) than in women (4.8 percent) (Stinson et al., 2008). Do these numbers represent a clinical epidemic? Not really. But what about the patterns of antagonism, entitlement, incivility, lack of empathy, and validation seeking that clearly appear to be on the rise? We do not have sufficient data on these trends to comment on whether these qualify as "epidemics" at this point in time.

Though woefully unscientific, simply looking at shifts in people's internet searches, the proliferation of books in the marketplace, and the viewing of YouTube videos on narcissism and other toxic relationship patterns, something is afoot. When "toxic" is the 2018 word of the year, when "narcissism" is the buzzword of our time, something is happening.

The Conundrum of Narcissism: A Playbook for Success?

When you have a list of traits that generally read like a corporate playbook for success, which is, in essence, a descriptive framework for a large proportion of financially and professionally successful celebrities, athletes, politicians, media figures, corporate wonks, tech titans, academics, billionaires of all stripes, and social media "influencers," are we really in a position to call it a "disorder?" Narcissism, as a pattern, appears to be associated with a greater probability of financial and occupational success and a greater likelihood of fame. It's an ironic juxtaposition—children are often told to wait their turn, be kind to others, share their toys, tell the truth, treat people equally, and show humility, all of which flies in the face of what are considered the tools for success in so many industries. It's as though efforts in elementary or primary school are the sole attempts to teach children the antidote to developing into a toxic person or to push back against narcissism. Then we release the children into a professional world in which these traits don't work. When do children start receiving the message that entitlement and selfishness will help them succeed? Is it a nascent cultural lesson? Is it coming from their parents? Their communities? The media? The right answer is likely all of the above.

Work is only one part of an emerging adult's life. The patterns that facilitate success, sadly, often do not work well in relationships. An unempathic person may make one hell of a CEO but a terrible husband. An entitled celebrity may curry lots of attention but would be an invalidating girlfriend. An arrogant and rageful athlete may be able to throw a ball better than anyone but is not likely to be a decent and attentive father.

The Medicalization of Bad Behavior

So let's get back to the narcissistic personality *disorder*. Most narcissists are doing just fine, do not report feeling uncomfortable, and rarely reflect on the fact that they are having struggles or difficulties in life. They plow through people and situations with little regard for the feelings of others, they live in grandiose universes where they are always right (and, frankly, they are often rewarded for their personality pattern), and they exploit people and situations to get their needs met with little regard for how their behavior impacts other people. However, with time, some narcissists do step up to the plate and say, "I don't like being this shallow," or, "I keep hurting people's feelings," or, "I have been a jerk my entire life; I don't know how to be any other way." They can have enough insight to recognize that their pattern is not nice, and they may actually get frustrated in therapy when they try to shake these patterns. These insights may come with advancing age, when their youthful swagger and professional success no longer hold much interest for the world at large, or when someone leaves them and they reflect on the emptiness that is left in the wake of that departure, and they aren't as interesting a romantic partner any longer, or they look around one day at their big, comfortable home and realize that they are all alone. Just at the time when people are facing existential demons and wanting to go deeper, a "self-aware" narcissist may find that going deep feels impossible, which can be very frustrating and result in despair. In a way, for narcissists to become aware of their narcissism can be worse than being in the dark. Awareness of their lack of depth can result in a sense of further emptiness and despair. But it is a step in the right direction. Growth hurts.

Allen Frances, psychiatrist, academic, a primary architect of the diagnostic criteria for narcissistic personality disorder, and author of the polemic *Twilight of American Sanity: A Psychiatrist Analyzes the Age of Trump,* raises concerns that we run the risk of medicalizing bad behavior when we slap the label "narcissistic personality *disorder*" on it. He believes that this diagnosis does not hold unless the person is experiencing significant emotional, personal, social, or occupational distress. Of late, theoreticians, psychiatrists, and mental health pundits have made their name discussing the label "narcissistic personality disorder" and how it pertains to world leaders—most famously, President Donald Trump. Frances believes that people who behave like Trump (who is the focus of his book) are not manifesting mental illness but are instead self-promoters, self-serving salespeople, and dangerous impresarios, and he writes, "To qualify for narcissistic personality disorder, an individual's selfish, unempathetic preening must be accompanied by significant distress or impairment." This is a tricky issue, because many narcissistic people do not experience distress or impairment. In fact, they tend to succeed brilliantly because they are so masterful at salesmanship, self-promotion, manipulation, and exploitation and are surprised and then angry when other people call them out on their behavior.

It is high time we stop thinking about this as a diagnosis—it gives people who behave in a narcissistic manner too much of an out. The label is actually quite unfair to people with mental illness, who bravely face down the challenges of their illness each day. It also takes our eye off of what is really going wrong in a world in which we implicitly view these traits and patterns as being valuable for leaders, not just in politics but across all industries.

Can a Narcissistic Personality Be Treated?

This raises a deeply challenging issue. For most psychiatric diagnoses—depression, phobias, obsessive-compulsive disorder, schizophrenia, bulimia nervosa—there is robust literature describing evidence-based treatments for these disorders. Some treatments are psychotherapies, some are pharmacological treatments, and others are psychosocial interventions. More often than not, a combination of these various techniques culminates in the most successful treatments. In addition, better detection of early signs of mental disorders can ensure early uptake of treatment to limit the disability engendered by mental illness. With each passing year, and with major developments in neuroscience, including epigenetics and better-articulated psychotherapies, we are making more and more headway into the treatment and management of mental disorders, thereby enhancing quality of life and physical and mental health for those living with mental illness.

Except for narcissistic personality disorder.

There is *very* little good evidence for treatments that work to treat this disorder in any long-term manner. Narcissistic personality disorder is a relatively stable disorder that does not shift much over time (Vater et al., 2014). There are studies that point to the utility of treatments to enhance specific behavior changes, such as attending appointments on time, or to manage anger and volatility, but the narcissistic person still remains a relatively callous or snarky "jerk." Therapy focuses on establishing rapport with narcissistic clients, developing a sense of trust, perhaps helping them connect dots between what may have been a difficult childhood for them and their current behavior, and carefully managing the boundaries of therapy (for example, they may want to go longer or start later, at their convenience). The literature on treatment has provided documentation of transient shifts in empathic recognition. For example, narcissistic people have intact cognitive empathy, and, if a therapist steers them properly, they will express it, but, without the therapist's guidance, they would not have gotten there on their own. In real time, outside of the therapy office, it can also be difficult for a narcissistic person to express empathy or understanding at the appropriate times, which can be bewildering and frustrating for those in any form of relationship with a narcissist. Cognitive empathy can be deeply unsatisfying and hollow, because it results in someone's "getting it" intellectually but not really being able to get there emotionally or behaviorally. Cognitive empathy can manifest when someone says, "I guess I understand why you would be angry"—but without the emotional energy behind it, it feels more like an intellectual exercise in empathy rather than the human experience of understanding.

There is virtually no evidence base pointing to the successful treatment of a person suffering from narcissistic personality "disorder" to a degree that his or her interpersonal relationships are significantly improved. "Successful" treatment may result in a narcissistic person's more readily taking responsibility for his or her behavior but may not *stop* the behavior. It is little solace to the spouses, partners, children, friends, coworkers, and employees of extremely narcissistic people that a therapist can train the narcissist to show up on time or occasionally take responsibility for narcissistic behavior. Even that will slide away very quickly—the first time a narcissist experiences disappointment, frustration, or stress, all bets are off, because narcissists tend to go right back to their usual ways. Narcissists are also extremely sensitive to stress, despite causing it for everyone around them. They tend to be very brittle in the face of it; as a result, even if they experience some small gains in therapy, their inability to regulate their emotions or experience empathy means that, in the face of stress, they will often return to patterns of rage, acting out, and poor frustration tolerance. Even in the midst of the rage, narcissists will acknowledge there is little they can do to stop it. By and large, the literature on treatment of narcissistic personality disorder focuses on very small numbers of patients, improvement requires many months or even years of therapy, and for every "successful" case reported in the treatment literature, it begs the question of how many did not improve. People with narcissistic personality disorder are also much more likely to prematurely drop out of psychotherapy. For every article or case study that shows progress, there are many individuals who make absolutely no progress. The main ingredient that appears to drive successful treatment is the ability of the therapist to make a healthy alliance with the client (not always easy with a narcissistic client), and with that trust, to journey into the darker issues. Bottom line, improvement in people with narcissistic personality disorder tends to be the exception and not the rule. I am a firm believer that, in general, therapy is better than no therapy, and that clients who are narcissistic or have narcissistic personality disorder can and do benefit from therapy; however, it is not likely to evince the level of change that enhances the lives of the other people in the narcissists' lives.

Narcissistic personality disorder and other disorders are often what we term "comorbid," meaning that narcissistic personality disorder can occur with other disorders, such as depression, anxiety, substance-use disorders, or eating disorders. Many times, treatment that focuses on the other clinical condition may result in some improvement, because the other symptoms have remitted (for example, there may be less irritability if the depression or anxiety is treated), but it's not likely to address the patterns that hurt other people, such as the narcissist's lack of empathy, insensitivity, validation seeking, or anger. The patterns of narcissistic personality disorder can make it more difficult to manage the other disorder, and that remains a major challenge for clinicians and therapists managing these complex clients.

Thus, at the core of it, narcissistic personality "disorder" is a disorder (or a pattern) that helps people become rich, powerful, and famous; facilitates success in many settings; makes people efficient; and does not have any known treatment that results in shifts substantial enough to enhance interpersonal functioning in the long term. The argument could be made, "Why label something a disorder if there is absolutely nothing you can do about it?" There has been some debate by experts in the field that, unless the person with a disorder is experiencing distress or discomfort because of the symptoms, then it does not qualify as a disorder. In general, we do not diagnose something because it causes *other* people distress. Keep in mind, the treatment literature and much of the literature on narcissistic personality are focused on the narcissist and trying to help the narcissist; little work in this area addresses how the narcissist affects other people and what happens to the victims and survivors of his or her abuse.

These arguments notwithstanding, narcissistic personality disorder is a disorder of self-esteem and self-regulation, and narcissism itself reflects pathological insecurity. A person who lacks empathy, seeks and needs validation, flies into rages, is grandiose, is shallow and superficial, and is deeply entitled is clearly compensating for something. However, narcissists' lack of insight and self-reflection means that they are unable to dig into that vulnerability and instead cover up the smell of their insecurity with the masks of entitlement and grandiosity. The grandiosity, in many ways, is a primitive attempt to protect their fragile egos; in fact, most of their behavior is organized to protect their fragile egos.

So can there be hope? I have experienced so much pushback from people who are narcissistic, sociopathic, and psychopathic, who have said, "I've been in therapy and I've made some changes. I don't like myself, and I know I've hurt others, so I'm going to fix it." Ultimately, one of the greatest predictors of whether someone is going to make a change in therapy is that he or she is committed to change. When a person gets elevated to a place where he or she can notice his or her blind spots and wants to change them, yes, there is hope. Many of these people will report difficult etiological backstories—abusive childhoods, emotionally impoverished families, cold and authoritarian parents, chaotic home lives—and that their emotional restrictiveness, lack of empathy, and propensity to rage are by-products of or even coping responses to their early life. For any person to be able to make a change, he or she has to recognize a need for a change, commit to making the change, and then commit to the daily work of sustaining that change. In this way, mindfulness becomes an important tool in the arsenal of managing the symptoms and patterns of narcissistic personality disorder. Mindfulness is a psychological stop sign, a moment to stop and think about the ramifications of an action before responding, and to not just automatically react in the usual ways or in the ways that they have been wired to respond over a lifetime. There is also the critical issue of teaching narcissistic people how to *respond* instead of *react*. Reaction is often automatic, thoughtless and rapid. Responding entails waiting a beat and behaving in a way that accounts for more elements of a situation.

When people are manifesting narcissistic patterns, they will also acknowledge that, even when motivated to change, to enter therapy, to try to be "better" for others, they come up short when the stress is on, when the interpersonal demands are high, and when their rage kicks in. How much change is enough to potentially make a relationship with a narcissistic person work? That is a subjective question. Each of us needs to be clear in what we expect from a relationship *and* what we can bring to one (whether as a partner, parent, friend, child, or colleague). If the narcissist cannot shift his or her patterns in a way that is workable for the other person, then there can be acknowledgment of change but also recognition that the change may not be enough. These issues and patterns are often intergenerational, and ending these cycles is essential and difficult.

For the purposes of this book, and all of my work in this area, let us no longer talk about it as a disorder. It means taking a longer view at the issue and acknowledging that we live in a world in which the traits that comprise narcissism are adaptive, so perhaps there is something diagnosable about the world at large. We should dump the idea of the *diagnosis* of narcissistic personality disorder and stick with the concept of narcissistic behavior, narcissism as a personality pattern, and interpersonally toxic patterns. We can organize the characteristics that represent the multifaceted nature of narcissism on the basis of literature going all the way back to the first commentaries on narcissism, which include clinical observation and empirical and theoretical reflection. When we call it a diagnosis, we get in trouble, and then we do not have a way to talk about these patterns, which are toxic, or narcissistic, or entitled, or just a source of heartache, heartbreak, and endless stress and strife. So let's return to the old adage, "If it walks like a duck and quacks like a duck...."

* * *

Call it what you want; it is more important for your own sanity and mental health to actually understand it. So let's develop a framework for what makes narcissism so toxic and difficult. In the next chapter, we'll examine the five overarching clusters of narcissistic patterns.

Chapter 2

The Anatomy of Narcissism and Interpersonal Toxicity

All cruelty stems from weakness.

—SENECA

L et us now create a system for what comprises a toxic person and toxic behavior. It is my hope that providing a framework that lists these patterns, and provides brief summaries as examples, will orient you to how nuanced this whole toxic person/narcissism/entitlement situation is. We can break down narcissism into five basic groups of traits; each trait has corresponding patterns of behavior that may be familiar to you if you have a narcissist in your life. This highlights how the patterns of narcissism actually cut across multiple areas of your life.

Each of these patterns will be described in a way to shed light on the normal version of some of these patterns as well as the darker patterns. This system will also index toxic people in terms of how they make others feel. As such, the kinds of feelings that each of these patterns tends to evoke will also be described. The reason many of these patterns can feel "pathological" is generally their consistency and pervasiveness; the toxic person regularly, consistently, or always engages in these patterns, whereas in the case of more normal manifestations of these features, it's something someone does rarely or occasionally—or if someone does them, he or she apologizes later, learns from the mistake, and never does them again.

The Five Clusters of Narcissism

Let's break narcissistic traits into five basic areas that are the reasons why they cause all of us so many problems. Each of the patterns within these clusters can affect us quite differently. The **interpersonal** ones make any kind of relationship challenging—and, often, the more intimate or close or important the relationship, the more problematic these qualities become. The **behavioral** patterns are often the ones we can observe more directly, because they translate into actions like buying expensive items and talking about them frequently or getting lots of cosmetic surgery. This is the reality-TV type of narcissism of vulgarity and visible bad behavior. The **dysregulation** elements are the ones that make the narcissistic person seem unpredictable or scary or do not always make sense, because they fly in the face of our inaccurate assumption that narcissists are confident and have high self-esteem. The **antagonistic** qualities are unpleasant and combative; they are the characteristics that are often the "essence" of what makes a toxic person toxic. These are also the qualities that often hurt us, even when we do not know the narcissistic person very well. The **cognitive** patterns speak to how toxic and narcissistic people think about and perceive the world. Any single group of these characteristics is difficult, and, when a few characteristics from each of these five sets of clusters are in a person, it can feel deeply uncomfortable, invalidating, and dehumanizing—in other words, toxic.

The next section of the book is a detailed map and guide to these toxic patterns. In writing about this issue, a question that often arises is,

INTERPERSONAL	BEHAVIORAL	DYSREGULATION	ANTAGONISTIC	COGNITIVE
• Lack of empathy	• Superficial	• Anger/Rage	• Grandiose	• Paranoid
• Manipulative	• Covetous/	• Validation	• Entitled	• Hypersensitive/
• Projection	envious	seeking	• Passive-	Petulant
• Lying	• Cheap	• Inability to be	aggressive	• Lack of insight/
• Poor boundaries	• Careless	alone	• Schadenfreude	Guilt
• Jealousy		• Fragile/Insecure	• Arrogance	• Skewed sense
• Gaslighting		• Shame	• Exploitative	of justice
• Controlling			• Lack of responsi-	• Hypocritical
			bility taking	
			• Vindictive	
			• Oppositional	

"I do some of these things—am I a narcissist?" Remember, narcissism is a pattern that is actually made up of lots of other traits, patterns, and behaviors. All of us engage in some of these behaviors sometimes; it is part of being a person. It is all about critical mass. If a person *consistently* exhibits the patterns listed in this chapter on a regular basis, with little self-reflection, then it creeps into the darker corners of toxicity and narcissism. Under stress, we all have the propensity to behave in a way that is less than elegant. We may become envious of a more fortunate sister, make a passive-aggressive comment to a friend who omitted us from his or her New Year's Eve party guest list, or be a bit too sensitive in response to comments about our vulnerabilities, but if that is not our primary mode of relating, or we catch ourselves and take ownership of our behavior and then change that behavior, we are typically not narcissists. At the end of each pattern is a brief description of the "normal" variant of that pattern, as well as the "pathological" variant. It can be confusing to know when these patterns become a problem, and this framework is meant to provide some benchmarks and clarification.

In addition, as noted above, when we talk about "classical" narcissism, we come back to the "pillars" of this trait: entitlement, grandiosity, lack of empathy, superficiality, hypersensitivity to criticism, emotional dysregulation, and validation seeking. In the absence of those, you may have a very difficult person, but he or she may not qualify as a narcissist.

At the end of each trait or pattern is also a description of how these qualities leave us feeling. Sometimes we cannot put a name to what these things are, but we are aware of how we feel, and working backward can help provide some clarity on these patterns. All of the words in the world, and descriptions and taxonomies, are no substitute for a feeling—and being in the presence of someone with narcissistic traits, despite their charm and charisma and confidence, can sometimes make the hairs on the back of your neck stand up. Pay attention; that may be all the sign you need.

Interpersonal

The interpersonal features of toxic people and narcissists are often the most challenging and painful. Because they are interpersonal in nature, they are the patterns that demonstrate how a narcissist interacts and behaves with us. These are the patterns that hurt us, make us interpersonally uncomfortable, confuse us, and are associated with negative effects, such as self-doubt, drops in self-esteem, sadness, anxiety, social withdrawal, and helplessness. There are eight typical patterns within a narcissist's interpersonal features: lack of empathy, manipulation, projection, lying, poor boundaries, jealousy, gaslighting, and controlling.

LACK OF EMPATHY

This is a lack of interest in or capacity for understanding the feelings and experiences of others. Lack of empathy also reflects a lack of self-awareness, an indifference to the wants or needs of others, and little recognition of how the person's behavior impacts other people. Lack of empathy can also be a driver of what can feel like an emotional "distance" or coldness that many experience with toxic and narcissistic people. Empathy drives the feeling of warmth people feel when they are understood. When you are with a person who lacks empathy, it is a bit like being in the presence of a mirror that does not reflect back, and that can leave you feeling unheard or uncared for, at a minimum or, in the extreme, it can leave you feeling as though you are losing your grip on reality.

Narcissists may be cognitively "capable" of empathy—meaning that, when a story is explained to them, they can understand why another person would be sad or upset—but they do not shape their behavior in accordance with that empathy. They may cry at a movie, but, when someone is genuinely suffering in front of them, they rarely show anything that resembles care, warmth, or concern.

No matter how clearly you communicate with them, narcissists do not listen, and, most of the time, it is because they do not care what other people have to say, especially people they view as somehow "less than" themselves (which is just about everyone). Not only does their lack of empathy hurt the people around them, but also lack of empathy typically translates into a lack of listening.

Lack of empathy is what makes narcissists problematic partners, parents, friends, coworkers—just about any relationship you can think of. Empathy is an inside job, and narcissists have underdeveloped psychological endoskeletons. As such, empathy, or the ability to maintain their internal emotional world and be responsive and engaged with the inner world of another, is beyond their reach.

Normal lack of empathy: This is not a pattern but, instead, it may reflect a difficult moment in time. An example may be rushing and not taking a moment to check in on the feelings of others or putting your needs ahead of someone else's from time to time, especially under conditions of stress, like when a family member is sick, you've just lost your job, or you are in the middle of a messy divorce. However, typically you apologize when you catch yourself, or you experience genuine feelings of remorse or guilt afterward, and you learn from the error.

Pathological lack of empathy: This is observed when the person rarely cares what anyone is experiencing or feeling, never listens, often interrupts (because he or she doesn't care about what you are saying), and always puts his or her needs ahead of others' needs. If this person asks how people are feeling, he or she doesn't really want to hear the answer. People with a pathological lack of empathy consistently minimize the challenges that other people may be experiencing and are often emotionally cold.

How does their lack of empathy make you feel? Unheard, misunderstood, invisible, hurt.

MANIPULATION

Manipulation is a bit like being a puppet master. The manipulator assesses a situation and then manages the situation and other people in a way that achieves what the manipulator wants, with little regard for how this may affect others. A really good manipulator can not only get what he or she wants and leave other people out in the cold, but also leaves those people who are out in the cold believing that they are still warm. Manipulation is salesmanship at its best. When you are manipulated, you feel "played."

Toxic and narcissistic people are so good at manipulation because it allows them to maintain their sense of self (which is entirely externally driven), and their lack of empathy means that they really do not care who gets hurt by the manipulation. They tend to be calculating and cold, because other people are largely objects to them, a means to an end, and they mentally work those angles and, ultimately, treat people as though they are disposable. Life is a game, and narcissistic people play it well. In fact, it is a zero-sum game for them—with one winner and one loser, and you can bet which side they need to be on.

Normal manipulation: When we engage in "normal" manipulation, this may manifest as buttering or fluffing someone up before you ask him or her to do you an unpleasant favor, like loan you money or drive you to the airport. Other examples may include when you do not want to do something and have someone else whom you know is respected (for example, an older relative or an esteemed colleague) get you out of it (because no one will say no to that person) or sharing gossipy details about someone else in the hope that it will make you look good. In the macro, this is never a healthy pattern, so even some of the "normal" manipulations we may be guilty of should be minimized and avoided. These patterns diminish trust and can hurt others.

Pathological manipulation: When manipulation is pathological, it entails getting what a person needs through interpersonal maneuvers with little regard for others. This can include when people regularly use unpleasant details about other people's pasts or a partner's past to induce feelings of guilt or shame and then capitalizing on that vulnerability to get what they need, chronically complaining about a situation in their lives (for example, financial issues or career conflicts) so that others will "rescue" them (even at great cost to the rescuer), and using lies to isolate a person from other advocates and then getting what they need from that person. At the extreme, manipulation can spin into exploitation, whereby the narcissist actually endeavors to take advantage of another person (for example, through blackmail or capitalizing on the vulnerability of that person) to the harm of the other and the gratification of the narcissist.

How does their manipulation make you feel? Taken advantage of, mistrustful, foolish, stupid, violated.

PROJECTION

Projection is a primitive defense—thus, it is a pattern in which a person engages without really thinking (psychoanalytic theorists would argue that it is occurring unconsciously, outside of our active awareness). The basic gist of projection is that people "project" their flaws, fears, short-comings, and other uncomfortable aspects of themselves that they may not like onto someone else (and this unconscious pattern protects the vulnerable self-esteem of the "projector"). For example, a person who is lying will accuse the other person(s) of lying; a person who is unfaithful will accuse a partner of being distant. This can result in unpleasant and inaccurate accusations and comments, and, in fact, those accusations may reflect something that the accuser is doing (for example, a cheating spouse accusing a partner of cheating or an angry and critical parent accusing a child of being angry and critical).

Toxic and narcissistic people are also fragile, and they are always monitoring their world for threats. Projection becomes a way of punishing other people for their own deficits, because they lack the insight or maturity to understand that these are *their* issues. It's as if their psyche knows they are behaving badly, but their conscious mind doesn't catch up with that and admit it, so, instead, they engage in projection. It is deeply frustrating to deal with projection, because, when you are on the receiving end, it can be confusing and off-putting. You are being accused of things you are likely not even doing (for example, lying, being cold), but that you *are* actually experiencing because the *other person* is doing them to *you*. (Simple projection hack: When you are being accused of something you are not doing but it feels like the other person is doing it, then that is projection. Don't defend yourself. If the person accuses you of being angry or bitter, don't say, "But you are the one who is angry and bitter." Instead, smile politely, say, "Okay," and gracefully step away.)

Normal projection: Projection, like all defenses, is a normal part of our psychological wheelhouses. Freud and other analytic theorists would argue that we project when we feel threatened or ashamed and unconsciously can't tolerate having those uncomfortable feelings about ourselves churned up, so we project them (it's like psychologically spitting out something distasteful, but then it gets on someone else). We all say things that are more about us than the other person. As long as it is not a pattern, or if we get called out on it and are willing to listen about it and work on it, then it's normal projection.

Pathological projection: Projection is pathological when it becomes a pattern and a primary way of dealing with feelings and other people. When a person is regularly accusing other people of his or her own shortcomings, or attributing patterns or moods to people that are simply not true on a regular basis, it is considered pathological. Freud and other psychoanalytic theorists would argue that projection is a primary defensive pattern observed in narcissism.

How does their projection make you feel? Confused, misunderstood, self-doubting, unheard, angry.

LYING

Toxic and narcissistic people lie repeatedly, and it does not feel good when you are on the receiving end. It is very difficult to restore trust after lying, but sometimes we are so desperate to trust someone that we keep writing excuses for that person. Narcissists' motivations for lying are manifold and may range from avoiding punishment or retribution for something they did to getting validation, but, mostly, they lie to retain or protect their fragile sense of self. Because narcissists are so prone to being able to rationalize rather than take responsibility, lying becomes part of the rationalization. They rarely understand the extent to which lies erode trust and hurt others, so lying tends to be a consistent part of their behavioral repertoire. They are practiced at lying because it works well for them, and, over time, it can be difficult to discern truth from deception.

Normal lying: This may fall more into the "white lie" category. Making up fibs as excuses for being late, canceling a night out, or cheating on a diet are things we all do from time to time. Normal lying is more about saving face and often does not hurt someone else if you are found out. It tends to be less of a pattern as well—just an occasional quick fix and one that "normal" liars often feel guilty about. However, it is one to stay on top of, because the literature suggests that the more we lie, the better we get at it, so it can be an easy habit to fall into if we are not careful.

Pathological lying: These are people who live in lies as much as truth; at the core of it, they are deceitful people. It is a pattern and frequent enough that it can be difficult to discern. It is often done in ways that can hurt others (lying about events, which, if found out, would cause distress to others or would have legal or financial ramifications). It is also done quite seamlessly—and the ease with which it is done can be disconcerting. Because pathological liars are so masterful at lying, it becomes easy to see how they can pull off a con such as "living a double life."

How does their lying make you feel? Deceived, unsafe, suspicious, mistrustful, angry, duped.

POOR BOUNDARIES

In many ways, toxic people and narcissists are what we call "impertinent," a rather formal word that implies being rude and disrespectful, or asking a person inappropriate or intrusive questions. Because of their high levels of entitlement, narcissists will offer unsolicited advice or inappropriate (or unkind) feedback or foist themselves into events or situations into which they may not have been invited. Toxic people are often accused of having "no filter," and sometimes we even validate this pattern and call them "brutally honest," but, ultimately, a boundary is being violated. Boundary violations can take in a lot of territory, from downright trauma and unwanted physical contact to weighing in on your life.

Poor boundaries can manifest in a variety of hurtful ways. Toxic partners and narcissists tend to be unfaithful in relationships, and that often starts with poor boundaries. Lack of empathy and entitlement can also feed poor boundaries (inappropriate electronic contact with coworkers or other acquaintances, feeling the rules do not apply to them, abuse of power). Toxic people often get away with this conduct because of fear, especially if they are in a position of power (for example, the range of sexual harassment and abuse cases perpetrated by wealthy and powerful people). Whether sexualized or not, boundary violations always make us feel uncomfortable.

Normal poor boundaries: There may not really be a normal variant of this pattern. Blurred boundaries are never good; however, what may look like enmeshed or poor boundaries to one person may be just family closeness to another. In assessing boundaries, the key is perspective. Reflect on what feels right to you (even if others just minimize it). Some friends talk ten times per day and show up on a honeymoon, but, if everyone is okay with this behavior, then perhaps there is no need to pathologize it. That said, it is good relationship hygiene to check in with those you are close with to ensure you are not encroaching on boundaries (not everyone may feel comfortable saying something). Boundaries can often slip over time and may require recalibrating from time to time.

Pathological poor boundaries: This behavior occurs when boundaries are violated on a regular basis. This can manifest in ways such as asking an assistant who is paid by your employer to pick up dry cleaning, watch your dog, or call your wife on her birthday for you. It can be sharing overly personal details of your life with someone who should not be privy to such information, as it could make the person uncomfortable (for example, talking about your sexual proclivities with family members or coworkers who may not want to hear about them). It can be sending romantic texts or making sexual overtures to a subordinate employee. It may also involve being inappropriately present or providing input into or criticizing adult children's lives and not allowing them to make their own decisions or live their own lives.

How do their poor boundaries make you feel? Violated, threatened, uncomfortable, guilty, and, in some cases, "special."

JEALOUSY

Jealousy reflects a pattern of envy and fierce protectiveness over the things a person values. Jealousy is a normal emotion that can grow out of multiple spaces: a competitive childhood, having experienced betrayal in the past, hypersensitivity, paranoia, insecurity, or fear of abandonment. It can be a normal response to a threat, especially a threat to an intimate or safe space. All of us have experienced some jealousy—of a sibling, a friend, a competitor for our partner's affections, a lottery winner, and so on. However, in a healthy person, it is a transient state. Narcissists are often deeply jealous, largely because they are insecure, hypersensitive, and, sometimes, almost paranoid.

Jealousy can take several forms. Relational jealousy is the most familiar—typically a jealousy about flirting, infidelity, or time spent with other people outside of the relationship. It can also manifest as jealousies within other close relationships, such as jealousy about a friend's success. Sibling jealousy is the sense that a sibling may have received or still is receiving more positive regard from a parent or parents or is more valued within the family. It can also be observed as a jealousy that one sibling has achieved more than the other (a sister has a big house, high-paying career, and takes lots of fancy vacations, while the other sister is living in a small house, is broke, has an unkind partner, and is in a dead-end job). Career jealousy can grow out of watching colleagues get promotions, better opportunities, or better perks at work. Jealousy, at its core, is about insecurity, and narcissists are insecure.

Normal jealousy: We have all been there. If your partner is working with a beautiful colleague on a project or when the people with whom you identify have "more" than you or are getting it more "right" that you, it is normal to feel jealous. In an age of social media, when everyone portrays envy-inducing lives ("I'm in Hawaii!" "Look at my new car!" "He finally asked [with three-carat ring flashing against the sandy beach]!" "My kid is the valedictorian!"), jealousy is a normal response. In some ways, the best way to beat back "normal" jealousy is to just cop to it. It can often help you let it go, and always recognize that a little is normal and that someone else is always going to have some things that you don't.

Pathological jealousy: This occurs when jealousy is the prevailing state of affairs, when anyone's good news raises mean-spirited rants, unkind emails, or insults. It means to publicly impugn another person's good fortune. Pathological jealousy can border on the paranoid and can translate into behaviors such as stalking, placing trackers on cars, using private investigators, and invading electronic privacy, such as secretly and regularly checking a partner's phone, email, or social media account. This can also manifest as frequent accusations about betrayal or telling the object of jealousy that he or she does not deserve good fortune or a happy life, or ruminating about the lives of others—what they have and how they live. Within a family, pathological jealousy can result in chronically uncomfortable family interactions about who has more, which person is favored, and over-perceptions of slights and past experiences when the jealous person felt left out.

How does their jealousy make you feel? Attacked, uncomfortable, hypervigilant, disrespected.

GASLIGHTING

Although gaslighting, in many ways, falls under manipulation, the classical elements of this dynamic are such a central and destabilizing part of any relationship with a narcissist that it deserves its own category. Gaslighting derives its name from a 1930s play and film called *Gaslight,* in which a husband succeeds in driving his wife mad by turning down the gas-powered lights in the house, denying that he is doing it, and telling her that they are no less bright. It is also reflected in the reality shape-shifting that toxic people are so easily able to accomplish and, in many cases, why their partners just go along with whatever they say.

Gaslighting is often cited as a form of emotional abuse. Classical gaslighting statements include "that never happened," "you have no right to feel that way," "you don't feel that way," and "I never said that." Gaslighting often consists of withholding ("I am not going to talk to you if you bring that up again"), contradicting (eroding your sense of certainty by telling you that you do not remember a situation correctly), or diversion (changing the subject to something more self-serving and to something that makes you look unkind or irresponsible, such as, "Remember that time you came late to my birthday party?"). Gaslighting also involves minimization of feeling ("You are being petty, getting upset about such a small thing") or abject denial ("That never happened"). Gaslighting has been termed "moving the goalposts," because, not only is it a shift in reality, but it is also experienced as a change in the rules, midgame. In some ways, gaslighting can often feel like "lawyerly" nitpicky arguments (a man who is found to be driving into his mistresses' driveway only to be confronted by his wife who waited in front knowing he was going there and says to him, "Ha! I finally caught you in your girlfriend's house." To which the narcissistic cheat will respond, "No, you didn't. You just saw me here on the street, I didn't go "in" to any house."). I suppose he is technically correct, but it is manipulative game-playing meant to toy with the reality of a distressed wife. That's gaslighting.

The phenomenon of gaslighting by proxy occurs when other people make excuses for the narcissist. This can be one parent making an excuse for the other parent, friends of a narcissistic partner making an excuse for his conduct, or other employees making an excuse for a toxic supervisor. This pattern can leave you doubting your reality in the same way. In fact, gaslighting by proxy can be even more profound in its effect, because it is the voice not just of one person, but of multiple people, which can fortify the impact, render the narcissist as more powerful, and leave you even more psychologically confused.

More than a few relationships with narcissists can be characterized by physical abuse, and sometimes people do not recognize it as physical abuse, because it may look like the narcissist's grabbing your arm and holding on too tight or being too rough during sex. At such times, it is not unusual for narcissistic people to engage in "physical gaslighting"— they will doubt your reality that it hurt when they grabbed you or hurt you during a time of physical intimacy ("Oh, come on, that didn't really hurt," or, "You are so sensitive; I didn't really grab you that hard"). This can be doubly destabilizing, because both your psychological and physical realities are being doubted.

Children are especially vulnerable to gaslighting, since parents are supposed to be honest and validating, and a child will doubt his or her reality before questioning a parent, in most cases. In adulthood, even though the adult child may recognize what is being done to him or her, the pattern of self-doubt may be pretty solidly in place. Gaslighting partners can leave a person feeling full of self-doubt, subsequently becoming over-reliant on his or her partner and, thus, even more susceptible to emotional abuse. A gaslighting boss can be particularly devastating, since you may carefully execute a task or responsibility only to be second-guessed to a point that it takes a toll on your mental health, or you may take the fall at work for something that actually reflects your boss's error. Gaslighting can also take the forms of both having your emotions denied by the gaslighter and denying your own emotions (for example, "I don't feel anything; it's not upsetting me"). It is as though, after years of gaslighting, you learn to gaslight yourself.

Normal gaslighting: I am not convinced that there is a normal variant of gaslighting, unless there is a moment when you truly believe that something was done correctly, when, in fact, you were wrong, and you stand your ground only to be found out to be wrong (for example, you insist that you put the cooler in the trunk for a vacation and then, when you arrive at the destination, it is not there)—but, since you did not set out to deceive anyone, it really does not qualify as gaslighting. In such a case, you would apologize and be more careful in your steely conviction in the future. Because gaslighting is a manipulation from the start, it is really never a healthy or normal pattern.

Pathological gaslighting: In the same vein, one could argue that all gaslighting is pathological, as it is meant to undercut another person's sense of reality and assuredness and infuse him or her with self-doubt. It is a form of control—and a classical part of abuse dynamics. Controlling parents can do it to children throughout their lifespan, controlling partners tend to start engaging in this pattern relatively early in a relationship, and toxic bosses or coworkers can do this at work.

How does gaslighting make you feel? Full of self-doubt, "crazy," confused, isolated.

CONTROLLING

Narcissists and toxic people are highly insecure and feel internally out of control, relying on the outside world for validation and to regulate their self-esteem. Thus, they often attempt to exert tremendous control over their external worlds, and this includes relationships, their environments, and other people. At the extreme is the kind of control observed in relationships characterized by domestic violence. In other cases, it may manifest as severe emotional control that can border on what is observed in psychopathy. Control may also involve controlling the decision-making and movements of family members. It is not unheard of for controlling parents to attempt to dictate every element of their children's lives—an extension of the helicopter and bubble-wrapped parenting observed in so many parents today. Well into adulthood, it is not unusual for parents who have the means to use trust funds and other financial incentives to purchase their children's obedience, devotion, proximity, or anything they want, and to use wills and estates to exert that same control from beyond the grave.

Their environments can also be dictated by tremendous control, and, if they have the means, they will have employees and housekeepers who maintain their offices and homes in rigid fastidiousness and will rage against any disruptions in their organized world, whether at home or at work. Cars are kept impeccably clean, and fury will ensue if anyone tracks in dirt. Disorder is not tolerated, and it may be that the highly organized structures of their outside world are an offset to the emotional dysregulation and inconsistent self-esteem they experience internally. It can have an almost obsessive-compulsive feel, and it can sometimes play out as what may appear to be a frank environmental sensitivity (the windows have to be oriented in the right direction, the precise type of cleaner has to be used, the light bulbs can't buzz, the gray in the walls can't be too dark). Stories of toxic, narcissistic, and entitled bosses screaming at underlings for a misplaced staple, a cup of coffee brought late, or a hotel room that is not on the precisely correct floor are not unusual. Interestingly, fear of being alone is something that peppers the world of toxic people and narcissists, a dynamic of which they are often unaware. As such, they will control others through any means possible—money, fear, strength—and it becomes a "controllable" way to create the belief that abandonment won't occur. In the early phase of a relationship, control can manifest as an insistence about spending as much time together as possible, something that can initially be labeled romantic but can become suffocating very quickly.

Finally, control can also manifest as an emotional control—an unwillingness to share vulnerability or to show other emotions they have branded "weak," such as kindness or sadness. Because of this, when toxic or narcissistic people experience these kinds of emotions, especially negative emotions such as sadness, the emotions may manifest as anger or rage.

Normal control: Some people value order in their environments and feel better for it; however, it does not take over their functioning and they are able to tolerate some disruptions to it. They may like to have their shirts organized by color but will not humiliate someone else if that goal is not achieved. Most parents offer advice to children and hope they will follow some of it, but that is quite different than trying to puppeteer a child's life.

Pathological control: This occurs when control becomes the prevailing dynamic in relationships. This is when the toxic person is more likely to view or engage with people as chessboard pawns than to engage with them as human beings with free will. In these situations, the demand is for order and control above all else, and narcissists find it nearly impossible to endure lack of order in anything. They may literally attempt to control whom a partner talks with and what clothes he or she wears, or a narcissistic child may restrict the movements of an older parent and block access to his or her own resources. Pathological control places partners, family members, friends, and employees on impossibly tight leashes. For a person living under the toxic regime of a narcissistic person, it can feel like a police state or constant surveillance of some form. In cases of domestic violence, pathological control is always observed, and it is often observed early in the relationship through isolation or chronic contact.

How does being controlled make you feel? Hopeless, helpless, ineffective, trapped, angry, frustrated.

Behavioral

The behavioral aspects of toxic and narcissistic people are the actions and attitudes that you can observe. They often relate to visible patterns, such as how these people look, what they buy, where they live, and how they spend money. These patterns are the overt manifestation of all of the other patterns (for example, the lack of empathy, the insecurity, the entitlement). Interestingly, the behavioral elements of a toxic person are often more annoying and are something that everyone observes and experiences when they interact with this person; however, different people may interpret these behaviors differently. One person may praise the person's "fabulous" Instagram feed, while another may view it as vain and cringeworthy. There are four typical patterns within a narcissist's behavioral aspects: superficiality, covetousness/envy, being cheap, and carelessness.

SUPERFICIALITY

For toxic people and, certainly, for narcissists, everything is a show, which is why luxury goods, expensive cars, cosmetic procedures, outlandish vacations, perfect bodies, visible accomplishments, or the "right" address is so important. The assumption that "the more perfect the Christmas card picture, the bigger the problems" often holds here—these families are fantastic at putting on a façade while, behind closed doors, a Tennessee Williams play is unfolding. Social media is the ultimate platform for superficiality and calls for edited images, perfect settings, and an aspirational life. For superficial people, it is not about living a full life or having a healthy relationship; it is about the "Instagrammable" life. They have a propensity for larger-than-life parties and soirees (mermaids in the swimming pool, ice sculptures, camels, fire jugglers, twenty bridesmaids, fifteen-tier cakes for a five-year-old—you get the idea).

Superficiality also takes in the territory of vanity, and, as such, narcissism and entitlement are big drivers of the massive vanity economy: cosmetic surgery, dermatology, dentistry, hair extensions, and body sculpting of all sorts. We are a culture that fetishizes and values youth or anything that resembles youth, and the superficial concern with outrunning aging and appearing young is a costly and time-consuming enterprise for many who fall into this bucket. Remember, *insecurity is the core of narcissism,* so gussying up a person's outsides means he or she does not need to worry as much about his or her insides.

Superficial parents often expect children to follow their path and live up to their ideals, and this could manifest in painful patterns, such as criticizing their children's weight, appearance, choices of hobbies, friends, and educational and career paths. It can also be manifested as children gravitating to activities the parents enjoy—with some children going so far as taking on hobbies or interests the parents enjoy simply to have more time with them and not out of any interest in the activity per se. As long as the child looks, behaves, or otherwise exists in a manner that the parent values, all is well. Basically, these parents are more concerned with how things look and appear to the world than of the quality of their children's inner lives.

Superficial friends are the ones who spend more time getting the selfie right and posting the picture than being present with you, and they will often react defensively when their self-referential life is critiqued or pointed out. A key dynamic here is status seeking. It is not uncommon for narcissistic people to seek out high-status friends or spend time in places or situations where they can meet these high-status people.

> **Normal superficiality:** In the age of posting about life via social media, most people will take the time to select the most flattering images or the images that make their lives seem "amazing" (for example, your fancy vacation shots from Fiji) to post. The world does judge a book by its cover, and most of us like occasionally pulling on a new outfit or sprucing ourselves up to have a night out. It comes down to how much time, money, and mental energy we devote to these pursuits.
>
> **Pathological superficiality:** It becomes pathological when a person judges everyone and lives by this superficial metric, such as expending significant resources (sometimes more than is affordable) on clothing, jewelry, handbags, shoes, homes, luxury goods, parties, cars, vacations. Snobbishly dismissing other people because they don't have the right "brand" or provenance, whatever that may be (club memberships, education, address, job, car, last name, clothes), is also a pathological form of superficiality. Superficiality becomes pathological when it entails being so focused on external variables that the person expends disproportionate resources on creating a "too good to be true" façade to share with the world. It's all skin deep.
>
> **How does their superficiality make you feel?** Bored, entertained, dazzled (for a minute), disgusted, uncomfortable.

COVETOUSNESS/ENVY

"Covetousness" is defined as "inordinate desire for wealth or possessions or for another's possessions" (Merriam-Webster, 2018). It is a form of greed mixed with jealousy. It is focused on "the other person," wanting your brother's car or simply a better car than your brother's, wanting the vacation a friend took, wanting a bigger house than your best friend's, in addition to just wanting "stuff." Covetousness can take up a lot of mental real estate. Covetous people tend to ruminate on their wants, spending lots of time researching and looking at the things they want.

Covetousness usually involves money and objects such as cars, houses, clothing, and jewelry, but it can also involve craving experiences (travel) or even people (attractive partner, wealthy partner, much younger partner). Covetous people can have a bit of a nasty edge to them. They are so motivated to possess that thing they want, that it can raise a specter of irritability in them until they get it. Sadly, covetousness is a beast that cannot be fed, a sort of materialistic gateway drug, and, if they do finally obtain the coveted object, it can be a setup to want more. A major driver of covetousness is our increasingly materialistic, consumerist, and debt-driven society (more on that later)—there are lots of goods to purchase, the marketers are brilliant at telling us we will feel better if we have them, and we can get lines of credit to purchase them. Sadly, once the coveted object is acquired, the debt remains, and the hole isn't filled. So the covetousness persists.

A key element of covetousness is envy—coveters not only covet what other people have, but also envy people who have what they want. And, in an interesting twist, they believe other people envy them, or, at least, they try to construct lives that other people will envy (social media helps with that). If other people have more than they do, people who are narcissistic or entitled experience it as a loss of self-esteem, and that is an uncomfortable place to be. Envy plays out in a fascinating way in narcissistic and toxic individuals. It results in speaking about a person they envy in absolutely grandiose and almost worshipful tones ("He is the coolest, richest dude around; I'll know I made it when I'm driving his car") *or* in absolutely disparaging tones ("Everyone knows that she slept around to get that stuff," or, "He only got all of that because his father is loaded; he's an idiot"). In families, this can play out in a tragic manner, especially when a parent covets what a child has earned or achieved—it can sap the enjoyment out of it and can also result in feelings of guilt for the child, whether that child is an adolescent or an adult.

Because narcissistic people believe that other people envy them, or *want* other people to envy them, they will make choices that they believe make them enviable. They choose the very objects they would envy to generate the enviable version of themselves (and often at the cost of debt, financial insecurity, and/or wrecked marriages or other important relationships).

Normal covetousness: We all want something—a home, a better car, a particular piece of jewelry, a trip to a certain place, a new pair of shoes. Sometimes it can become a passion project of saving up, and perhaps we even harbor a bit of envy for those who are already in possession of it. However, if a person is not putting himself or herself into financial danger or castigating the person in possession of the coveted object, person, or situation, then it may likely be filed under "a passing coveting."

Pathological covetousness: Pathological covetousness is all-encompassing. The person does feel rather Gollum-y (the creature who coveted the Ring in *The Lord of the Rings*) in his or her single-minded obsessiveness about the things or people he or she wants and can't let it go. Often these people lose sight of their initial drive for the things they want or hold unrealistic expectations about what obtaining these things will actually get them. In addition, the covetousness tends to creep into other areas of their lives, and they may find themselves often talking about it, referring to it, risking themselves financially for it, and criticizing or envying people who already have it. At its extreme, it can look like an outright obsession.

How does their covetousness make you feel? Uncomfortable, bored, frustrated, put off, disgusted, concerned, and sometimes empathic.

BEING CHEAP

The grand irony is that, for folks who are so concerned with appearance, status, material goods, and superficial pursuits, toxic and narcissistic people are notoriously miserly and cheap. In many ways, spending money serves an instrumental purpose for them (to purchase a luxury item that will give them status, to purchase a new car that will give them satisfaction, to be generous to others they want to impress or win over). The fact is, once you are won over, they may not be forthcoming with any resources—money, time, or presence. It can be an agonizing dichotomy, because it is not unusual for a toxic, narcissistic, or entitled person to have plenty of wealth and then use it as a tool of power and manipulation within a family or business system.

It is the paradox of the modern era—executive compensation has never been higher, and low-wage workers cannot catch up. The cheapness of toxic and narcissistic people is the reason that "trickle-down" theories do not work—the lack of empathy, the entitlement, and the need to regulate self-esteem from the outside mean that toxic and narcissistic people are not going to share their goodies, toys, or money. And their penchant for rationalizing anything that is self-serving means that they are able to sleep at night, even when they make untold millions while their employees struggle.

This can be confusing in a relationship; blinding generosity during the courtship phase will be followed by restriction and questioning about how money is being spent. Toxic and narcissistic people will hand over a credit card and then criticize you for using it. They no longer "need" to be generous once they "get the girl (or the guy)." In light of their paranoia, it is quite common for them to believe that they are being taken advantage of or used for their money, and they can become suspicious about spending it on others, even though they themselves may have set the tone for spending money on other people. This isn't just about frugality or good financial planning, but rather one more way for narcissists to manage their self-esteem and control other people. It can also be startling to watch them transform from generous to cheap in a short period of time or to be generous only when there is an audience (purchasing expensive rounds of drinks or dinner for a large group when everyone will publicly applaud them, but being miserly and cheap in one-on-one encounters, on things a family member needs, or with someone whose status is of little interest to them).

But this is not just about money. When we think about someone's being cheap or stingy or miserly, we typically think about money, but it can extend to time or simply generosity of spirit. This "cheapness" of spirit can be experienced as a coldness and a distance, or simply a lack of responsiveness to good things—such as being cold or bored when a child shares an accomplishment or experience or distracted when a person in a group is recounting a happy tale.

Normal cheapness: "Cheap" and "frugal" are not the same thing. Cheapness gets at the concept of having the resource and not being forthcoming with it at appropriate times. Frugality relates to being careful with money. Sometimes we are particularly frugal, especially if we are saving up for a goal, and that may lead us to be less generous than usual. A good rule of thumb: If you feel the need to get the calculator out at a fast-food restaurant to split the check because your friend ordered the larger French fries, that's cheap. If you avoid eating out for a few months to save up for a car, that's frugal. That said, even if you are careful with money and may be reluctant or unable to be generous with cash or gifts, also reflect on your ability to share your time. If you have time and are willing to share it, then that is a good sign.

Pathological cheapness: This can manifest as being miserly even when the resources are there. For example, being stingy when you are behind closed doors with someone but ultra-generous when there is an audience. This can also be a strategic use of money, such as their being overly miserly with a family member who could benefit from it but then giving their resources of time and money to people whom they wish to impress. Pathological cheapness can also be observed in a person who is able to switch gears from being generous to being less than generous after he or she wins you over. In addition, pathological cheapness can also manifest in the person who may step up and offer financial assistance or some other resource, and then keep reminding you about it for such a long time that you just wish you had gone to a bank.

How does their cheapness make you feel? Devalued, confused, uncomfortable, frustrated.

CARELESSNESS

Lack of empathy means narcissists remain indifferent to the needs or wants of other people, as evidenced by their dismissive behavior. They rarely inquire about your well-being, do not appear to care about your difficulties or triumphs, will make decisions with little consideration of how they affect other people, or will say things that are insensitive.

When narcissistic people are confronted by these patterns, their responses will range from defensiveness ("I didn't really mean that when I said that; stop putting words in my mouth") to dismissive ("Stop being so sensitive; you know what I meant"), and even, in some cases, apologetic ("Sorry about that. I didn't mean it; sometimes I just say things without thinking about it"). A key difference between toxic or narcissistic people and psychopathic people is that narcissists don't typically set out to hurt someone else. It is the fact that they are psychologically stunted, impulsive, emotionally restricted, and incapable of stepping out of themselves that often leaves them saying inappropriate or unkind things to other people. Psychopaths, on the other hand, know exactly what they are saying or doing and can masterfully use words to hurt, and often will do that. That is not to say that narcissistic people cannot or will not do that, but, more often than not, they are merely careless.

It all boils down to carelessness. They do not filter, they do not censor, and they engage in the callous luxury of saying whatever they want, whenever they want. Filtering, censoring, and thinking about what we say are effortful—each takes a moment, and it requires empathy or some regard for the other person or persons in the conversation or interaction. It takes work to hold back from saying something at certain times, and we hold back to be sensitive to the feelings of others. Narcissistic people do not play by those rules; their impulsivity means that they just blurt something out and assume they can remedy the situation by minimizing it or apologizing for it after the fact.

Carelessness can really hurt; intention does not always matter. A hurtful word is a hurtful word, whether it was intended to be as such or not. Here's a simple analogy: Imagine that someone slaps or punches you in the face. It hurts. And then the person says, "Oh, I didn't mean to do that. I was practicing punches earlier today and just did that without thinking." The bottom line? When you were punched, whether it was intended or not, regardless of the reason, it hurt. We may be able to psychologically "process" something hurtful better if we understand the intention, but how many times can we revise our reaction to careless words?

Carelessness also implies a devaluation. The assumption is that "if you mattered," the toxic or narcissistic person would take a minute before saying or doing something thoughtless. It makes you feel like you are not worth filtering for. By and large, toxic people are equal-opportunity perpetrators. The *only* time narcissistic people will get it "right" is when they perceive the other person in the interaction to be very important or valuable in some way (such as having more wealth, power, or fame, or could help them achieve an opportunity they are hoping for). But, even then, because toxic people are so accustomed to talking without thinking, they often quite easily get it wrong even with the people who matter to them.

Normal carelessness: We are all guilty of it. We forget to check in with a friend who is going through a difficult time, because we are too busy. We throw off a comment that could be perceived as criticism, because we are not being sufficiently mindful during the conversation. We say something insensitive to someone who is struggling, because we did not think it through. And, in normal patterns of carelessness, when the pattern is pointed out to us, we are typically contrite, we apologize and take responsibility, and we try harder in the future to be more present and mindful.

Pathological carelessness: Again, it is a pattern—a pattern of making dismissive, unkind, or thoughtless statements or gestures, which are often followed by (insincere) apologies. It almost becomes a cycle: Say something hurtful, get called out, apologize, do it again. When carelessness is so consistent that disappointment or hurt is a regular part of the menu, and the careless individual has a collection of excuses ("I'm busy," "I was distracted," "It's just how I am; I didn't mean it"), it is likely more of a pathological pattern.

How does their carelessness make you feel? Dismissed, devalued, undeserving, "less than," unseen, unheard.

Dysregulation

Toxic and narcissistic people cannot control their emotions, and, in part, that is due to the fact that they regulate their self-esteem from the outside in. Ultimately, narcissistic people and most toxic people are deeply insecure, and, when people are insecure, they perceive themselves as being chronically under threat. As such, they do not soothe their negative emotions well and practice either denial or projection. When they are frustrated, disappointed, or stressed in any way (especially in a way that feels threatening), they often blow up, and their rages invariably appear out of proportion to the situation that set them off. Thus, they are prone to rages because they feel jealous, rages because they feel disrespected, rages because they feel unappreciated, rages because they feel someone "got one over" on them, rages because they did not get what they want, and the list goes on.

The patterns subsumed under dysregulation relate to narcissists' own fragility, which is why they are always trying to manage emotions, such as anger, through external means, and this can include seeking validation and avoiding being alone. In addition, it is not unusual for narcissistic and toxic people to engage in other dysregulated behaviors, such as drug and alcohol use, spending/shopping, gambling, and even compulsive sex to attempt to regulate these emotions. There are five major patterns that fall within a narcissist's dysregulation: fragility/insecurity, anger/rage, validation seeking, inability to be alone, and shame.

FRAGILITY AND INSECURITY

Narcissism equals pathological insecurity. The pattern of fragility and insecurity is actually more of a *reason* for dysregulated patterns such as rage. The role of fragility and insecurity in narcissism often takes people by surprise. Narcissistic people are traditionally so antagonistic, abusive, disrespectful, and generally difficult (and can be confident and interpersonally suave) that it can be difficult to view them as being fragile. Their fragility emanates from the fact that they are deeply insecure and have to regulate their self-esteem based on what other people think about them. As a result, they are completely reliant on other people's appraisals of them. They wither at a mean tweet but, since they are narcissistic, they don't cry about it—they launch a counterattack. Their fragile self-esteem ties into their hypersensitivity, and they cannot endure even gentle constructive feedback (I have even had narcissistic students complain that their A was not high enough and attempt to file grievances as a result). Any rejection, critique, constructive criticism, or even suboptimal feedback or lighter praise than they had hoped for, is ego crushing and will almost always result in anger and rage. As a result, it is nearly impossible to ever help narcissistic people improve, because they are unable to accept constructive feedback and are more likely to sue than to implement thoughtful guidance.

Because their self-esteem is entirely tied into more fleeting characteristics, such as appearance, their fragile self-esteem becomes more fragile with time. The usual fallbacks of appearance, youth, and career, in most cases, tend to lose their luster with time. As such, the rages can get worse as narcissists get older. This all ties into dysregulation, because their pushback when they feel their self-esteem is being threatened is often quite explosive or exaggerated; they become deeply glum or rageful when things do not go their way. Because insecurity is rarely understood to be the foundation of narcissism and toxic people in general, the dysregulation often also seems illogical, but understanding the fragility that undercuts narcissism helps the patterns make more sense (though it does not necessarily make them more tolerable).

Normal fragility and insecurity: We all have Achilles' heels and vulnerabilities, and when people "go there" or we experience criticism about those things, our reactions may be disproportionate to the critique, or we may be unable to hear what someone is saying because we are so upset. In the normal version of this, people will catch themselves, apologize for an overreaction, be self-reflective, communicate about this particular vulnerability, and return to their stable sense of self.

Pathological fragility and insecurity: Any bit of feedback, advice, or criticism unsettles the fragile sense of self-esteem and sends the narcissistic person spinning—almost always into a rage, but, in a small percentage of cases, into sadness or even depression. Anything that does not maintain his or her ego is poorly received, and there is no opportunity to provide feedback, because it is too unsettling for everyone involved and the narcissistic person will always overreact. Thus, narcissists often do not receive feedback about their behavior, because other people just don't feel it is worth the bother and the tantrum.

How does their fragility and insecurity make you feel? Like you're walking on eggshells, censored, inauthentic, anxious, frustrated, confused.

ANGER AND RAGE

Hell hath no fury like a pissed-off narcissist. Toxic, entitled, and narcissistic people cannot manage their emotions, and, when anything threatens their sense of order, privilege, entitlement, justice, or convenience, they lash out explosively. The news coverage in the past year of

50

rageful bosses (Harvey Weinstein, Matt Lauer, Donald Trump) often references their terrifying rages, which cast fear in everyone around them and allowed them to wield their power mercilessly. But this does not happen just in companies—it can occur in families, in classrooms, and amongst friends. It is this dynamic that leads people to walk on eggshells around them, because they can go from zero to sixty over what can seem like the tiniest issue. Over time, the entire system organizes to insulate toxic people from anything that can anger them, because everyone else is afraid of their rage. Rage that culminates in verbal or physical abuse is never acceptable. Never.

It is the dynamic of anger and rage in toxic people that can result in toxic strangers' impacting us. All of us have been in a restaurant, subway car, airplane, children's park, parking lot, or other public place in which someone threw a tantrum and spewed rage at a person in that setting. It is difficult to witness these tantrums, and it takes a toll on the observers, even if they are not part of the interaction. In this way, toxic people can impact us, even if we have no relationship to them.

Growing up with parents like this can make the world feel like an unsafe space—both for children and for the adults that they will become. Having a boss like this can result in severe stress that can impact physical and mental health. Obviously, this is also a dynamic often observed in domestic violence situations, with the roller coaster of anger, rage, and violence punctuated by empty apologies, and then the whole cycle begins again. Even amongst friends or siblings, or in any other group in which a toxic person runs the show through anger, it can be destabilizing—and, ultimately, it sets the tone for all interactions.

Normal anger: We all get angry—it's a normal response to frustration and disappointment. Anger is a negative emotion that we can express appropriately to share these feelings. Rage is a stronger emotion, and, at times, there can be normal rage, such as when it is a reaction to a horrible injustice, an abuse of power or abuse within a system, or a sense of powerlessness in the face of helplessness. However, rage is not a healthy emotion in the long term. It is a stressful emotion, putting real wear and tear on our physiological systems (Siegel, 2005), and is frightening and threatening to the people around us.

> **Pathological anger and rage:** Consistent displays of disproportionate anger, frequent use of insults instead of appropriately expressing anger about a situation, rapid ramp-up of anger into rage that feels out of proportion to the stimulus, reacting with anger and rage to almost every disappointing or frustrating situation, and controlling other people who are afraid of this rage and never "rock the boat" are all examples of pathological anger and rage.
>
> **How does their anger and rage make you feel?** Unsafe, fearful, helpless, hopeless, angry, anxious, detached, vulnerable, avoidant.

VALIDATION SEEKING

Imagine someone cut off your air supply. You would use all the strength you have to get some. It's the same for narcissists and for many toxic people when it comes to validation. They require the admiration and validation of the world outside of them to survive. As long as a steady stream of compliments, gifts, success, and adulation is coming in, most narcissistic and entitled people are fine (though they always crave more). Social media has fast-tracked validation, so now a person can just sit in the comfort of home, edit and post photographs, and wait for the likes to come in. These days, you don't even need to go through the headache of a conversation or a human relationship to get validation. But, like any drug of abuse, validation seeking eventually starts losing some of its power, so you need more and more validation. At some point, ten likes is not enough; now it needs to be a hundred. So many people are living lives in the service of Instagram rather than in the service of life, making choices about vacations, family outings, restaurants, the clothes they will wear, and how they will spend a Sunday morning in the name of validation seeking.

Validation seeking is the way that narcissists regulate their self-esteem. Because they are so insecure, they need the world to help them regulate their fragile sense of self by telling them they are wonderful or attractive or smart or amazing. Narcissists need to hear and receive validation on a constant basis. In the absence of it, they become quite glum.

In any relationship with a narcissist, this results in a one-way street in which everyone has to bring heaps of validation to the narcissist (this is something called "narcissistic supply"); in essence, it is the equivalent of feeding an insatiable beast. Narcissistic supply is the validation provided to the narcissist, and this can be attention, validation, admiration, compliments, blind adoration, fans, Instagram followers, Facebook likes, trophies and awards on the wall. To be in a relationship with any narcissist, the price of entry is provision of narcissistic supply. It's the equivalent of shoveling coal into a furnace, the relationship stops working once you stop providing supply. It is never enough. There is no reciprocity in this quest for validation—narcissists ask for it endlessly but rarely offer any. Sadly, when they do offer any validation, it is often in the name of manipulation or to get something they need, rather than really offering genuine praise or mindful recognition of the triumphs or goodness of another person.

Normal validation seeking: We all like being told we look nice or are nice but, ideally, we do not *need* it. Most people do light up when they receive a compliment, but a healthy person recognizes that he or she was always that good person even before the validation. Normal validation results in people's using social media not solely for likes but also because they are genuinely curious about the lives and opinions of others and want to reciprocally share the events of their own lives.

Pathological validation seeking: It is very unhealthy when other human beings serve primarily as sources of validation and admiration. This can often play out as, "Enough about you, tell me more wonderful things about me." Pathological needs for validation are observed when narcissists push out the people who are not yes-men or validation providers. There cannot be enough compliments for them (their self-esteem constantly needs to be fed), and it starts anew each day—it's as though the compliments and validation don't stick, and so they need more every day. If they give you a gift, be prepared to have to say "thank you" for a *very* long time (in many cases, the gift is not worth it). Without validation, these folks become depressed, dejected, and irritable. As noted, this can manifest in an unhealthy devotion to social media—with a life organized around getting approval, likes, and followers.

How does their chronic validation seeking make you feel? Exhausted, unsatisfied, bored, used, frustrated, unheard, disgusted.

INABILITY TO BE ALONE

For many narcissists, to be alone with their fragile self-esteem, insecurity, and need for validation is very difficult, so they will seek out spaces where they are not alone. The personality trait extraversion is actually significantly higher in narcissists (Holtzman et al., 2010), especially grandiose narcissists (Jauk et al., 2016), because they are always "people seeking." The challenge is that they are seeking other people not necessarily for affiliation and closeness but rather for validation. They become distressed, dejected, and even panicky when they have to fend for themselves. The inability to be alone can also manifest via manipulation (such as guilt) to "force" other people into their purview.

In the age of social media, narcissists will stare at and check and recheck their social media compulsively to ensure that people are still out there and paying attention to their posts, and that no one else's posts are better than their own. They also chronically check their phones, hoping for text messages, DMs, phone calls, or emails. They may roll their eyes and pretend that the many people trying to reach them are a nuisance, but, without those pings, dings, and rings, they would actually feel like deflated balloons. Narcissists often love to entertain, not because they want to treat other people well or be gracious, but to ensure that they will not be alone (when the party is at their house, they are sure to be invited). They use entertaining as a way to grandstand and show off and expect lots of ring-kissing and, ideally, for guests to envy their lives a little bit too.

It gets tricky over time, because the more bridges that narcissists or toxic people burn, the harder it may be for them to find people to spend time with them. If a narcissist has money, he or she can typically find enough "pay to play" friends and family members, especially if the narcissist is willing to pick up the check or pay for the plane tickets or concert tickets. Many wealthy narcissists are able to ensure that they are never alone by "buying" the people who spend time with them or having lots of "employees" around them who run their errands but whom they also expect to stick around for dinner.

Narcissists who are alone are often a sad sight. They can look lost, anxious, irritable, and sad. Think about it: Their fragile self-esteem crumbles without validation from other people, so being alone is typically unacceptable. More vulnerable narcissists can find being with other people exhausting at times because they are a reminder of their "lack of success," but will be angry when they cannot find people to spend time with them at their convenience.

Normal inability to be alone: Solitary confinement is considered to be one of the cruelest forms of punishment that can be inflicted on a person; as such, few normal people would want to be alone 24/7. There are times when all of us want to spend time with friends and family, and this can vary based on how extraverted or introverted we are. The more extraverted a person is, the more challenging it can feel to be alone for long periods of time, and extraverted people may gravitate toward jobs in which there is a lot of social contact or toward living arrangements that involve other people. However, this normal desire for wanting to be with other people is counterbalanced by the ability to tolerate and even welcome being alone.

Pathological inability to be alone: This is observed when the person is deeply uncomfortable with being alone—even the thought of having to eat a meal alone fills the person with immense anxiety and feels like an embarrassment. At such times, there is a tendency toward self-pity and for the narcissists to start calling everyone they know until they find someone to agree to spend time with them, because it would be too uncomfortable otherwise. People who have a pathological difficulty with being alone may also lash out angrily at other people when they do not agree to spend time with them.

How does their inability to be alone make you feel? Suffocated, bored, frustrated, guilty.

SHAME

Shame is a public emotion. It happens when a person does a bad thing and is judged by the public, which results in a negative feeling for the person who did the bad thing. The man who cheats on his wife is found out, is called a homewrecker, and that feels bad—because he *looks* bad and is being tried in the court of public opinion. Guilt is a different animal. It's when people judge themselves badly (whether or not the world ever finds out). It is more mature and psychologically healthy to evoke guilt rather than shame to regulate behavior, and, as you can imagine, narcissistic and toxic people are much more driven by shame than by guilt. The feeling of shame is not a pleasant one, so it is not unusual for the shamed person to act out angrily at the world, by not taking responsibility, by blaming the people who called him or her out (rather than being contrite about the behavior), by pointing out the flaws in other people instead of owning his or her own transgressions, or by throwing rageful tantrums. In comparison, a guilty person will often turn inward and may become depressed, anxious, socially withdrawn, and uncomfortable. A guilty person will typically not go on a social media tear and point fingers at others whom he or she believes are behaving badly.

Research using a tool that can examine brain function, called functional magnetic resonance imaging, studying small samples of people, has revealed that the neurobiological substrates of shame and guilt in the brain are actually different (Michl et al., 2012). With that said, even if narcissists know they did something bad, their tendency is to focus on their shame and humiliation and loss ("You can't imagine how difficult this has been for me and my family") rather than transcend to focus on the pain of those they hurt. They may not understand that they did something wrong, and, even when authorities or other structures penalize them or call them out for what they did, they tend to focus on themselves, revealing an astonishing lack of insight. For example, in the weeks and months after Harvey Weinstein was called out for multiple misdeeds, on a very shameful and public platform, resulting in major personal and public losses, several sources indicated that his main rallying cry was to find out "who did him in," rather than expressing sincere contrition about his wrongdoing.

Skilled publicists, whose job is to issue convincing apologies that convey sufficient guilt, will often make it appear as though the shamed transgressor feels bad, but it doesn't ring true. A standard trick in the narcissist's playbook is to state, "I am sorry that my behavior hurt other people," rather than, "I did a bad thing and I regret my behavior." While that may be a legal maneuver, it still feels as though there is little insight about the bad behavior. Instead, it feels as though they can only acknowledge that people got hurt by the behavior with no understanding that the behavior itself was problematic. At such times, narcissists and other toxic folks are quick to call any landscape of accusations toward them a "witch hunt," which turns them, as the perpetrator, into a victim. It's a clever gambit and reflects more shame and less guilt (or simply lack of insight).

Social media has made shame something that is easier to disseminate. Wrongdoings or bad behaviors can be hinted at more widely through social media networks or to wider circles of friends and family. Does shame result in any significant behavior change? Not typically. Maybe for a minute, a week, or even a few months, but, until a person can regulate his or her behavior from the inside, rather than the outside, it is unlikely to change. Or, as Gabriel García Márquez once wisely wrote: "Shame has poor memory."

Normal shame: We have all done bad deeds and we have all been called out on them, and we felt really bad afterward. In most of these cases, we felt guilty, and, if we were found out, we also got the double displeasure of shame. But, if the guilt predates the shame, then it means the apparatus is working right—and, since, for a normal person, these feelings are so bad, they can act as a deterrent to engaging in that bad behavior again.

Pathological shame: It becomes pathological when the person never learns to regulate on the basis of guilt or simply learns to do the right thing. Instead, he or she keeps behaving badly, getting called out, experiencing shame, and maybe apologizing a few times or getting angry or both, and then doing it again. The entitlement often means that the person does whatever he or she wants, with little regard or concern for consequences. The lack of empathy means that there is not a natural drive to reflect on how the behavior affects other people. Then, if someday, these people do get called out on their behavior, their reaction tends to be shame, defensiveness, and characterizing themselves as victims rather than perpetrators.

How does their shame make you feel? May leave us feeling ashamed ourselves if we are drawn into the scandal; hurt, embarrassed, revictimized.

Antagonistic

This is the part of the toxic and narcissistic pattern that feels deeply unsettling and threatening—and that negatively affects anyone in the toxic person's path, whether a stranger or a partner or a family member. These are the qualities that reveal the narcissists and toxic people to be bullies, tyrants, braggarts, jerks, and assholes. The antagonistic traits are those apparent in the "cinematic" narcissist: the Wall Street tycoon, the cruel dictator, the vindictive boss, the abusive parent. In families, these antagonistic patterns can leave the other family members frightened, and the family system often organizes in a manner to avoid evoking the anger of the antagonistic bully. There are nine common patterns within a narcissist's antagonistic repertoire: grandiosity, entitlement, passive aggression, schadenfreude, arrogance, exploitation, failure to take responsibility, vindictiveness, and oppositional behavior.

GRANDIOSITY

Grandiosity can run the gamut from showmanship to delusion. In general, it's a tendency to exaggerate accomplishments, talents, and experiences. Narcissists' fantasy worlds are overly developed, and, if they are not already successful, they will spend lots of time talking about their dream wedding, massive career, money they are going to make, or lives they are going to change someday. In some ways, it's like watching or listening to intoxicated people (and when grandiose narcissists are drunk or high, it can get worse)—they talk big, but the talk doesn't really make sense. At the extreme, it can seem delusional ("I feel as though I am the vessel for faraway universes; all the knowledge in the world runs through me, and, when I am ready, I will share it"). At times, they can sound like cult leaders and conspiracy theorists. By and large, they just look like they have very little insight or self-awareness. At times, grandiosity can be entertaining, such as when they talk about their grand plans for their new app, or their new business strategy, or their new company—these plans often do not come together, but they can be interesting to witness and hear. And, at those moments, it becomes clear why grandiosity is frequently observed in visionary people. They have big, seemingly unreachable ideas (Uber, the iPhone, social media) that are actualized and change the world, and that only fosters more grandiosity and fertilizes it for the many people who want to be just like them. Over time, these conversations can feel vulgar, especially with people who have already achieved financial success and are yammering on about private jets and ten-carat diamond rings, or even on a smaller scale about their brand-new car, swimming pool, or vacation to Hawaii.

The grandiosity often leads them to live in a world that does not really exist. They talk about their gorgeous girlfriend as though they are already dating her, about the mansion they will have as though they are already living in it, and the wedding dresses they will wear despite not yet having located their groom. In that way, they are already living in their grandiose world, which can be confusing for other people—their grandiose fantasy becomes a reality. It can also be exhausting to listen to these grandiose ramblings, especially when you are trying to keep real life running—getting real bills paid, real kids to the bus stop, and real deadlines met. In a relationship, this can also create the feeling of "not being enough." The grandiose fantasies are repeated so often that it may leave a person questioning whether he or she is the right prop for the grandiose life the narcissist is striving for. In essence, narcissists set unattainable goals, so they can talk about them as though they are really happening, instead of the far duller topic of the day-to-day hard work involved in pursuing a series of smaller and more realistic goals.

Within a family, parents' wants for their children may be so grandiose that they stop attending to the daily needs of their children (the sports practices are often focused on conversations about pro sports contracts and the Olympics, rather than simply the love of the game; or it can be off-putting for other parents, having to listen to the narcissistic and toxic parents share their child's Ivy League achievements or other grand aspirations). Dynamically, the grandiosity is a defense against the emptiness and insecurity that the narcissist and most toxic people experience inside. Grandiosity protects the fragile ego in a rather immature manner.

The grandiosity is also often a trap and sets the seeds for patterns such as love bombing that will be detailed later in the book (see Chapter 7). Many people will admit that they fell for the grandiose person who courted them and showed them an over-the-top good time, and that they believed the fantasy fairy tale placed in front of them. In the grandiose world in which we live, lots of people fall for the hype that bigger is better. Not in relationships.

Normal grandiosity: All of us have told at least one fish tale in our lifetime ("I once caught a fish *this* big"). You may occasionally stretch the truth so people enjoy your story; you may overstate a relationship or an experience to give you some "cred," to dazzle, or to help you feel better. You may occasionally say that you are going to do something spectacular (take a major vacation, have an adventurous experience, apply to a competitive job or school) but really do not have a plan or an intention of following through (or literally do not know how). You may talk about it as a dream of yours but have to quietly swallow the likelihood it will not happen. Or you may overblow an experience on social media. Sadly, our world actually seems to pull for grandiosity, as though our ordinary lives are not sufficient. The key is to recognize the extraordinary within the ordinary.

Pathological grandiosity: Grandiosity becomes pathological when people exhibit a constant pattern of exaggerating experiences and achievements, stating things that are untrue and overblown, exaggerating relationships (for example, with a famous person), making bizarrely unrealistic statements about their own prowess or abilities ("Nobody in the world could do this better than I can"), talking about a larger-than-life future, or regularly portraying themselves as invincible and bulletproof. Pathological grandiosity also pulls people out of their real lives to the point where they start to believe the constructed fantasy and find it difficult, unsatisfying, and even distressing to pop back to the humdrum daily stuff of life.

How does their grandiosity make you feel? Confused, annoyed, bored, incredulous, insecure, not enough, entertained.

ENTITLEMENT

Entitlement is the signature characteristic of a toxic person and is one of the central issues that is driving the new epidemic of human toxicity. Sadly, entitled behavior is quickly becoming the new normal. It is the foremost driver of the "Don't you know who I am?" movement. Entitlement is the assumption that people deserve special treatment for no other reason than that they perceive themselves to be important, or that some "special" aspect of them entitles them to better treatment than everyone else. That is sadly how the world does work in actuality—the wealthy, the powerful, the famous *are* treated differently, but, when that is *expected*, they start drifting into the territory of entitlement.

Entitlement is often facilitated by factors such as celebrity, wealth, and power; however, there are many broke and unknown people who don't have anything resembling power, who are also extremely entitled—and their entitlement can be particularly brittle, because there are few people who actually facilitate it. Anyone who has worked in any form of customer service has come up against entitlement on a daily, if not hourly, basis. And, if it is not something we face at work, we may suffer with it when everyone is made to wait because an entitled person decided to show up late and the trip was delayed for him or her. Entitled people are often quite oblivious to how their demand for specialness and their lack of regard for others negatively impact others, and, more important, they do not care. Entitlement and lack of empathy go hand in hand—entitled people will often demand special treatment, even if it means someone else loses out.

Normal entitlement: You are rude to a receptionist or flight attendant on rare occasions because you are being made to wait an inordinate amount of time or because you are tired. You sometimes expect special treatment because you have been a regular patron of a business or in another setting. You use your credentials to make your frustration at a situation known ("As a doctor, I must say I am really put off by how you treat your customers"). In most cases, you are embarrassed by your tantrum afterward and reflect on it before ever doing it again.

Pathological entitlement: By definition, most entitled behavior is pathological. When entitlement cuts through everything the person does—an unwillingness to engage in or endure any of the normally expected rituals we humans have to experience, including waiting in line, following the speed limit, and paying our dues at work—it is a problem. It comes down to the "Don't you know who I am?" of it all and people's belief that the world is their playground, to be experienced with impunity. They frequently express frustration and anger when consequences follow their behavior. While many structures out there foster the idea that some people deserve more special treatment than others, it is an antagonistic way to go through life.

How does their entitlement make you feel? Angry, frustrated, shocked, disgusted, devalued.

PASSIVE AGGRESSION

Passive aggression often feels more "victim-y" than many of the other antagonistic dynamics and patterns of toxic people and narcissists. It's a backdoor form of antagonism. At the core of it, narcissists are insecure and fragile, and this can manifest as vulnerability. In fact, people who have the pattern of vulnerable narcissism often look so "whiny" and "needy" that they do not fit the typical pattern of a narcissist as a bully or show-off or combatant or mean person. However, it has the feeling of an antagonistic trait because many people feel as though they need to defend themselves in the face of passive-aggressive remarks. It also goes back to emotional regulation, because narcissistic people cannot regulate their emotions and their own self-esteem. Either they attack when disappointed or they paint themselves as victims in order to get the support and validation of others.

Passive aggression is a psychologically immature and indirect way of attempting to get needs met and of issuing criticism or insults. The passive-aggressive person will often cast himself or herself in a victim/martyr role that can result in feelings of guilt or discomfort by the person who is hearing it (e.g. "glad you had fun on your business trip, must be nice to go to sunny Miami while the rest of us freeze—life here is the usual misery, but glad that you had fun."). The phrase "must be nice" is often the tagline for passive-aggression. This pattern can cause you to question your reality and does not allow for direct communication to take place. Passive-aggressive people often portray themselves as long suffering while pointing out your shortcomings, instead of coming out directly and stating their discomfort with a situation. In that way, there is actually a fair bit of entitlement and grandiosity built into passive-aggressive patterns. Passive-aggressive patterns typically co-occur with petulance and a tendency to temper tantrums with lots of "woe is me" tossed in. Later, when we talk about subtypes of narcissism, I will reveal how this passive-aggressive pattern is very much a part of something called "covert narcissism."

Normal passive aggression: Sometimes when we feel hurt, we may have a tendency to engage in "woe is me" ideation, and then punish the person who hurt us in an indirect manner ("It's okay, I don't mind that I wasn't invited to your birthday; I love binge watching TV on Saturday nights. But it's a shame we don't have enough extra tickets for you to come to that concert next week"). Social media can sometimes fuel these flames—when we see via social media that we were not invited to an event, the tendency may be to say, "No problem, I really don't like that band, it's a terrible venue, and I have tons of work to do, so I probably can't make it to our yoga class in the morning." Admit it. We've all done it. The key is to lick your wounds, grow up, and, if something makes you uncomfortable, come out and say it clearly.

Pathological passive aggression: This is when passive aggression becomes a regular pattern and a consistent way of responding to perceived slights and disappointment. This can result in others around the narcissists trying to please them constantly, just to avoid the feeling of guilt that follows from anything they perceive as an insult or an oversight.

How does their passive aggression make you feel? Guilty, uncomfortable, frustrated, pitying, defensive, angry.

SCHADENFREUDE

"Schadenfreude" is a German word that is defined as "malicious joy," or, in the Cambridge Dictionary, as "a feeling of pleasure or satisfaction when something bad happens to someone else." It's a trait that builds upon so many of narcissists' other vulnerabilities; their need to regulate their self-esteem on the basis of validation (which means that, if someone is doing better than they are, they cannot tolerate it), their tendency to envy and covet, their lack of empathy, their hypersensitivity, their deformed sense of "fairness" and justice, their entitlement, and their grandiosity all come to reside in this phenomenon of taking joy in others' failures. It tends to be pronounced when the toxic person may have wanted the experience or material item that the other person has. This can play out as macabre joy over a friend's getting into a car accident in his new German sports car, or a toxic mother tut-tutting at a daughter who is failing at a job that her mother believed was too good for her, or an embittered unmarried friend becoming cheerful at a friend's relationship breakup, or a former boss's feeling glee when your entrepreneurial endeavor fails. Toxic and narcissistic people are often the first to issue a bemused "I told you so" when someone fails or falters.

In this way, toxic people can often be wet towels at happy occasions that are not about them. First, they cannot tolerate not being the center of attention; and, second, they can't tolerate watching someone achieve or potentially get ahead of them. Many people will report that attending a wedding with a narcissist feels like the seventh circle of hell because of his or her mean-spirited comments, rancorous laughter when things go wrong, and cynicism about the couple, the event, and the guests. Sadly, we live in a time when Twitter has become a schadenfreude delivery device for everyone from the commander in chief to late-night comedians to disgruntled celebrities to trolls mocking the tragedies of the day.

Normal schadenfreude: Though none of us cares to admit it, we have all had a momentary malicious-joy moment—maybe when an overly confident friend got taken down a few rungs, an arrogant coworker didn't get the sales award that month, the high school rival ages poorly, or the perfect daughter of the perfect couple did not get the perfect test score. We all do it—it's human nature—but if we catch ourselves, and it is not a pattern, then it's simply being human (and, interestingly, many of us tend to become more "schadenfreude-y" when it is the toxic narcissist who loses out—karma sometimes feels good).

Pathological schadenfreude: It's pathological when it becomes a pattern and is even launched at people who really worked hard and earned something or people who are more vulnerable. Pathological schadenfreude can feel uncomfortable—in some ways, you want to distance yourself from someone sharing these comments. It feels mean-spirited and typically disproportionate. People who engage in chronic schadenfreude may visibly laugh at an inappropriate time after someone has failed or gotten hurt or may even shame or excoriate in a public manner the person experiencing a failure. They will rarely offer sincere congratulations, may skip out on celebratory events that herald the accomplishments of other people, or may make underhanded comments on a regular basis that a certain accomplishment was not earned but came about through less meritorious means.

How does their schadenfreude make you feel? Gross, uncomfortable, unpleasant, hurt, angry, intimidated.

ARROGANCE

"Arrogance" is defined as "proud in an unpleasant way and behaving as if you are better or more important than other people" (Cambridge Dictionary). In this way, arrogance is a riff on entitlement—entitlement is a belief or a perception, and arrogance is how it manifests. Arrogance comes off as haughtiness, cockiness, swagger, snobbery, and dismissiveness. It tends to be a relatively repugnant trait, but, somehow, it has become conflated with success and confidence (if someone is that cocky, it is presumed that he or she must have the goods to back it up), and it's not unusual for people to believe someone is allowed to be arrogant because he or she is accomplished at something ("He's the best chef in town—he has earned his arrogance"). However, if someone is genuinely confident about his or her abilities, arrogance is unnecessary. People's arrogance typically reflects an insecurity, a need for posturing, as though their "excellence" (real or perceived) won't be noted, or that their "excellence" is somehow insecure or unstable, and that they are doing you a favor by being with you. The arrogance seeps out when they are interacting with someone they believe is "less" than them (which is just about everyone), for example, of lower social class, not a member of their club, someone more junior or less skilled than they are, a different race or religion, from a less affluent part of town, or holding a lesser position or job than they do. It can be painful to watch—and even more painful to experience. In short, it often feels like simple snobbery. Arrogance is ultimately based on perception—there is typically no meaningful reality to the hierarchy the arrogant person creates. Arrogance builds upon the contempt that narcissists appear to feel for most people, and they maintain a chronic disdain and even disgust for people who do not measure up to their grandiose and superficial metrics.

Arrogance often makes us think of less-than-favorable descriptive labels like "asshole," "prick," "dick," or other anatomical insults. It can make a relationship difficult, and it can be embarrassing when a new person is introduced to it; you may be used to it, but people newly meeting an arrogant person may be put off. Arrogance is a trait that persists *long* after the achievements that may have facilitated the arrogance evaporate. For example, there are fraudsters in prison who long ago lost their power and cachet and still retain their arrogant swagger. Arrogance is a signature sign of a narcissist, as well as a classical element of narcissism.

Normal arrogance: I'm not sure this is ever normal; it could manifest as a strongly spoken confidence to make a point, but usually the person gives a disclaimer or qualifier first ("I know this sounds arrogant, but I am one of the most experienced fishermen I know, and that bait is not going to work"). The disclaimer takes away the sting of the haughtiness, but you can make this work only from time to time.

Pathological arrogance: By definition, arrogance is pathological—it is antagonistic, is oppressive, and creates an environment of dismissiveness and inequity. When it is pathological, it colors all interactions and emerges when there is a power differential of any kind. There are never any disclaimers issued, because these people truly believe that they are better than others and act in accordance with that presumption.

How does their arrogance make you feel? Dismissed, devalued, "less than", unheard, uncomfortable.

EXPLOITATION

Exploitation is (sadly) a natural part of relationships with toxic and narcissistic people. Since they view other people as objects designed to achieve some goal (status, validation, task completion, ego gratification, sexual gratification, companionship), exploitation comes naturally. This pattern can occur in a range of ways, but, largely, it looks like taking advantage of someone, and often taking advantage of their vulnerabilities. Examples include a person's pursuing a relationship with someone to whom they are not at all attracted in order to access his or her money or power, or a moneyed or powerful person's taking advantage of someone much younger or in a less empowered position. It can manifest as using someone for his or her connections to get something as mundane as concert tickets all the way to big-ticket jobs. Toxic and narcissistic people can also be notoriously disloyal, and exploitation is often a part of that dynamic. And it is not always in the direction you would assume. A young, beautiful person with few resources can exploit someone who is older and better resourced by playing on the older person's vulnerabilities and fleecing him or her out of cash and gifts.

Anyone who has been taken advantage of by a narcissist knows how harrowing exploitation can feel. This can be incredibly damaging when you openly and honestly enter a business partnership with someone, and that person pulls the rug out at the eleventh hour. This can happen when a person enters into a business relationship with a narcissist on the basis of a handshake deal (the narcissist will often say, "We don't need a contract—I've got your back," or will even use manipulation and feign hurt: "I can't believe you think we need a contract—I thought we were friends"). It can happen when a toxic parent or sibling promises a loan "with no strings" when a child is in dire need of money, but, when the child is ready to pay the money back, the parent throws an onerous interest rate on the loan. Exploitative people are expert at sussing out who the good "marks" are and taking advantage of them. And it feels awful when it happens to you. Especially when that person is close to you—a friend, parent, partner, or coworker/business partner.

Normal exploitative behavior: There's no such thing. While we may all have once in our lives buddied up to the kid we really didn't like but who had a swimming pool or the newest computer game, anything much beyond that is basically taking advantage of someone else, and that does not fall under the realm of "normal" or "healthy" under any circumstances.

Pathological exploitative behavior: This is the ability to construct relationships solely for personal gain—and to do it repeatedly. Folks who do this may look like smooth politicians or slick businesspeople who tend to make relationships solely to achieve an advantage. While they may be able to rationalize such conduct on the premise that it is the nature of the political or business game, these folks can rarely turn it off in their personal lives. Exploiters sniff out all human relationships from a position of advantage or status and then parlay those relationships into as much gain as possible.

How does exploitation make you feel? Used, diminished, manipulated, foolish, hurt.

FAILURE TO TAKE RESPONSIBILITY

Narcissistic people rarely take responsibility for their misdeeds, the messes they make, and the hurts they cause. This is unsettling because, in some ways, even when people make errors, others can offer some forgiveness if the perpetrator is willing to own up and take responsibility, and that can be enough healing to foster moving forward. But the unwillingness of a person to take responsibility speaks to a lack of awareness that can feel almost dehumanizing.

There are a variety of reasons that narcissists are unwilling or perhaps unable to take responsibility in the face of a hurtful action or cruel words. Foremost is their lack of insight—their lack of self-reflection and self-awareness coupled with their lack of empathy, which results in not even considering the feelings or experiences of the other, and that means that taking responsibility does not even register for them (they simply do not care that they hurt someone else). Their arrogance and entitlement can result in a belief that they were in the right, or that the hurt feelings of another may just be collateral damage and "not that big a deal." Toxic people are also master revisionists and rationalizers and may not take responsibility because they may perceive their behavior as payback or a vindictive quid pro quo, of sorts ("Remember that time when you did this to me? Now we are even").

Interestingly, a major dynamic that may be fueling the swerve away from many people's taking genuine responsibility for their actions anymore is the pervasiveness of litigation. In the US in particular, where civil litigation is becoming normative, it is axiomatic that, in all settings—legal, employment, political, neighborly disputes—people not take ownership of their behavior lest it come back to bite them. Overzealous lawyers stand behind clients and remind them to keep mum about anything and to apologize only after they get called out. It becomes a situation in which people are told to just "keep quiet," in case their words can be used against them—not exactly fertile ground for anyone to take responsibility.

Normal failure to take responsibility: "Officer, I didn't see that stop sign" could be a classic example of a normal person's not taking responsibility. Like children, for a moment, we do like to think we can stumble and deny our way through a misdeed in the hope that we can avoid a penalty. But, in the big-ticket situations, most people are mobilized by a moral core that implies that taking ownership is the only way to move forward. Most people recognize that taking responsibility for something that has occurred can allow everyone to heal and proceed in a more informed and honest way. We have all failed to take responsibility from time to time, especially when no one is harmed by it, but only from time to time.

Pathological failure to take responsibility: This is the consistent projecting of blame onto others, deflecting, lying, or just generally avoiding any ownership of misdeeds and bad behavior. Responsibility deflectors will often delay taking responsibility until an external entity puts their feet to the fire, or incontrovertible evidence such as video or photographs forces them to do so, and, even then, they will craft complex rationalizations or will deflect and call the accuser(s) out on bad things they once did to them. For many narcissists, the motto is "deny or die."

How does their failure to take responsibility make you feel? Revictimized, disappointed, invalidated, angry.

VINDICTIVENESS

Although toxic and narcissistic people often commit many wrongdoings that leave others seething, most of their victims let it go, move on, or don't take up the fight. Regular people generally (and rightfully so) believe that expending more emotional capital on negative thoughts after a conflict means that the other person has won. Normal individuals may not have the time to launch an offensive either, so, for their own self-preservation, will let it go. To be vindictive is to be predisposed to seeking revenge and to be driven by this to an unreasonable degree. In a divorce, toxic people are not content to peaceably and honorably divide assets—they will go to war. In a family, they will cut whom they believe to be a disrespectful or ungrateful family member out of the will entirely (and they will use the family trust or will as a battleground, threatening or making changes any time they do feel wronged).

Vindictiveness-focused folks will push the limits of propriety, outing a partner on social media, secretly letting others know humiliating details about someone whom they feel did them wrong or hurt their feelings. It gets tricky because toxic and narcissistic people are hypersensitive (we will get to that) and, at times, almost paranoid, so they often perceive wrongdoing where it does not exist and may launch vindictive campaigns against unwitting and blindsided victims. Toxic and narcissistic people are often prone to vindictiveness because their external image governs them, and anything that punctures their public image, that otherwise threatens their self-esteem, or that risks bringing shame onto them is unendurable, so they fight back the only way they know, which is via antagonism rather than negotiation, compromise, or diplomacy. In essence, because they are so insecure, they engage in grand gestures to show others "who is boss." They enjoy making examples of other people.

Vindictiveness also manifests in the people who "lawyer up" when they do not get their way. Their sense of entitlement means that they will relentlessly harass people they want to punish for any variety of reasons. Letters written on thick legal letterhead can exert muscle and frighten people who may not understand the terminology or ramifications or may not have the means to fight back. Because narcissists and toxic people are obsessive about the idea that life has to be "fair" (for them, at least), they will spend resources and waste other people's time and resources to ensure that they feel that it all turns out even (for them, at least).

Hell hath no fury like a toxic narcissistic scorned. And many people with narcissistic and toxic people in their lives will admit that they have often not challenged or taken them on because of their fear about vindictiveness. Years and vast amounts of money can be spent fighting a narcissist's vindictiveness, and it can shatter a person's sense of well-being and hope.

Normal vindictiveness: Because vindictiveness tends to be a disproportionate and deeply antagonistic reaction to any perceived threat, there is not really a normal version of it. *Wanting* revenge is actually quite normal (as hard as it is to admit), and it is understandable to get some pleasure out of the downfall of someone who has wronged you (watching the ex who cheated on you be cheated on—for most people, that's a good day). But vindictiveness is an active state—it means *seeking out* revenge, and that is never healthy; and to do so often means that whoever harmed you is still exerting influence in your life.

Pathological vindictiveness: This occurs when someone sets out for revenge at nearly every slight and frames it as a matter of pride. People who do this will chronically make an example of others who they believe wronged them by threatening them, suing them, publicly humiliating them, or otherwise making their life a living hell. "Letting it go" is not in the toxic person's playbook.

How does their vindictiveness make you feel? Scared, threatened, inconvenienced, publicly shamed, anxious, silenced.

OPPOSITIONAL

"You can't make me do that…" "I refuse to do that…" Oppositionality is a defiant stubbornness that can evoke a tantruming three-year-old. It is a refusal to adhere to the request of another person or follow a rule, especially if that rule or request is perceived to be inconvenient by the narcissistic person. As in many situations, narcissists' hypocrisy comes through, and while they have no problem making demands on other people, they resent deeply when anything is asked or required of them. They sometimes expend more energy trying to avoid a requirement than actually just following it.

Control is a major dynamic in narcissism, so when being asked to do something or follow a rule, they will often bristle because it can feel like a loss of control. In addition, oppositionality is also related to entitlement. Entitlement, as we already discussed, is a sense that the rules do not apply to them, so oppositionality is also an expression of that entitlement, a sort of behavioral "stand" against rules that they do not really believe apply to them.

In close relationships, oppositionality can manifest in varied annoying ways—refusing to take out the trash, refusing to finish some other longstanding task, refusing to share a piece of information that would be helpful or soothing to you ("I don't have to show you my phone, this is a free country"). In workplaces it can slow down everything, and oppositional people are rarely team players. They really do adhere to chapter and verse of their job description, and will regularly refuse tasks that fall even slightly out of that description even when everyone would benefit (including themselves!). In many cases, it can become exhausting enough that you will often relent and no longer ask them to do anything just to avoid their defiant outbursts. Oppositionality is exhausting to witness and experience, and can leave you wondering about the developmental age of the oppositional person who looks more like three than thirty-three at the time of one of their oppositional showdowns. Oppositionality represents the crossroads of entitlement, arrogance, lack of empathy, a need for control, and impulsivity.

Normal oppositionality: We all have our moments when we are a spoiled teenager and may whine about not wanting to empty the dishwasher, but it would be unusual for us to downright refuse it. We may also refuse to do something that flies in the face of our values (for example, patronizing a business that has offended us with its business practices) or that leaves us feeling at risk (jumping off of a cliff into the ocean). When it is rare, episodic, and is not delivered with petulance or a poorly thought out rationale, then it may not fall under oppositional behavior.

Pathological oppositionality: This is oppositionality that tends to be pervasive and reflects a consistent refusal to engage in or complete any task, request, or behavior that they do not feel they should have to do. It may be termed stubbornness or defiance but it goes beyond that—to a petulant unwillingness to engage in behaviors that can often benefit other people such as those in a household, workplace, or the world at large.

How does their oppositionality make you feel? Frustrated, angry, helpless, befuddled, bemused.

Cognitive

When we talk about the cognitive features of toxic and narcissistic people, we are, in essence, talking about how they think. Narcissistic people often manifest distorted thinking or contorted rationales. At times, these patterns of thinking appear to defy the reality of the majority, bolstered by the narcissists' insistence that their thinking is right and everyone else's is wrong, with little willingness to budge on their point of view. The cognitive features of narcissism are important to understand, because thinking typically shapes behavior; thus, understanding the thought processes can provide insight into their behavior. There are five main patterns within a narcissist's cognitive features: paranoid, hypersensitive, lack of insight, skewed sense of justice, and hypocritical.

PARANOID

"Paranoid" may be a strong word, but it is not unusual for toxic and narcissistic people to regularly feel that other people are out to get them, persecute them, or take advantage of them (in some ways, it is a massive projection). Paranoia is defined as a strong tendency to feel that you cannot trust other people or that other people have a bad opinion of you. It is a cognitive pattern, as it impacts how the person processes information about the world and the people in it. Because narcissists are so hypersensitive and insecure, they experience everything as a threat, and this can escalate to the level of paranoia. Narcissists are not psychotic, so their paranoia is not at a delusional level; it's just a chronic sense that, when things do not go their way, the world is unfair, and the people in it are conspiring to make their lives more difficult.

They often believe that other people envy them or impede their success or aspirations. Possibly because they do so many bad things—they have left a lot of broken hearts, broken souls, and broken spirits in their wake—they believe that people are plotting against them. They are prone to misinterpreting events in their world or environment as malevolent and threatening ("Why is that guy looking at me like that?"). They are also very prone to thinking that their partners are unfaithful or otherwise taking advantage of them (again, ironic, since they are far more likely to be the cheater and not the one who is being cheated on). In some ways, because they take advantage of other people so often, it's a setup for their own paranoia because they have just enough insight to know that karma is a bitch and that, someday, someone is going to figure out where the proverbial bodies are buried. Sadly, many narcissists are prone to isms—racism, sexism, nationalism, classism. Because they maintain a stance that people are out to get them, they tend to group entire classes of people as a threat. This can even culminate in dangerous rhetoric and a tendency to paint all people who are different than the narcissist or toxic person as a threat, or as somehow bad. It's not lost on me that, just as we are seeing more painful and divisive conversations in the realm of the isms, we are also observing what appears to be a societal uptick in narcissistic patterns.

Normal paranoia: Those who have less privilege in a given situation (for example, racial/ethnic minorities, immigrants, women, LGBTQ individuals, persons living with disabilities, older adults, religious minorities) often do encounter real bias and discrimination, and it can definitely sensitize perceptions of negative motives in other places (but that is not paranoia, as it is often true, and this phenomenon, which can be quite adaptive, has sometimes been labeled "healthy cultural paranoia"). People who have experienced trauma or people who have experienced betrayal in some form (at work, in a relationship) may also sometimes harbor a loss of trust, a suspiciousness, or an extreme caution that can border on the paranoid, but, over time, with ongoing healthy and nonbetrayal experiences, they can return back to non-sensitized perceptions of the world.

Pathological paranoia: When people have pathological paranoia, there is an overarching belief that everyone is out to get them. Obviously, if it is frank paranoia (the belief that aliens are reading one's mind or stealing one's information), then this may be a sign of more severe mental illness, such as schizophrenia, other psychotic spectrum disorders, or bipolar disorder, or may be a by-product of substance use. Pathological paranoia, as observed in narcissism, can manifest as spending significant amounts of time on witch hunts, trying to smoke out betrayers of trust, or believing that others (family members, partners) are betraying trust with little substantiation. Pathological paranoia can result in workplaces that are tense and mistrustful, with everyone concerned about informants amongst them, people's feeling like they always need to look over their shoulders, and inappropriate monitoring of communication. Such workplaces often grow out of a paranoid person's running the show. In close relationships, it is not unusual for paranoid partners to use cameras in the household to watch the comings and goings of visitors, trackers on cars, phone location services, and private investigators to track a partner's movements, all with the goal of "catching" a person who may be betraying them (did someone say "stalking"?). Finally, we may see prejudicial and divisive discourse or even the spewing of what feel like conspiracy theories that may be more at home on an inflammatory news network than as a part of normal circumspect conversation.

How does their paranoia make you feel? Confused, on edge, suspicious, betrayed, violated.

HYPERSENSITIVE

For people who are hypersensitive, even the slightest joke can be experienced as an insult or a character assault. They are permitted to make jokes at anyone's expense, but the first time someone makes a tiny jab at them, it's the end of days. They have two standards in the world: the way they are permitted to treat other people, and the way they expect to be treated. This can make it difficult to ever be authentic with them, because you are often censoring yourself for fear that you will say something that will be misconstrued or misinterpreted as an insult. A hypersensitive parent will be the one who will become hurt or enraged because you purchased him or her a gift in the wrong size or because his or her birthday card came a day late. A hypersensitive teenager will feel that the comment you made about his or her rosy complexion was a comment on his or her acne. A hypersensitive boss will castigate the employee in the meeting who may make an off-handed comment about the furniture in the conference room. A hypersensitive partner will interpret your conversation with a cousin as your dissing him or her, or your off-handed compliment about a brother's new home as a comment on his relatively lower salary.

Hypersensitivity, in some ways, also relates back to dysregulation, but it is, by and large, a chronic misinterpretation driven by insecurity.

In fact, life with hypersensitive people feels like a big misunderstanding. Their insecurity means that the world can feel like a very threatening place—a place full of people who can stop validating them and superficial fantasies that may not come true. The hypersensitivity also relates to their grandiosity (they do not want to hear anything that punctures their fantasy version of themselves) as well as their entitlement (as though they are entitled to never having to experience discomfort). If you spend enough time with a hypersensitive person, you may feel as though it takes a long time for you to get a thought out—and that may be because you are thinking of all the ways that what you are saying can be misheard before you actually speak. Their hypersensitivity can render them petulant and "tantrum-y." It is this quality that often results in toxic and narcissistic people's getting into heated social media exchanges with other people, even if they do not know them, because they cannot endure criticism, even from someone they have never met. In addition, they tend to over-personalize everything. Personalizing matters can make them more sensitive and activating—and the lack of boundaries combined with the fragile ego experienced by narcissistic and toxic people means that even a passing comment, a late response, or a confused expression on the face of the other is personalized and responded to as a threat or an insult.

In daily life, their hypersensitivity can also result in their becoming sullen when they feel as though someone was mean to them, which can be quite uncomfortable for everyone involved. In order to avoid having to deal with these tantrums and periods of sullen withdrawal, people will often walk on eggshells to appease narcissistic hypersensitivity.

Normal hypersensitivity: We all have vulnerabilities (our weight, our appearance, our bank account, our parenting abilities, our background), and, when we feel that someone may be slighting those things, we may overreact or become overly defensive. Over time, those close to us may learn that each of us has a bit of a "no-fly zone" that is harder for us to regulate, but that, by and large, in most realms of life, we can handle ribbing (good-natured or otherwise), criticism, or a lost thank-you card or forgotten invitation. We may also become more prone to hypersensitivity in times of fatigue, stress, or mental exhaustion, but perhaps, during those times, it is merely sensitivity (and not *hyper*sensitivity).

Pathological hypersensitivity: This means taking everything personally—too personally. Any feedback, even feedback that is actually good but may still require a revision or a change, is experienced as an insult rather than as a mere critique. You may say a hundred nice things about people with pathological hypersensitivity, but they will zoom in on the one thing you said that they felt was a slight (for example, you may describe someone as a visionary and brilliant artist, and talk about how beautifully he or she has triumphed after a bad review once received, and the artist will be angry that you mentioned the one bad review and may become sullen or withdrawn for the rest of the evening). They will overreact to even the smallest slight or hold a grudge over such slights (not being invited to a party that largely involved people the hypersensitive person did not know or making a small innocuous joke about a hypersensitive sibling's spouse). Interestingly, they can even be somewhat "environmentally hypersensitive," as though they are dogs hearing a high-pitched sound. They may become rude or agitated if they do not like the pitch of someone's voice, the way someone may shake a leg, a person's use of ketchup, or even the color of the walls in a hotel room.

How does their hypersensitivity make you feel? Hypervigilant, inauthentic, overly careful, censored, exhausted.

LACK OF INSIGHT

Lack of insight reflects poor self-reflection and lack of self-awareness. It is as though the person cannot connect the moral, ethical, and personal dots to recognize that a behavior was "bad" and may have hurt someone, to know that genuine apologies and self-reflection should naturally follow, and to learn from the episode. Often, when toxic people say whatever outlandish thing they want, they themselves will acknowledge, "I didn't think." Anyone who has had a toxic family member, partner, coworker, boss, or friend knows what this lack of insight looks like—we tend to look at people like this with "seriously?" written all over our face. Sadly, many times they get away with it, because people tend to write it off as, "That's just how they are—they have no insight into how they affect other people." Social media and comments sections for news sites are terrible playgrounds for people who lack insight, because tweeting and other kinds of posting can happen at all hours—and there is no stop-gap mechanism to prevent them from hitting "post." As such, numerous regrettable tweets and other social media posts have gone out there, only to be recalled shortly thereafter (but since everything lives forever online, there is no way to un-ring that bell). The lack of insight means atrocious sentiments can be posted with little regard for the impact on others or for the implications for their own lives. Many a kingdom has been brought down by a poorly conceived tweet (Roseanne, anyone?).

Giancarlo Dimaggio and Giovanna Attinà, psychologists at the Center for Metacognitive Interpersonal Therapy in Rome, Italy (Centro di Terapia Metacognitiva Interpersonale) write about the tendency of the narcissistic individual to be a storyteller of sorts, and to intellectualize their experiences and lives instead of actually being able to talk about themselves. In this way, even when they are talking about their own lives, it feels as though they are telling a story about someone else. This can not only make it difficult to connect with them, but also foster this lack of connection to their own inner world. These researchers also describe the narcissist as being in a "never ending fight with an internalized oppressor." But because they are unaware of this dynamic, they are not in touch with their own arrogance, antagonism, argumentativeness, aloofness, and insecurity.

Lack of insight likely reflects a cognitive error driven by lack of empathy ("I don't care"), entitlement ("I can say what I want"), and grandiosity ("No one can touch me"). The concrete and primitive defenses of a narcissistic person mean that they are almost childlike in their inability to reflect on how they impact other people. In this way, people who lack insight are often not very good candidates for therapy. While therapy may be able to flash a big, hot spotlight on their lack of insight and perhaps serve as a wake-up call, in the absence of insight, therapy can move rather slowly or not at all.

Normal lack of insight: All of us have times when we say something insensitive, but, when it is a normal lack of insight, we recognize our error immediately or shortly thereafter, feel terribly for it, and address our wrongdoing. We may also be thrust into a culture or system different than that to which we are accustomed and run the risk of not having insight or awareness around what is considered appropriate behavior in that circumstance, but, after learning about our errors, we address the behavior.

Pathological lack of insight: This is when someone just doesn't get it, just does not care, or doesn't want to put the mental effort into understanding his or her behavior. When people lack insight, they often do not understand why other people are offended by their conduct and are sometimes genuinely surprised when it is pointed out to them. And toxic people may also get quite angry and upset that people are criticizing them for being offensive. Pathological lack of insight is a pattern—again, they just don't get it. Even with well-rehearsed PR statements, it feels like they are reading someone else's words or will talk about their own hurt and loss before acknowledging the pain of those they hurt. Their lack of insight often drives a lack of guilt. In this way, pathological lack of insight renders someone a "serial hurter" of other people.

How does their lack of insight make you feel? Pained, confused, bewildered, hurt, betrayed, angry.

SKEWED SENSE OF JUSTICE

"That's not fair." Somewhere along the line, toxic and narcissistic people did not get the memo that life is not fair—especially in matters of love and other people. In fact, "That's not fair!" may be on par with "Don't you know who I am?" as a narcissistic mantra. They maintain a skewed sense of fairness, in which circumstances are experienced as "just" if their personal needs are met. They are not nearly as concerned about whether circumstances are equitable for others. They are acutely aware of the quid pro quo. If they give you a gift, they may not expect to receive the same caliber of gift in kind, but they will expect you to be disproportionately grateful and to tell other people how generous they are—in other words, they need a validating payoff for their good deed. Gratitude often represents "justice" to them. If they do you a favor, they will remind you of it for years, to the point that you will often regret taking the favor, as the gratitude and karmic payback are far more than the favor was worth. Narcissists and toxic people tend to keep "emotional ledgers" in which they maintain a careful accounting of grievances and things that are "owed" to them—and will get their debt paid back in one way or another (ironically, they never keep a second set of books about all the nice things people have done for them over time).

Life is inherently unfair, and, if the balance sheet works out in the end for you, then you are doing better than most. It is a tough calculus, because exactly what constitutes "fairness" is also challenging. The fact is that really bad things happen to really good people, and vice versa. In many family systems, one adult child will take almost complete care of ailing parents, and toxic siblings will still fight that person on the estate when the parents die. It feels unfair, it is unfair, and there is typically little we can do about it. For narcissistic and entitled people, the idea of fairness is interesting, because, from their point of view, fairness occurs only when the outcome benefits them. For example, let's say there is a workplace group of twenty people and only five tickets to a gala benefit. The company does a lottery or other similar event to fairly distribute those tickets. If the narcissistic person does not get the ticket, then "it's not fair," but if he or she does win one of the tickets, then he or she would applaud the lottery system as supremely fair. Narcissistic people tend to approach the world as a five-year-old would, expecting each child to get the same number of cookies, or blocks, or slices of birthday cake. But, because their idea of fairness is not real fairness, it can rankle even more. It can make relationships very thorny—there is lots of keeping "score"— "How much did you spend on my mother's birthday gift? I spent more on yours," "I spent six hours at your family's Thanksgiving, now you have to spend six hours at mine," "you have an ex-boyfriend on your social media, so it's okay for me to message my ex-girlfriend." With a narcissist, it always feels like tax day and everything has to balance out.

It is in this way that the role of privilege is often completely incomprehensible to them. They believe their privilege is deserved, or they have little insight regarding their privilege. For example, narcissistic and toxic parents will chronically remind children of all they did for them years later (to which most people want to say, "Yep, it's called being a parent"). I have even witnessed one family's handing their adult child a bill for "services rendered" at the time their adult child reached middle adulthood, despite this child being a hardworking, self-supporting individual. This obsession with "justice" can be manifested in extremely petty behavior: expecting a certain seat at a family function, to be accorded a special role in a ceremony, or to be the recipient of an award because it is "their turn." They frequently will want to hash out old hurts and may bombard you with old texts, emails, and messages about what they did and what you owe them. The obsession with "justice" and fairness is often a product of the entitlement, dysregulation, and antagonism observed in narcissism. The "Don't you know who I am?" of the world is often at play here—it's a tagline for expecting special treatment, which, in their minds, is just. The sense of justice is often a manifestation of simply being a spoiled child.

The sense of justice can also climb into spaces in life in which it is impossible to really engage in any form of "accounting," such as love, kindness, compassion, mentoring, or emotional support. Narcissistic people will certainly try to find a way to quantify these processes. It is not unusual for them to say, "You can't feel that way. Don't you remember when I listened to you ten years ago?" or, "You owe me after all the times I was your cheerleader." And, on the other side of that coin, they really do not like to see someone thrive after leaving a relationship with them (this relates back to the concept of vindictiveness). Toxic people will often assert that it is not fair that you may have found happiness after leaving any form of relationship with them, as though there is some form of suffering (more than you already endured) that you need to experience or a punishment that needs to be enacted because you had the chutzpah and courage to distance yourself or walk away from the toxic situation altogether. In the sickest and most savage variants of this are narcissistic partners who are embroiled in messy breakups or divorces who fight for custody of children they are not interested in raising, but just to get revenge on the other parent or who stalk, assault, or even murder their estranged partners and even children.

Finally, as noted earlier, in their zeal for justice, toxic and narcissistic people often over-rely on the legal system to provide some form of remedy to the perceived slights of the world. This can manifest as frivolous lawsuits, threatened litigation, or thinly (or not) veiled threats written by attorneys. The belief in justice becomes so entrenched that toxic people believe they are entitled to it and will often attempt to achieve it through expensive legal means. Sadly, because mounting a legal battle is often beyond the financial or energetic capabilities of most people, litigation-wielding narcissists frequently do achieve their sense of justice this way, getting settlements or other judgments that can harm or even destroy other people and that satisfy the obsession for justice and general interpersonal bloodlust that can motivate narcissists.

Normal sense of justice: All of us have some expectation of fair play—paying for a service and receiving it, completing requirements and being recognized for doing so, following the rules and not being penalized. If things do not happen as they are agreed upon, we will often seek out legal or financial remedies. We do expect certain reciprocities to play out in relationships—and some of these do relate to resources. For example, expecting to be paid back on a loan, having your friend pick up your kids since you have done it before for him or her, having a mindful plan for holidays each year that accounts for extended families, receiving a thank-you for a thoughtful gift. When this does not happen, it can be frustrating or even unsettling for us. We may also have moments when we are more concerned about resolving our own crisis than about resolving the crises of others (a flight gets canceled and you do not concern yourself with who "deserves" to get a new flight resolved most quickly). However, we can perhaps cry or grumble our way into acceptance, because, in fact, acceptance is the only meaningful antidote to feeling that the world is an unjust place.

Pathological sense of justice: Examples include being unable to let go of perceived injustices for years, particularly when they are minor; expecting extreme validation and gratitude in the face of a favor or gift, and becoming angry and petulant when it is not received; keeping play-by-play or item-by-item mental records regarding other people, brooding about them, and raising them regularly; making everything about "fairness," even when it is not in the best interest of others (for example, custody battles); using attorneys or other expensive remedies to achieve a sense of justice that works for them; or escalating to violence, stalking, or other forms of assault because they perceive an injustice within a relationship, particularly when the relationship ends.

How does their skewed sense of justice make you feel? Uncomfortable, minimized, devalued, controlled, petty, threatened, fearful.

HYPOCRITICAL

"Hypocrisy" is defined as "a feigning to be what one is not or to believe what one does not: behavior that contradicts what one claims to believe or feel" (Merriam-Webster, 2018). Hypocrisy is endemic, and it is a pattern that makes people very uncomfortable—a sort of two-headed beast that entails doing something bad and then turning around and condemning the behavior in others. It is omnipresent in world politics today and is, in essence, a "Do as I say, not as I do" approach. The inherent inconsistency of hypocrisy is what contributes to its distaste. The classic example of this is the person who publicly criticizes, excoriates, and shames someone who has engaged in marital infidelity and is then found out to have been committing infidelity in his or her own marriage.

This moral and behavioral inconsistency is a hallmark of narcissism and toxic people. In general, politicians are the patron saints of hypocrisy, breaking promises and preaching false morality. Hypocrisy is frequently observed in politicians, private-jet-traveling preachers, and other folks who claim to be pillars of morality and sacrifice (businesspeople, community leaders, university administrators). By and large, hypocrites tend to be quite self-righteous, which often manifests as a holier-than-thou stance. That type of stance is a signal of hypocrisy, as well as a pretty bright red flag suggestive of toxicity and narcissism.

The irony of toxic and narcissistic people is that they often portray themselves as paragons of "how life should be lived." They focus on their visible successes—their businesses, their homes, successes of themselves and those within their families—and are self-righteous enough to believe that their path is *the* path. In this way, toxic and narcissistic people will go into moralizing professions, ranging from cult leader to tyrannical church leader or even self-help guru (irony duly noted).

Hypocrisy needn't occur just on a public stage. It can manifest in close relationships and families (for example, people tell friends that they put family first but never show up to their child's soccer games; or they shame a partner for posting a sexy selfie on a social media site but then like numerous similar pictures of other people) or in the workplace (for example, the boss receives a big award for valuing the rights and dignity of employees but is then found to have sexually abused young women or men in the workplace). Toxic and narcissistic people are often vulnerable to this conduct because they present, value, and display themselves solely on the expectations of the external world. As long as that gets them validation, they do not really care if the conduct is consistent with their inner world. In addition, their entitlement can drive the belief that the rules do not apply to them. Hypocrisy can sometimes almost feel like a form of gaslighting, since they are saying one thing and doing another, which can be maddening and confusing.

Normal hypocrisy: Everyone engages in some form of moral outrage, and yet we don't always have our i's dotted and t's crossed. We may come out as advocates of good public education and then send our children to private school, we may believe in cruelty-free products but then turn around and purchase one that is not, or we may hold a strong position about a certain group (support of LGBTQ rights or refugee rights) but patronize a business whose ownership has not had a good track record with that group. When caught in the hypocrisy, if we own it or correct it, it may be a simple slip and not character-defining hypocrisy.

Pathological hypocrisy: This relates to the big-ticket and hurtful inconsistencies—when people come out strongly against a behavior or policy to small and/or large audiences of people but conduct themselves in private life (or even in public life) in a way that is completely at odds with that presentation. It happens when a person attacks the moral quality of another person, but his or her own morals are suspect. It is consistently criticizing a family member, partner, friend, or associate for a certain behavior and then engaging in that same behavior. When hypocrisy is pathological, it is consistent and resistant to feedback and change.

How does their hypocrisy make you feel? Duped, betrayed, angry, annoyed, mistrustful, confused.

* * *

Can one narcissistic or toxic person have all of these traits? Probably (hopefully) not. Most toxic, narcissistic, and entitled people have at least one from each category, and, if you are seeing two or three from each category, you are describing a *very* unpleasant, antagonistic, high-conflict, and toxic person. Remember that the core pillars of narcissism—lack of empathy, entitlement, grandiosity, validation seeking, and dysregulation—are the key factors, and, in the absence of those, the person may not be as toxic. But where those patterns go, the others tend to follow. For all of these patterns, insecurity and variable self-esteem is the constant backdrop.

Read on to learn about how these traits can combine to create different kinds of toxic, difficult, and narcissistic people. Read carefully to determine which patterns you may be encountering in your life, because they require different strategies. Sun Tzu wrote in *The Art of War,* "If ignorant both of your enemy and yourself, you are certain to be in peril." This book will allow you to become knowledgeable about narcissistic, difficult, and toxic people and also to reflect on yourself. Armed with that, you can hopefully get out of peril.

Chapter 3

What Flavor Is Your Narcissist?

Nothing is easier than to denounce the evildoer;
nothing is more difficult than to understand him.

—DOSTOYEVSKY

When you have thirty-one traits and patterns in five categories, that implies millions of possible combinations. Thankfully, there are not millions of possible types of narcissists or toxic people (although there are millions of narcissistic people out there). The media and popular discussions largely give coverage to the two most obvious and problematic forms of narcissist: the malignant narcissist and the grandiose narcissist. These represent the classic toxic narcissistic people who are bullies, liars, tyrants, and cheaters, and vulgar, insincere, and entitled. Even though these patterns often manifest quite early in a relationship, we will also address why we still allow these people into our lives and cut them slack, even when we can see them coming and even when they behave in such dehumanizing and invalidating ways.

There are subtypes of narcissism that may be harder to spot, and, in fact, many people do not even recognize them as subtypes of narcissism and interpersonal toxicity. These patterns hurt just as much as the others, but they can be quite confusing. In this chapter, we'll explore the five major types of narcissists as well as why it can be so difficult to walk away from them. You'll also learn the distinction between psychopaths, sociopaths, and narcissists.

The Grandiose "Classic" Narcissist

This is your classic narcissist, and though initially he or she may not present as toxic, once you scrape away the top level of charm and charisma, the toxicity and antagonism manifest rather quickly. This subtype encompasses the arrogant, entitled, charming, grandiose, superficial, vain narcissist. These types of narcissist are the show-offs, the braggarts, the superficial party boys and girls. They care about appearances above all else and measure success in money, possessions, appearances, and power. The other adjectives that come to mind with this subtype are "slick," "egotistical," "full of themselves," and "(overly) confident." But, just like all narcissistic and toxic people, they lack empathy, have a tendency to lie and engage in projection, and, when frustrated, disappointed, or cornered, become very rageful. These are the people who are very easy to get drawn into, because they are so charming and successful; they often appear to be "pillars of the community" and do very well as public figures or leaders. It can feel exciting and intoxicating to become acquainted with them and their larger-than-life worlds. They have a tendency to boast about their accomplishments, possessions, children, family, and job, but, when you start talking, they will either yawn, check their phones, or claim that they are too busy to keep talking.

A common error is confusing narcissism and confidence—and this error is made most often with grandiose narcissists. In our society, we frequently do not recognize that confidence is a dish best served quietly. A truly confident person does not feel the need to talk, share, post on Instagram, and otherwise broadcast every detail of his or her life. The tendency to shout from the rooftops about virtues and wins often seems like confidence, because most people do not do it. Because narcissists are more often materially successful than the average person, we assume that this braggadocio or actual ability is what got them to their success (they did not). *True* confidence is a bit more restrained and quiet, and tends to be backed up with an accurate assessment of one's ability, an appropriate manner of communicating those abilities, the willingness to hear about other people's skills or perspectives, and enough humility to put others at ease.

Why Is It So Difficult to Walk Away From Them?

They are great salespeople (which is why you got drawn in in the first place), and, just as you are walking away, they will attempt to sweeten the deal. Their grandiosity is tantalizing, elements of the relationship can be exciting, and, even though the lack of empathy and entitlement are draining and soul sapping, the excitement of winning them over feels good. It's a bit like a casino—you keep going back to the blackjack table or the slot machine for one last hit, because this may be the time you hit the jackpot (it never is). Grandiose narcissists can also take a toll on your self-esteem, and that can most often manifest as self-doubt and sometimes as guilt ("What if I end up alone?" "She did raise me," "I may not be able to find a better job"). Grandiose narcissists are exciting and draw you in on the basis of that charm and excitement, and hope is often what keeps relationships with grandiose narcissists going.

The Malignant Narcissist

This is the toxic narcissist and the most aversive form of the narcissistic person. The existential psychologist Erich Fromm coined the term "malignant narcissist" and described it as "the root of the most vicious destructiveness and inhumanity." This form takes the grandiose narcissist and adds a more exploitative, antagonistic, Machiavellian, and, at times, seemingly psychopathic overlay. Malignant narcissists are well put together and typically score high on measures of self-esteem (Hickman et al., 1996). At the most extreme, this narcissistic type conforms to something called the Dark Triad—a term coined in 2002 by Delroy Paulhus and Kevin Williams, both of whom are researchers at the University of British Columbia—which takes in territory including psychopathy, Machiavellianism, and narcissism. These are people who are charming, political, manipulative, and narcissistic, and who lack any remorse. As such, they can be dangerous, cunning, exploitative, and can do tremendous damage. Malignant narcissists drive people to the edge and leave them feeling betrayed, fearful, manipulated, tricked, and devastated. The boundary between the malignant narcissist and the psychopath or sociopath is blurry at best (more about that in a moment). At some point, the label does not matter; their patterns of behavior are dehumanizing—and take a tremendous toll on anyone in this type's wake. Anyone who thinks he or she can outwit, outsmart, or outplay this type may have to be more malignant than the malignant narcissist. It's never a battle worth taking up.

As difficult and downright mean as they can be, malignant narcissists are actually not always as easy to spot as you might think. Given that many of the forward-facing traits of malignant/overt narcissists include entitlement, grandiosity, and superficiality, they just seem like the classic banker/lawyer/businessperson/pro athlete type. They are what Tom Wolfe terms "Masters of the Universe" in *Bonfire of the Vanities*. But they are dangerous, and while most probably will not engage in violence toward you, their abuse of power, lack of empathy, bending and breaking of rules, slippery ethics, and general sense that people are disposable can be soul sapping. Many people will report that, after a relationship with a toxic malignant narcissist, they feel as though they have endured a trauma and will report symptoms similar to those observed in people experiencing post-traumatic or acute stress disorder, including anxiety, rumination, reliving the experiences, social withdrawal, nightmares, and hypervigilance, as well as physical reactions such as headaches, muscle tension, skin rashes, and gastrointestinal difficulties.

Why Is It So Difficult to Walk Away From Them?

Fear. This is the most frightening form of narcissism, and, at times, it may feel like psychopathy (described later in the chapter). The fear of retribution, vindictive behavior, or worse is often quite realistic and can make the decision to leave terrifying. Even when things are not that perilous, it can be destabilizing to have spent any period of your life being dehumanized, invalidated, controlled, and threatened. This type of narcissism can leave anyone who has been in contact with it—children, partners/spouses, employees, siblings, friends, family members—shaken to the core and plagued by fear, confusion, self-doubt, and worthlessness. In the absence of enough self-esteem to believe you can thrive on your own, staying can be just a manifestation of the defeat these relationships bring, or the paralysis induced by fear.

The Covert/Vulnerable Narcissist

This is a "stealth" form of narcissism but is a very difficult one nonetheless. Covert narcissism has variously been labeled vulnerable narcissism, hypersensitive narcissism, and fragile narcissism. Historically, while there has been more of a focus on the classical "overt" narcissist, there has always been a theoretical body of work that has addressed this less obvious but equally difficult narcissistic personality style. Covert narcissism is characterized by lack of empathy, projection, entitlement, hypersensitivity, arrogance, paranoia, passive-aggression, sense of justice, resentment, and insecurity. Covert narcissists are not showy or grandiose in an obvious manner. Rather, they believe the world does not understand them or their special, unique, or great abilities (more of a masked grandiosity). Other more vulnerable patterns such as anxiety, depression (especially in the face of disappointment or shame), and social withdrawal are also commonly observed in this pattern. In 1997, Holly Hendin and Jonathan Cheek, a graduate student and a professor at Wellesley College, respectively, addressed the measurement of covert narcissism—work they updated in 2013 with a revised scale—and basically argued that covert narcissists are actually grandiose, but they don't advertise it. Instead, these people are stuck in their own head, wondering why the world never gave them the recognition they deserved, and they may actually feel like forgotten geniuses. They also believe the world owes them something and maintain a brooding anger about not having received the things that they believe they deserve. They tend to be resentful of the world, of people in their social sphere and in their family, and of anyone whom they perceive to have a better life than they do (which is just about everyone).

Their interactions with other people tend to be hostile, and it is in this way that covert narcissism most closely resembles more traditional narcissism. Covert narcissists are believed to be more likely to hold what is known as a "hostile attribution bias," which is a style whereby people will interpret or over-interpret the motivations (and, by extension, behaviors, communication, actions) of others as hostile. Not surprisingly, because they think others are driven by hostility, their responses mirror that hostility. Consistent with this finding, personality researchers W. Keith Campbell and Joshua Miller (2013) apply other research to speculate that covert narcissism is the subtype of narcissism that is more likely to be associated with early environments characterized by abuse and neglect. A child exposed to chronic neglect and invalidation is going to have been exposed to more hostile motivations and become more attuned to combing their environments for hostile threats.

Covert narcissists can be hypersensitive to criticism and cannot let go of anything that resembles a critique. As such, they will ask for reassurance in the face of a criticism, and any criticism or lack of recognition fortifies their belief that the world does not quite understand their "special" qualities. This form of narcissism is not captured in our traditional ways of measuring the trait of narcissism, so these people often get missed. They generally appear introverted, unhappy, glum, hangdog, and sullen. But, just when you do think they are vulnerable or depressed, they will launch into an overly intellectualized debate about something and try to "beat you" at it (everyone has one covert narcissistic relative who holds the table hostage with a conversation in which he or she needs to be the expert and humiliate or at least "get one over" on anyone who may share that expertise). They often feel inferior to others (because, like anyone who is narcissistic, they regulate their self-esteem from the outside, and they do not perceive or actually receive sufficient validation) and are immensely dissatisfied with their lives (Cooper and Ronningstam, 1992; Wink, 1991). Unlike their more classically narcissistic doppelgangers, these folks are not well adjusted, and, while the classical overt narcissists tend to maintain higher levels of self-esteem and lower levels of depression, the covert/vulnerable narcissists do not fare as well.

People in relationships with covert narcissists may think that the latter are depressed (they can be) or have low self-esteem (they do) and will often pity them or want to help them. Thus, they are frequently surprised when their attempts to be gentle or offer warmth or kindness to the covert narcissist are met with anger, rejection, insults, or coldness. Paradoxically, if you were to try to end the relationship out of exasperation at his or her antagonism, coldness, or distance, it would not be unusual for the covert narcissist to cry or behave in some other similarly vulnerable manner. Close relationships can be very difficult with covert narcissists, and they manifest more of an anxious/avoidant attachment style in close relationships (Campbell & Miller, 2013). All of this can make covert narcissism a very confusing space. Covert narcissists can also present as socially unskilled (unlike the classically overt narcissist, who is typically quite charming, engaging, and confident at first blush), which, again, may lead others to either avoid them because they may seem socially awkward or ignore their lack of empathy in lieu of their apparent vulnerability. They also tend to maintain the mentality of a victim and perceive threats, harm, insults, and persecution on a regular basis. As noted above, the pattern of the malignant narcissist often borders on the pattern of psychopathy. Interestingly, because of the relative lack of social skill, the more reactive temper, and the brooding resentment, covert narcissism, especially in its more virulent forms, can resemble sociopathy.

An important factor that rears its head in all forms of narcissism, but particularly covert narcissism, is contempt. Roberta Schriber, a research fellow at Arizona State University, and her colleagues explored the concept of dispositional contempt and found that, much like covert narcissism, it is a bit paradoxical. They defined "dispositional contempt" as "the tendency to look down on, distance, and derogate others who violate our standards." Basically, it is a tendency in a person to be judgmental in a sort of "sneering" way. They found that dispositional contempt was associated with coldness, a sense of superiority, disagreeableness, and racism, but also self-deprecation, emotional fragility, low self-esteem, insecure attachment, and feeling a bit "put upon" by the world, which they believe places unrealistic, perfectionistic expectations on them. In this way, the covert narcissist often looks like the brooding angry person who constantly bears a grudge, is socially isolated, holds venomous and cold opinions about other groups (particularly already marginalized groups), and is quite mediocre in their outcomes (they are likely overrepresented in certain sectors characterized by high levels of contempt, such as internet "trolls").

Entitlement is still very much present in covert narcissism—there is an ongoing disaffection with the world at large, which these types feel does not recognize their specialness or grant them the honor and attention they deserve. There is also a prevailing sense amongst covert narcissists that they did not get the life they deserved, and they tend to blame other people for that circumstance ("If only I had different parents, a different spouse, a different education, different friends, a trust fund, less people from other countries competing with me for a job [and so on], I would have been an amazing success"). While it does not tend to be the grandiose "Don't you know who I am?" entitlement (though it can be), it quietly flows under the surface and is masked by an unhappy, sullen exterior. They remain arrogant, perhaps not coolly arrogant but arrogant nonetheless, and often feel like the annoying and angry know-it-all on the bar stool next to you.

92

Why Is It So Difficult to Walk Away From Them?

This is a confusing form of narcissism, and, at first blush (or even later), it can look like depression or anxiety. Many people would not leave these relationships, because they feel guilty leaving someone who, on the surface, seems so vulnerable, and they may even pity the individual and try to "rescue" him or her. These relationships are often kept in place by a sense that, once something "good" happens to the covert narcissist (the promotion or the hoped-for recognition), things will become better.

The Communal Narcissist

You know this person—he or she is jetting off for an eco-charity tour, building new huts in a village, holding babies in slums, rescuing a variety of animals, building in time at a posh resort on the way out, attending or organizing charitable galas, and then Instagramming the whole thing. Communal narcissists may feature frequent posts on their social media or personal website showing them interacting with those "less fortunate" than them and drawing attention to their charitable deeds with hashtags like #savingtheworld, #feelsgoodtogiveback, #charitygoals, #iloveeveryone, or #elephantsarepeopletoo. Then they sit back, expect validation from their followers ("Wow, you are amazing," "You have the biggest heart ever," "Keep saving the world—and you look hot in your bikini") and then bask in likes and comments about their giving nature. They tend to cast themselves as altruistic, and, while their less communal narcissistic counterparts are more likely to view themselves as successful or better than other people, communal narcissists are more likely to view themselves as helpful, and, to get their self-enhancement needs met by being viewed as helpful, giving, and charitable people (Gebauer et al., 2012; Rogoza and Fatfouta, 2018).

Jochen Gebauer, a professor at the University of Mannheim, and his colleagues, presented this concept of communal narcissism in a research paper in which he distinguished communal narcissism from the more traditional form of narcissism (he labeled this traditional form of narcissism as agentic narcissism, and, in this book, it is called classical or grandiose narcissism). He argues that communal narcissists are motivated by the same needs as other narcissists (e.g. grandiosity, self-enhancement, etc.), but that they meet these needs through communal means (e.g. engaging in activities that would be viewed well by the world or which ostensibly help others). In essence, their research suggests that a communal narcissist may want to be viewed as a "living saint," which reflects a grandiose self-assessment and need for public reverence and awe.

We have to be careful here; there are many well-intentioned people who really do put others first and who give the best of themselves and endless uncompensated hours to charitable endeavors. The real issue is the motivation. Communal narcissists are motivated by validation, and, if others do not take notice of their "goodness," then the communal narcissists can get a bit prickly, frustrated, and even angry. In addition, they may give up dozens, if not hundreds, of hours to plan a charitable event but become mini tyrants when doing so, making it feel more like a bad job for the other well-intentioned volunteers. Communal narcissists may seem like they care very much about people facing challenges around the world—and be the first to jump on a flight to dig a well or help hurricane victims—but, in their own life, they can have all of the usual narcissistic relationship patterns, including detachment, lack of empathy, entitlement, and anger. This juxtaposition can be *very* confusing for partners, family, and friends, who see these people being viewed by the world as the great givers, yet, at home, they are anything but. Communal narcissists do value their place in the community, whether it is their town, their children's school, or their place of worship, and they derive tremendous validation from it. What they do not do well is one-on-one relationships.

Communal narcissists may be the dictatorial PTA president; the donor who gives and expects names on buildings and lots of press and publicity, as well as lots of fawning by the entities that benefit from the largesse; the dog rescuer who chronically abuses a boyfriend or girlfriend; or the social media-savvy global savior who also takes the time to post with hashtags about his or her goals, tan, and brand of sneaker, all while cleaning plastic from the oceans. The juxtaposition of giving to the world but withholding at home can make this a perplexing and frustrating scenario for someone close to this pattern. In many ways, the communal narcissist derives a sense of self from the idea of being a "giver" but maintains little insight into his or her entitlement, antagonism, or lack of empathy in other close relationships.

Why Is It So Difficult to Walk Away From Them?

Who walks away from a "saint"? The world often thinks the communal narcissist is like Mother Teresa or some other saintly or presumably altruistic figure. You may even feel double teamed: The communal narcissist is invalidating in his or her relationship with you, and, in turn, the people in your world may be invalidating because they find your concerns about your relationship hard to believe, given what a "charitable" soul the communal narcissist is. There is a sense of not only guilt but also discomfort that you are leaving or criticizing a person who the world may brand as a "giver." The inconsistency of the public persona and the person's conduct in your relationship can make this a challenging dynamic to leave, especially if you value or are swayed by the opinions of other people (even people who may not be privy to your relationship).

The Benign Narcissist

These may simply be jerks or attention-seeking fools. Their lack of empathy may be experienced as a cluelessness, their entitlement as clumsy, their grandiosity as childlike. Their tendency is to talk about themselves or make your story about them. They hold the narcissistic traits, but at a milder level that lacks the malignancy or toxicity that results in hurt or anger. There is a superficial immaturity to benign narcissists, and diagnostically this may conform to a pattern termed "histrionic." They care, with adolescent zeal, what people think about them and crave being the center of attention, they are the adults who are glued to their social media with the obsessiveness of a sixteen-year-old, they post pictures of every outing and tag everyone, they may say thoughtless or insensitive things that make you look twice at them, but it all feels more like the lack of a filter than a deep-seated lack of empathy or willful cruelty. They are the people who act foolishly in a bar and may even be fun to talk with at a party. But, in the harsh light of day, their narcissism may just feel like a headache and a waste of time.

A relationship with a benign narcissist may not be experienced as abusive, but it may be unfulfilling, because it tends to be shallow, can feel immature, and can be experienced as one-sided. The benign narcissist may be the self-obsessed mother who rarely asks you how you are feeling (but cares deeply about what you are wearing), the vapid coworker who wants everyone to know the provenance of her handbag, the life-of-the-party partner who is incapable of having a conversation much beyond the events of the weekend. These people are relatively harmless. They are definitely not the people you would turn to for a meaningful discussion of deep spiritual issues or a personal crisis, but they can be entertaining to have at a party. If you learn to not turn to them for the things they cannot provide (such as emotional depth), then this form of narcissism does not feel too virulent.

Why Is It So Difficult to Walk Away From Them?

In some ways, you don't need to. You just need to ensure that you do not double down on them. They are the folks who may frustrate you because there is a friendship there that can be good fun but, when you really need them to be there, they don't deliver. Like many relationships, relationships with these people can be difficult to leave for reasons including nostalgia, laziness, complacence, or simply because they are not really disrupting your life that much. Benign narcissists can be keepers as long as you do not turn to them regarding issues for which you may need deep empathy and understanding. They may not be a good choice for a long-term partner, and, if the person is a family member, then you may just have to adjust to a relationship that is relatively superficial. In cases in which the benign narcissist is a parent, there may be some unresolved resentment about the parent's immaturity, and as an adult, it may feel as though the parent is emotionally stunted, while you have progressed and leapfrogged your parent into adulthood.

Entitled People

A driver of toxic, difficult people and of narcissism is entitlement (remember, this is one of the patterns that falls under the antagonistic trait). Entitlement is the problem of our time. It has always existed amongst those in power and those who hold privilege. However, it is now commonplace in everyone. Somehow, the prevailing wisdom is that everyone is *entitled* to special treatments or benefits. This is the one pattern that is becoming so prevalent that we are beginning to see it in everyone from social media followers to five-year-old children to high school students to airline passengers to fast-food customers to parents to strangers in parking lots. All of us encounter entitlement during our daily errands, in our workplaces, with our families, in our classrooms, on public transportation, while we get our hair cut and purchase our groceries, and in our social media feeds and our celebrity culture. The challenge of entitlement is that no one is born this way (other traits, like introversion, extraversion, and agreeableness, are, in part, temperamental and, as such, inborn). People learn it. It is developed because someone told them it is okay. Obviously, some learn it quickly because they are born into vast privilege (children of corporate titans, world leaders, celebrities, royalty) and never experience any other reality (until they do, if they do). Others learn it over time because society, their parents, or their peers permit it or even reward it.

Entitlement is, in many ways, a visible pattern. We see it when someone is yelling at a receptionist, when someone feels he or she should not have to wait in line and cuts to the front, when someone asks that a deadline be adjusted because he or she wants special dispensation, and when someone is told to not use a phone in a movie theater but does it anyway. This is in contrast to lack of empathy, which is more of a feeling—while it can manifest in some behaviors (literally looking away while we talk or not asking us how we feel), it is something we experience more emotionally than visibly.

Where do people get the idea that they deserve special treatment, that they are somehow above or exempt from the rules? A few places. First, it is taught—typically by parents. Most often, children learn it from watching it; they watch their parents' entitled behavior, how their parents treat other people in the world and within the family, how they treat the children's teachers, or how they may treat someone who helps them, like a babysitter. When the parent either overtly or covertly communicates that the other person is "less than" and that the parent deserves special treatment, the child, by extension, will learn that pattern. In addition, an entitled parent is unlikely to correct a child when that child is behaving in an entitled manner. In part, it also emanates from parents who do not check their children or teach them to regulate their behaviors or feelings. Children tend to be entitled by nature. They just do what they want; it is the job of the parents, family, and teachers to teach them that there are rules and structures around appropriate behavior. When they don't, we end up with entitled little people, but addressing the behavior requires the parents' recognizing the entitled behavior as wrong.

Children may also learn entitlement from the cultures they populate, including schools, sports teams, or clubs. If the coaches, leaders, or teachers foster a culture of entitlement, then the child will believe it. There has been a fair amount of debate about the idea of a "trophy for every child"—this is often a setup for a child's feeling like there always has to be an ostensible "prize" at the end. That can lead to poorer frustration tolerance in the face of loss or failure or if there is a lack of recognition for simply showing up. This need to overly commemorate even nonexceptional events may yield a greater likelihood of asking for "special" dispensation, or even a redo. As a college professor, I have faced down many an entitled student at the end of a semester who wondered why he or she did not receive an A. These students are often quite ashen when they are told they did not earn it. For many of them, the belief was that showing up entitled them to an excellent evaluation. Think again.

In addition, there has been an overcorrection in reaction to the more authoritarian, emotionally distant, and even militaristic child-rearing approach of prior generations, with a subsequent focus on chronic self-esteem enhancement. This can reinforce the unrealistic assumption that "everyone is special." Everyone *is* in fact special and unique; however, that does not entitle everyone to special and unique benefits. Remember, the entitled person believes that he or she deserves special treatment, even at the cost of other people (like with the lifeboats on the *Titanic*).

Our culture is also set up to foster entitlement, with VIP lines, preferred parking, front-of-the-line passes, first-class airplane seats, and first-class waiting areas. Entry to these spaces tends to be not earned but purchased. The increasing gap between rich and poor in the US and around the world only fosters these assumptions of entitlement. We are increasingly becoming a culture that is cruelly dismissive of those who have "less" and reveres those who have "more" (regardless of how they acquired it). We are in the era of the genetics of luck—if you are born to the right parents, the rules don't apply to you.

From a psychological perspective, entitlement is actually not good for people. It may get their needs met in the short term. However, entitled people can have significant difficulty with ever hearing the word "no." In my clinical work with either narcissistic clients or simply deeply entitled clients, I have seen that they experience *significant* difficulty when they are told no, and there is nothing they can do about it. In the face of frustration, they often experience symptoms of depression, sleeplessness, anxiety, obsessive thoughts, distractibility, and a greater likelihood than non-entitled people of relying on drugs and alcohol to cope. Because our entitlement culture is based on the idea that money can fix any-thing, when a situation arises in which that does not work, the person falls apart. These situations typically involve other people—the entitled person may lose a relationship and want it back and the other person cannot be bought or manipulated, or the entitled person receives a bad grade in a class and really cannot bribe or threaten a professor (though he or she does try).

Entitlement can also manifest as self-righteousness. Entitled people rely on a convenient form of morality in which the rules don't apply to them and believe that their worldview should universally apply to other people. It is for this reason that entitled people can often suggest dra-conian social policies that can seem particularly hurtful to vulnerable groups (such as really harsh views about groups such as the homeless, economically struggling mothers, or immigrants) while also demonstrat-ing an unwillingness to recognize their privilege and luck. Entitled people also use litigation as a tool to enact their sense of personal righteousness, filing expensive and, at times, frivolous lawsuits and using attorneys to turn divorces into bloodletting and to punish any variety of slights. On the flip side, they get enraged when they receive the same treatment and will often start screaming about injustice, slander, libel, and defamation when someone uses the "weapon" of the law against them.

Wealth can result in something called "acquired narcissism" or "acquired entitlement." Not all rich people are bad people, but life does treat them differently. They often do not have to manage the day-to-day indignities the rest of us more regularly endure, such as cleaning our own homes, folding our own laundry, sitting in a middle seat on an airplane, worrying about paying for college, stressing over medical bills, carrying our own bags, running errands during rush hour, and sitting in traffic day after day. As such, the world can seem like a well-oiled machine to wealthy people, and that can result in a higher set of expectations, a greater unwillingness to endure anything but the easiest of circumstances, a certain lack of resilience, and a tendency to be dismissive of other people or to view them as functionaries or conveniences. The litmus test then may become whether you can snap them out of their bubble and remind them that the person fetching their coffee or cleaning their home or driving their car is, in fact, a human being and deserves humane and decent treatment. When called out, many people of means who behave in a dismissive manner will snap out of their "entitled hypnosis" and be quite apologetic. That is what is meant by acquired narcissism or entitlement—it is a product of people's circumstances but not who they really are. But, when people really do take the stance that, in fact, due to their social station, money, title, or power, they can do what they want and treat "lackeys" as lackeys, then we *are* dealing with toxic entitlement and, most likely, narcissism as well. If you are a secure human being, you never need to dehumanize another person, regardless of your bank balance or societal position.

Which Subtype Is Your Narcissist? (Hint: The Thirty-One Traits Can Help)

Most narcissistic and toxic people will fall into one of the above subtypes but, given how many patterns of narcissistic and difficult/toxic people we have discussed thus far, when we reflect on the thirty-one traits that comprise the various facets of narcissistic or difficult/toxic people, it can help to consider the trait that is the most noticeable. For example, you may have a grandiose narcissist, an entitled narcissist, a superficial narcissist, an arrogant narcissist, a cheap narcissist, and so on. Just consider the trait that is most salient (think about the toxic people you know and their most forward-facing qualities—you can see how each of them has a slightly different face, but none of them is attractive).

The overarching theme is that all of these patterns represent some form of toxic interaction. For example, grandiose narcissists will simply brag endlessly about their accomplishments, entitled narcissists will always complain when they do not get special treatment, and superficial narcissists will focus only on how people look and the car they drive, and focus on those traits within themselves. Their front-facing "type" will flavor their particular brand of narcissism. It is important to understand their subtype, as it will give you a better strategy for how to manage them, and you can tailor your approach to this subtype. For example, grandiose narcissists can be managed by fluffing them with compliments, entitled narcissists by treating them in a special way just to shut them up, and communal narcissists by tossing them ten bucks for their charity du jour and "liking" their charitable endeavors online. These strategies obviously are not pleasant or sustainable, but they may forestall frustration, conflict, and futility of interactions with narcissists.

Psychopath vs. Sociopath vs. Narcissist: A Toxic Continuum

This is a distinction that people seldom get right, and, even in the field of psychology, there is a fair amount of disagreement. Criminologists, sociologists, psychiatrists, and psychologists approach these terms and phenomena through different lenses. These words represent a mash-up of clinical terms, sociological terms, and trait labels. They are often used interchangeably, and perhaps they are best viewed as points on a continuum and different facets of overlapping syndromes. There are, in fact, some toxic narcissists who look like psychopaths, and some covert narcissists who look like sociopaths. It has been suggested that "psychopathy" is a term that has more specificity and clarity, while "sociopathy" remains an evolving term and still lacks the kind of specificity we need to use it in a meaningful way. Let's break this down so you know what you are dealing with. There are actually different techniques that you would use with a psychopath versus a narcissist.

Psychopathy researchers Hervey Cleckley, Robert Hare, J. Reid Meloy, and William Reid have offered some of the most comprehensive descriptions of psychopathy. Cleckley, in his classic work *The Mask of Sanity,* labels psychopaths "grossly selfish, callous, irresponsible, impulsive, and unable to feel guilty or be able to learn from experience and punishment," and he highlights issues such as low frustration tolerance and blaming others for their problems. Hare labeled psychopaths "social predators who charm, manipulate, and ruthlessly plow their way through life...violating social norms and expectations without the slightest sense of guilt or regret." Robert Hare and Paul Babiak, in their book *Snakes in Suits: When Psychopaths go to Work,* build upon their research on the construct of psychopathy. They make a key distinction between psychopathy and sociopathy, describing the psychopath as an individual who

101

maintains no sense of morality or empathy (while manifesting traits such as superficial charm and lack of remorse), while the sociopath *does* have a sense of morality and a conscience but does not maintain a sense of right and wrong as held by their culture. In other words, they know what constitutes moral and decent conduct toward other people but choose not to engage in such conduct. Stephen Dinwiddie, a professor at Northwestern University, suggests that "sociopathy" may be a less precise term than "psychopathy" and more consistent with a broader definition that takes in a more varied population of people who behave with no empathy, little remorse, callousness, and norm-violating behavior, whereas psychopathy as articulated by Robert Hare is a far more precisely defined pattern. Jack Pemment in the Department of Biology at the University of Mississippi highlights that we are still articulating the differences between psychopathy and sociopathy, biologically, cognitively, and behaviorally. He recognizes that sociopaths do know the moral code of a culture but think and behave in dangerous and marked contrast to those moral rules. He argues that "the key to understanding sociopathy has to be in the power that ideas exert on the brain."

Sociopaths look very similar to psychopaths in terms of their disregard for others, lack of remorse, coldness, and irresponsibility. There is a body of empirical support indicating that psychopathy has genetic underpinnings and that psychopathic brains may be different, with studies examining brain structure and function revealing that psychopaths respond to stress differently, have different levels of autonomic nervous system reactivity, and may simply be wired differently in terms of how they think about rewards and consequences. Increasingly, research is also revealing the neuroscience of sociopathy—and this work continues to evolve. Some have suggested that sociopathy is more consistently a byproduct of neglectful and abusive households or associated with an early history characterized by trauma or other violence. In addition, sociopaths are a bit "sloppier"—they do not have the cool efficiency of the psychopath. Instead, they tend to be more agitated, and, when they do engage in behavior that violates the rights of others—whether it is violent or not—they are generally more impulsive, and they do not plan as well. Because of this, they are easier to spot and often live on the fringes. People are less likely to be charmed by sociopaths, as they are often cold and emotionally distant. Sociopaths are more broodingly angry and are at risk for reacting impulsively to aggressive feelings or even mere frustration or disappointment. They can look like covert narcissists without remorse. Sociopaths are prone to explosions of rage—and are not as seemingly cold and calculating as their psychopathic counterparts. Sociopaths are the guys who get into brutal bar fights; psychopaths are better as hired assassins who leave no trace. The rage of psychopaths tends to be more quietly menacing. They wear a cold smile that hides the terror that they will perpetrate when they are ready. Sociopaths are messy and bombastic with their rage.

Both patterns are similar. A significant proportion of psychopaths were raised in homes and settings characterized by violence and neglect, but psychopaths tend to be more coolly efficient and interpersonally skilled, so they may appear as glib and superficially charming. They are much more skilled at manipulating people and, as such, psychopaths make better criminals than sociopaths do, perhaps because, according to researchers like Robert Hare, they really do not have a grasp on that which is "morally right," which makes it a bit more seamlessly simple to violate laws and norms. Neither group is particularly pleasant in the long term. However, especially in the case of the psychopaths, their superficial charm can make them tempting as potential partners, business associates, or leaders (estimates vary widely but suggest that anywhere from 5 to 21 percent of CEOs and other corporate leaders are psychopaths or have very strong psychopathic tendencies). Interestingly, they have little use for closeness or intimacy, but they do welcome the idea of exploiting other people for status, sex, money, power, or just because they get off on exploiting people. They are very good at this game and can be so charming in the beginning that the evil they are ultimately able to perpetrate can be extraordinarily unsettling for the people who fall into their traps.

"Psychopathy" and "sociopathy" are not diagnostic terms. The diagnostic manuals most widely used internationally are the *Diagnostic and Statistical Manual for Mental Disorders*—fifth edition (DSM-5) and the *International Statistical Classification of Diseases and Related Health Problems*—tenth edition (ICD-10). Neither of these books uses these terms, instead using the term "Antisocial Personality Disorder," which is defined as "a disregard for or violation of the rights of others" and characterized by egocentrism, self-esteem derived from power or pleasure, absence of prosocial internal standards, lack of empathy, lack of remorse, incapacity for mutually intimate relationships, and use of dominance or intimidation to control others.

Narcissism is a somewhat "milder" variant. An easy way to understand it is that all psychopaths are somewhat narcissistic, but not all narcissists are psychopathic. Narcissists rely on validation from other people to prop up their self-esteem and stabilize their insecurity, while psychopaths derive their self-esteem from power, intimidation, control, and the pursuit of pleasure (and do not really care what other people think). Narcissists tend to have superficial relationships and rely on other people as sources of validation, while psychopaths and sociopaths, as a rule, tend to exploit and abuse other people. Narcissists are undercut by a real sense of insecurity, and a need for admiration, whereas psychopaths are not plagued by insecurity, but they are brilliant at exploiting it in others. Ultimately, it is the lack of remorse that really differentiates the two. Narcissists are prone to shame, and they care so much what other people think that when they do a bad thing, they may actually feel bad—not necessarily because they feel bad for the other person, but they are ashamed at being called out because it is not validating and it threatens their already vulnerable self-esteem, as well as their sources of validation. Psychopaths and sociopaths, on the other hand, don't care what other people think about them, so, when they do a bad thing, they simply do not care about its impact on others, as long as it gets them what they need or want. Their ability to view people as expendable makes it likely that they will exploit others, with little regard for the harm it causes. A relatable example could be that, when narcissists are unfaithful, they will try to hide it, deny it, minimize it, and may even feel a little bad and ashamed about it. When psychopaths are unfaithful, they will firmly believe it is their right, will keep doing it with impunity and, other than the resulting inconvenience, do not care if they are caught. The psychopaths tend to be a more severe variant of malignant narcissism, while the sociopaths tend to be a more severe variant of covert narcissism. This is not meant to be an exhaustive review of these complex diagnostic and etiological distinctions. Ultimately, these are subtle scientific issues, and the science of the neurobiology and genetics of psychopathy is yielding a stronger evidence base for the origins, treatment, and understanding of psychopathy and sociopathy.

So, if we view antagonistic, high conflict, toxic personality styles on a continuum, it may look like this:

TOXIC & INVALIDATING PEOPLE: THE ICK FACTOR

MORE TOXIC AND DAMAGING →

Entitled People/ Benign Narcissists	Communal Narcissists	Covert Narcissists	Grandiose Narcissists	Malignant Narcissists	Sociopaths and Psychopaths

In all cases, these are wolves in sheep's clothing; otherwise they could not do the damage they do. Psychopaths and sociopaths are chilling because they do not feel remorse, and they bask in their impunity. They rely on a combination of factors, not only superficial characteristics such as charm, charisma, and confidence but also accomplishments and skill sets (for example, brilliant tech guru) that often result in the support and complicity of governing bodies, institutional leaders, and other authorities. For example, in reading the case of Larry Nassar (the physician who was convicted of sexually abusing and assaulting dozens of female athletes at Michigan State University), he was empowered and enabled to inflict maximal damage because he perpetrated under the color of authority and hid behind a cloak of respect placed on him by various administrators. As such, parents believed him and so he was literally handed his victims. Until the very end, he defended his actions as appropriate medical treatment and complained about how much of a toll the legal proceedings were taking on him, with little to no regard for the harm he had brought upon these young women. This cycle was more recently reproduced at the University of Southern California in the wake of allegations about a gynecologist at the student health center who now faces accusations of abuse, which occurred over decades, and reports suggest that complaints were made by patients and staff and little was done. The Catholic Church, for years, covered up numerous cases of sexual abuse perpetrated by the clergy, with thousands more cases emerging recently, and the clergy were protected by the church, which maintained secrecy about this horrific abuse. In these settings—universities, health centers, and churches—people do not have their "predator goggles" on and assume they will be safe. Interestingly, in many of these settings, the perpetrators were people who held heaps of privilege by dint of their race, gender, education, job title, and the institutions for which they worked. These are just high-profile cases that have arisen in the news in recent months; however, similar cases are reproduced in courtrooms, boardrooms, bedrooms, and classrooms around the world every day and, often, the perpetrators face no consequences, nor do they ever express any regret. Their victims often carry the scars, self-doubt, self-blame, and numerous other symptoms of psychological fallout for years. When the institutions that are meant to foster safety betray it and allow remorseless perpetrators to harm others, it's a wake-up call that our systems may support narcissism, sociopathy, and psychopathy rather than meaningfully address and limit them.

Narcissistic Patterns in Other Disorders

All of this has to come with a disclaimer. Some of the *patterns* observed in narcissism can also be related to other mental health issues a person is experiencing. Remember, narcissism is not a *diagnosis*; it is a *pattern*, and it is broadly characterized by a lack of interpersonal awareness, as well as interpersonal antagonism, and dysregulated moods. Elements of this pattern can also be related to other mental health issues and embedded within other patterns of mental illness. For example, people with substance use disorders can lack empathy, behave in an interpersonally antagonistic manner, behave in a grandiose manner when intoxicated, or be singularly obsessed and focused on using drugs and recovering from using drugs; people with borderline personality patterns may be conflictual, may be hypersensitive, or may have unstable moods, and have empathy that varies from deeply intense to a lack of awareness when their rage and distress overwhelm them; people with autism spectrum disorders may be experienced as lacking empathy or as being interpersonally distant or unaware; people with mood disorders may also be experienced as lacking empathy, irritable, or emotionally distant (or, in the case of mania, grandiose); people with anxiety disorders may require lots of reassurance (which could be interpreted as validation seeking) or as so socially uncomfortable that it could be experienced as a lack of empathy; or people with PTSD may be experienced as emotionally restricted or distant. As a result, understanding narcissism and isolating it as a pattern is not as simple as it seems. Some of these patterns may emanate from

106

other clinical causes and require a different set of expectations, as well as a need for specific and evidence-based treatment for that person's pattern or disorder. The more you know about people and their backstories, the more conversant you can be in understanding those people and your relationships with them. Nonetheless, these patterns are still interpersonally difficult and still require you and others to set appropriate boundaries and realistic expectations. It is never your responsibility to rescue another person. You can be compassionate and self-preserving at the same time, and, in fact, that may represent the optimal balancing act for your holistic sense of self and well-being, as well as for sustaining healthy families and communities. And you can do this in a way that does not require you to maintain unhealthy patterns within chronically invalidating and destabilizing relationships.

* * *

This book is meant to serve as a guidebook, map, and framework for what toxic, high-conflict, difficult people are all about. Narcissistic people are a subset of toxic people, and, while nearly all narcissistic people are toxic, not all toxic people are narcissistic. What may be toxic to one person doesn't affect another. The word toxic may represent an interaction or a pattern, but, ultimately, if it's toxic, it's making you sick.

But this isn't just about individual relationships. Next, we are going to talk about how every one of us who is living in the world as it currently is, is in a toxic relationship and may not know it. The world has slid into a constant backdrop of incivility, narcissism, and toxic entitlement, and it is affecting nearly all of us. It also makes it more likely that, as this becomes the new normal, we will tolerate toxic people more easily and may even be more likely to fall for them, work for them, or even raise them.

And that is very bad for us. All of us.

Chapter 4

Toxic Universe:
The Narcissistic World Order

When one with honeyed words but evil mind
Persuades the mob, great woes befall the state.

—EURIPIDES

I recently came across a cautionary tale that was lurking in a tabloid story about a young woman. She shared a story of woe about spiraling into more than $10,000 in debt to create a social media-worthy lifestyle. This, in essence, entailed spending money on clothing, accessories, and high-end travel and posting the imagery of her lifestyle. She was creating a false aspirational self who had the money and spare time to create an enviable lifestyle, in the hope that others would follow her, believe her, and covet her lifestyle. Perhaps she believed that, if she faked it long enough, it would become real and she would be able to monetize the illusion. Her self-disclosure via the tabloid pages revealed that she wound up financially tapped out, and she claimed she was now going to pursue a less superficial lifestyle. The current focus of the world on having "stuff" and larger-than-life experiences, and people's need to ensure that the world knows about them, is fostering a sense of insecurity in everyone. No matter what you have, there is an Instagram post telling you that you do not have enough.

News coverage on a minute-by-minute basis features people who are anointed with power and platform through political office, media punditry, celebrity, or wealth engaging in diatribes, insults, assaults on human rights, or dehumanization of anyone who is perceived as the "other." This can be observed in insults issued to dying senators, to children with developmental disabilities, to women who have been sexually assaulted, or to people who are homeless. We are becoming accustomed to a world in which empathy is rare, entitlement is commonplace, and the pursuit of power and wealth is considered so noble that hurting other people is permissible to achieve these goals. The new world mantra is "It doesn't matter how you get there, as long as you get there." We are no longer shocked or bothered by any of this. An optimist might argue, "That's great—people are resilient, and they adjust and do not let any of this bother them."

Wrong.

When we adjust to this, we normalize it. And perhaps what happens on the evening news does not feel relevant to your daily life and relationships, but, in fact, it is. When civility disappears; when mocking vulnerable people is considered normal banter; when powerful people can defend their abuse and assault of employees and others with less power without irony, insight, or contrition; when we don't think twice when someone starts screaming, "Don't you know who I am?"; *when we don't question these things, when we just accept them as the way things are, we give them permission to occur.* And, when we give these things permission to fester and foster, when we reward them and give them vaunted status, we incentivize them. There becomes zero incentive for people to change their abusive behavior; if anything, this raises the rewards for being abusive. It can be easy to perceive bullying, entitlement, and general "assholery" as a path to success, security, and power. The world has become a petri dish of sorts in which the toxic elements are festering, and we need strategies for how to manage this—because what we are currently doing is not working.

In this way, the world gradually became narcissistic and, right now, the narcissists and the most toxic amongst us appear to be controlling the narrative and shaping our reality. I have long written, spoken, taught about, and treated people based on the idea that, when we spend time with toxic people, difficult people, narcissists, psychopaths, sociopaths, and/or assholes. it is not good for us. It erodes our self-esteem, infects us with self-doubt, increases the likelihood of stress-related illnesses, and makes us less efficient, because we spend our time walking on eggshells and trying to protect ourselves against their careless, mindless, and sometimes downright cruel words, actions, and manipulations. Over time, we may even start believing their insults and castigations. We live blindly in the hope that it will somehow resolve itself and things will get better. In this chapter, we'll take a look at how our society and culture, with the trappings of fame, social media, materialism, and money, can foster this rise in narcissistic behavior, so that we can become more aware of its lurking presence. The first step in conquering toxic behavior is acknowledging its existence.

Why Do We Fall for Toxic People?

Why do we fight for them, keep going back for more, admire them, elect them, share our holiday dinner with them, agree to a third date with them, model our lifestyles after them, work for them, or fall in love with them?

Insecurity.

Insecurity explains nearly all of it. In the most simplistic telling of the tale, if we address insecurity, the toxic people would not be able to inflict the same damage as they do now. We would be better able to neutralize them if we eliminate the fear. If the world felt stable, and we ourselves felt stable, then narcissistic and toxic and difficult people would not stand a chance.

Narcissism is based on insecurity, and narcissists get to this insecurity through a variety of paths. Most likely, something goes wrong in the early years—safe and secure attachments are not given the chance to develop, people do not learn to regulate their emotions, and they learn to manage their emotions from the outside in and seek validation, so they can manage their self-esteem and sense of self. There is also likely something "constitutional" or temperamental that they are born with; it is as though they are born with a hypersensitive temperament that manifests early on (and they turn into colicky adults). Not everyone who has been exposed to a childhood that lacks safe and secure attachments becomes interpersonally toxic. In fact, some who are exposed to invalidating or abusive

110

early environments become "too" kind and accommodating, become overly empathic, and run the risk of being victimized by manipulative and unempathic people. In addition, some people grow up in consistent, loving, empathic families with secure attachments, and yet they still veer into a toxic space.

Toxic and narcissistic people grow out of an interaction between an inborn temperament and their environment. Their insecurity results in insecurity in the people around them as well. In that way, *insecurity is like a psychological virus that can be passed along unless we have a vaccination against it*—and this book is meant to serve as part of the vaccination that can help protect you from being infected by their insecurity.

So toxic and narcissistic people are not only insecure themselves but also create more insecurity in the world. In fact, they flourish under conditions of insecurity and chaos. In addition, they prey on insecurity. Healthy people who have a secure sense of self are either willing to call a toxic person out—call them out on their arrogance, their grandiosity, their entitlement, their lack of empathy, or their general bad behavior—*or* they will simply walk away from that person. Secure people do not feel the need to prove that they are "enough" to someone else. Where this sometimes goes awry is when secure people meet toxic people and become convinced that their own goodness, their love, can "rescue" the toxic person. It does not work that way, and many a life has been ruined by the transformational fantasy of love saving the beast. The idea that love can rescue a narcissist is a fairy tale.

Obviously, toxic, narcissistic, difficult people don't lead with lack of empathy, grandiosity, unmitigated rage, manipulation, and lying. If people led that way out of the gate, we would run away. In some ways, Mother Nature has mastered this paradigm. Think about brightly colored fish that are poisonous or beautiful venomous butterflies that resemble nonpoisonous butterflies. They have to draw their prey in first or deter their enemies. In human beings, what is the equivalent of colorful feathers and camouflage?

Charm, charisma, confidence, attractiveness, success, intelligence, and articulateness.

Narcissists, psychopaths, and many toxic people are skilled storytellers and salespeople. They can and will make you feel as though you are the only person in the world. For all of their lack of empathy, they are able to study people and suss out their vulnerabilities. Once they understand those vulnerabilities, they do not protect them; they tend to exploit them. Toxic, narcissistic people charm other people in one of two ways. The first is the devil-may-care approach, whereby they simply say what they want with little regard to whether other people will be hurt by their words. Those in this group are often classified as being "bold," "headstrong," and "mavericks." In some ways, they are the kids who are willing to act foolishly or behave badly in the classroom, as the other children look on with envious admiration for their chutzpah. These are often the more classically grandiose narcissists. The second way is the data-gathering approach. Once those in this group identify someone whom they may want to draw in, they pay very close attention to him or her. They learn that person's strengths and, more important, vulnerabilities. They figure out exactly what to say and do to convince the person to get close, and, once they have him or her in their web, they know exactly what to do to control the person (this is sort of the *Talented Mr. Ripley* approach). This can happen over a very long time (in the way a toxic narcissistic parent will come to control a child) or during a far briefer period (such as during a courtship).

The Three Cs of Narcissism

We often confuse characteristics associated with strength or wisdom, such as charm, charisma, and confidence (what I have often termed "the deadly three Cs" of narcissism) with other good qualities, such as protection, leadership, and "visionary-ness." It is easy to fall under their sway, because we are told that the three Cs are signs of strength and success. Unfortunately, the interpersonal qualities that keep us healthy in our long-term relationships, such as kindness, compassion, respect, vulnerability, warmth, and genuineness, are often devalued, especially in men. Men with these characteristics are sometimes labeled "weak," and that labeling can start at a young age through their own fathers and other male authority figures, media, society, and peers. The narcissist's confidence is also alluring but deceptive. We are often comforted by the apparent confidence of a person, especially since most of us tend to be more self-effacing. Confidence leaves us feeling safe, as though confident people will be able to deliver on what they say, a dynamic that is very reassuring. Personality researcher Theodore Millon has astutely pointed out that the narcissist's confidence is often hollow and characterized by what is almost a hip coolness or insouciance. Narcissists can appear nonchalant, unusually calm, not affected by emotions around them (positive or negative)—*until* their ego is threatened and their confidence shaken—and then their rage bubbles to the surface.

Narcissistic and toxic people are like well-feathered peacocks—they have the right feathers to get noticed. Those feathers may not necessarily be their appearance; they can also be their power, their stature in the community, their wealth, or their potency because of their role in your life, such as being a parent or other family member. We are rarely told to take a careful look at whether a person is kind or warm, but often view people with respect and awe when they are "successful." That paradigm has to change.

The next step is that, once toxic people are in our lives, our own insecurities can make it difficult to evict them. We fall into the traps of writing narratives about them to build them up, even once they start behaving badly. If I had a dollar for every time someone said that the reason they had fallen into a toxic relationship and were having a difficult time getting out was because that person initially had been so charming, I'd be a wealthy woman. Then the person created a story about the toxic person that was so convincing that, even after the psychological abuse, the lying, the gaslighting, the projection, and the meanness set in, he or she was stuck in the early narrative about how charming and exciting it all was. I have worked with clients who are holding on to stories about two good months of fun in the beginning of their relationship ("He took me dancing, we traveled to places I have never been, we would eat at the best restaurants, he would drive out of his way to pick me up, he remembered my best friend's birthday"), despite fifteen years of a nightmare. They focus on the trip to Miami ten years ago, and they conveniently forget the abusive words, the neglect, the cruelty, and the gaslighting that happened last night.

I have noted that maybe the safest bet is to steer clear of charming, charismatic, and/or confident people. It's a bit tongue-in-cheek because, if these traits are accompanied by warmth, humility, kindness, and empathy, then that is a rare combination—enjoy it. People who are more inward in their focus, or who are more circumspect and wise, often do not build up their external and charismatic muscles; it's rare to find both characteristics in the same person. That said, if a person leads with charm and charisma and plenty of confidence, sit up straight and pay cautious attention. Make sure that there is empathy, that entitlement is not at play, that the person is genuine, that there is respect and, frankly, that he or she has the goods to back it up. Don't let the charisma and charm blind you and stop you from looking deeper for the rest of it.

Because the toxic and difficult folks, especially the narcissistic ones, lead with the "good stuff," they get a foot in the door and, once that happens, they are often in. However, this "good stuff" paradigm does not always apply to "nonoptional" relationships, such as family members. People do not get to choose their parents or siblings, or even their coworkers, in most cases. But I have no doubt that those very parents, or grandparents, or stepparents, or in-laws who behave in toxic and invalidating ways can put on a hell of a show for other people (the narcissistic mother who charms the neighbors, the difficult father who is considered to be a pillar of the community, the toxic coworker who is able to charm the boss, the charismatic sibling who has stuck a knife in your back, the mean-spirited daughter-in-law who has charmed your son but quietly insults you when no one is looking). They charm someone—it just may not be you.

The InTOXICation of Fame

When YouTube took hold in 2005 and social media platforms such as Instagram proliferated, an increasingly universal drive for fame accompanied it. Human beings have long been drawn to fame but, in the past ten years, anyone with a cell phone, time, persistence, and a hook can potentially go viral. Some authors posit an evolutionary reason for wanting fame: social belonging. We humans want and, in fact, need social belonging and connection. Being part of a group once could have been the difference between life and death, since our group/tribe may have been the only means to keep us safe. In addition, we are biologically wired to avoid social rejection, and we experience social rejection in the same way that we experience physical and emotional pain. Social psychologists and professors of psychology Roy Baumeister (who is presently at the University of Queensland) and Mark Leary (who is a professor at Duke University) argue in their 1995 work that the drive to fame may actually largely be our need for social belonging. Perhaps fame implies permanent social belonging because the person will be recognized every-where he or she goes. Work by psychologist Dara Greenwood, who is presently a faculty member at Vassar College, and her colleagues reveals that the need to belong and narcissism are both associated with fame, but that narcissistic people are more focused on the recognition and VIP status that fame brings rather than on fame as a means to connect to other people. It brings to mind someone I once worked with, someone who desperately wanted to be famous, and, when asked why, he said, "So I am never lonely again."

Fame is now something that feels accessible in our culture, and it fulfills a basic need, thus more and more people are behaving in ways that will get them that fame. That may mean money spent on being an Instagram star; endless documentation of every trivial detail of a life, which is shared on social media via live streams; having experiences for the sake of sharing them rather than the experiencing of the event itself; auditioning for any number of talent-based reality shows; or hoping to go viral through any number of social media or YouTube shenanigans or even dangerous stunts. Over time, the quest for fame can pull people out of their lives, foster entitlement ("I deserve to be famous"), and move the focus to sharing experiences rather than actually enjoying them. This drive is also more likely to be observed in narcissistic individuals, given their need for validation and the perks of fame, including special access and special treatment.

Most people will never be famous and, for most people, that is okay. But the pursuit of fame and the external self that it fosters play to the strengths of a narcissist. Our society often reveres fame, and this celebra-tion of fame, the desirability of fame, and all that goes along with it make it more likely that more and more people will pursue it. In this way, the focus on fame has become a contributing factor to the "narcissization" of our culture and fosters a more toxic society.

The Toxic Playground: Social Media

Some mental health professionals I have worked with have termed social media a "tool for inducing envy" that is often designed to share an ideal and carefully curated version of the self (Vogel et al., 2014). Interestingly, this research suggests that, the more idealized the image a person puts out there, the lower his or her self-esteem (and perhaps the self-esteem of the people viewing those images). A friend's travel pictures from Greece, a cousin's new car, an ex-partner's wedding, portrayals of families that appear to be faring better than ours can all feel personal, especially if our lives feel sparse in comparison (even though social media posts rarely tell the full story).

For toxic, narcissistic, and entitled people, social media is a double-edged sword. In one way, it is their mother ship, a way to mainline validation from the comfort of their own home or vacation by posting dispatches from a sumptuous life or sharing accomplishments or painstakingly edited images of themselves—they get the external validation they need to offset their insecurity. In another way, narcissists often get slapped by social media because they have the tendency to envy and may believe that someone else has it better than them. A conference paper by Marijke De Veirman, a faculty member in Political and Social Sciences at the University of Gent, and her colleagues reported on an experimental study examining the impact of highly luxury-focused Instagram sites on self-esteem. They found that the negative effects of viewing consumerist and luxury-driven Instagram posts had a more pronounced negative effect on self-esteem in more materialistic individuals.

Finally, narcissistic people, because they are so dysregulated and entitled, often cannot keep it together on social media. They have a propensity to post mean-spirited and unkind comments, or to post politically divisive, polarizing, and inappropriate content—in both cases, it reflects a lack of empathy, a lack of self-reflection, a lack of insight, and carelessness. Many toxic people, ranging from some of the most powerful people in the world down to your difficult relative, will find themselves locked into Twitter wars or Facebook spats because they could not filter their negative words, and they will sometimes find themselves having to issue a mea culpa after the fact. Toxic people tend to shoot first and apologize later, and social media can be a dangerous space for that personal style.

Because narcissism is a pattern underwritten by insecurity as well as variable self-esteem, social media has exploited the weaknesses of the narcissist. Social media by definition is based on social comparison, and overwhelms users with images and information that are often used for uncomfortable social comparison. For a person with a healthy identity, this may rankle at times, but doesn't devastate. For an insecure person, the complex stew of social media images, frustration about a life that doesn't measure up, and an inability to express emotions has resulted in a world full of disproportionate reactions to disappointment, seething envy about the better lives of others, and a dysregulated anger that pervades the media, cultural communication, and the populace at large. Instagram + Envy x Insecurity = Rage.

Social media and internet media have developmentally impacted an entire generation (Digital Youth Project, 2008). A survey conducted in 2017 revealed that when six- to seventeen-year-olds were asked what they wanted to be when they grew up, 34 percent answered "YouTuber" and another 18 percent answered "vlogger." Long gone are the days of aspirations of firefighting or doctoring—now, offering up makeup tutorials, videogame narration, or stream of consciousness from a parents' basement is a career aspiration that will carry with it the validation of fame and fortune. It's impossible to train an entire culture away from the temptations of fame and fortune, but we have to be mindful that the roots of these quests go deep. How do we create people of depth who are empathic, connected, and driven by mutuality in their relationships within the new world quest for fame and fortune?

Superficial Selfies

The selfie is the coat of arms for a narcissist. The goal of the selfie may not quite be fame, but it reflects a need to document one's life for the consumption of others. Some researchers have referred to a trend of "selfitis"—obsessive selfie taking at the level that looks like an addiction. In 2016, Ji Won Kim and Tamara Makana Chock, a graduate student and a faculty member at Syracuse University, respectively, conducted research documenting that narcissism is associated with a greater likelihood of posting solo selfies and editing selfies and, interestingly, they did not find that the "need to belong," which appears to be an important part of fame seeking, is associated with selfie taking. Because narcissistic people are not particularly geared toward establishing connected, close, and reciprocal intimate relationships, selfies work for them, as they allow them to demonstrate and maintain one-sided superficial relationships, which sustains their quest for admiration. Basically, it's like having a relationship with a mirror.

Internet Trolls

Social media has provided a platform for people to easily engage in antagonistic and cruel attacks. Unless the moderators of a site intervene, the attacks and insults can be issued and seen by many. These can be defamatory, humiliating, mocking, and shaming, and are almost always hurtful. Internet trolls, as a rule, tend to be covert narcissists, with a lot of malignant narcissism thrown in. On the individual level, the troll's comments and reflections are designed to be divisive, polarizing, hurtful, and even threatening. Their rhetoric and attacks are often focused on already marginalized or vulnerable groups. Internet trolls are generally psychologically immature individuals who are unable to appropriately modulate their thoughts, feel a brooding sense of resentment bordering on paranoia, and are largely incapable of empathy.

Once upon a time, when a person wanted to express a strong and perhaps toxic opinion, there were lots of hoops to jump through. You would have to write a letter to the editor of a publication, which involved getting a piece of paper, writing the thought down, finding an envelope, finding a stamp, and going to the mailbox. Then an editor would serve as a gatekeeper and have the opportunity to choose whether or not to publish the letter (which he or she typically would not, and, instead, would bar this kind of vitriol from getting the kind of public play it gets now). That is far too many steps and barriers for a troll-like individual. But now, without leaving their bedrooms, they can launch endless inflammatory invectives against other people.

Trolls hurt people—their words turn news sites, social media sites, and other collective posting spaces into toxic spaces. Even when the reader is aware that the person posting such vitriol and hate is, at best, a coward operating from the anonymity of an alias, simple exposure to this hateful, uncivil, baiting, and cruel abuse contributes to the larger toxicity in which we are all currently living and that is negatively impacting everyone's health and well-being.

Social Media, Materialism, and Envy

Social media has also transformed into a sort of "materialism theater." Americus Reed at the University of Pennsylvania has noted that social media is "where we curate an idealized version of ourselves." And that is largely conducted through users and "influencers" who turn themselves into living, breathing billboards, draped in clothing, sunglasses, handbags, and shoes that they feel compelled to feature with a hashtag to foster consumption of those products. It becomes a toxic display in which a person's position in the hierarchy can be vaunted, inducing envy, reminding other users that they may not have these things, and fostering subsequent insecurity and then more consumption. Hashtaggers and Instagram influencers may have no goal other than profit, self-promotion, and self-enrichment (getting freebies from the brands they are flashing, and more followers), but the impact on everyone is widely felt. This impact can be particularly profound in more impressionable groups, particularly younger people.

Ultimately, social media and participatory media have fanned the flames—if not acted as an outright accelerant—on the epidemic of toxic entitlement and narcissism. They have pulled a significant proportion of the population into more superficial exchanges that are brief, often one-sided, and targeted toward surface-level qualities, including consumerism, luxury, and appearance. The ubiquity of these platforms has made them a normative space for interaction, and, as such, bubbling under all platforms is the need to share, belong, seek validation, and be seen. Not everyone is using social media to induce envy, but enough people are, and that can skew the experience for many users.

Scandals involving Facebook—indicating that the perception of Facebook as being free and open was not accurate, and that Facebook was engaged in more behind-the-scenes gerrymandering with people's data than most users believed—have cast a small pall, but, at this point in history, social media remains a primary mode of connection and communication. Because it is such a stronghold of toxic people, it is essential to remain aware of how it supports and fosters toxic people, narcissism, incivility, and insecurity; how it impacts our health; and how to better and more critically consume and use it. Otherwise, we can quickly get pulled into the toxic riptides without even being fully aware it is happening.

A Balanced, Responsible Approach to Social Media

It is not realistic to propose any solutions that involve eliminating or even minimizing social media reliance or use. Most people would argue that we would have to pry their social media from their cold, dead hands, or they defend it ("Everyone is using it," "It's a great way to stay in touch with my family," "I need it for my business"). And, as with just about anything we are discussing, it is not *all* bad. Social media has become a tool whereby people have actually found a space for connection and empathy: Far-flung families can watch violin recitals and share wedding pictures, small groups can attempt to reach wider audiences, groups who may have difficulty connecting due to geography or physical limitations (people who live in rural areas, people who are homebound due to illness) can find emotional support, groups who have faced stigma or marginalization can seek community and information, and the simple exchange of information can occur across disparate groups of people. But, just as with any tool, it has to be used responsibly and with self-awareness. As young people live and die by the number of likes they get and experience genuine sadness, anxiety, and a decrement in self-esteem when their images and posts are not noticed, they are developing within a space in which they are relying on external validation to shape their sense of self. This runs the risk of becoming a recipe for an entitled and narcissistic adult (more on that later) and creating distance from real living, breathing, human relationships. Social media is a tool that could awake the narcissistic and toxic beast within each of us and make us reliant on external barometers such as likes and retweets to regulate our self-esteem. Its proliferation has normalized validation-seeking patterns and made us more likely to endure narcissists, give them larger platforms, make more excuses for them, and also distract us from our healthier pursuits of live connection, self-reliance, and deeper rather than superficial empathy. There is a danger of getting pulled down into the narcissistic swamp.

It all comes down to balance. It's too simple to demonize social media without taking a longer view. Research is increasingly revealing that, while virtual interactions are not truly substitutes for real social relationships, they can be a meaningful enhancement, providing the opportunity for people to maintain connections, share interests, gain information, and better understand themselves. The proliferation of social media happened very quickly, and the social landscape transformed in the blink of an eye. Parents, educators, and academic and occupational curricula all need to focus on building digital literacy and social skills. Critical thinking about all things media is absolutely essential, must start at a young age through the schools, and should be a central pillar of all K-through-12 and post-high school curricula. As with most things, social media and related technologies have two faces. It is incumbent on all of us to understand how to use them in a healthy manner.

Follow the Money

Which came first, our obsession with money and material goods or toxic narcissism? It's a tough question to answer, because we cannot do the kind of research that would truly allow us to answer these questions. We do know this: The wealthy have less empathy, less interest in other people, greater entitlement, higher levels of shoplifting, and less ethical behavior. Paul Piff at the University of California, Irvine is conducting fascinating research on these issues, and he and his colleagues have published work in which they experimentally manipulated a person's sense of being "wealthier." When people were made to feel richer, they were more likely to endorse unethical decisions, such as stealing office supplies or taking candy (Piff et al., 2012). This body of research also supports the notion that the wealthy are more likely and willing to behave in selfish and unethical ways to get ahead and are actually less likely to be charitable (Piff et al., 2010). Is this how they became wealthy? Were they more willing to take the unethical, selfish, and uncomfortable path that many people are not willing or comfortable taking? Piff's research argues that believing you are wealthier can also shift a mindset to being less generous, so perhaps any of us would become more entitled if we believed we were wealthy. Piff and others who conduct this work support the argument that, when we consider ourselves to be somehow "better" than those whom we deem "lower than us," we create the belief that we are actually better, more important, and more deserving, all of which sets up a platform for greater entitlement. The greater the inequality, the lower the generosity—not just of money but of spirit.

Capitalism, especially our current form of capitalism, is predicated on success and profit above all. Under these conditions, even when the economy improves, the sheer amount of social inequality means that we are not going to see an overall uptick in happiness for everyone (though some people are as happy and satisfied as can be, because the system favors them). Being empathic can be economically inefficient. A profit-driven system has a singular focus: to build profits. The eighteenth-century

Scottish economist Adam Smith's theories that propelled free-market capitalism were based on the naïve assertion of the "invisible hand"— a metaphor that maintains that society and business can both benefit indirectly in the face of individual self-interest across many people. The individuals do not have to intend to bring about these benefits; the benefits just come because people are promoting their own interests. It's a shame Smith never met Freud, because that's not how people work. Smith's theory comes up short, because he did not account for unempathic, detached, and entitled self-interest, largely propelled by ego. When people promote self-interest, in the absence of any regulations, or checks and balances, inequality blossoms. However, these economic theories have underwritten our systems for centuries and were co-opted into trickle-down economics and deregulation. While some people benefited, most did not.

Shifts in migration also impacted workforces, and the removal of regulation meant that imbalanced models could be put into place. Profits went to shareholders and bonuses for corporate bosses and were not used to improve communities or create jobs but to fatten the pockets of those at the top of the corporate food chain, while wages did not keep up with the cost of living for everyone else. Main Street died out, and the mom-and-pop stores of our youth were replaced by large chain stores that sell everything from shoes to televisions to ice cream to shaving cream. It was naïve of Federal Reserve heads to truly believe that Wall Street and other financial sectors could regulate themselves! That's like believing a four-year-old will take just one cookie from the jar if the mother is not looking and will share that cookie evenly with siblings (though I am willing to bet that the four-year-old would behave more ethically than a large investment bank). Our current world of robber barons has definitely fostered the normalization and culture of narcissism and toxic relationships through which we are currently limping.

A report by the Institute for Policy Studies, which draws data from the 2017 Forbes 400 and the Federal Reserve's 2016 Survey of Consumer Finances, delivers some rather sobering statistics. The three wealthiest people in the US hold more wealth than the entire bottom half of Americans combined. The entire Forbes 400 list now holds more wealth than the bottom 64 percent of the US population (approximately 204 million people). And yet, at the same time, 20 percent of households have zero net worth or a negative net worth. The interesting assumption is that those who accumulated all of that wealth earned it, while those who are upside down or struggling are irresponsible. It sets up a tricky paradigm. Most people believe that, if they work hard enough, they can succeed—and rarely account for luck, inherited wealth, or timing as the key. Our society reveres the wealthy and is loath to think they got there by luck. So we run the risk of also valuing the patterns and traits that get people there and keep people there. There is a certain lack of empathy in mocking those who may have less and in assuming that they do not work as hard. There is an arrogance and a naïveté in presuming that those who have incomprehensible wealth worked hard for it. These dangerous mindsets perpetuate the slow, steady drumbeat of narcissism across all sectors.

There is no putting this genie back in the bottle, and we live in a time of tremendous economic disparity. Because the tendency is for toxic, narcissistic, entitled, and, in more than a few cases, psychopathic people to cluster at the top of the corporate ladder, their lack of empathy, grandiosity, selfishness, vindictiveness, and arrogance implies that they are not very likely to want to share their profits, to turn down massive bonuses, or to ensure that the rank and file are well looked after. Americans and, increasingly, the rest of the world get funny and morally rigid about these matters. Everyone wants to believe it is a meritocracy. It's not.

But we also need to be careful. Not all wealthy people are toxic or narcissistic or entitled, just as not all people who struggle financially are lazy or morally bereft. Sociologist Rachel Sherman wrote about these issues in her book *Uneasy Street: The Anxieties of Affluence*, which presents the tensions voiced by people of wealth. Based on interviews with fifty wealthy families, she offers some astute and incisive observations on wealth. Wealth does not imply braggadocio or vulgarity. Many of her interview subjects are invested in being perceived as "normal" and maintain ambivalence about being affluent (they certainly appreciate the conveniences and luxuries it gives them but also know that it attracts a certain level of envy, suspicion, or a general sense of "You didn't really earn this on your own"). They maintain awareness that wealth is associated with snobbishness, entitlement, superficiality, or vulgarity. Sherman also notes that they showed discomfort in talking about their own wealth, and this means they actually run the risk of denial and missing an opportunity to accurately view their advantages. The topic of inequality makes for an uncomfortable conversation. So, no, not all people of wealth are toxic, but there does need to be consideration of the problematic distributions of wealth. Sherman's book reveals that it may be viewed as acceptable for people to have lots of money, as long as they are nice people. Our society's drive for money against the backdrop of a few having too much, and many having so little, creates social conditions that are *optimal* for the growth of toxic entitlement and narcissism. There is a cultural blind spot in place that is allowing the incentivization of narcissism to proliferate quickly.

Since this book is not meant to be a treatise on the American and global economy, you may be thinking, "Who cares? Who cares that any of this happened? What does this have to do with my narcissistic husband or my toxic mother?" Many staunchly believe that our current economic system works and works well—and that America is the land in which hard work is rewarded equally. The fact is—whether you believe in our domestic and global economic systems or not—we *all* need to care, because our current economic structures consistently reward narcissism. In most corporate environments, having narcissistic traits makes a person more likely to be successful. That the willingness to advance your own cause and simultaneously throw another person under the bus, the ability to put profits before employees or consumers, intimidation, or the skills to use manipulative strategies to keep competitors or even colleagues at bay is rather consistently associated with or even required for success, means that we have turned the diagnostic criteria for narcissism into a veritable "guide to corporate success." Most strikingly, I recently had a student come to me after a lecture on narcissism, a student who also had a day job in marketing and sales, and implore, "Teach me how to become narcissistic," because he thought it would help him get ahead in his company. (He was right—it would have, and no, I did not accept the request to mentor him in the dark arts.)

The Measure of Success

Maya Angelou wrote, "Success is liking yourself, liking what you do, and liking how you do it." Other surveys out there highlight factors such as happiness, engagement, and close family ties as being indicators of success. Most Americans associate financial success, career achievement, educational attainment, and family as barometers of success. Success has both a status element and a subjective element, which is often what makes it confusing. The status element is where the narrative about "stuff" (money, career) fits, while the subjective piece often takes in happiness, authenticity, and connection to others. The narrative that Americans care about happiness more than wealth doesn't always hold water; Americans are starstruck by rankings of the wealthiest Americans (such as the Forbes 500), but there does not seem to be an analogous list of the most authentic, kindest, or friendliest Americans. The fact is we like quantifiable indices of success—income, SAT score, GPA, profit versus loss—and those metrics tend to favor the narcissists.

The challenge becomes how rarely we look at someone who lives a life of relatively limited material goods and money, or has a simple job, or lacks validated cultural benchmarks such as children or marriage, and genuinely label that person successful. While I do wish we lived in a Maya Angelou world of success as being authentically committed to yourself, we don't. I am heartened to see that, year after year, when I ask my students at California State University, Los Angeles to define "success," I get descriptions that are equal parts material success and equal parts genuine happiness; however, they will acknowledge that, in the classroom, they are more concerned with getting the A, rather than just learning or self-enhancement. Many of our scripts and narratives of success are dictated by other people—our families, our cultures, our media—thus, finding an individual roadmap for success can prove to be challenging, especially for young people. If people get too caught up in the paradigm of success's being a material outcome (salary, house, car), it can leave them more vulnerable to the more narcissistic stomping grounds of money and materialism and the potential toxic impacts and attendant insecurities of focusing largely on those outcomes.

Psychological researcher Marion Spengler, while at the University of Luxembourg, and her colleagues from around the world examined data from a forty-year study of 745 people from 1968 to 2008, and, amongst their findings, they noted that those who broke the rules and defied parental authority had higher incomes. Timothy Judge, a professor of psychology at Notre Dame, and his colleagues actually got the data to support the idea that "nice guys finish last." In a series of studies, they found that agreeable people earn less money, and this finding is even more pronounced for men. The authors suggest that these findings uphold the idea that "men earn a substantial premium for being disagreeable." And, since disagreeableness is an element of antagonism, which is an element of narcissism, it does hold up the argument that narcissism is good for your bottom line. Unfortunately, it is likely that those who earn more money are more likely to be disagreeable but yet also end up serving as "role models" and aspirational targets for people who are attempting to achieve the status elements of success. Once again, without thinking about it, we value narcissism and antagonism.

UC Irvine professor Paul Piff's research again provides some interesting illumination here. He and his coauthor, Jake Moskowitz, also a researcher at UC Irvine, found that people who were wealthier expressed happiness through feelings that are self-focused, such as through pride, contentment, and amusement. Individuals in their survey who had less money were more likely to agree with statements that were focused on others, statements that addressed issues such as compassion, love, and awe. Piff and Moskowitz argue that, when you have more money, you really do not need to deal as much with the details of life and the needs of other people, and so happiness can derive from the self, personal accomplishments, and status. People with less wealth actually need one another to survive and may, as a result, derive more happiness from being able to connect with others. Since we have established that wealth and the traits associated with narcissism hang together, it makes sense. Wealthy people may not have empathy and, frankly, may not need it, as they are more insulated from the challenges of the world and of other people, and their joys are more insulated too (their joy may derive from an expensive new object they have purchased rather than from the happiness of another person).

Narcissists change the value of psychological currencies. Compassion, empathy, reciprocity, mutuality, gratitude, and loyalty are the main currencies of healthy and close human relationships. In a more entitled and narcissistically driven world, compassion has lost its value in terms of deriving societally validated "success." That is not to say it is not precious—it is, and it is essential. However, people who practice compassion in their lives can get very confused and hurt when they encounter narcissistic and toxic people or narcissistic and toxic institutions, because narcissists tend to discard or devalue compassion. In addition, it is even more destabilizing when currencies such as manipulativeness, exploitation, dishonesty, and cruelty seem to increase in value as a means of succeeding.

Once upon a time, we named buildings after heroic figures in our culture and community—soldiers, people who fought for the rights of others, community and civic leaders, and scientists and scholars. Those days are gone. Nowadays, the naming rights for anything are sold to the highest bidder; stadiums and buildings are named for corporations and donors. A recent controversy was raised in Abington Township, Pennsylvania, when the local high school, which had carried the town's name for years (Abington High School), was facing the prospect of being named after a Wall Street–investor type who had graduated from that high school many years before, in exchange for $25 million. But, as with all gift horses, it came with strings: namely, administrators would change the name of the high school, place his name over a certain number of doorways, and prominently place a portrait of him in the foyer of the school, along with other demands. The school board thought this was a good idea; the community thought otherwise.

University presidents, school boards, and community leaders who are all scrambling for resources, as public budgets dry up, offer up buildings, schools, park benches, even trees to be named by the highest bidder. This represents a major shift in our society, in which the billionaire has become a person to venerate and who can purchase memorialization and monumentalization while alive rather than earning it or having it issued posthumously. Because of society's adoration of all things wealthy, billionaires represent that pinnacle of achievement and are imbued with virtues, such as hard work, ethics, morals, philanthropy, and even a sort of divine energy. They are placed on those pedestals because they have what most want—and we rarely ask any questions about how they got there (no one really wants to know what the sausage is made of). Solely on the basis of their wealth, they represent demigods living amongst us. To a narcissist, they are the holy grail, with enough external validation and material success to guarantee a lifetime of happiness and a steady stream of homes, cars, adulation, sex—all of the basic food groups for the narcissist. Are all billionaires narcissistic? Obviously not. But are the rates of narcissistic traits amongst them higher than for the general population? The best guess there (in the absence of hard data) would be absolutely yes. The traits that are almost required in our world economies to get ahead and stay there are predicated on the central pillars of toxic entitlement and narcissism.

Toxic Masculinity

The concept of "toxic masculinity" or "traditional masculine ideology" is a concept that entered the public purview in the last few years and was highlighted in 2018, when the American Psychological Association (APA) released their Guidelines for Psychological Practice with Boys and Men. Ad campaigns focused on this (most notoriously the Gillette razor advertisements), and backlash followed. Many men apparently (and more than a few women), did not welcome this analysis of their world order.

For years, men were assumed to be the reference group and the specific issues faced by men with regard to societal expectations, socialization, privilege, and gender roles had actually not been specifically addressed by the field of psychology and mental health. Within the APA guidelines, the issue of traditional masculine ideology (others have more negatively framed this as toxic masculinity) referred to a pattern of devaluation of emotion in men, discouragement of emotional expression, and stoicism. In addition, it also referred to the reinforcement of the "tough guy" persona—being tough, cold, and emotionally distant, even when others (e.g. their spouses, partners, children) may have benefitted from their emotional expression. Finally, traditional masculine ideology also refers to the overvaluation of power as *the* societally validated motivation in men, which then extended to a greater likelihood of violence—the articulation or manifestation of that power. This was detrimental not only for the overall mental health of men and boys, for whom vulnerability, emotional expression, and distress were discouraged or even pathologized, but for the world at large. This was not good for the partners, spouses, and children of men who never learned to manage and manifest their emotional worlds and find appropriate outlets for them. Within this ideology, men who did evince vulnerability would be dismissed as weak, and these patterns are not only inter-generational but also globalized, and this traditional masculine ideology is, in fact, even more entrenched in cultures outside of the United States and Western Europe. In fact, most of our history books appear to be stories of masculine ideology gone awry.

What does this mean for the core topics of this book? Specifically, narcissism, entitlement, and incivility.

Everything.

While toxic masculinity or traditional masculine ideology are not, by any means, synonymous with narcissism per se, the top notes are very similar. These patterns can foster a sense of insecurity in men, which underlies the core of narcissism. In addition, the impoverishment in emotional expression that society reinforces in men can undercut empathy or empathic responsiveness and, instead, move the focus to superficial posturing and validation seeking as a means of soothing unaddressed inner emotional worlds (why share a feeling when you can buy a fast car instead?). It's much more complex than simplistically opining that Sunday afternoon football is nothing more than an outlet for men's emotional worlds. But too many men, including many men I have worked with clinically, never got the opportunity to "practice" their emotional vocabularies. And this ended up coming out in numerous ways that were not good for them or the people around them—including substance abuse, violence, lack of empathy, poor communication, social withdrawal, and rage. Some of this brooding rage and unresolved emotion are often what underlie covert narcissistic patterns—characterized by resentment, passive aggression, hypersensitivity, and a self-conception characterized by victimhood. When we didn't teach men how to "be" with emotion, they never learned to regulate it. And narcissism is—at its core—a deficit in emotional regulation.

While *both* men and women can manifest narcissism, entitlement, incivility, and a whole slew of other antagonistic patterns—these patterns are, in fact, more common in men. Most importantly, while most men and boys are vulnerable to the expectations of traditional masculine ideology, the majority do *not* manifest "toxic" masculinity, and it is unfair and inappropriate to paint all men with this brush. However, the ways we socialize our boys and men definitely ups the ante and the probability of narcissistic and entitled patterns in our society. Until we can shift the paradigm on emotion, vulnerability, sharing of distress, and new models of masculine "strength" that are not wedded to power, privilege, profit, and intimidation—we can expect that the antagonism that is seeping into all corners of our lives and worlds will continue to plague families, relationships, workplaces, schools, and society at large.

Education

In an ideal world, education teaches us not only reading, writing, mathematics, and critical thinking but also how to be solid human beings. It teaches us the importance of qualities such as patience, discipline, honor, loyalty, compassion, respect, and tolerance. This stance is not one that is always welcomed. Many people actually believe that education should stay out of the ethics-and-morals business, as though those are family matters. We also tend to do a better job of teaching about kindness and civility to younger children, when edicts about fair play and kindness to friends are easier to discuss, and the biggest crisis of the school day may be who is the line leader or who gets to pass out the apples at lunchtime. The civility appears to fade as children head into middle school and significantly diminishes in secondary school, at which time the economic expectations of the "real world" loom large. The charm of giving every kid a turn tends to get eclipsed by parents who want to ensure that their child is the one at the head of the line, the child to achieve the elite college admission, to get the plum internship, and to be a starter on the sports team when college and professional scouts come sniffing.

The "branding" of education, and Darwinian subterfuge of high-end college admissions have become so captivating that, in March 2019, they culminated in a college admission bribery and cheating scandal termed "Operation Varsity Blues" that became an international cause célèbre. A group of well-heeled parents, including celebrities, investment bankers, attorneys, and academics attempted to subvert the system, and these deeply entitled, arrogant, grandiose parents believed that, just as they purchase every other high-end trinket or toy they want, a brand-name college became one more thing to acquire. At some level, these parents had become so accustomed to getting what they wanted, when they wanted it, that they assumed they could employ similar tactics for college admissions, effectively indoctrinating a new generation of entitled adults. These parents and others like them sullied the very brands they revered.

These players in this drama clearly lacked any kind of empathy or self-awareness, unethically and illegally usurping seats at the universities from more deserving applicants. They did not reflect on the potential ramifications of their actions on their children, higher education as a whole, or students they have never met. This scandal raised the hackles of everyone in America—it was a sad affirmation that university admissions did not reflect a meritocracy and were bought and sold to the highest bidder. The story was a crucible of the blindness of narcissism and entitlement, and confirmation that centers of higher education were being co-opted into social clubs that perpetuate the blights of entitlement, narcissism, and incivility.

As a university professor myself, I have been in the education world for over twenty years, and it is getting harder to have discussions about ethics, decency, and civility. Multiple forces have conspired to make this more challenging, including a greater focus on objective learning outcomes than on the less quantifiable focus on the whole student, a heavier teaching load and fuller classrooms, students who are looking for a credential rather than an educational experience, and the high cost of the higher education that students believe (realistically so) they need to be able to translate into marketable skills and not just philosophical conversations about ethics, critical thought, and compassion.

But it is in our educational settings that we sow the seeds for the overvaluation of toxic patterns such as entitlement. Children and adolescents get confused and made cynical by patterns that are hypocritical. In one breath, we talk about being a "good person," and, in the next, we witness advertisements for expensive preparation courses for achievement exams designed to get students into Ivy League and other elite universities. Toxic and entitled parents often hijack a school as their own fiefdom to advance the interests of their child and their family. What message does this send to a child? That he or she is special and the classmates less so? Will this influence these kids as adults? Probably yes. Because not only have they been learning these patterns from their parents, but also they may witness these techniques working with the school to help them achieve their goals. Children can then be socialized to become quite Darwinian, to ensure that their needs are fully met before considering others in their environment. When schools and universities foster a sense of privilege and entitlement in their students—and in theory, these are supposed to be our future leaders—then our educational systems become part of the problem. Schools are increasingly becoming businesses, attracting "customers" (students), "donors" (wealthy alumni and parents), and "patrons" (corporations). This approach shifts the model from growth, critical thinking, and education to pleasing and fluffing to ensure that the customer is satisfied, and that happy parents and patrons keep donating.

We are starting to view universities and the degrees they proffer as "brands." Thus, Harvard is becoming no different than Chanel. Once education gets viewed through a materialistic lens, then are we no longer developing students who are getting opened up to varied perspectives to be stewards of a society, but rather we are developing well-heeled and privileged people who run the risk of promoting consumeristic and materialistic values and the attendant insecurities. In that way, even our higher educational systems become key contributors to the proliferation of valuing interpersonally toxic traits and maintaining the sense of insecurity that generates fertile ground for the epidemic of toxicity and narcissistic patterns to grow unchecked. Interestingly, children who are more focused on materialistic aims have higher goals oriented toward performance and fewer goals around mastery of their schoolwork (simply put, "As long as I get the A, it does not matter what I learn").

Consumerism and Materialism

The "Rich Kids of the Internet"; $800 shoes; $25,000 handbags; engagement photographs featuring multicarat diamond rings; celebrity Instagram accounts that feature fetishized imagery of 1,000-square-foot closets, full of perfectly organized shoes, bags, and watches; fairy-tale weddings; $50,000 children's birthday parties; and tricked-out Lamborghinis all reflect the heightened materialism of our culture. Americans are carrying $13 trillion in debt. Spending, displaying, branding, and believing that more is better are core issues in the toxification of our culture.

Capitalism relies on consumerism, and consumerism runs the risk of being a tool that people use to regulate self-esteem. The message in America, and increasingly around the world, is that stuff can make you happy, and billions of dollars in advertising are spent to communicate the ideology that designer labels denote accomplishment, success, status, and specialness. Why work on inner growth and self-actualization when a pair of sneakers or a Gucci handbag can get you there quicker?

Tim Kasser is an expert on materialism and consumerism and has written two books on these issues (*The High Price of Materialism* and *Psychology and Consumer Culture*). Kasser characterizes materialism as an overvaluation of making money, generating wealth, acquiring material possessions, maintaining a certain image, and being famous or, at least, popular. Scales that measure material values suggest that people who are more materialistic believe that money and objects bring happiness. Research suggests that materialistic people are more competitive, less empathic, and more manipulative and selfish—and, not surprisingly, that materialism and narcissism are clearly associated with each other. And there is a paradoxical juxtaposition—these patterns are unhealthy, yet materialism is deeply incentivized by a capitalistic economic system that is reliant on overconsumption. As such, we get the daily, perhaps hourly, message that our lives would be better with a particular car, or dress, or watch, or handbag, or vacation—and that, in turn, we would actually be better people as a result.

Advertisers tend to be better psychologists than actual psychologists and have no ethical dilemma about exploiting vulnerabilities to separate consumers from their money. Many of the statuses we most value in our society (physical appearance, fast cars, organized kitchens, eternal youth) can largely be achieved only by spending money. These things often achieve status because we are *told* to value them. The media also plays into this insecurity in the form of improvement shows—about weight loss, plastic surgery, and home improvement—in which the message is that spending money and the attendant transformation will make us better. These programs serve only to magnify the insecurity that comes from living in a world in which we are told that we could *be* better if things just *looked* better. In this way, narcissistic people often make the best salespeople, because they fully believe in the values of materialism and inherently are able to promulgate the insecurity that consumerism requires.

Kasser highlights two pathways to materialistic values: materialistic messages and insecurity. This is an interesting dichotomy, because *all* of us are exposed to these materialistic images (billboards, signs in subway cars, pop-up ads on websites and our phones, TV and radio commercials); you would have to be a Luddite residing in a forest to be insulated from them. But the insecurity piece highlights the specter of narcissism and toxic entitlement. Remember what we said earlier: Narcissism is, at its core, a problem with poor self-reflection, inaccurate self-esteem, and insecurity. Kasser points out that people manifest greater materialism when they feel insecure or their sense of self is threatened. Interestingly, that is also the dilemma of narcissists—they are insecure. Thus, many narcissistic people may acquire lots of stuff to insulate themselves from those feelings. Not surprisingly, research suggests that higher materialism is also associated with higher social media use.

Materialism is driven by insecurity and superficiality, and so is narcissism. Thus, it makes sense that narcissism and materialism go hand in hand. But, in a capitalist, consumerist, and materialist world, the measure of success is typically material success (car, house, purse, credentials, money, stuff), and, as such, the narcissists appear to be successful and "winning" at the game of life in these cultures (and this message is increasingly creeping into all cultures). Changing the paradigms and measures of success is a tough sell.

Materialism is definitely a narcissist's ground game and one that is not good for any of us. It sets a tone for incentivizing acquisition and superficial validation and for rewarding narcissism and toxic entitlement. It is not good for our health, for our families, or for the environment. But, sadly, it doesn't appear to be changing anytime soon.

New Age Narcissism

In the haze of this difficult world in which we are finding ourselves, with corporate malfeasance, White House scandals, polarizing politics, chemical weapons being used on children, American families working harder and having less, and angry words from Washington, D.C. and beyond, we are all struggling to find our true north. Instead of calling this out as the outcome of placing narcissists and other toxic folks in charge of a critical mass of governments, institutions, and organizations, many try to find more mystical solutions. Whether through yoga, meditation, positive affirmations, "The Secret," putting intentions into the universe, daily gratitude, spiritual gurus, crystals, retreats, enlightenment hierarchies, cults, dietary changes, or a focus on blind optimism, there is some risk in trying to think or chant the myriad injustices, problems and antagonisms of our current world away.

Many of the activities listed above, such as yoga, meditation, mindfulness, and eating healthier food, are good exercises and daily practices—they have been shown through research to have some beneficial physical and mental health effects. But they are not cure-alls. And the challenge comes when zealots start running with these platforms. New Age gurus on YouTube and Instagram, such as those pushing weekend retreats (white robes and turban optional), often preach a mosaic of hybridized Hinduism, Buddhism, and positive psychology that focuses on love, light, and a just universe delivering what you ask for. At the same time, many of these gurus and programs preach intolerance of negative mood states or words. Sadness or other difficult emotions become forbidden in these settings, all magically solved by joy and one's inner light. The fact is that negative mood states sometimes need to be played out. *In challenging times, it is okay to question, to feel irritable, and to have a normal reaction to an abnormal situation.* The challenge is that, many times, the people promoting these New Age manifestos are businesspeople and are selling only half of a message. Their approaches raise the question of whether they are selling happiness, love, and light as a brand or whether there is an authentic commitment to the growth of their clients and disciples.

There is also a tendency for some of these folks to fall under the umbrella of communal narcissism, spouting off sunshiny affirmations that do not account for a person's holistic and personal experience ("You can love his narcissism away," "You can meditate away his negative energy," "You can learn tantric sex and the magic will win her over"). The intolerance of any negativity in these spaces can mean that the "head guru" and his or her followers may abruptly ostracize or censor anyone who does not agree with the canon of love, light, and rainbows—as though a single negative thought could bring the whole happy pyramid down. In a world where people are seeking answers, too many people do not have access to good mental health services, and folks are feeling vulnerable, there can be a dangerous opportunity to take advantage of these vulnerabilities. This is especially true in the realm of narcissism, in which good information is essential, and sometimes that information is hard to hear. While love and light may have their place, information and awareness are essential tools to push back against narcissistic abuse and get command of past or current narcissists in your life and the attendant psychological issues you may be experiencing in their wake.

Sometimes the self-help indoctrination and New Age seminars and wellness polemics can also fall into a darker space, with these "growth gurus" veering into rather cultish spaces, not allowing people to experience negative emotion, providing simplistic palliatives ("Say two affirmations and call me in the morning"), making people reliant on the cult leaders and the functionaries within the cult, charging increasing fees as you proceed "up the levels," and leaving people feeling as though they are somehow ungrateful for having a negative thought. As a rule, cult leaders are narcissistic and perhaps even psychopathic, as seen in their grandiosity, exploitation, manipulation, and control (and news reports about leaders of varied cult-like "healing" groups have revealed allegations of sexual abuse, isolation, and psychological abuse). The New Age narcissists deny negative moods because happiness sells better, and also because such negative thoughts and feelings puncture their superficial and unempathic bubbles. People who have been victims of narcissistic abuse are vulnerable to the love bombing and recruitment strategies employed by cultish systems. The children's film *Inside Out* got it more right than most of these New Age hucksters by acknowledging that joy is joy only when you invite sadness along for the ride to give it texture, meaning, and contrast.

Once again, materialism, consumerism, and superficiality play on the communal narcissism of New Age fads, and, while some of these systems *do* originate from well-intentioned places, it is important that people do not outsource their souls to the most compelling guru, yogini, teacher, or spirit guide. After going through narcissistic abuse, many people want to be rescued and want to believe that a New Age cure and a few crystal beads will magically make things all better. It is not that simple, and part of healing the abuse is to grieve the loss and dig deeper into your own psychology so you do not fall prey to narcissism again (and you may be vulnerable to a narcissistic guru when you are trying to heal from the self-doubt and insecurity that accompany narcissistic abuse). The feel-good palliatives may also block our ability to take a good, hard, and honest look at what is happening in our world these days and to develop more informed and authentic responses to the increasingly toxic, entitled, and narcissistic world we face. I have sat in far too many conversations in which people say, "No, no, I don't want to hear any bad things—it's easier for me to pretend things are good." *That kind of blindness to real issues can be what fosters the existing toxic frameworks we have in place* and gives the narcissists and bad guys amongst us free reign to continue breaking our hearts, polluting our workplaces, and destroying our health.

What's Your Brand?

Somewhere we went from asking, "Who are you?" to asking, "What's your brand?"—and individual human beings became commodified entities that are no different than a can of soda or a pair of jeans. Obviously, branding is a central part of a business model, but what happens when it is applied to individual human beings? Business consultants may talk about the strengths and weaknesses of this approach, but, from a psychological standpoint, it can be argued that the individual gets lost in the brand, and it is a setup for viewing the self through an externalized lens ("How can I sell 'me'?"). There is little research on this topic, but it would stand to reason that a person who is more superficial or validation seeking would be better equipped at pushing his or her personal brand, disseminating it on social media as an influencer, and having less shame about selling his or her angle to anyone. But, just like all business endeavors, not all brands succeed. What does the failure of a brand imply for an individual? Is it a failure of the self? It's one thing to build a new widget and try to sell it, and, if it does not sell, then it is the widget that fails (people may not need a velvet can opener), but, if you are selling your personal brand, it can take more of a toll (people may not need you).

This push for people to commodify themselves can foster the normalization of narcissism—and our willingness to tolerate it. It has become so endemic that few people second-guess it; even your grandmother's friends are branded and selling stuff on social media ("Click here to order Grandma's home-knit mittens"). It is slowly becoming normal to feel that everyone is working an angle, and that runs the risk of sucking the authenticity and genuineness out of relationships. The world can start feeling empty when people are storefronts instead of people.

* * *

Narcissism is a growing trend in our society, fueled by social media, mainstream media, materialism, capitalism, and how we measure success, not to mention our obsession with fame and attention. Even our approach to education has shifted away from teaching critical thinking, ethics, and empathy in favor of quickly teaching whatever will guarantee the most financial and career success. When everyone feels the need to create a brand around his or her identity, how do we cultivate genuine interpersonal relationships? In the next chapter, I'll offer some background of how narcissism develops, along with some important formulas explaining how you can inadvertently raise a narcissist.

Chapter 5

How (Not) to Raise a Narcissist

*My dad had limitations. That's what my good-hearted mom always
told us. He had limitations, but he meant no harm.
It was kind of her to say, but he did do harm.*

—NICK DUNNE in Gillian Flynn's *Gone Girl*

How does one create a narcissist? Where do narcissists come from?
How exactly does a toxic person come into being? How do you
create a person who could willfully and unapologetically hurt another
person? What would possibly lead someone to walk around the world
in a "Don't you know who I am?" mindset? At this juncture, you know
the finer points of narcissism and interpersonal toxicity. You know how
narcissists behave. You are aware of the different subtypes, and hopefully
you can identify a toxic person much more quickly now.

The simple question "Why are they like this?" may be the question
that is raised most often, especially by people who are suffering the most
at the hands of a narcissist. The assumption may be that, if people could
understand how the narcissists or toxic people came to be as they are,
then the behavior could be fixed. There is no one right answer—there
appears to be more than one path to becoming narcissistic, difficult,
antagonistic, toxic, or deeply entitled. The only consistency is that the
condition likely represents a mash-up of certain inborn temperamental
and environmental factors. However, there are no guarantees. There are

plenty of people who are raised by negating, invalidating, and even abusive parents who turn into kind and empathic adults, who then go on to become excellent partners, parents, and people. There are also plenty of people who are raised in deeply loving, empathic, and consistent homes who become quite toxic and narcissistic. As with all things human, there are many exceptions, but there are also some clear patterns and probabilities, which we'll explore together in this chapter.

Armed with a guide about how to raise a narcissist or a toxic person, most people will hopefully opt out. However, since many people lack awareness of their own demons, they blindly raise more and more narcissistic people. In addition, these children are raised in a world that, for the many reasons we have discussed, rewards and reinforces narcissism. Even the best-intentioned, most loving, and solid parents have to constantly bring their A game to ensure that their children do not get swept into the current of entitlement, narcissism, grandiosity, toxicity, and the accompanying choruses of "Don't you know who I am?" that have become normalized.

A Framework for Understanding the *Why* of Narcissism

Various models in psychology have been termed "bioecological models," the most renowned of which was developed by a psychological researcher named Urie Bronfenbrenner. He viewed a nested series of systems that children reside in and examined children's development through their interaction with their environments and culture. A riff on his and other models can be used to organize what we know about the structural foundation of narcissism.

INDIVIDUAL TEMPERAMENT	FAMILY	COMMUNITY	SOCIETY
• Sensitivity • Motivation • Biological "vulnerability" • Reactivity	• Attachment • Parental mirroring • Inconsistency • Conditional love • Regulation of emotion • Rewarding of behavior and emotional expression • Abuse/neglect • Modeling and shaping behavior	• Modeling and rewards • Emotional regulation • Measures of success • Skills valued in schools and other pursuits (e.g. achievement vs. empathy)	• Materialism/consumerism • Measures of success • Rewarding entitlement • Inequality • Fostering incivility • Gendering of emotional expression

Narcissism evolves from numerous pathways: how a person is parented; the way local communities and community-based entities such as schools interact with a child (sports, other activities, spiritual communities, neighborhoods); the values society imparts to all of us. All of these pathways intersect with an individual's temperament. Not everyone who is raised in an invalidating environment will develop the same way. And, at some level, *all* of us are vulnerable to the societal pressures of narcissism. Each part of this model can be protective or potentially harmful (for example, loving, consistent, and present parents can help a child be more resistant to societal pressures for superficial consumerism). Overall, however, each structure supports and reinforces the others. Let's break down some of these pathways.

The Tempest of Temperament

Although narcissism is, in fact, a personality style, it's not quite that simple. While there are no "toxic" babies per se, all babies come into the world "selfish"—they do not have insight, they require other people to take care of them, and they do not have the cognitive capability to recognize that the caregiver may have something else to do or may be too tired to do something. They believe they are the center of their own universe. They cry and protest because they cannot take care of themselves. But we do not label babies narcissistic, because we recognize that babies' behavior is oriented toward survival (they can't feed themselves, change themselves, or communicate, and are chronically confused about other people). But, as infants develop, they learn. They learn that they cannot always have their way. From the standpoint of probabilities, it could look like this:

	High Biological Vulnerability	Lower Biological Vulnerability
Highly Invalidating Early Environment	*Highly* likely	Likely
Normal Early Environment	Possible	Not Likely

This is a framework offered by author, researcher, clinician, and borderline personality disorder theorist and expert Marsha Linehan. She devised the biosocial framework for borderline personality disorder, but it also very likely fits for narcissism. She argues that there may be a "biological vulnerability" and this may relate to temperament, emotional regulation, or reactivity. This biological vulnerability often plays out as a hypersensitivity that is present from early in life, which then interacts with the early environment. This implies that, even under the best of circumstances, in the face of a biological vulnerability, it is quite possible that a narcissistic or otherwise very difficult and dysregulated adult could emerge, but the one-two punch is when the biological interacts with the environmental.

Over time, children's brains develop, the events of real life provide a reality check, and children slowly learn that they cannot always have what they want, or, at a minimum, they have to wait. They discover that they may be the center of their own universe, but that other people also have other stuff going on too and may not be able to drop what they are doing to attend to them. Because of this, children learn to regulate themselves—to delay gratification and endure frustration, and, with time, may even check in to determine whether someone else in their world needs their help. Ideally.

Interestingly, adult narcissists often look like an infant, or, at least, a toddler: They "cry" (or yell) when they do not quickly get what they want, assume that people will come running when they cry, and become agitated when they don't come running, don't really care about the needs of the people around them, and believe that they are truly the center of the universe. Ultimately, narcissism is actually one of those things that you ideally develop *out* of, not *into*.

Family: The Power of the Parent

It is unlikely that anyone sets out to raise a narcissistic child or a child who develops into a toxic person. However, there are parents who simply may not be up to the rigors of parenting, and actually don't care about the kind of person their child grows up to be, and there are parents who may be narcissistic, entitled, and quite toxic themselves and actually believe their children are superior to others. These children receive that message, both directly and indirectly, which may facilitate their development as narcissists. Even without trying, there are definitely patterns that set a higher probability of developing a narcissist than others. Many parents wither under the daily trials, tribulations, and demands of a child—and this withering will be far more pronounced if the parents themselves are narcissistic.

Just as a recap: People who are narcissistic have difficulty with internal psychological dynamics—they are unable to regulate their self-esteem as well as their emotions. They attempt to regulate their self-esteem, sense of self, and emotional states from the outside, through validation and achievement. As such, their emotional regulation varies with how their external world is treating them on any given day. When they are going through a good day or a good period of their lives, they are almost unrealistically cheerful and maintain a grandiose exterior and belief that they will own the world. However, when things turn south at all—if someone criticizes them, they get into trouble, their business goes south, their friends start making more money than them, someone rejects them—their moods turn very dark, very quickly. In that way they are extremely vulnerable to the vagaries of the world. Wealthy or privileged narcissists often keep this under control by paying people to keep disappointment away from them, but even they are not immune from things like broken hearts, getting caught in misdeeds at work, or rainy days. Families that have narcissists in them will often go out of their way to protect the narcissist from bad news or other stressors, just to avoid their wrath and rage.

MIRRORING

Heinz Kohut focused on the process of *mirroring*, which, when done correctly, means a parent is present. Mirroring entails parents' offering emotional mirroring, appropriate approval, and feedback in a consistent and realistic manner. There are many reasons a child may not be adequately mirrored: parents who lack empathy, who are more concerned with their own validation, who are distracted by life stressors or simply their own interests; parental narcissism; or mental illnesses such as depression, substance abuse, or other personality disorders that may pull a parent away from parenting if those disorders are untreated. Please note: A parent's having a mental illness does not make him or her a bad parent. A parent who has a mental illness (as with any illness) or very difficult personality patterns needs treatment and support. In fact, it can be argued that all parents need support. In the absence of those supports, and a lack of awareness, there is a real risk of missing out on adequately addressing a child's needs. There may also be cultural factors at play, including cultural factors that may discourage parental warmth or emotional expression, as well as cultures that rely on deeply authoritarian models of parenting. When the caregiving mirror is inconsistent, the child cannot develop a realistic sense of self and maintains an unrealistic and undeveloped worldview. Without mirroring and provision of a more realistic sense of self, adults can maintain the same grandiosity they had as a six-year-old child (and still believe they are a fairy princess or a superhero) and also not be able to draw together a coherent sense of self.

Mirroring also teaches children how to manage their emotions. Ideally, the parents' or caregivers' mirror should teach them to recognize their feelings and then allow them to learn to manage them on their own. People who lack this mirror keep looking outside of themselves for emotional regulation. In short, it's like being a forty-year-old man and still hoping someone will stick a pacifier in your mouth. Without adequate mirroring, Kohut argues, emotional regulation is thwarted, and narcissists are prone to abrupt flare-ups of anger, rage, and frustration (much like a four-year-old throwing a tantrum). They project their emotions onto other people, because they are unable to tolerate those emotions within themselves, and then they accuse other people of being angry. In the midst of all of these powerful emotions, they try to find an adult version of a pacifier to soothe themselves, which can take the form of sex, drugs, alcohol, or spending (or all of the above).

COMPARTMENTALIZATION

Otto Kernberg believes that, when children have unempathic, cold, or distant parents, they remain emotionally malnourished. Without this emotional nourishment, their psychological "insides" never fully develop, and, instead, they are forced to develop their outer world. They learn to develop the superficial skill sets that will win over their emotionally unavailable parents, which may include being a pleaser, being physically attractive, excelling at sports, overachieving as a student, or overdeveloping some other niche skill, such as playing an instrument, dancing, or winning spelling bees. This dichotomy of having underdeveloped insides and an overdeveloped outside allows them to become compartmentalized. They may become grandiose about their outer worlds and talents, and, if they do experience moments of vulnerability or weakness, they will deny that vulnerability. This is a process called splitting. It's as though they experience themselves in two distinct ways and are unable to integrate the two: the "strong and good" version and the "weak and vulnerable" version. As time goes on, this compartmentalization is often why they can seem to be two-faced, or to be able to do bad things and jump right back into their usual lives. For example, they may be able to cheat on a spouse, come home from their mistress, and still play at being a devoted family man, or be rageful at night and then expect things to be forgiven and return to normal in the morning. Their compartmentalization also makes them prone to projection.

SECONDARY NARCISSISM

Freud also weighed in on the topic of narcissism in his work *On Narcissism* (1914). In its simplest form, Freud viewed narcissism from the perspective of affection targeted toward something or someone outside the self, which is then directed back onto the self. This phenomenon of secondary narcissism manifests as a person who becomes isolated from society and the people within it. In his description, these narcissistic individuals will have low self-esteem because they cannot successfully love other people or be loved. He also clearly delineated dynamics of guilt and shame typically observed in narcissists, as well as their reliance on defenses such as projection. He believed that narcissism is a chronic search for self-preservation and the need to protect the psyche. In his telling, the origin of narcissism is likely some form of unresolved conflict from childhood that is playing out in adulthood. In one of the wisest descriptions of narcissism, Freud stated, "Whoever loves becomes humble. Those who love have, so to speak, pawned a part of their narcissism."

ATTACHMENT THEORY

Attachment theory focuses on our earliest relationships, typically with our parents or other early primary caregivers. Mary Ainsworth and John Bowlby were the developers of this theoretical framework, and they focused on understanding how infants reacted to separation from parents. Their focus was on the availability and responsivity of the caregiver, as well as the closeness and connectedness of the contact with the caregiver. If the caregiver is not available or responsive, then the child will be anxious and will search his or her environment or will cry or make vocalizations to call for the caregiver. If the caregiver does not materialize, then the baby will experience despair. It is normal for young children to become upset when their caregiver leaves, and it is normal for many children to be quickly soothed by the caregiver when he or she returns.

The attachment styles listed by Ainsworth and Bowlby include *secure, anxious,* and *avoidant*. With secure attachment, we witness a child who is sad when the parent leaves and comforted when the parent returns. The anxious attachment style is observed when the child becomes extremely distressed when the parent departs and has a difficult time being soothed by the parent when he or she returns. In this attachment style, the child will waver between wanting to be comforted and wanting to punish the parent for leaving. Finally, in the avoidant attachment pattern, children do not get too upset when the parent leaves, and, when their parent returns, they actively avoid them.

In 1987, researchers Cynthia Hazan, who is presently a professor at Cornell University, and Phillip Shaver, now a professor at the University of California, Davis, postulated that these patterns manifest in adult relationships as well. Securely attached adults are sad when they have to say goodbye to their partners and genuinely happy and elevated when they are reunited. Anxiously attached adults are chronically worried that other people do not love them and become frustrated when their attachment and intimacy needs are not met. Avoidant adults do not care about close relationships and don't want to be dependent on other people. People who are narcissistic most often look anxiously attached—they are always worried that their love object won't return their love, and they get vociferously angry when their needs are not met. Because of the narcissism, they are often inconsistent, cold, rejecting, and unempathic with their partners and act surprised and upset when they are rejected. In addition, narcissists can become "obsessive" in relationships, especially with partners who are believed to bring cachet to the relationship (youth, beauty, wealth, fame, power) and will find themselves caught in an obsessive push-pull with a partner, with lots of dramatic arguments, anxiety, stalking, and begging the partner to come back. It's the anxious attachment come to life in adult form.

HUMANISTIC THEORY: CONDITIONAL LOVE

Humanistic theorists such as Carl Rogers maintain a positive view of human nature and would not ever want to take as bleak a view as I do on narcissism. They would argue that narcissists had far too many conditions of worth placed on them. In a humanistic model, all human beings are viewed as having the potential for "self-actualization," a sort of transcendent state that finds the person authentic, fully formed, deeply genuine, empathic, capable of offering unconditional regard, and in full possession of his or her strengths, vulnerabilities, and humanity (self-actualization, in many ways, is the opposite of narcissism). If we were to use the humanistic theory to understand narcissism, the argument could be made that narcissistic adults had conditions of worth placed on them as children. Instead of simply feeling loved, they felt that love came attached with conditions—love if they got good grades, behaved well, scored a goal, or kept quiet. This can become even more complicated if the conditions were also variable (*sometimes* they were loved when they behaved well, but sometimes they were not). The humanistic model maintains that children be loved and know that they can love, and this comes only from a person's being loved in a genuine manner without conditions attached. This requires that the parents be confident in their own ability to love and be loved. Unconditional positive regard leaves a child feeling secure, with a well-developed sense of self and the ability to withstand and regulate frustrations such as disappointment and failure. The easiest way to remember this is the idea that *the phrase "I love you" should never end with the word "if."*

MODERN TAKES ON NARCISSISTIC ORIGINS: SHAME, HUMILIATION, AND MATERIALISM

In the years since Freud, Kernberg, and Kohut published their work, authors have developed newer theories of narcissism. More recent theorists like Alexander Lowen have postulated that narcissism relates back to shame and humiliation during childhood because the parents were controlling and emotionally cold or distant. In this scenario, the parents would issue disproportionate punishments or chronically criticize, invalidate, or shame the child for his or her emotions. The child then learns that power is the means of managing close relationships and that expression of feelings is a weakness. In this way, children who ultimately become narcissists are often more prone to rebellion, especially during adolescence, which may represent an attempt at using rebellion as a manipulation to gain power within the family or to shift the balance of power.

Finally, another brick in the wall of understanding narcissism may derive from the work of researchers like Richard Ryan and Tim Kasser, who address extrinsic and intrinsic value systems as well as materialism. Materialism—the drive to consume, possess, and show off external objects and achievements—is a central characteristic of narcissism. Given that narcissists are externally driven, it stands to reason that they would be materialistic (which has been supported by existing research). Ryan and Kasser argue that extrinsic value systems—value systems that are targeted at validation from the outside—are the value systems associated with materialism. Given that narcissists regulate their self-esteem from the outside, materialism becomes one more tool by which to regulate self-esteem. (Who cares if you have low self-esteem if you drive an expensive car? The car becomes the manifestation of the self-esteem.) It also connects with theories about the origin of narcissism, as their work illustrates that extrinsic value systems are associated with greater emptiness, fragility, lower self-esteem, and greater need for praise and are negatively correlated with empathy. Extrinsic values translate into being less prosocial, less community oriented, and less attuned to the needs of others. Thus, against the backdrop of a more materially oriented society or system, narcissism is more likely to proliferate.

BEHAVIORISM: ARE WE JUST RATS IN A MAZE?

One of the simplest premises in psychology is this—if you reward a behavior, it is repeated. And that was the basic premise of behavioral theorists Edward Thorndike and B.F. Skinner that formed the foundation of behavioral theory. A rat could be trained to correctly walk a maze or press a lever simply on the basis of being rewarded food. Acquisition of narcissistic behavior may also be that simple. All of us are vulnerable to this. Go to a coffee shop, get a stamp each time you purchase a coffee, you keep going in and buying coffee to earn a free coffee. Child gets a gold star, child repeats the behavior that earned the star. When we deconstruct the patterns that comprise narcissism, that may mean that a child gets rewarded (perhaps inadvertently) for tantrums, bullying, impatience, whining, entitlement, bragging, or other unpleasant behavior. A child may also get differentially rewarded for scoring a soccer goal, getting all A's on a report card, being a prima ballerina, or winning a spelling bee, while being relatively ignored or at least unnoticed while appropriately expressing feelings, simply being kind to a sibling, or engaging in a compassionate act. We shape behavior in the way we reward it. In that way, narcissism may simply be a reflection of how children's behaviors are shaped into adulthood by parents, extended family, teachers, communities, and society at large.

MODELING BEHAVIOR

"Do as I say, not as I do." Modeling matters. Psychologist Albert Bandura postulated a model called social learning theory, which simply holds that children do what they see, especially when the "model" or person engaged in the behavior is particularly relevant to the child (a parent, a sibling, a peer). He also developed a theory of "vicarious conditioning" which builds upon this premise and holds that a person will watch a model engage in a behavior and observe the consequences that the model receives from the environment. A person can observe whether that model was rewarded for the behavior (or not), and learns whether or not the behavior is rewarding simply by watching whether the model was rewarded. It is understandable that behaviors such as entitlement can be learned simply by watching a model (e.g., a parent or other significant person) be rewarded for engaging in such conduct.

A child who observes parents reading, reads. A child who observes parents hitting, hits. A child who observes parents eating well, eats well. And a child who observes entitled behavior is likely to be entitled and tend towards the "Don't you know who I am?" behavior. Many parents do not recognize that their child is watching and listening with rapt attention when they are yelling at a teacher or a coach or a cashier (or maybe they don't care). Children are paying attention when a father disrespects a mother; they are noticing when a parent is fixed to a phone screen and does not lift his or her head to listen to them. And, whether parents or other adults are in the children's purview, our children are watching all of us. The big question is, what happens to a generation of children who observed adults buried in devices? Time will tell.

Biology

Neuroscience research continues to highlight the biological substrates of many mental disorders and provide more insight on the origins of mental illness, as well as treatments targeting the neurobiological bases of a range of disorders ranging from depression to anxiety to bipolar disorder. However, when examining personality patterns such as narcissism, the biology remains a bit more elusive. While research has substantiated that certain brain regions subserve key psychological functions, such as empathy, much of this research has focused on more severe personality pathology, such as psychopathy. Robert Sapolsky, a Stanford professor and author of the comprehensive book on the biology of behavior *Behave: The Biology of Humans at Our Best and Worst* does an excellent job of taking uncomfortable behavioral patterns, such as violence and aggression, and boiling them down to biology. Hormones such as testosterone, neurotransmitters such as dopamine and brain areas such as the amygdala and frontal lobes are all players in so much of our "bad behavior." Notably, he points out that the amygdala is not just central to our experience of fear and anxiety but also aggression. He notes that we, as humans, are programmed to trust, but that the ever-vigilant amygdala learns distrust, while hormones such as testosterone play a key role in the maintenance of hierarchical status, and a blind willingness to get and maintain that status. Most importantly, he makes the critical observation that the social context around us impacts how our central nervous system works, because it comes down to how we interpret events. Accordingly, to Sapolsky, the challenge is not that testosterone is associated with aggression but that society rewards aggression. So perhaps, a brain is a brain, and the social context into which one is embedded, starting early in life and moving forward into adulthood, means that one person's fear is another's aggression, one person's random act of kindness is another's bar fight. Beliefs about the world and the people in it translate these brain functions into very different behavioral responses. Basically, a narcissistic person's brain was shaped differently, and continues to be rewarded differently by the world. The biology of the various elements that comprise narcissism, including lack of empathy, impulsivity, and emotional dysregulation, is beyond the scope of this book. However, ongoing work into the neurobiology of narcissism and other antagonistic personality styles may over time provide us with more frameworks for treatment and prevention (here's hoping…).

Motivation: The Role of Community and Society

Finally, we can also reflect on the issue of motivation. There are myriad theories of motivation within the field of psychology. The one many may remember from introductory psychology is Maslow's hierarchy of needs, which starts with survival needs like food, shelter, and water at the bottom of the pyramid and ends with the highest-order motivations of esteem and actualization at the top. Motivation researcher David McClelland believed that we learn motivations and that there are three motivators we are all driven by in varying degrees: the need for affiliation (belongingness, choosing the needs of the group over individual needs, and avoidance of uncertainty); the need for achievement (a person is goal oriented and may prefer working alone to achieve those needs); and the need for power (a drive for control over others, enjoyment in winning arguments and competition, the pursuit of status and recognition). These needs are shaped by our families, cultures, and communities, and by our treatment by these institutions and groups. All of us are driven by these motivating forces to varying degrees, with one of them serving as a dominant motivator. For narcissists, sociopaths, psychopaths, and high-conflict, toxic, or antagonistic individuals, that dominant motivator is the need for power. If your motivations are not aligned with those of someone you choose as a partner or friend, or with a parent, it can result in conflicting worldviews and different ways of relating to people. This motivational "style" or "need" dominates in a way that colors a person's character and results in that style's coloring who they are and what they do. The need for power is very much an overlay of a narcissistic style.

So the alchemy of our early environments—parental relationships, attachments, rewards, punishments, motivation, and how we are loved—sets the complex architecture for the psychological underpinnings of narcissism. And all of this occurs against the framework of our society, culture, and communities.

The Paradoxical Issue of Indulgence

In many ways, the origins of narcissism are a paradoxical hybrid of overindulgence and underindulgence. Personality researcher and theorist Theodore Millon characterized narcissism as a disregard for the "sovereignty" of others and believed this derives from the entitlement and the extremes of either overindulgence or neglect. What Millon was saying is basically that narcissism arises from a spoiled child *or* a neglected or even abused child, and any of us who have talked with or interacted with narcissists have observed that they are typically either one or the other.

In some cases, a narcissist can be both. Narcissists are often *overin-dulged* with regard to money, toys, experiences, and hearty congratulations when they succeed at what their parents want (for example, their parents will spend piles of money on special sports teams and coaches so they have a shot at the big leagues—the parents will show up at every game, keep the trophies polished, and talk endlessly about their children's successes on the playing fields—or the parents will devote resources to fostering their children's admission to an Ivy League university and spend endless hours and dollars carefully engineering their children's social and academic lives). In the same breath, narcissists are often *under*indulged with regard to their emotional worlds. As long as the conversation is about golf, or basketball, or an upcoming game or match or recital or success, the parents will move heaven and earth to be there, but, when the conversation shifts to the children's emotional needs or vulnerabilities, or simply the need for empathy, the parents do not have the bandwidth to provide that. This can establish a cycle of guilt and confusion in which the parents are ostensibly available and publicly appear to be cheerlead-ers, but the children grow up feeling deprived in terms of any emotional connection. The children grow up believing that their value is in *what they do*, rather than *who they are*.

Much of this comes down to how a child is taught to manage frus-tration. It is the inability to manage frustration in any way that is the Achilles' heel of narcissists. As a culture, we are becoming worse and worse at this, but our tools for managing frustration are developed while we are young. As schoolchildren, we are made to wait in line, take turns, share a toy, and anticipate a holiday or a birthday party. Childhood is also a time to learn in a protected manner that things may often not turn out our way. We may not get the toy we want or the experience we hoped for. It may rain during the parade, or we may not be invited to a birthday party. Life itself slowly schools us on the idea that life is not fair and that we can endure it. Even board games are designed to teach some form of frustration tolerance, waiting your turn, sometimes losing. Interest-ingly, children are actually better at delaying gratification today than they were about thirty to forty years ago. Stephanie Carlson, a professor at the Institute of Child Development at the University of Minnesota, and her colleagues from around the country replicated Walter Mischel's infamous "marshmallow test" and found that currently kids are actually able to wait longer for a reward than in the original study conducted fifty years ago. The researchers attributed this to a shift in how we educate children and an increasing focus on executive functioning, which is associated with inhibition. However, delaying gratification and tolerating frustration may be two different things.

Managing their discomfort at times when they "want what they want," and adjusting to having to wait in line or share something they want with someone else, may be two of the most valuable skills we provide to children. These experiences instill children with the belief and the skills to tolerate those moments when things do not go their way. However, if parents give their children the implicit message that they do not have to wait in line, if they model entitlement and "Don't you know who I am?" tantrums, that can be a problematic setup for the inability to tolerate frustration in the future. Teaching a child to manage impulsivity is one of the greatest challenges faced by both parents and teachers— and the fact is it is more difficult for some children than others. Some children are able to successfully inhibit their impulses in a consistent manner, whereas others have a very difficult time, and this pattern can dog them into adulthood. Children's brains are still developing; the part of the brain that helps us regulate these impulses, the frontal lobe, develops right through adolescence. But it is the role of the adults around the children to give them the tools to manage their impulses and their frustration. The trait of disinhibition is common in narcissistic individuals, and most simply manifests as acting or speaking without thinking. For this reason, it is not unusual for persons with narcissistic styles or full-blown narcissistic personality disorder to have co-occurring attention deficit hyperactivity disorder (ADHD), or even mis-diagnosed ADHD since the impulsivity may be part and parcel of the narcissistic personality and not an attentional issue per se.

However, maybe, as a parent, you did foster empathy, and model good behavior, and cultivate their emotional worlds, and practice unconditional love, and teach them to wait their turn, and you still have a narcissistic adult child. Maybe you and a sibling had very similar childhoods, and yet one of you is narcissistic and toxic and the other is not. That's because, even if you do not follow this roadmap, we cannot underestimate the importance of disposition, temperament, personality, and constitution. People do come into the world with a temperament, which is believed to have a genetic component. That constitution can set up a vulnerability or a lifelong "difficult edge"—or, on the other hand, a sweetness that persists throughout life.

Are We Stuck in a Generation of Parental Overcorrection?

Perhaps this is a generation that is trying to make up for the generation before; despite witnessing models of parenting for a long time, we are seemingly overcorrecting now. Trying to ensure that the hurts we may have endured from a prior generation of authoritarian or disengaged parents is addressed by trying to be all things to our children. Some are pushing their children less; others are encouraging their children to shoot for the stars. Helicopter parents are bubble-wrapping their children to protect them from danger and disappointment, maintaining poor boundaries with their children, and attempting to engineer optimal outcomes. Parents who may have come from more limited economic means may welcome the opportunity to open doors and provide resources for their children that were not available to them. In addition, parents who are often well intentioned may be trying to prepare their children for the dog-eat-dog world into which the children are entering. Interestingly, the research on helicopter parenting suggests that these parents are not doing their children any favors, with recent research suggesting that helicopter parenting is associated with diminished autonomy and sense of mastery and has negative impacts on future relationships and sense of self.

Parents may feel as though they are thrusting their children into a *Hunger Games* landscape of economic disparity, overly competitive college admissions, and the need for STEM-specific skill sets, such as writing code, computer programming, and robotics, that are incentivized in the marketplace. Children are being tossed into a world with a far higher cost of living, fewer well-paying jobs, and a political landscape that has created unrest and divisiveness. Many economists and sociologists are predicting that, for the first time in a long time in the US, the present generation of emerging adults will not collectively prosper and maintain the same level of economic security as their parents. Specifically, economist Raj Chetty and his colleagues at Harvard University found that, while 92 percent of children born in the 1940s earned more than their parents did, only 50 percent of those born in the 1980s did so. As such, there is a desire to keep children safe by ensuring they have the credentials, tools, and resources to fight the good fight. This can shift the focus from building a good, kind, empathic kid to building more of a warrior who attends the "right" school, has the "right" major, gets the "right" job, does the "right" sport, marries the "right" person, drives the "right" car, and lives in the "right" town. The concern is that, by trying to overcorrect the hurts and missteps of a previous generation of parents, parents may still step into the proverbial pile of parenting shit and be drawn into a well-intentioned, albeit externally validated, space of "success" rather than an internally mediated space of authenticity and sense of self. This is a setup for entitlement, challenges with regulation, an inability to cope with disappointment, and a need for external validation.

While past generations of parents did get it wrong in many ways, they were far better at letting their children experience disappointment and get through it. That may be the most important lesson children get, and one they may be better equipped to handle if they come from a place of empathy, consistency, and self-awareness. It's painfully simple and yet painfully difficult. If children could be loved unconditionally and taught to love themselves, then we could outmaneuver this upswell in narcissism. But that requires parents who love themselves. These intergenerational cycles are long—and cast long shadows. The sweet spot is parents who can be emotionally present for children and to be a mirror of their feelings but still allow them to fail and face the consequences of their behavior, and to do all of this from a place of empathy and genuineness. It's a long game.

The Child as Hyperconsumer

The tech world is ahead of us, always. And all things tech—computers, cell phones, social media, tablets, gaming sites, virtual reality, artificial intelligence, the internet, internet-enabled things—are a means of rapid delivery of advertising and generation of revenue (just as TV and radio once were). Our ability to google obscure facts while in a remote café on the other side of the world comes at a cost. Critical thinkers can try to tune out the tailored ads, pop-up ads, big-data manipulations on social media feeds, email advertisements, fake news, real news, and everything in between. All of these ads play on our vulnerabilities and insecurities—body image, aging, masculine prowess, financial fears, global threats. If the ads are constant enough, they get through and morph our reality (no matter how good our critical thinking is).

Children are not as discerning, and the old adage "taking candy from a baby" takes on a new tenor here. Children are being impacted by the pop-up ads and the constant cacophony of imagery, sounds, and promises offered up by their devices. Some of this advertising is incentivized, and children are encouraged by the "gamification" of internet advertising to watch and re-watch an online ad or to enter branded websites. The typical child between the ages of eight and ten spends an average of eight hours on media per day, and, for older children and adolescents, this number jumps to eleven hours. Children now spend more time on devices and watching TV than they do in school (Rideout, Kaiser Family Foundation, 2010). Which means they are also being exposed to a wide variety of advertising being delivered in a wide range of formats. Targeting children through advertising is as old as Tony the Tiger and Ronald McDonald, but the constancy and tailored nature of the imagery represent a chronic shift in children to their being acquisitive and materialistic. Thus, they are becoming more extrinsically oriented at exactly the phase of development when children would be best served by developing their inner worlds and regulatory mechanisms.

Children get shaped in multiple ways: the experience of want/need for the items and experiences being advertised, the feeling of being "less than" if they are unable to acquire these things, the message that they are somehow lacking, and reinforcement of the belief that external "things" can improve their status. Children are in the process of integrating their external and internal messages into a consistent sense of self. If they are already being raised in a negating or inconsistent environment, these marketing, advertising, and commodification gospels have even more potency. For a child growing up in an invalidating environment, these gospels are even better able to fortify the message of "you are not enough" or that the external matters more than the internal. This sets children up with a belief system that organizes around consuming and regulating their sense of self through acquisition of objects outside themselves.

Very often, the "rewards" we give children for both intrinsic and extrinsic successes (high grades, a clean room, a good deed, a soccer goal) are purchased—a shopping spree, a new toy, a theme-park trip. Less often is the reward something that may carry more psychological meaning and foster the development of strong relationship skills, self-valuation, and self-reflection, such as time alone with a parent perhaps embroiled in a craft project, building something, walking in the woods, tossing a Frisbee, or splashing in the ocean. The way we provide rewards for children sets a tone, and our reward systems actually foster the growth of the child as a consumer, rather than as a celebrator and a valuer of experiences with others, experiences in the world, curiosity, and creation. Certainly, every child—and, in fact, every person—will welcome rewards of a physical nature (toys and so on), but the equation is becoming increasingly imbalanced. And the fact is, in our busier worlds, with greater financial demands (perhaps we are all working more hours to maintain the materialistic narrative), it is much easier to launch a few keystrokes on an internet toy store website to acquire that prize or reward for a child than to unplug from our lives and give children that afternoon with finger paints or that day in the park.

A Formula for Raising a Narcissist

In a nutshell, there are a few formulas for narcissism, but there is enough randomness (inborn temperament and disposition) to ensure that there are no guarantees. So, armed with a lot of theories, perhaps we can issue a cautionary tale about how to raise a narcissist. The following actions and behaviors will increase the likelihood of raising a child who turns into a narcissist, or who is more likely to be a toxic player in his or her world.

1. **Be emotionally unavailable.** Very few parents out there set out to do this, but it happens inadvertently. Ironically, one factor that has played a role in pulling parents out of parenting is our reliance on devices. Our devices are a blessing and a curse—they have become a simple tool to maintain contact with children, schools, playdate parents, and babysitters but have also pulled us out of the psychological availability that children need. Many are the times when parents are staring at a phone rather than at the

child in their arms. Most of us have witnessed a parent putting off a child for a minute longer while being entranced by something on a phone or computer screen. This obviously hampers the mirroring that a child needs. (I have often considered that one of the most fortunate tricks of timing I personally have experienced is that smartphones did not exist when my daughters were small. When I breastfed them, there wasn't much else to do but stare at their sweet faces, but I could see how it would be tempting to stare at a phone and catch up on emails and other responsibilities, especially since caretaking a newborn or small child can get to be rather monotonous over time.) Emotional unavailability is not just about staring at devices but also about being present when you are present. This is not to say that parents have to be 24/7 caregivers—children need some time to play and explore on their own—but, when you are present with them, be present. Parents need to be more mindful than they once were. Lives are busier and distractions are plentiful, so it is an act of will to remain available to a child.

2. **Buy them their own tablet and smartphone when they are one year old.** Babies appear to be able to operate tablets and smartphones and press buttons to get their favorite imagery up. While this is sweet and engaging, it may also impede opportunities to actually connect, mirror, and attach. The nature of the imagery and the interfaces offered by digital devices can be very engaging for children, but they can result in missing other opportunities which are critical including language development and social interaction. Minimize the use of these devices, particularly in the earliest years. The American Academy of Pediatrics in 2019 issued a blanket recommendation that children under the age of twelve months should not interact with screens and devices.

3. **Make them feel the world is a dangerous place.** This can be done by being inconsistent or unavailable, or, as they get older, by teaching them that the world is full of threat. No matter how big or small your space, children who are securely attached because they feel confident that their parents are responsive will feel safe enough to explore. Be there for them and create a safe little space

for them. This is true confidence, not brash bravado. There are enough media forces out there telling us the world is a dangerous place. Make your children prudent and streetwise but not anxious.

4. **Deny their emotions.** Too many people are uncomfortable with negative emotions, and boys especially are at risk for being told that vulnerable emotions are a sign of weakness. Actually, do not turn off when they are going through a difficult time, and do not make negating statements like "Don't be sad." If they are sad, acknowledge their sadness; don't try to rush its resolution. If children can feel confident in their ability to manage their emotions and not be afraid of them, as well as feel that those emotions are valid, then they will take that into adulthood and allow those emotions to be felt instead of trying to deny or project them.

5. **Fix their problems for them.** A bad grade shouldn't mean a nasty phone call to the teacher. It should mean letting them share their feelings, take responsibility for their performance, tolerate the discomfort of the problem, and generate their own solutions with your support.

6. **Behave in an entitled manner in front of them.** They really do as we do, so our actual behavior as parents matters. Do not imply that there are two sets of rules—one for you and one for the rest of the world. Children are not able to endure those kinds of dichotomies. Be mindful of how you interact with teachers, service employees, family members, and strangers. Modeling is also a key element of how we learn to behave. If children observe entitled behavior, they learn it. The "Don't you know who I am?" mantra is typically learned at a parent's knee.

7. **Never let them be disappointed.** Learning to be disappointed and to tolerate the discomfort associated with it is key to becoming a well-regulated adult. It is difficult to observe children be hurt or sad or disappointed, but, at those moments, it is crucial to not try to fix it but instead be there for them, let them know that they are a good person, let them cry it out, and let them know that a new day will dawn. Learning these internal regulatory practices is critical and may also protect them from other issues, such

as psychiatric disorders associated with dysregulation (substance abuse, impulse control disorders, eating disorders, gambling, shopping, dysregulated anger outbursts).

8. **Compliment superficial attributes.** Don't over-focus on external attributes like appearance, weight, physique, height, hair, or how fast they can run. These are low-hanging fruit and easy to focus on, but, if you do so, children's sense of self and validation then starts to derive from their appearance and veer into a more extrinsic worldview, as well as a physically defined sense of self. It's more important to compliment their kindnesses, work ethic, grit, resilience, and good deeds. This can push the focus to who they are, instead of how they look or their external achievements, and enhance self-valuation from the inside. I have worked with many adult clients who reflected on the fact that they were praised endlessly for their cuteness or beauty as a child and taught to use their appearance to get what they needed from the world, something they now struggle with because their psychological worlds were never valued. In our culture, beauty is conflated with youth, and, once adulthood hits, external beauty can cruelly be viewed as a depreciating asset. From a psychological perspective, children and young adults who are socialized solely on the basis of their appearance, may become stunted in other manners, and. when their youthful visage and figure no longer attract them attention and acclaim, they may have tremendous difficulty coping with aging and no longer being the recipient of attention for their appearance.

9. **Develop extrinsic value systems.** Don't spend the weekend just shopping; spend it with others, as volunteers, with family and friends, at children's events, at the park. Become involved in the lives of others through volunteering, children's civic activities such as Girl Scouts, visiting family members, or spending time outdoors. In our device-heavy world of children's entertainment, they are bombarded with advertising around the clock. Forty-eight percent of parents report that restricting device time for their children remains a constant battle (APA, 2017), so this has become the new abnormal normal. And check your own material

consumption and value system—model the prosocial for your children.

10. **Insult and criticize your child.** Criticizing, verbally assaulting, insulting, and hurling hurtful words at your child are simply not acceptable. Doing so can leave permanent psychological scars, and these kinds of interactions with your child do not occur on an even playing field. Even as a child gets into adolescence and feels like an adult, he or she is, in fact, still your child. Engaging in this type of behavior not only harms children's developing sense of self but also can set them up to feel "less than" and set them on a lifelong pattern of self-devaluation. It can also normalize this pattern and make your child more likely to throw cruel and insulting words at peers and adults, or to live with a sense of self-loathing, and to carry these patterns into adulthood.

11. **Put your child in harm's way.** Parents can and do sadistically expose a child to abuse, whether at their own hands or the hands of another (though, tragically, it does happen). However, many children are exposed to trauma that reflects intergenerational patterns (e.g., members of the family system who are known to be abusers are permitted to be with children), or poor monitoring by parents who themselves may have experienced childhood trauma. Poor judgment by a parent who may knowingly or carelessly put a child within the purview of an abuser can have far-reaching psychological consequences, including the types of insecurity and regulation deficits observed in narcissism. While none of us can completely shield a child from every danger in the world, parents can, at a minimum, put their child's safety first and have their eyes open to the kinds of people we bring into a child's life. As parents, we are the gatekeepers, and our decisions have lifelong psychological consequences.

* * *

You should now have a better sense of the origins of narcissism and the various factors that contribute to its development in children. Mindful and informed parenting plays a key role, as does modeling compassionate, empathic behavior. But the world also plays a role, and, while none of us as individuals can do much to change the world at large, we can alter and remain aware of how and why we consume the things in it. In Part I, we explored the different types of narcissists and narcissistic patterns as well as some of the reasons behind why narcissism appears to be growing exponentially in our culture. But what can you do if a narcissist is having a direct and very real impact on your life? In Part II, we'll examine the toxic people in your life—whether they are your romantic partner, parent, boss, coworker, sibling, friend, in-law, or even your own child— and I'll provide concrete strategies for how to manage these relationships and take care of yourself. This is a guidebook that can be personalized. If your parents were not narcissistic, then that may not be an area of the book that will garner much attention from you, but a narcissistic sister may have hijacked your family system. You may be struggling with a workplace colleague who is brutally toxic but not a spouse. Ultimately, the strategies remain the same, but these relationships are all qualitatively different, and so each type of relationship gets different coverage. The goal of this book is to help you, if you're struggling in any form of relationship with a narcissist or narcissists, to understand it at both the individual and societal levels and to keep yourself from being blindsided by the very people you may have once trusted.

Part Two

THE TOXIC NARCISSISTS IN YOUR LIFE

Freedom is what we do with what is done to us.

—SARTRE

Chapter 6

The Narcissist in Your Bed

Often it is the most deserving people who cannot help loving those who destroy them.

—HESSE

If you have already read *Should I Stay or Should I Go? Surviving a Relationship with a Narcissist*, or if you have ever been in a relationship with someone who is narcissistic, entitled, or just simply toxic, you know this territory. The evolution of these relationships reads like a modern dark fairy tale. Girl meets charming, charismatic boy. Charming, charismatic boy takes her on fabulous dates, love-bombs her, promises her the world, and makes her feel like she is the only girl in the world, and everyone around her is fully charmed too. Red flags often appeared within the first six weeks (bouts of rage, unwarranted jealousy, insistence on spending all your time together, yelling at a waiter, fights followed by big apologies, preoccupation with his cell phone or social media, criticism, distance, inattention, coldness, long stories about how difficult his life has been), but everything else is going so well, and the clock is ticking, and who is to say the girl will meet anyone else? She has always worried about being enough, and she sure hopes she is enough for this charming guy. (And, in the interest of time and space, change "girl" and "boy" as needed to make this fit your story—it goes down the same way every time, regardless of gender.)

Everyone else around you is telling you he is a great guy; the ones who aren't telling you he is great are probably jealous or bitter, and all relationships have bumps in the road, right? If he's jealous, that's because he's so into you. After a few months, perhaps years, perhaps decades, you are a shell of yourself; maybe you were cheated on; the rage is a regular event; you haven't experienced anything resembling empathy since the first few weeks of the relationship; you feel chronically undermined, dehumanized, and invalidated; you no longer trust your own decisions; you have withdrawn from other people who matter to you and do not really feel confident enough to push yourself; and you may even be depressed. You are full of self-doubt, because he questions your reality on a regular basis. I have heard this story from people in the US and the UK, Australia and South Africa, India and China, Switzerland and Sweden, Myanmar and Canada. I have no doubt this story repeats in every country and every corner of this world.

What starts like a fairy tale ends up as a psychiatric case study. Your narcissistic, entitled, and/or toxic partner may also have been so skilled that he or she was able to hide his or her meanness from the family, often being quite generous at family dinners out or vacations together, further making you feel like you are losing your mind, and perhaps you were even termed selfish or unrealistic for having "high expectations" by the very people you rely on for guidance. In the most fortunate telling of these stories, your family and friends actually do recognize that your partner is narcissistic and toxic and support you (in fact, are almost willing to carry you) out of the relationship and it may be you who is resisting, because you cannot break out of the mindset that "maybe she/he will change."

Having been privy to these stories for years, I have heard of people giving up lives and enduring a variety of emotional atrocities at the hands of toxic and narcissistic partners, including leaving rewarding careers, moving away and losing contact with beloved family members, having partners demand that they pursue abortions (or they deny a child is theirs), forgiving cheating partners a dozen or more times, having family heirlooms stolen, learning about partners who had other families in other parts of the country or the world, having children alienated, and handing over life savings to fund the grand plans of a manipulative, narcissistic partner. The people who did these things were not foolish, or stupid, or ridiculous—they truly believed that they were in a committed relationship and, at the time, these actions made sense. Over time, the relationship sapped them of their sense of self. It happens slowly, over time—not overnight.

Narcissistic and toxic relationships leave you feeling depleted in a variety of ways: feeling like you aren't good enough, chronically second-guessing yourself, often apologizing, and/or feeling as though you are losing your mind, helpless, hopeless, sad, depressed, anxious, unsettled, no longer getting pleasure out of your life, ashamed, guilty, and exhausted. There is a sense that you can turn the ship around if you get it "more right"—if you are thinner, prettier, wrinkle free, and have flatter abs or if you clean the house, make more money, perform better sexually, keep the children in line, and try to get along better with his or her family. Even more complicated is that narcissistic people expect you to be a mind reader—and to literally anticipate their needs before they happen. It's a tall order, and you are bound to get it wrong more often than not—no matter how hard you try.

All of this misses the central premise (except in relatively rare cases): *A narcissistic or toxic or deeply entitled person will not change enough to make a close relationship sustainable in a meaningful way.* And you will never be enough for him or her. No one will. In this chapter, you'll learn why narcissists are so skilled at attracting you, how hope—and fear—often keep you hanging on, what love means to a narcissist, how to manage your expectations, how to coparent with a narcissist, and important strategies for dealing with a narcissistic partner. In an ideal situation, you are reading this before you even enter into a narcissistic relationship and learn to be a better gatekeeper, not falling for traps such as love bombing and allowing their insecurity to become your own.

The Cautionary Tale

In October 2014, a successful businesswoman from Southern California named Debra Newell went on a date with a man named John Meehan. Ms. Newell had been married prior and had four adult children. By many reports, John was rakishly handsome and engaging, and, with her children grown and her business successful, she was open to the things most people want in their lives, love and companionship. On their first date at a local restaurant, she was attracted and engaged, but also sensed a few red flags....

So began a relationship that would be memorialized in a true crime series entitled *Dirty John* by journalist Christopher Goddard, which was featured in the *Los Angeles Times*, and which went on to become a widely subscribed podcast and a series on *Bravo*.

It was the classical tale of the toxic relationship. Any read of the story reveals Meehan to be psychopathic, and the romance had all of the standard top notes of a relationship with a psychopath or narcissist—lies, aliases, inconsistencies, menace, abuse, financial trickery, control, isolation, apologies, more abuse, second chances, charm, charisma, confidence, vanity, gaslighting, manipulation, and fear. It also had all the warning bells of a toxic relationship—intense intimacies shared too soon, moving in together too fast, getting married too quickly, getting blinded by grandiose compliments and day-to-day niceties, against a perilous backdrop of "things aren't adding up."

Dirty John is a modern love story for the true crime era. It was an unsettling cautionary tale of mating and terror in an era of right swiping and online avatars. While the technology may have changed, the top notes of a toxic relationship remain the same: invalidation, inconsistency, dehumanization, intimidation, deceit, and abuse.

What was more compelling to me was not the story itself (which is, in fact, *very* compelling), but the reactions people had to Ms. Newell on a range of online portals and comment boards. Many of the commenters vilified her and mercilessly criticized her for her decision making, her willingness to give him second chances, and her "blindness" to his deceit and manipulation. It is easy to tell a story backwards and make the puzzle pieces fit. It is easy to read a psychopathic or narcissistic love story and assume we would not make the same mistakes, that we would have seen this coming from a mile away. Love stories with narcissists and psychopaths are easy to judge, but not always easy to avoid. Perhaps Ms. Newell was criticized because she was older, as a woman over fifty, as a mother, she should not have been making the rookie mistakes of an ingenue or a younger woman. It's not that simple. Toxic partners have a way of rendering people colorblind so they cannot see the red in the red flags. Without an understanding of these patterns, it is easy to repeat the same mistakes. The story of *Dirty John* was a reminder that narcissists and psychopaths are able to get into their partners' hearts and minds by figuring out the little things their partners crave, providing them, and seemingly erasing the heartaches of the past. Ms. Newell was sometimes simply grateful that John Meehan would run her errands or sit by her side at a doctor's appointment. Little things that masked the myriad warning signs around her. Ms. Newell believed in love stories, romance, and second chances. She herself acknowledged the mistakes she made in her life and felt that it would be hypocritical to judge her flawed partner so quickly.

The criticisms of Ms. Newell reminded me that people in these situations are often confused and may not know where to turn for help. Ms. Newell's family raised concerns, and, when the time came, helped her the best that they could. The dismissive nature of other people who judge a person for going in and out of a toxic relationship may leave a person feeling more isolated when he or she is in this situation. The people close to sufferers of these relationships may be equally confused, and there is a dearth of information on what to do when you find yourself in a narcissistic relationship. Not all therapists are trained in these patterns, and even the professional guidance can be contradictory.

Our choices and decisions represent a lifetime of experiences and the stories we tell ourselves. Childhood histories and traumas, societal messages, rewards, punishments, fairy tales, cognitive errors, narratives, good experiences, and bad experiences. Ms. Newell had her own back story. Her family was deeply wedded to the ideas of forgiveness and redemption. She herself had endured past relationships with narcissists, the tragic loss of a sister to domestic violence, and societal messages about love, romance, and dating. What she didn't have was a guidebook, a map, or some other form of relationship GPS. Sadly, most people don't, which is why so many people repeatedly fall into the abyss of these kinds of relationships.

When people are in the throes of a relationship with a narcissist, many of them do not listen to reason. The gentle feedback from friends and family, the sideways looks, even abject concern from those close to them are often ignored during the early phase of the relationship when it is all about love bombing, the seduction, the romance, the excitement, the "magic," and the chase. When people are told to get out of these kinds of relationships, they often grind their heels in deeper and "prove" to the world that they can get this right. After being raised on fairy tales, people want to believe them. They want the frog to become a prince, the beast to become a boyfriend, the tyrant to become an angel. They want the "too good to be true" to be true.

The *Dirty John* tale almost ended in abject tragedy but, even though the ultimate tragedy was thwarted, there was still so much ruin in its wake. That's the tragedy of all relationships with narcissists, psychopaths, high-conflict, difficult, and toxic people. *Dirty John* was not terrifying because it was unusual and atypical, but because it was formulaic. Without a road map, it's all but impossible to navigate these relationships without becoming confused and lost, even though the road is quite predictable. Read on to learn about why we fall into these traps, why it is so hard to get out, how to avoid them, and how to survive once you get stuck.

Transactional Narcissistic Relationships

Sadly, human relationships are becoming more and more "transactional." While most people do not want to view them that way because it feels horribly cynical, it is easy to fall into the trap of viewing a relation-ship with a "balance sheet" mentality. There are lots of quid pro quo expectation that waft into a relationship. When we put something into a relationship, we often expect it to "come back" in some way. Narcissis-tic and toxic relationships are notorious for feeling transactional. People who invest resources in a relationship frequently report living with a fear of being taken advantage of, and some believe they bring a certain asset to a relationship and should be rewarded in some way for that. In my clinical work with people who are narcissistic, the transactional demands are typically transparent. Narcissists may provide housing, a car, jewelry, shoes, clothing, and/or entertainment and be very clear on what they expect in return—and this can range from specific sexual demands to the partner's being available to them as desired, to the partner's simply being their yes-man (or yes-woman).

Perhaps, as mating became a more technologically mediated process, and materialism became a stronger life force, transactional relationships became an inevitability. The quid pro quo of these relationships may not be as extreme as a person believing that the gift of a diamond necklace translates to a certain number of sexual acts, hours spent cleaning the house, or nights on the town (but sadly it can be!). Yet, there is sometimes the skewed belief that mutuality, love, companionship, and presence can somehow be quantified and commodified in a way that the balance sheet comes out even. Women increasingly are sold the narrative of the fantasy of marrying the billionaire or the prince. Toxic, narcissistic relationships are plagued by this transactional nature. This pattern not only can damage the fabric of love and intimacy but also may be fostering the landscape of toxic relationships. In addition, the greater likelihood of financial success in narcissists means that people may view them as a path to financial security, a sort of "fairy-tale dream." That dream has often left people completely financially dependent on a partner, and, decades later, when they decide to leave, they have no work history, few independent assets, a messy divorce, and a fear of starting again. Transactional relationships imprison people. If you are *very* fortunate, you may walk off with a hefty financial settlement after such a relationship, but, in a relationship with a narcissist, you can be certain it will be the fight of a lifetime.

Love Bombing: The Gateway to a Toxic Love Affair

It's easy to get drawn into these relationships. Narcissistic people tend to be attractive, well put together, successful (or are able to convince people that they are successful), intense, charming, and charismatic, and often know how to put on a hell of a show. Their entitlement initially may look more like confidence or authoritativeness or simply be labeled "manliness" or "assertiveness." It's not as though they are going to lead with lack of empathy or abuse. The early weeks and months with these folks can be intoxicating, and they are masters at the phenomenon of love bombing. The love bomber puts on a full-court press with grand gestures, gifts (enormous bunches of flowers sent to your home or workplace, high-end items, or even lots of small gestures that are somewhat intrusive—sent to your home or workplace, left on your car—in essence, letting the world know that you have someone in your life), exciting experiences, expensive nights and days out, and often intense trips early in the relationship. The weapons in the love bomb arsenal are things like horse-drawn carriages, helicoptering to a picnic, or a white-gloved dinner set up on the beach with liveried footmen and $300 champagne. The focus is on grandiose and attention-getting behavior that is cinematic and Instagrammable.

Love bombers will typically bring you into their life a bit too quickly (as a rule, Thanksgiving dinner with extended family is not a sensible third date). It's a cunning tactic, as you may now find it more difficult to leave, because you may feel more accountable to more people. Love bombers will also be pretty insistent with the communication, with lots of romantic texts, DMs, and emails (and they will get angry if you do not keep up with their communication barrage). Their communication can also be quite intense, with clichés like "This is a once-in-a-lifetime love story," "We are living the true real-life fairy tale," or the greatest narcissistic ringer of them all, "No one will ever love you the way I do." This love bombing can be a bit disarming, but, by and large, it is deeply romanticized. It does feel like a real-life fairy tale, and especially for someone who is young and vulnerable—or even someone who has been bashed in other relationships—it can feel like the ship and the prince (or princess) have come in. Love bombing is a classic red flag. A few romantic gestures are lovely in a courtship but, quite inevitably, love bombing is followed by scorched earth—the grand gestures abate, the texts may drop in frequency (unless the narcissistic or toxic person is deeply controlling, and then they will continue but will change in tone from sweet nothings and sexy goodnights to angry demands about your whereabouts and whom you are with), and all references to a grand love story get forgotten. It can be confusing. The love bombs may continue to fly at times when the validation matters to the bomber (lavish weddings, big expensive destination birthday parties), and it no longer feels like a fairy tale but more like a self-serving circus. Narcissists have very little inner world to offer, so they offer a rather vast external world—nights out, gifts—and it is easy to get so distracted by it that you do not take the time to really notice the person.

The early excitement can make it harder to see and respond to the red flags. The numerous interviews I conducted for this book and for *Should I Stay or Should I Go?* revealed that, in all cases, the red flags became apparent in the first few months, and usually in the first few weeks. This was reported in relationships that had lasted forty years and in relationships that had lasted four months. But, for any number of reasons—the feeling of being not good enough, the idea that no one better would come along, practical reasons, fear, confusion, discouragement by others, the belief in "Someday it will better," the rescue fantasy, or just still being in love and under the narcissistic, toxic partner's spell—the people stayed.

Why Do We Stay?

One of the major questions that comes up around entering a narcissistic relationship is "why?" "How could I have fallen for this? Why did I stay in this? It was so clear from the beginning." Most narcissistic people start their game strong and, as noted earlier, they are overflowing with charm, charisma, and confidence—the three seductive Cs. I maintain my assertion that these traits should leave you very concerned because, in some ways, they are distractors. They can pull you away from digging deeper and understanding the other person or really paying attention to the core qualities that make for a strong relationship, including respect, empathy, compromise, reciprocity, and kindness. In all of my years doing this work, not once did someone, when describing the early months with a narcissistic partner, describe the person as kind, respectful, or warm. The more common adjectives were "fun," "exciting," "charming," "life of the party," "commanding," "charismatic," "good on paper," "smart."

Once that early narrative sticks, and they are in the relationship, most people fight to keep the relationship going. This can happen for a variety of reasons, including a sense of duty or responsibility, "stick-to-itiveness," cultural reasons, financial reasons, routine, simplicity, and pity. However, the most compelling reason may be fear—fear of leaving this relationship but also of then being alone, or of having to start again, or fear that maybe this is as good as it gets. And, since the narcissistic and toxic relationship undercuts any sense of confidence and fills people with self-doubt, they no longer trust their judgment. It becomes easy to think that the problems are "temporary" or perhaps that you are "overreacting," and it can become quite simple to fall into the trap of "trying harder," "loving more," and "making more sacrifices." A courtship with a narcissist is more of an indoctrination than a love story.

Codependency

There are some who believe that narcissistic relationships remain in place because their partners are "enablers" who participate in the toxic spiral because the narcissist "feeds" their vulnerabilities, while the "codependent" partner keeps providing narcissistic supply. It's a risky paradigm. Co-dependency is a term that originated in the clinical literature on addiction (and has origins in the language of twelve-step programs, such as Alcoholics Anonymous). It describes a family system characterized by denial, lack of communication, and restricted expression of emotions. Co-dependent individuals often deny their own healthy needs, and attempt to save or rescue the "problematic" person in the family system (e.g., the alcoholic) whether by denial of the problem or by repeatedly rescuing them with caregiving or money and other resources. Definitions of co-dependency have since broadened beyond addiction to other difficult family dynamics, including abuse and other mental illnesses and personality dynamics.

In my experience of working with hundreds of people in this situation, I have observed that being raised in an invalidating family can create the risk of a person's feeling as though he or she is not enough, and either observed or participated in denial of problems within the family. In their adult relationships, people from invalidating family systems may then transition into playing the role of rescuer and caregiver with the goal of "winning over" his or her unwinnable partner (a replay of trying to win over the unwinnable parent). Interestingly, even though they grew up in family systems that played out this dynamic, they do not recognize it in their adult relationships. Instead of questioning the unhealthy dynamic, they accept it because it is all they know. Becoming educated about the pattern, and the revelation that it is not likely to change much, rallies many people out of their blindness and awakens them to make a change. The risk of dismissing these patterns as largely codependent, and casting the person in a narcissistic relationship in the role of an enabler, can be a precedent that pathologizes a person for simply wanting to make a relationship work (until he or she recognizes it never will). Narcissists *do* persist because the world *does* enable them—it often starts with parents, and then narcissistic patterns can be "enabled" by school systems, friends, workplaces, and the world in general, which may praise them for their cool efficiency, their charm, their confidence, and their success. In that way, perhaps we are all codependent with the narcissistic people and systems around us.

We Know Better

What's interesting is that everyone knows better. We really do. Take a look at any romantic comedy or "chick flick" you have ever seen. The story is the same. Girl meets a guy. He is a slick, charming narcissist (invariably with slicked-back hair or better skin than anyone else in the film), he always has a fast or noisy car and a tricked-out bachelor pad, and he tends to be successful, glib, and charismatic. Shortly into the film, we learn that he is up to no good—cheating, lying, insulting, or just being generally mean or unpleasant. Enter the somewhat bumbling, slightly socially awkward guy: If it's high school, he is a musician, is good at science, or writes poetry; if he is an adult, perhaps he's living in a garage apartment. But he is a rumpled, handsome guy. In these stories, typically, he is a teacher, or an artist, or runs a nonprofit (or intends to do these things). He is rarely a man of means. Although the woman in the story has managed to score the slick narcissist and everyone is so happy for her, she strikes up a friendship with the rumpled guy who is respectful, kind, empathic, and compassionate, and listens to her (because she isn't getting those needs met with the narcissistic guy). Over time, she finds narcissistic guy more repellant or cold or distant and realizes that the sweet, financially unsuccessful guy is the one she wants to grow old with. All of us are rooting for the sweet guy, not the narcissist. And the filmmakers know this, so even Hollywood, the *most* narcissistic industry around, sets up the story so the narcissist does *not* win. The happy ending occurs when the woman does not end up with the narcissist. Why do we root for the sweet, empathic guy in the movies but not in our real lives?

The female version of this entails a man's being the browbeaten supplicant to a woman with a beautiful physique and great hair, and who also tends to be wealthy and deeply materialistic (and she is often much younger than him). He works tirelessly to ensure she has her materialistic yearnings met, and they attend vapid social events. Then, one day, he meets a sweet woman with messy hair who wears vintage or other secondhand clothes, who tells him to pursue his dreams. If all goes well, the superficial narcissistic woman ends up going off with the slick-haired glib narcissist, and the sweet man and woman live in a ramshackle cottage in a gentrifying neighborhood somewhere. Hollywood still remains very heterosexist, and as we see more LGBTQ love stories, my guess is that we will see the same tropes play out—with the glib narcissist losing out to the kind, empathic person. Perhaps someday culture will support real life happy endings, and not just save them for the silver screen.

The Toxic Toll on Your Health

Interestingly, and not surprisingly, toxic relationships take a toll on your health (as do all toxic things). Narcissistic and toxic relationships tend to hijack our brains, leaving our bodies to do the heavy lifting. Over the years, I have had myriad clients who spent decades contriving complex rationalizations and excuses and downright amnesia for a narcissistic or toxic person's behavior. And then, one day, their bodies gave out. They experienced hospitalizations, illnesses that did not dissipate for months, horrible rashes and hives, or exacerbations of autoimmune conditions—literally their bodies were trying to tell them to get out, even as their minds kept devising excuses to stay. Many people lost their livelihoods and their life savings on these illnesses and their treatments. Ultimately, their bodies told the truth and, at that point, when their minds believed the toxic person or people in their lives would "rescue" them when they became sick, they were treated as an inconvenience and left to fend for themselves. Listen to your body; it tends to be more honest and it is better at sussing out a toxic relationship than your mind.

The great challenge is that it is very difficult to systematically research these issues. It is possible that the stress of a dysfunctional relationship of any kind is also mirrored in other stress—work, financial, other social issues—or that people who remain in dysfunctional relationships may somehow be different and that it may not be the toxic relationship per se, but characteristics of people who find themselves in these relationships, that may make them more vulnerable than others to a variety of stress-related health issues. Observationally, the fact that a person's health improves upon leaving or modifying such relationships certainly suggests there are benefits to stepping away—but the mechanisms of any such improvements remain unclear. Research that has been done on the impact of conflictual marital relationships and health has shown that conflictual relationships are associated with changes in immune function (for example, research by health psychologist Janice Kiecolt-Glaser and her colleagues).

A recent study by Sarah Stanton, a professor of psychology at the University of Edinburgh, and her international colleagues actually does provide some data to suggest that, over a twenty-year period, something called perceived partner responsiveness is associated with higher risk of death. Perceived partner responsiveness was defined by the authors as the perception people have that their romantic partners understand them, appreciate them, and care for them. In that way, this construct sounds a bit like empathy. The research yielded a somewhat subtle finding, basically suggesting that the perception of a change in partner responsiveness over ten years was associated with negative emotional reactions to stress, which was subsequently related to a greater risk of death ten years later. In simple terms, Stanton et al.'s research suggests that, when people perceive a drop in their partner's emotional responsiveness, over time, this may be related to poorer emotional coping with the daily stressors of life, which likely places a person at risk for negative health consequences and death. Further work would be needed to further tease this all out, but this work provides empirical support for what clinicians observe quite often. Over time, the sense that one's partner is not responding is an unpleasant experience and may render a person more vulnerable to negative stress reactions. Whether this translates into poorer self-care, higher physiological levels of stress, greater psychological distress, or some other process that undercuts a person's health, these findings lay out a compelling framework for the long-term effects of experiencing a relationship characterized by drops in empathy and emotional responsiveness. It would be premature to suggest that being in a relationship with a narcissist may presage earlier death, but these data certainly hint at the sinister relationships between emotionally unsatisfying relationships, stress, health, and disease.

These relationships can leave people thrown off in all areas of their lives. People who are in marriages or relationships with narcissistic, entitled, toxic partners will report having problems with decision-making at work and in other areas of life; apologizing to everyone, even for issues that are unrelated to them; a fear of making plans or setting goals, because there is the assumption that they will not be realized or that the people cannot make those plans happen because they are not good enough or will not be allowed to pursue them; avoiding other people or withdrawing from other people, perhaps out of shame or confusion or just plain exhaustion; and engaging in unhealthy patterns to numb their emotions, including taking drugs, smoking, consuming alcohol, spending, eating, or over-exercising.

The False Hopes That Keep Toxic Relationships Afloat

Romantic and intimate relationships with narcissistic people are often kept in place by misassumptions and fallacies. The primary reason these relationships happen is twofold: One, you do not understand what you are dealing with; and two, you don't trust yourself. Even when it starts turning south, instead of trusting your instincts, you are able to say, "Maybe I'm being too critical" or, "Everyone deserves a second [third, fourth, fifth] chance" or, "This doesn't feel good, but it was so good when we first met, and I'm sure we will get there again" or, "If I break up with him, he will meet someone else and she will get the better version of him" or, "I don't want to hurt his [or her] feelings." The exception of the early courtship phase gets turned into the rule despite the years of neglect, negation, invalidation, and, at times, dehumanization. One of the key dynamics that keeps these relationships in play is the almighty *rescue fantasy*. Short version: "If I love him enough, then it will get better." It's the *Beauty and the Beast* of it all, and, in fact, it is the trope that cuts through so many love stories: With enough love, the bad guy can be turned around. Not true. You will notice that *Beauty and the Beast* never had a sequel—that's because it probably did not end well.

Love is an extraordinary emotion, and it is not just a romantic notion. It is really a life energy that we can arc into our lives in so many healthy ways above and beyond a romantic partnership—we can flow it into ourselves, our children, our work, and those around us. We often use the word "love" selectively, and much of the "sell" of love happens around romantic and caregiving relationships (wife, mother, husband, father), rather than our viewing it as a healthy and healing energy we all have. It is unfortunate when we give our love to someone who is incapable of receiving it, misuses it, and will not reciprocate in a meaningful way. Love is great; loving a narcissistic person is not.

One question that arises is, "How many good days are enough?" If narcissists were awful and abusive every single day, then you may not have gotten in, and you certainly would not have stayed. There were enough good days and good times to keep you hooked. Even in the aftermath of months, years, or decades of neglect, disrespect, verbal abuse, lies, deceit, and meanness, it is astonishing how often people in narcissistic relationships can still get lost in how wonderful the trips are or were, the concerts, the sex, or the dancing together. Narcissistic partners are like "Disneyland dads"—they are able to perform beautifully on the fun days but are not of much use when the rest of life happens. Vacations can be extravagant, nights out positively seductive, and their charisma can light up any event. These red-letter days become lily pads, and people in narcissistic relationships often jump from one to the next and hold on to these special days as if they are precious relics, as evidence that the relationship *does* work, and they are unable to let go of the relationship because they had one good weekend in Maui. Only you can do the math and determine whether your memories of a sun-kissed holiday or box seats at a concert are sufficient recompense for the daily sensation of not being enough. There will always be good days in a relationship—be careful that you are not holding on to distorted memories of them or the misguided hope that you can get back to the early days of fun and fantasy.

No, you cannot rescue narcissists no matter what you do. When I work with clients who are coming out of narcissistic relationships or are confused about their narcissistic relationships, as we start doing the postmortem, the pattern becomes very clear: No matter what rescue strategy they tried, nothing ever got better. Many people in these relationships find that a survival strategy is to not spend too much time thinking about yesterday, or the day before that, but rather focusing on the "someday" when it might get better. Frankly, looking at the number of days behind you when nothing worked is awful and would require a change in strategy. Relationships with narcissistic, toxic, and entitled people are kept in place by hope. Hope that, someday, things will get better. Hope that they will be back to their good self when the deadline passes, when the taxes are done, when you finally get a house, when they get the promotion, when the kids are no longer sick, when they finish school, when the deal is closed. *Hope can be a dangerous emotion when you are in a narcissistic or toxic relationship.*

The rescue fantasy gets some of its fuel from the vulnerability that bubbles under the surface of every narcissist. Unlike psychopaths or sociopaths, who are pretty immune to vulnerability, narcissists may cry some rather convincing tears or issue a reassuring "I understand" speech, or say something compelling such as, "I get it, and I will change for you." If you pull off a grand gesture like packing your suitcases or hiring a divorce attorney, they may issue the plaintive apologies and mea culpas you had been praying for. It is that moment when you believe that they finally "got it." And, sometimes, the wakeup call that you may move out and move on can actually translate into weeks, months, and even years of peace and rebooting. But then narcissists slide back, as they always do, because their core characteristics have not changed. Remember that narcissistic people are masterful at putting on a show, so they can sweat through "good" behavior for a while, but then it lands right back where it was. That can feel devastating—especially when you recognize that you put more time and more heart into it only to end up in the same place, having wasted *more* time.

Another version of the rescue fantasy involves being rescued yourself. For myriad reasons, often stemming from difficult childhoods, many people want to be rescued. Someone to step in, take care of them, provide a sense of security, and take away the anxieties of life. People looking to be rescued often want someone to do the job their parents did not do—they are often just looking for someone to reassure them and take care of the stuff of life the way a parent was supposed to. The swagger and false confidence of the narcissist can play into this fantasy. Narcissists may have the financial means to ensure that basic needs of life are met. It can also be easy to confuse control and caregiving. Someone wanting to be rescued may view the extreme control a narcissist exerts in a relationship as almost "parental" and meant to keep them safe (rather than seeing it as a means of wresting away their sense of independence and autonomy and making it much more difficult to leave as things deteriorate within the relationship).

A common theme in many relationships with narcissists, especially narcissistic partners, is that perhaps, in the right conditions, *they* might rescue *you*. This would typically play out around medical conditions. After years of rationalizations and heartbreak over why they would ignore you, insult you, criticize you, or invalidate you, when the moment came when you were *sick*—you had an injury, an accident, a miscarriage, cancer, a fainting spell, heart palpitations—the fantasy would be, "Of course they are *finally* going to help me—I am sick." Perhaps the fantasy was that, upon seeing your physical vulnerability and a "legitimate" illness, they would step in as a white knight or savior. That they would drive you to the hospital and hold your hand. That they would sit by your bedside and feed you ice chips. That they would sit with the doctors and nurses and ask concerned questions. Perhaps it is the soap opera fantasy of the cinematic moment at your bedside, when they finally recognize how much they love you. That this would be the moment when they finally get it right. And that would make everything else better, because they would nurse you back to health.

It's a faulty assumption. After years of your mental health, soul, and mind not mattering, why would your physical health matter? If anything, in most cases, narcissistic partners view the sick person as an inconvenience and would minimize the health concerns with statements such as, "Are you really that sick?" or, "You are making a big deal out of this" or, "This is going to take a lot of time out of my day to drive you to the doctor." Sadly, if you do actually get the ride from them, their coldness and rejection in the hospital or clinic can be even more upsetting than if you were sitting there alone. Also, think ahead. If your broken arm, or your fever during a pregnancy, is being viewed as an inconvenience, what are the odds that these people are going to nurse you back to health when you are older and may not be able to afford other help? Do not wait for the emergency-room rescue fantasy. And do not be surprised at their lack of empathy when you are sick. Illness is inconvenient for narcissists—and the lack of empathy can increase your suffering because you are psychologically devastated.

What Is Love?

In the context of narcissistic relationships, some reflection on love is needed. Human beings want it, and most psychologists would argue that humans need it. To not want love or to even eschew it would be classified as an abnormal pattern in a person. And yet, the words "I love you" remain the most essential and the most vexing in any language.

So let's return to the question, "What is love?" The answer may be, "It depends who is asking." A major stumbling block in many narcissistic relationships is the subjective nature of this word. I believe that, in the first ninety days of a relationship, the two people should sit down and have a *required* discussion about the meaning of love to them, so they can ensure they are using the term similarly. I have worked with and spoken to numerous couples and individuals who say, "If he loved me, he would not do this" or, "I don't believe she loves me, even though she says she does." It really just depends on their definition of love. For some people, love is showing up; for others, it's paying the bills. Depending on whom you ask, it means respect, or romantic gestures, or loyalty, or looking good together. There is no need to judge another person's definition of love but, if you are in a relationship with that person, you'd better have a shared definition.

Narcissists are rarely plugged into their emotional world deeply or insightfully enough to truly articulate what love means to them. Imagine on a third date hearing, "To me, love means getting lots of validation. I don't intend to give much back and, in a few months, I'm going to get bored. When that happens, I may be coolly rejecting or worse. I will rarely show you empathy, unless it is convenient for me, and my needs will always come first. I am special, and I expect you and the rest of the world to recognize that, and I really do not think the rules apply to me, so, if you love me, you will not place rules on me. I will take care of your material needs and ensure that our relationship looks good to the world. That's what love is to me." If they do say that, and you stay in the relationship, then that's on you. In most narcissistic relationships, they wouldn't say this aloud, but their behaviors are likely in line with this definition of "love" from the very beginning. If this *is* their definition of love, and they behave badly, then perhaps their behaviors are consistent with love, and when they say, "I love you," they mean it—it's just their (skewed) definition of love.

A *healthy,* loving relationship is reciprocal, respectful, patient, compassionate, empathic, kind, and supportive. That's it. If, in the midst of that, it is fun, exciting, romantic, sexy, and adventurous, then wonderful—that's the icing and the cake. Sadly, especially as more and more narcissistic relationships proliferate, more and more relationships are largely characterized by control, fear, and desire. Increasingly, people are conflating control with solicitude or attentiveness or confusing fear with excitement and, "This is my one and only." Desire is a superficial state—often one that draws people into romantic unions—but it is not sustainable. It is a bright light that burns out quickly. Desire can devolve into fear if it is the only thing keeping the relationship going, and it can make the relationship more about superficial possession of a gorgeous object than about the big-ticket items that make a relationship healthy, solid, and sustainable. It's like falling in love with the smell of the pollen but never getting to know the flower. As social media and traditional media too often uphold the possessive, materialistic, exciting, enviable, attractive relationship as a standard to achieve, it can push the *essential* ingredients of authenticity, reciprocity, mutuality, respect, and the rest of it out of sight. In this way, the world is glorifying the narcissistic relationship as desirable. If you have read this far, you know that this kind of relationship never ends well.

Love and Fear

Our personal vulnerabilities and insecurities are often what complicate the idea of healthy love for us and make us vulnerable to entering into narcissistic relationships. Fear is the most common emotion that propels people into narcissistic relationships: fear of being alone, fear of not deserving better, fear of not being enough. Another factor that increases the likelihood of entering into a narcissistic relationship is unclear motivations. Many times, people can get lulled into a narcissistic relationship simply because they "want to be wanted." That is in marked contrast to wanting to be respected, wanting to be valued, or wanting to grow. Many times, the narcissist's love bomby approach (constantly calling, texting, DMing, liking social media posts, checking in, asking you where you have been) is not loving or intense curiosity—it is control. But, in your desire to be wanted, it is easy to be blinded and to forget to pay attention to the other person's values, empathy, compassion, and genuineness. Love is the most complex simple emotion in the world, and it requires us to be honest with ourselves about our own psychological susceptibilities and blind spots, while being clear on what the other person's definition of "love" is. It may be *very* different from yours, and it may not be healthy, particularly if that person is narcissistic. The bottom line? *Get your soul and psyche in order before falling in love.* We get back only as good as we give; the world mirrors back what we are. When you put your insecure self out there, the likelihood you will receive narcissists increases, because they are the best mirrors for insecurity. Fear and love do not belong in the same sentence…always remember that.

The Mantra of the Narcissistic Relationship

Whether a person stays in these relationships or leaves them, the two-part mantra remains the same:

The narcissistic, toxic, entitled person will not change enough for it to make a difference,

thus

you have to manage your expectations.

This dysfunctional mantra applies to *all* narcissistic relationships. Mom and dad. Husband or wife. Daughter and son. Boss and colleague. Brother and sister. Friend and neighbor. And any other relationship you can think of.

The "they will not change" part is the most difficult part for people to get their head around, because, just like that, the hope is pulled out from under their feet. There is also often quite a bit of anecdotal pushback, and even some case material that will show some good evidence of change in narcissistic people after individual, couples, or family therapy, a period of time spent in rehab, or a significant event occurs in that person's life (typically a tragic event such as a death, natural disaster that directly impacts them, or significant loss of property, such as a house burning down). *Sometimes* these kinds of events are a wake-up call, but only sometimes; at other times, these kinds of events make them even more combative and angrier. Sometimes, when people have financial problems, yes, they win the lottery. That doesn't make buying lottery tickets a sensible financial strategy. It's the same way with narcissistic relationships.

The Rubber Band Theory

The "rubber band theory" of personality can help make this clear. Our personalities are, in essence, our psychological fingerprints. They do not tend to change much with time, they are patterns, and they give other people a predictable sense of how we will respond in a variety of situations. The rubber band theory argues that our personalities are like rubber bands and, in fact, can be stretched out at certain times and under certain conditions. It is possible that, after a partner packs his or her bags, finds a new place to live, and moves out with the kids, the narcissistic spouse will go to therapy and change his or her behavior significantly—for about three to six months (nine to twelve with some luck). That is because narcissistic people will exert every bit of mental control they have to act differently—to be attentive, to put down their phone, to find different ways to react and tamp down the anger, to be more empathic and listen, to be mindful of their words. The rubber band is stretched. The partner who left, returns, full of hope that the narcissist has "changed" in a permanent way. Then time goes on and it becomes clear the partner is going to stick around, a stressful day happens at work, the kids keep waking up in the middle of the night, the partner raises the possibility of pursuing a long-term goal, or the narcissistic person's ego gets bruised at work. Because enough time has passed and because of stress, the rubber band returns to its original size and the narcissistic and toxic patterns return: They stop listening, they get angry, they cut the partner off, and they go back to their entitled, cold, and unkind baseline.

This is observed in families too. Many people with narcissistic parents are well acquainted with a lifetime of these patterns. They will go to great pains to prepare their parents for the holidays—"This year please don't do [X or Y]"—and they lay out ground rules, and they believe that this year will be different. And it's not. The rubber band of personality will almost invariably return to its usual state during evocative and stressful periods, such as holidays. There will always be a side of gaslighting and verbal abuse along with the yams at the holiday dinner. So the unrealistic expectations get set and dashed on a yearly basis.

The rubber band almost always returns to its original size over time, and the process can be sped up by anything that threatens a person's ego, like stress or a disappointment. The most honest look at a person typically occurs under conditions of stress. Anyone, including toxic people, can keep it together and bring their A game from time to time. A relationship with a toxic person or with a narcissist requires almost daily recalibration, and the best that one can hope for is the days the rubber band is stretched and the "new and improved" version of the person emerges. Enjoy it for the short period it is, because, just as with a rubber band, once you let go of it, it will return to the original size.

Infidelity

This is an issue that arises often with narcissistic and toxic partners. "Infidelity," in and of itself, is a difficult term to firmly define, as it means different things to different people. There is sexual infidelity or "cheating" in the form of a person in a committed relationship's having sexual relations with someone outside of the relationship without his or her partner's knowledge or agreement. There is emotional infidelity, in which a person in a committed relationship is sharing confidences and intimate emotions with, and has romantic feelings for, a person outside of the committed relationship. There is "microcheating," a phenomenon whereby a person engages in what may be viewed as somewhat "shady" or uncomfortable behavior (direct messages via social media to an attractive friend, texts to a coworker outside of work hours, coffee dates the person "forgets" to tell a partner about). Microcheating is tricky and may vary from relationship to relationship—one person's microcheating is another's "friendship." Infidelity can take the form of a one-night stand or a long-term love affair. It can represent betrayal, disloyalty, poor boundaries, and/or impulsivity.

Are all cheaters narcissistic, psychopathic, or toxic? No. Research finds that infidelity can occur for a number of reasons and serve a number of functions, and not all relationships end after infidelity. In fact, well over half of couples stay together after an episode or episodes of infidelity.

Narcissism and infidelity go together because, in many cases, infidelity reflects a lack of empathy and a lack of consideration of the feelings of the partner. There is definitely an undercurrent of entitlement (as though people feel they have the right to pursue this relationship or gratification). It can be a superficial and grandiose endeavor, especially if the new love object is someone younger and perhaps more attractive than the committed partner or brings some other gratification or excitement to the cheater's life. The infidelity often represents a form of validation seeking—a fresh source of narcissistic supply with all of the bells and whistles of excitement and courtship. The arrogance of narcissists and other toxic sorts means that they often are confident that they will not get caught, or they simply do not think forward to the consequences of their conduct. Ironically, many people assert that they will and have endured years of emotional abuse or invalidation or humiliation at the hands of a narcissist and they stuck around but, somehow, their partner's cheating was the straw that broke the camel's back.

Despite the narcissist's propensity for cheating, hell hath no fury like a narcissist cheated on. As already noted, narcissistic folks tend to be suspicious to the point of paranoia. While they expect absolute privacy and lockdown on their devices, they do not tend to respect that for their partners and will often inquire about a partner's whereabouts, friends, and exes; who the person talks to at the gym and gets texts from; and an accounting of all Instagram followers; and will be highly suspicious of all comings and goings. It can feel like a double standard, because it is. Infidelity is a normative part of the narcissistic landscape, whether emotional, sexual, microcheating, or all of the above.

Coparenting With a Narcissist

With narcissists, "coparenting" is a misnomer. You do not truly coparent with them; you are the sole parent trying to manage a toxic situation. Coparenting with a toxic partner, whether with your ex or current partner, is perhaps the most difficult shared responsibility a person can have with a narcissist. As a healthy parent, you want to protect your children; support and encourage them in their goals; give them an emotionally rich vocabulary; teach them critical life skills, such as compassion, respect, and empathy; minimize entitled behavior; and raise them to be good citizens, peers and, perhaps one day, partners and parents. If your coparent is a toxic narcissist, then you will face more than twice the work—not only to impart these life lessons in the first place but also to undo the damage wrought by your narcissistic coparent (for all the reasons described in the parenting chapter). People who attempt to coparent are often at wit's end, figuring out how to balance parenting their children while managing their partner. In general, when you are in a relationship with a toxic narcissist and attempting to coparent, you are, in essence, a single parent with an elephant on your back; you have all the responsibilities and are undermined on a daily basis. It would be easier to be an actual single parent. You will spend vast amounts of time trying to get your children back on track after time spent with the narcissistic parent, and your life can be spent getting your children back into a schedule or routine just to have that routine disrupted again.

This can all become exponentially more complex if the relationship ends. The courts *do not care* if your partner has a narcissistic, borderline, psychopathic, antagonistic, high-conflict, or passive-aggressive personality style. In fact, people with these personality styles are often masterful at manipulating the cast of players in a toxic divorce, including attorneys, judges, mediators, family therapists, and custody evaluators. The courts are singularly wedded to equitable division of assets, including children, and, unless you have ironclad documentation of a toxic parent's conduct, you are unlikely to prevail in the family courts (and, even if you have that ironclad documentation, the unwillingness of the system to recognize the damage wrought on children by exposure to these toxic parents, as well as the lack of any consequences or penalties that act as a real deterrent to toxic parents and their antics, means that the toxic parent will still be given far more custody than is healthy). Narcissists rarely face real penalties, and their sense of power derives from the control they are able to wield over an ex-partner by using children as pawns. This can result in abject helplessness, hopelessness, and despair as you wend your way through a revolving door of court hearings, attorneys' offices, and financial ruin, as you keep visiting and revisiting every stipulation in custody agreements. It is not unusual for people in these situations to experience clinically significant levels of depression, anxiety, suicidal thoughts, difficulty sleeping, lack of self-care, and difficulties with concentration.

You got out—and that is a Herculean journey in its own right. However, if you had children together, then, in many ways, the hardest part of the journey is beginning. A toxic narcissistic person does not like losing. Sadly, many times, narcissists' asking for more custody of children (more custody than they may be prepared to manage given their work schedule, or more than may be optimal for the children) is a gambit meant to hurt the other parent (they may have little actual interest in their children, but they get a sense of revenge in keeping them from the other parent) or a way to dodge child support payments, which multiply when custody is not evenly distributed.

In all cases, as will be noted in the chapter on narcissistic parents, the parent views the child as a source of narcissistic supply. So, just as in every other relationship toxic people maintain, they look upon other people as "conveniences" that either meet their needs or are "inconveniences"—and their children are no different. The paradox of children is that they are the ultimate source of narcissistic supply, since they are often viewed as an extension of the parent, but children, by definition, are incredibly inconvenient. They are noisy, unpredictable, demanding at times, capricious, mercurial, and prone to tantrums, and that can be very off-putting for narcissists, who do not want to put the messy needs of other people (including their children) ahead of their own. In addition, because toxic narcissists view people as objects, it is easy for them to use their children as pawns to exert their ego and control over a situation.

Coparenting: If They Left You

If toxic narcissists do the leaving, it can be particularly galling since they likely left for someone else or the idea of something bigger or better. They may even embark on making a new family with their new partner, either because the new partner has children and they want to blend the kids into some kind of narcissistic and dystopian Brady Bunch or because their new partner is much younger, and they embark on "Family—Part II." In some cases, if you are incredibly lucky, they will have flown the coop and have no interest in the children, but this is rare. However, this scenario can still lead to other toxic situations, such as insufficient child support, inequitable division of assets, and confused children who may wonder where their father or mother went.

If your toxic partner left you and wants to play at making another family, he or she may reappear in your children's lives to help convey the image of a devoted mother or father. This can be a lovely time for your children, who may have attention lavished on them, but you can set a clock by the fact that, once the posturing has passed, the narcissistic parent will return to being distracted and will bring inconsistency back into your children's lives.

Because toxic parents are rarely interested in their child's well-being above and beyond their own, they may take you back to court if they find a new partner and believe the children will be a nice addition to that picture. However, it can also go the other way, as toxic parents move on. They may not want the balancing act or the headache of their existing children, and it can be devastating and confusing for children to witness the parent just move on and start again, without them.

Coparenting: If You Left

Good luck. You may face the custody battle of a lifetime, and that could last until your children are adults (and persist in many ways even after your children are adults). This battle may be a punishment to you for leaving; after a while, it isn't clear whether it really is about the children or if it is about punishing you. The ongoing specter of being pulled back into court, having custody arrangements renegotiated, having child support manipulated and shifted, and being forced into regular contact with your ex because you are supposed to "coparent" feels unbearable. You will also receive inane guidance from a variety of people who may not understand narcissism and toxicity and expect you to be cordial with someone who abuses you at every turn. One text message can turn into eight hours of battle. A simple inquiry about having a holiday dinner with your children can result in your ex-partner's spitefully exerting his or her "parental rights" and ensuring that special events established for your child would be hard won or otherwise ruined. Even planning a vacation can require attorney's bills and court orders.

In order to punish you for leaving, the real toll becomes your child, and I have worked with countless clients who have spent years living in fear of angering their ex-partner further and having a workable custody arrangement threatened. Mediators will naively suggest you craft a solution together, leaving you even more frustrated—again, the legal, judicial, and social service systems rarely recognize the phenomenon or impact of toxic coparenting—and this negotiation and renegotiation process can leave you feeling revictimized and even traumatized. While, in an ideal circumstance, you never have to communicate with your toxic ex again, leaving it to attorneys and other third parties can get expensive and untenable. Sadly, the way the system is set up, you have to find a way to walk a razor-thin tightrope and protect and parent your children.

Despite these patterns, you do not need to (nor should you) demonize their toxic parent—your children will learn the truth over time. However, when your children ask you about their parent's behavior, or just need a sounding board, do not sugarcoat it or promote the same false narrative that has allowed this toxic person to get into and stay in your life and likely hurt numerous others. Normalize your child's experience, try to stay focused on the toxic parent's behaviors and do not comment on the character of the other parent, consistently check in with your children, and ensure that they have good mental health services (because there is sometimes the requirement of two-parent consent for medical and mental health services, and narcissistic or other types of toxic parents are notorious for blocking access to mental health services for their children; if the services can be deemed essential, working with an attorney and the courts may be the only way to ensure mental health services for children). The fact is that one good parent can protect children, and the damage of narcissistic parents often happens when no one checks in with the children or validates their experience. Sadly, none of this is a guarantee. You can carefully follow these kinds of guidelines, and, if the other parent succeeds in their campaign, and uses other tools such as money to their advantage with your children, it can be devastating to have a child at any age who bought into the polarizing, dishonest, and deceptive narrative of a narcissistic parent, and rejects you as their parent on that basis.

Coparenting With a Partner Who Has a Narcissistic Ex-Partner

This is a situation that can be extremely befuddling—it happens when you marry or enter into a relationship with someone who already has children, and that person's ex is narcissistic and toxic. This is likely a pattern you become aware of as you spend more time with your partner. Narcissistic ex-partners can wreak havoc on your new relationship and make it all but impossible to be a healthy influence in your partner's children's lives. Toxic ex-partners may still have an axe to grind, may still be dragging your new partner into court, are likely to keep manipulating and shifting custody agreements, and may consistently engage in boundary violations, such as sending your new partner inappropriate messages, showing up at all hours, and trying to draw you close into a friendship so they can encroach into their ex-partner's new relationship. It can feel all but impossible to be a healthy stepparent in such a situation, and, in fact, you may be unable to provide healthy parenting guidance to your new partner, because it will all be undone when the child is with the narcissistic ex-partner, or your own partner has been rendered unable to be the kind of parent he or she wants to be. It can also tarnish your view of your partner, especially if you feel he or she is being railroaded by the ex-partner.

In these situations, you may feel like you inherited someone else's problem, and, in many ways, you did. These circumstances can devolve into something that is quite frightening if the ex becomes fixated on you and is poking into your life through social media, asking the children for information, or, as noted above, attempting to become overly familiar with you. A toxic ex-partner is often a problem that is not going to go away, and it may require you and your new partner to consider couple's therapy as a place to discuss the reality and limits of the situation, and for you to reflect on your endurance or appetite for this situation. If you are already in a situation like this or married to and perhaps have a blended family with a person who has a narcissistic ex-partner, you need to do the same due diligence as those who themselves have a toxic ex-partner. Ensure that you document everything. Consult with an attorney on ensuring that custodial and financial matters are as clearly articulated as possible, maintaining strict boundaries, and recognizing that this is baggage that you didn't ask for but that came as part of the new relationship. Feelings of resentment at having your life upended by your partner's narcissistic ex and a sense of helplessness are not unusual in these situations, because you, your new relationship, and perhaps even your own children you are bringing into this situation are being negatively impacted. Your ability to enact much change may also be limited, given that it is not your divorce, your ex, or your biological children.

Domestic Violence

It is necessary when writing about relationships with narcissists, sociopaths, psychopaths, other unstable personalities, and overall toxic behavior to also address domestic violence (sometimes termed "intrafamilial violence" or "intimate partner violence"). In the most classical form, domestic violence manifests as an intimate partner's (husband's, wife's, boyfriend's, girlfriend's, fiancé's, fiancée's) verbally, emotionally, financially, and/or physically abusing his or her partner. One in three women and one in four men have been physically abused by an intimate partner (Black et al., 2011), and we do not have reliable statistics on the rates of emotional abuse that partners face.

As a general rule, all domestic abusers are narcissistic, difficult, and antagonistic. They are controlling, vindictive, rageful, and entitled, and they lack empathy. The ability to inflict harm and violence on someone they purport to love reflects the lack of a healthy psychological core and the presence of deep insecurity. I have heard every explanation of how many abusers come from violent homes and so on. The fact is the majority of people who come from abusive homes do not perpetrate violence or abuse, and perhaps it is a moral question about whether there is any absolution or true rehabilitation for the person who perpetrates such acts. Ultimately, since nearly all perpetrators are narcissistic, they are not likely to change enough to sustain a healthy intimate partnership, so staying in hopes that their next apology will be true is the equivalent of punching yourself in the face. In addition, a large proportion of domestic violence takes the form of emotional, psychological, and financial abuse—forms of abuse that do not leave visible scars or result in restraining orders or other legal remedies. In fact, the scars of chronic emotional abuse run far deeper and often psychologically harm survivors for far longer. Nearly all physical abuse is accompanied by the other forms of abuse, so it can be difficult to tease it all apart. In general, the rule of the land is that, once abuse is perpetrated within a relationship, the DNA of the relationship has changed permanently. The short answer? *Get out.* However, for all the reasons discussed in this book, leaving may not feel like an option, may be dangerous, or may be impermissible in certain cultures. Hope and fear collude to maintain this deadly cycle of domestic abuse. Many people do not have an option; many cannot get out. Perhaps the only answer to any of this is a world in which we can teach people about these patterns, so they do not enter these relationships in the first place.

Domestic violence is often intergenerational. Adults who were raised in homes marked by domestic abuse or domestic violence often inadvertently choose partners who are abusive, and this may be for practical reasons (they are fleeing their violent family of origin and will relent to the first partner they find who pulls them out of it—not exactly fertile ground for making a good decision). Or they may be more likely to be perpetrators. Either way, both perpetrators and survivors of domestic abuse tend to reflect an intergenerational pattern. In addition, it is not unusual to observe patterns including narcissism, psychopathy, sociopathy, substance abuse, or PTSD in perpetrators, and PTSD, substance abuse, anxiety disorders, mood disorders, and other disorders that reflect dysregulation (such as eating disorders, self-harm, and impulse control disorders) in survivors. Until we start modifying societal structures, including better support for women and men who are victims of abuse, better foster-care systems, provision of high-quality psychological services to survivors and perpetrators, penalties and deterrents that have teeth to address perpetration, judicial and legal policies that recognize recidivism and stop blaming and retraumatizing victims, and education that teaches children that abuse is wrong—until we start witnessing those macro-level shifts—these intergenerational cycles will not end.

While domestic violence is most often perpetrated from partner to partner, keep in mind that any intrafamilial or intra-residential violence qualifies, and this means violence between adult children and parents, siblings, other family members in residence, or even roommates. Both women and men can perpetrate domestic violence, and male victims are frequently underrepresented in the statistics because of an unwillingness to report. Finally, same-sex couples have higher-than-expected rates of partner violence. The bottom line? No one is immune.

Law enforcement, legal, and judicial systems are not set up to adequately address domestic violence. American laws result in victims being retraumatized through investigative and judicial processes, restraining orders often result in an increase in violence by perpetrators, and law enforcement is often limited in their ability to respond until there is an actionable offense. Finally, victims may recant their allegations, because they are plagued by self-doubt, fear, and practical concerns including finances.

Domestic violence is a severe and often life-threatening situation. While all of the dynamics laid forth in this book are relevant, the process of getting out of an abusive relationship can be quite dangerous and require different and more acute intervention through law enforcement, domestic violence programs and shelters, and other means of safety, which are beyond the scope of this book. If you are currently in a violent relationship in the United States, please contact the National Domestic Violence Hotline at 1-800-799-SAFE (7233) or online at www.thehotline.org, and, if your partner or other perpetrator monitors your devices, please ensure you erase any search histories from your device, computer, or phone to better ensure your safety. Ideally, use a computer or device in your workplace, a public library, or that belongs to a friend or family member so that shared devices and cloud storage do not reveal your search history either. If you reside outside of the US, please turn to whatever resources may be in place through local governmental offices, consulates, law enforcement, or nongovernmental organizations, depending on the appropriate resources in your region.

Takeaways: Toxic Partners

Should I Stay or Should I Go? offers a compendium on how to manage toxic relationships, and is a far more detailed resource for how to manage these intimate relationships with narcissists and entitled people on a step-by-step basis. Here is the condensed version:

1. **Manage your expectations.** What does that really mean? It means realistically maintaining expectations. In the winter in Chicago, you do not expect an eighty-degree day. When you stick your hand into a fire, you expect to get burned. In the morning, you expect the sun to rise in the east. You do not become upset when the Chicago day is cold, you do not act surprised when your hand gets burned in the fire, and you would not hold out hope that the sun will rise in the west. The same absolutes matter here. If the toxic, narcissistic, or entitled partner has always expected special treatment, rarely or never shows empathy, is almost always focused on superficial factors, always gets rageful whenever criticized or frustrated, and is a liar, then that is how it will always be. So, when he or she does not ask you about your day or is rude to the flight attendant or rude to you in public, or takes you for granted, or cheats on you or lies to you, don't be surprised. Being surprised expends lots of psychic energy. Just nod your head as you would when you draw your jacket around you on that cold Chicago day.

2. **If you leave one of these relationships, expect a mess.** There may be lawyers, money used as a weapon, vindictive behavior, accusations, verbal abuse, manipulation of children, and public vilification of you (and, in some cases, it can become very dangerous). Narcissistic people do not like being left, even if the relationship was a mess and even if they already have a new partner waiting in the wings. These divorces and breakups can haunt people for years, *but never has a person said he or she regrets leaving a narcissistic relationship*. Make the practical preparations you

need to make before the proverbial shit hits the fan: Get your financial ducks in a row, ensure that you have essential documents, arrange a place to stay if needed, and let other people know what is happening. This will be a journey, and all journeys require preparation.

3. **If you stay in one of these relationships, you need to become somewhat "inauthentic."** It can definitely take a toll on your soul in the long term. You cannot talk about your life, accomplishments, or anything meaningful (because you know you will be criticized, minimized, or ignored). You also cannot share bad experiences (the broken refrigerator, the bounced check), because narcissistic or toxic partners will become enraged that you inconvenienced them and blame you. Nor can you share bad news that leaves you vulnerable (a sadness, a fear, or an illness), because they will offer no empathy and that can feel awful. I often counsel people to generate a list of neutral topics (the weather, a new business being built in town, the neighbors' new succulent garden) and not take the bait on controversial topics that their partners may dangle. Take away their power by no longer offering the core of yourself to them. Many people feel saddened by this recommendation. They feel that they signed up for a relationship, a life partner, a person with whom to do stuff. Sadly, that is not how this is going to turn out. It may mean taking some separate vacations and even crafting separate lives. Your reasons for staying or leaving are very personal, so craft a solution that works for you. Build up a network of friends, supporters, and others who want to hear your good news and can support you through your bad news. Many people spend decades telling a narcissistic, toxic person their highs and lows, aspirations and woes, just to have those things minimized. They often give up on real dreams and, ultimately, devalue themselves. Find a healthy group to share your authentic self with and be clear with yourself about why you are staying in your narcissistic relationship. Your authentic self will suffer when you stay in one of these relationships—you simply have to cut off too much of what is genuine about you to make

it work. But, if you do stay, ensure that you have outlets for your genuine self to flourish.

4. **Don't get lost in the "The next person will get a better version of [him or her]" fantasy.** This is the reason many people stay in relationships with people who are narcissistic, entitled, and toxic. They maintain that incorrect assumption that the narcissistic person can significantly change, and then they believe that the next partner will get an empathic, unentitled, kind, normal version of their toxic ex-partner. That's not going to happen, because that version does not exist. Give it enough time, and I can all but guarantee that his or her new partner will have the same experience you did. Again, this is about managing your expectations. You can waste a lifetime staying in the relationship waiting for something that is never going to happen, or you can pass the ball to his or her next unfortunate victim and start rebuilding your own life. (It can be tempting to think you are playing the martyr by writing the new partner a message about what awaits him or her—be clear on your motivations. This is the new person's lesson to learn. By trying to thwart your narcissist's new life, you are still trying to retain a relationship with that person. Let him or her go.)

5. **Consider psychotherapy.** Even a few sessions can help but find someone who understands narcissistic and toxic relationships and get the support and sounding board you need. Toxic and narcissistic relationships leave people feeling full of self-doubt and confusion, and there can be some frank psychological fallout, like depression, anxiety, and other symptoms. But, if your therapist offers negating guidance such as, "Are you sure you gave your relationship a chance?" then find another therapist. Often people feel like they cannot discuss the relationship with friends or family, and therapy provides a safe and objective space for that. Take the time to find a therapist with expertise in antagonistic patterns such as narcissism, so they can hear your experience from a realistic perspective, and provide guidance that does not leave you confused.

6. **Don't take their bait.** They will bait you. Over and over. If you have kids, it may relate to custody. If not, it may just be a rehashing of old grievances. They will try to get you into the mud with them. Remain aware that they will not change enough to make a difference in your relationship, and they will gaslight and deny your reality and project their stuff on you. Do not defend yourself, because you are then playing their game. If they insult you, just nod your head and walk away. The longer you defend yourself and keep taking the fight, the longer you allow this relationship to run your life.

7. **It's not you—it's them.** Ultimately, in most relationships, there are two people and some level of shared responsibility (but I tread very lightly here, because I refuse to view it this way in the case of abusive relationships—someone who is too afraid to leave is not "contributing" to his or her own abuse). That said, while there may be some level of dysfunctional communication that has overtaken a narcissistic relationship on both sides, ultimately, much of this dysfunction originates from the toxic person's lack of empathy, entitlement, coldness, manipulation, control, grandiosity—yep, it's him or her. So stop making it about you, stop trying to change yourself, because nothing will work. But also take some ownership of your life and own up to the true state of your relationship and your partner.

8. **Distance yourself.** A popular term in the community of people who have endured or are still enduring relationships with narcissistic and toxic people is "no contact." This implies cutting off all possible contact—blocking their number, blocking their access to your social media, blocking email access, and avoiding people they know and places they go. Obviously, this is possible only to an extent, depending on the type of relationship you are in with a former narcissistic partner; if there are children, there may need to be some contact, but that can be brief. If you cannot go no contact, consider a technique that has been termed "gray rock." This technique entails making yourself as uninteresting and inert as a gray rock. It means communicating via one word answers, offering little engagement, and making no demands. Over time,

when you provide no validation, no opportunities for conflict, and are rendered completely boring, most narcissists, and psychopaths, will lose interest. In the most extreme cases (though this can get expensive), any contact can be brokered through attorneys. But distance yourself as much as you can, and, if you don't need to be in touch, don't be.

9. **Engage in some form of self-care and self-preservation.** This is not meant to be self-indulgent weeks at a spa or eschewing your responsibilities. It can be giving yourself a short break with a cup of tea and a book, or just sitting in the car for five minutes before you go into the house to be with children or having regular coffee dates with a trusted friend. You will need something that uplifts you after the abnegation of a relationship with a narcissistic or toxic person. After years with a narcissist, it has likely been a long time since anyone has taken care of you. This guidance applies whether you stay in the relationship or whether you leave it. People who have been in relationships with toxic or narcissistic people do not even believe they deserve to take care of themselves or feel guilty doing so. It can sometimes be more useful to think of it as "self-preservation" rather than as self-care, and as an attempt to save yourself before this relationship does any further damage to you.

10. **Keep your relationship issues off of social media.** In the reality-bending insanity of a narcissistic relationship, it can be tempting to lambast your partner on social media, advertise your fun nights out as revenge, or complain about your "woe is me" life in the wake of your narcissistic partner. This is not an appropriate way to foster social support, and your narcissistic partner can play this game far better than you. In addition, if you are navigating a divorce, and especially if there are children involved, it is unfair to the children and can actually hurt you in legal proceedings, since social media feeds are discoverable. This is a place where you can go high when the narcissist goes low. Block your narcissist and people who enable him or her, gain strength from your friends and followers, but keep things clean.

11. **Generalize the lessons to the other narcissists in your life.** In an ideal world, leaving a narcissist can be an exorcism of sorts—finally seeing the relationship up close, seeing that it would never change, and recognizing that you are functioning better with it behind you may cure you of your drive to keep engaging with narcissists. Once you "get it," it can be a purging of demons and give you clarity not just about this relationship, but also about other narcissists you have endured or still are enduring in your life. In that way, while this relationship has taken a toll on your life, maybe it was an essential step in releasing the past and protecting yourself in the future.

12. **Embrace radical acceptance.** Managing expectations and setting boundaries are necessary and key ingredients whether you stay or go from a relationship with a narcissist. However, the final step is an internal process that is essential in ANY relationship with a narcissist. Radical acceptance is the absolute acceptance that "this is how it is." It will not get better, it will not shift, there is little that anyone can do about it, and that is that. This is not meant to render a sense of helplessness or hopelessness, but acceptance. In this way, you can put your emotional and mental bandwidth to better use. Instead of trying to change the unchangeable or being frustrated and distressed, you can focus on other issues (e.g. enhancing your children's lives, cultivating friendships) that will benefit from your effort.

Chapter 7

The Narcissist Who Raised You

Children have never been very good at listening to their elders,
but they have never failed to imitate them.

—JAMES BALDWIN

Many people met their very first narcissist on their first day on this planet. It was their mother, their father, or both. People with narcissistic parents often have no other reality—as such, it shapes who they are and become. It can take some heavy psychological lifting to get past growing up this way and making healthy choices as an adult. A toxic parent engages in the established patterns of narcissism: lack of empathy, self-centeredness, arrogance, unchecked rage, grandiosity, and deep entitlement. Basically, it is a situation in which the parent chronically puts his or her needs first and the needs of everyone else second. There are myriad possible reasons for these toxic patterns. Parents who are toxic are often narcissistic, but there may also be other patterns, ranging from untreated psychopathology, personality disorders (particularly borderline, narcissistic, and antisocial personality disorders as well as passive-aggressive patterns), and substance abuse to the parents' own history of having toxic parents—this can be a transgenerational issue. No matter what the reason, it is not the child's responsibility to be patient with or address a parent's issues. Period.

Children do not have the luxury of knowing or even understanding that their parent is a narcissist. With few exceptions, children want to believe their parents are heroes and caregivers and will give their parents thousands of chances to get it right. Partially, this is adaptive; if the child does get the validation of the parent, then the child will be kept safe by the adult. But, mostly, it is reflexive, and most parents start from an advantageous position: If you feed this little person, he or she will like you. The job gets more demanding as it goes.

Parents set a primitive tone for us, and the fact is that no one gets it *just right.* Parents' sadness, worries, disappointments, psychopathology, and distraction all become the stuff of their children's development and become the only reality or "normal" the child experiences. Parents are people, and their history does not magically disappear when they have a child. Extending that to what we discussed before about habituation (adjusting to a given situation), these familial patterns become normalized, and we often replay them in numerous ways in adult life. One narcissistic, entitled, toxic parent can steer the course of a childhood in a permanent way and can impact adulthood until the end of life. Parenting and narcissism do not mix. The key requirements of parenting—consistency, empathy, compromise, sacrifice, self-awareness, discipline, and equanimity—are precisely the qualities that narcissists lack.

The analogy I have used with numerous clients when we discuss family-of-origin issues is that the experiences we have or endure as children are like etchings or echoes. These experiences don't define people, but they also cannot be denied—the echo, the faint mark, is always there. At the most extreme, it is like experiencing an injury in childhood; it may always give you some aches and pains as an adult, but it doesn't have to restrict you. The awareness of these dynamics, how they impact a person, and how they continue to play out can be used to enable behavioral change and different kinds of choices.

The Key Characteristics of a Narcissistic Parent

In writing this book, I spoke with dozens of people with toxic or narcissistic parents. Their stories are heartbreaking, because not only did the narcissism make for difficult and painful childhoods, but also the scars and damage wrought by their toxic parents impacted their sense of self-worth and their decision making in relationships throughout their adult lives. Their stories, however, are sometimes triumphant. They did not allow their parents' toxicity to do them in, they found strength within themselves, and they took their lives back despite their self-doubt.

Some key themes emerged over the course of the interviews (while these were not true of every parent, these were themes that multiple respondents highlighted, in terms of how their parents' toxicity manifested). These themes ranged from invalidation and emotional distance to control and competitiveness to inconsistency and poor boundaries.

Invalidation

Toxic parents make everything about them—your triumphs, your losses, the day you give birth, a family funeral, the day you go in to get chemotherapy. Regardless of the topic or situation, they turn it back to themselves. Their children's needs are secondary and typically met only if they align with the needs of the parents. They lie to their children about family issues and chronically second-guess and gaslight their children well into adulthood, often asking questions like, "Are you sure?" or stating, "You don't know what you're doing." Narcissistic parents engage in petty quid pro quos: If they feel slighted by their children, they will punish them in some way. This could range from not speaking to you to deliberately forgetting your birthday, to not coming to an event that is important to you. Again, these are patterns that respondents reported happening during their childhood and adulthood with toxic parents. Any feelings that are (or were) expressed are often denied or minimized, which represents the worst of both gaslighting and invalidation.

Another theme that surfaced was the feeling that other people in the family system want the person to "get over it" just to keep the peace and avoid having to face down the toxic family member. This means that other family members do not listen to the person, which becomes a form of family gaslighting. Toxic parents also participated in parental gaslighting. Parents denied the events that occurred during the childhood of those interviewed—and, after finding the courage after years to confront their parents, their recollections and feelings were doubted or denied by their parents.

Emotional Distance

The people I interviewed also reported that their parents were cold and distant. This is a form of parental abandonment, because the parents could not handle, manage, or be bothered with parenting. The parent may have provided for basic needs (meals on the table, clean clothes), but there was absolutely no emotional "get" from the parent—either warmth or empathy. This also arced into literal abandonment, and respondents shared stories of being left with the other parent, stepparents, or grandparents and being unclear about when the parent would return.

Control and Authoritarianism

People who have narcissistic parents said they were authoritarian, controlling, tyrannical, and demanded blind obedience. They often split family members so that, if the child created a close alliance with the other parent, the toxic parent attempted to undercut that. The toxic parent also attempted to do this if siblings banded together, or if a grandparent, aunt, or uncle allied with the child. They impeded adolescent children from becoming more independent or criticized them in a manner that sapped their independence. Narcissistic parents can be quite inconsistent, at times shaming their children for lacking independence, and then impeding their children when they attempt to be individual. Toxic parents also sabotaged friendships that might have provided the child with confidence and other support. This also included relationships with close family members, coaches, or other mentors or teachers in the community. Respondents reported a consistent pattern of parental gaslighting, acknowledging that, when they experienced physical discomfort or had an emotional reaction, their parents told them that they were overreacting or being too dramatic. The parent's mood and expectations were the law of the land, and anyone who did not adhere to these edicts would face harsh consequences.

Poor Boundaries and Lack of Safety

Poor boundaries included encroaching into their child's life in a way that was intrusive, behaving inappropriately with their child's friends, and showing up unannounced. These parents demanded that their children become high achievers or engage in activities, jobs, or fields of study that were consistent with the parents' interests or aspirations, with little regard for whether their children found these activities interesting. As adults, respondents admitted that their toxic parents would criticize the respondents' own parenting, especially if that parenting was characterized by warmth, empathy, flexibility, and connection.

A few interviewees talked about the experience of family mobbing, whereby narcissistic and toxic parents would organize the other family members and curry their favor to scapegoat one child within the family system, and if that person decided to distance himself or herself from the family, he or she was written off as ungrateful, aloof, or a "problem child."

The narcissistic parents also made choices that put the child in harm's way, including allowing people into the home that may have sexually or physically abused the child and keeping that dangerous person around because it fed the ego and needs of the parent, despite the harm coming to their child. Respondents also mentioned having fearful parents who were in the relationship with the toxic parent and did not protect the child but, instead, continued to single-mindedly provide narcissistic supply for the toxic parent (resulting in the negligence of their children).

Sometimes both parents were toxic and would act as a tag team and defend each other ("Why do you criticize your mother?"). This would be particularly damaging and painful, because the child would not have a "reality check" of any kind within the family system. This is a dynamic that continued into adulthood for several respondents.

Superficiality

The people I interviewed also reported that their toxic parents expressed disproportionate concern about what other people would think about their family and less genuine concern about the children. Their parents were chameleons who were able to put on a good show for other people, which was confusing for the children, hearing that their parent was so helpful or wonderful when they were having a very different experience at home. Due to their own grandiosity, these parents expected their child to be great, so, while there was a sense of being encouraged and cheered on in whatever activity they were doing, it was in the name of greatness for the parent and the public face of the family and not necessarily for the pleasure of the activity or the happiness of the child.

The Impacts a Narcissistic Parent Can Have on a Child

Because I interviewed adults, they all shared the impacts that growing up with a toxic or narcissistic parent had on them in adulthood. The effect of this kind of parent, especially when they did not understand it, often lasted long into adulthood. However, once they became educated about their parents' narcissism, sociopathy, passive-aggressive behavior, and other toxic patterns, many were able to heal and create full and satisfying lives. Some of the most common impacts they experienced included:

- A childhood riddled with insecurity, confusion, a lack of safety, a sense of anxiety, fear, sadness, lack of confidence, and loss of their sense of self.
- Punishment if they ever attempted to advocate for themselves, and the clear message that to advocate for themselves was unacceptable.
- A sense of "survivalism." Children in these situations learned to do what they needed to do to please or appease their toxic parents. They also became masterful at jumping through hoops and addressing their unpleasable parents' needs, regardless of the toll it took on the child.
- Having to meet their own needs on the sly or in secrecy in order to protect themselves.
- Experiencing a range of physical symptoms was not uncommon for these children. It is stressful to grow up like this and, not surprisingly, several people reported having varied physical symptoms during childhood, including migraines and headaches, cold sores, chronic gastrointestinal issues, hives, and skin rashes.
- Chronically having to appease the parent, but their parents would rarely appease them; instead, they would more often criticize them.
- At one point, nearly every child believed he or she was the problem and kept trying to be "better" so that his or her parent would be happy.
- Confusion about feelings of just wanting to leave the parent when they were old enough to move out, but a lack of confidence or a sense of guilt from "abandoning" the parent.

The kinds of impacts that trailed people into adulthood included:

- Psychiatric and psychological issues:
  —Low self-esteem
  —Depression

—Anxiety

—Eating disorders

—Using drugs or alcohol to manage their feelings

—Suicidal thoughts

—Self-harming behaviors

- The inability to value themselves or feel that they are worthy or that they are "enough."
- Choosing a narcissistic, toxic, and/or controlling partner. Choosing partners who are invalidating, demeaning, critical, contemptuous, dehumanizing, or abusive. For many of them, this was a cycle that repeated for years—and felt like a natural extension of their childhood pattern of providing narcissistic supply, silencing their own needs, and living under conditions of insecurity and inconsistency. Sadly, being with an abusive person, at a primitive level, felt like "home."
- Difficulty accepting kindness or assistance from other people.
- Having their own challenges with empathy and entitlement as adults.
- Being overly empathic with other people as an adult and being taken advantage of because of this.
- Not feeling as though they had the right to boundaries with their parents or with anyone else in their lives.
- Running themselves into the ground and trying to do too much for other people. After the fact, many of them recognized that this was a pattern that was a by-product of feeling that they were loved only for "doing" and that this was the only way they thought that someone would want to have them in their lives.
- Losing out on professional opportunities because they did not feel confident enough to accept a promotion or other advancement or struggling at work because of indecisiveness and self-deprecation.
- Periods of grief. Several people reported feeling "robbed" of a childhood or a family once they realized what the patterns were. They recognized that they had fought for having a sense of family or childhood, and kept throwing themselves back in because they so desperately wanted to have loving parents and a sense of family.

The Unstable Foundation Laid by a Narcissistic Parent

A toxic and narcissistic parent can impact a child in numerous ways, as we've seen from the behaviors and experiences reported by those interviewed. In the following section, I will outline some of the most common patterns, their effect on a child, and how these patterns can play out into adulthood.

Persistent Neglect and/or Negation

Narcissistic parents may be so caught up in their own lives and pursuits that they are unwilling or unable to make the sacrifices that all children require. It can impact the child in very real and practical ways: The parent does not prepare appropriate meals at appropriate times, does not show up on time to pick up the child from school or activities, or does not adhere to a bedtime or other routines. The subtle impacts are even more far-reaching and often manifest as not listening to the child, interrupting the child, maintaining little interest or curiosity in the child, and criticizing, belittling, or humiliating the child. If the toxic parent is not interested in the child at any given moment, he or she does not notice the child. This is not to say that a busy parent will always get it wrong—many people beautifully balance the demands of careers, other life stressors, and parenting; it's about being consistent, present, and mindful.

This does not always manifest as physical or environmental neglect—the child may be well fed, clothed, housed, enrolled in school, and taken on vacation. It is more of an emotional neglect (see the "Over- and Underindulgence" section later on in this chapter). There is little interest in the child's internal world, but the physical is managed well, and sometimes very well, leaving other people thinking that the child actually has a perfectly lovely life. It's like having plenty of food but still starving to death.

EFFECT ON THE CHILD

In cases when needs are not being met, obviously this can leave children not only physically at risk but also without a consistent mirror as described earlier in Chapter 5, or with an insecure attachment to the parent. These children may chronically attempt to curry the favor of their parent but, over time, if the neglect is persistent and pervasive enough, the children may simply lose interest and withdraw entirely.

HOW DOES THIS PLAY OUT INTO ADULTHOOD?

Some people in this situation have become fully estranged from their family and parents. They may have been forced to be self-reliant and have often succeeded in that, or the situation may have forced them into risky or suboptimal situations, such as dropping out of school or entering into a dangerous relationship to secure a place to live. Sadly, some people coming from this situation will find that they have numbed themselves and cut off their emotional worlds, and are now unable to connect to others as adults, often feeling distant and disconnected. But it is also possible that this sets up a need for validation that pushes a child raised like this to keep seeking validation in some form from others—teachers, peers, the world at large—while never becoming confident in his or her sense of being "good enough." Sadly, sometimes the patterns of childhood neglect and negation can result in adults who look narcissistic themselves, which makes sense, since the core dynamic of narcissism is insecurity. Unfortunately, narcissistic parents can leave their children feeling "not good enough" in perpetuity. This need for validation can play out rather badly in adult relationships: The adults may seek out narcissistic partners who allow this dynamic to repeat or other negating situations in which a lifetime can be spent trying to prove themselves, as though doing so will fix the neglectful, negating childhood.

Inconsistency

Toxic and narcissistic parents are inconsistent in all ways—not only in practical matters, such as routines, but also in how they interact with their children. At times, they are overinvolved and almost inappropriate with boundaries or indulgence, and, at other times, they are completely disconnected and uninterested. These vacillations typically vary based on the parents' needs, with little regard for the child. If the parents need attention, they will turn to the child for it. If the parents cannot be bothered with the headache of a child, they will ignore the child or only intermittently interact with him or her. Narcissistic parents regularly break promises and have complex rationalizations for breaking them. They rarely follow through on obligations on a regular basis, often not showing up to concerts or soccer games, or rarely showing up on time to pick children up from school or some other place. Narcissistic parents engage in conditional parenting, showing these children affection when they do what their parents want but withholding it when they do not.

In many ways, narcissistic parents treat children as conveniences (or inconveniences). When the child is convenient (there are guests in the house and they want to play at being the "uberparent," or their child has just given a brilliant performance and they want to soak up the adulation being placed on their child), then they will be highly attentive to the child. But, at times when the child is an impediment (making demands when the parent wants to be doing something else or asking to play the same board game for the hundredth time), the narcissistic parent will tune out. Or, even at times when the child is making no demand but the parent is having a bad day, the narcissistic parent will be unable to step out of himself or herself long enough to check in with the child. No parent gets it right all of the time; as psychoanalysts such as Donald Winnicott note, it is enough to be the "good enough" parent—that is to say, to get it right much of the time. Sadly, the narcissistic parent falls well under that threshold, and the "not good enough" parent yields a child who retains the "not good enough" sense of self for decades.

EFFECT ON THE CHILD

Inconsistency can leave children confused, anxious, destabilized, insecure, and feeling like they are always walking on eggshells. Over time, they may get savvier at figuring out the parent's "patterns" and will get wise. They may determine whether it is at specific times of day or under other conditions when they are valued and focus on those. The children also start to learn that they are valued only for certain aspects of themselves, which can set them up for recognizing that the only way to bring any consistency into their lives is to live conditionally and provide a parent with what the parent wants. This kind of inconsistency can result in chronic anxiety for the child, who may start to have difficulties in school or with attention or may even evince unusual behaviors.

HOW DOES THIS PLAY OUT INTO ADULTHOOD?

Again, much like neglect and negation, this pattern can also impact attachment, and it can make the world seem like an unsafe and unpredictable space. In adulthood, this can play out in several ways, including the extreme of being overcontrolled to an almost compulsive degree to get the sense of consistency that often eluded them. The inconsistent mirror and inconsistent sense of self can also result in difficulties with emotional regulation, a sense of not being enough, and an almost painful sensitivity to others—to the degree that people who come from this type of environment may be at greater risk of monitoring all of the people in their environment and constantly shape-shifting to please them. This can set someone up for falling into narcissistic relationships of all kinds in adulthood.

Competitiveness

Toxic and narcissistic parents tend to be highly competitive with their children, which can manifest as a pattern of jealousy, particularly as the child becomes older and they are in competition with their child. Even when their children are young, toxic parents may grow resentful that their child is garnering more attention than they are receiving or may push their children to fight or try harder. This can play out in a number of ways, including frank competition with the child (actually trying to be better at the thing the child is doing or reflecting on their glory days of that particular activity), playing down the child's accomplishments ("Back in my day, it was much more difficult to win at one of these competitions"), not showing up to a competition or performance, or leaving the room when the child's achievements are being discussed. Paradoxically, it is often toxic or narcissistic parents who shunt the child into the single-minded pursuit of excellence in a particular activity—and yet it is also their inability to get their own ego out of the way that blocks them from praising their child's efforts. The child may be praised only when he or she wins and never recognized for effort unless it culminates in a win. The narcissistic parent may be covetous or jealous—a pattern that can persist through their relationship with the child.

EFFECT ON THE CHILD

The effect on the child is commonly guilt at outshining the parent or making the parent feel uncomfortable. In some cases, there is also resentment, but guilt is often the leading emotion here and can even make the child ambivalent about his or her achievements. This can even present as self-sabotage to avoid winning, or discomfort with winning, which can ultimately manifest in adulthood as an inability to "own" accomplishments or the feeling of "survivor's guilt" for succeeding. They may look humble, but the humility is often a frank denial of their achievements. Finally, children raised under these circumstances may experience significant anxiety and may become physically ill before a competition, as well as experience a loss of the love of the game because the entire process has become so co-opted by the competitive needs of the parent. For these children, holidays and birthdays are often ruined, because the toxic parents cannot endure other people's receiving attention, or people are not behaving precisely as they want during the family gatherings.

HOW DOES THIS PLAY OUT INTO ADULTHOOD?

In adults, this bizarre parental competition can actually become even more heightened. If you do actually wind up having greater success than your parent, he or she may still criticize it and devalue the quality of your career, home, or objects. If your spouse is kind and loving or different than in the relationship you had with your parent, the parent may denigrate your spouse or your marriage. Narcissistic parents are threatened by their adult children's accomplishments or joys and minimize them, trivialize them, or take responsibility for them.

Sadly, people with toxic or narcissistic parents often will keep trying to please them and impress them, whether that is purchasing them gifts big or small (I have heard about people who did have significant success and went so far as to purchase a toxic parent a home or a car, only to have the parent complain about its features or location, and the adult child looked as devastated as a small child whose parent may have mocked a drawing that he or she made). Many people report that the competitive parent ruined their wedding day, because the parent encroached upon the arrangements as though it was his or her big day and found it difficult to tolerate the adulation heaped upon the bride or groom, or because the narcissistic parent needed to ensure it was a big enough "show" to outshine other family members. This competitive dynamic can also result in a feeling of guilt, especially if the child's life or outcomes far surpass that of the competitive narcissistic parent. Instead of being able to enjoy well-earned accomplishments or even just lucky twists of fate, there can be a sense of guilt that pervades all successes. The toxic parent can cast a long shadow.

Rage

Parenting is difficult and, even on the best day for the best parent, it can be frustrating. Since toxic or narcissistic people do not tolerate frustration or disappointment in any form, parenting can be a disaster for them, as there is a propensity for terrifying rage in the face of normal parenting moments. The rage can be targeted at anyone, and, at times, the rage is unrelated to the child's behavior but may be a manifestation of other issues in the parent's day, including relationship problems, work difficulties, or just because something in the narcissistic parent's life did not go the way he or she wanted. Parental rage may manifest as loud screaming, cruel insults ("you ruined my life"), throwing objects, unreasonable and disproportionate punishments, physical violence, or storming away without letting the child or others know where they are going or when they will return.

EFFECT ON THE CHILD

It is terrifying to grow up with a rageful parent. It foments a sense of unpredictability, and the children will often wind up spending their childhood walking on eggshells to ensure that they do not contribute to the likelihood of an explosive rage or that they get out of the way of one. This can also communicate and model to the child that dysregulation is acceptable or can contribute to a sense of fear.

There is much excellent work and writing on child abuse, and this is not meant to be an overview of these issues, as they are beyond the scope of this book. Abuse can put a child at long-term psychological and physical risks, as well as at behavioral risks that can have long-term ramifications, including mental illness, substance abuse, self-harm, risky behavior, or criminal behavior. For further and more specific reading on these issues, please search out resources specific to adult survivors of child abuse; there are many excellent nonprofit organizations that provide referrals, information sheets, and advocacy.

HOW DOES THIS PLAY OUT INTO ADULTHOOD?

Consistent exposure to rage in childhood can have various ramifications in adulthood, depending on the extent and impact of the rage. Obviously, the most abusive rage and that accompanied by direct or observed physical violence can contribute to the likelihood of mood and anxiety disorders, substance use, and impulse control disorders, PTSD, or personality disorders. If the rage manifests as chronic verbal abuse, such as screaming and yelling, it can lead to a greater likelihood of anxiety, difficulties with distractibility and concentration, post-traumatic symptoms, and self-doubt, as well as foster a hypervigilant walking-on-eggshells style after years of growing up in an unpredictable, rageful situation. Dangerously, this can increase the likelihood of entering into an abusive or toxic relationship. Exposure to this dynamic may increase the likelihood of rage in adulthood in the child exposed to it—or, at least, difficulty regulating strong emotions such as rage.

Scapegoating

Narcissistic parents can sometimes scapegoat one child in a family system. Often, they will choose the child they are most threatened by. It's paradoxical, as they may scapegoat the child they most "need" because that child is a source of validation or is a high achiever. They may also scapegoat this child for reasons that otherwise threaten their public persona (for example, the child may exhibit characteristics or have an appearance that the parent feels is unacceptable). It is as though the shame of needing the child results in projection of negative thoughts and behaviors onto that child. Among many of the people interviewed for this book, the scapegoated children were either the oldest, more successful, had more friends, or were more intelligent than their siblings (or posed some other threat to the ego of the parent). The parent may even have felt competitive with the child. This is an extraordinarily painful dynamic for a child, who may feel as though the entire family system is conspiring to bully him or her, and highlights fears of ostracism and isolation. It is not unusual, within a narcissistic family system, in addition to the scapegoated child, for there to also be the "golden child," a role that is not always a simple one. They may receive the best of the narcissistic parent's acclaim, but they may also feel beholden to the parent, responsible for the parent, or even a sense of survivor guilt for being "the chosen" one while another sibling was being scapegoated. Interestingly, many golden children will report that they found it even more difficult to distance themselves from the narcissistic parent as adults for a complex set of reasons, including guilt, fear, confusion, duty, and obligation.

Narcissistic parents' inability to differentiate between themselves and their children can lead to patterns such as projection and envy. They will rally the other children or other stakeholders in the family system against the child, and siblings may join in to create a stronger alliance with them, because these siblings too may feel competitive or jealous of the child or fear the narcissistic parent. In the most extreme cases, the scapegoated child in this system will be abused, while other children do not experience abuse, a dynamic that negatively impacts all siblings within the family system.

EFFECT ON THE CHILD
Isolation, fear, and post-traumatic symptoms can be observed. Children may also be deeply confused as to why they are the sole target of a parent in a situation in which there are other siblings. This dynamic is obviously psychologically and potentially physically harmful to a child, but it also negatively affects other siblings in the family system who may subsequently feel guilty for participating or have survivor guilt for not being the target of the abuse or for not attempting to "save" their sibling. It may also model scapegoating behavior for the other children in the family, which they may take into future relationships.

HOW DOES THIS PLAY OUT INTO ADULTHOOD?
The scapegoated child may be very untrusting as an adult and may find it difficult not only to trust in intimate relationships, but also to trust other systems. There can be real fear that, within groups of friends, in school, or in work settings the scapegoating dynamic may replicate. There may also be long-term psychological and psychiatric fallout, manifested through mental illness, risky behavior, and other maladaptive behaviors such as substance use.

Over- and Underindulgence
Parents who are narcissistic and entitled are on when it works for them to be on and off when they are off—their on-ness and off-ness do not tend to mirror what the child needs; they just reflect where the parents are. When narcissistic parents do accurately mirror what the child wants, it is typically just a happy coincidence, which can be even more difficult for the child in the long run, who believes the parents *can* get it right, not

knowing that the times they do get it right are likely just luck of timing, rather than the parents' being connected in any meaningful manner. This pattern tends to be materially and superficially **overindulgent** (the theme park parent who is good for the big moments; the parent who purchases all of the latest electronic gadgets) but emotionally **underindulgent** or altogether absent (has no interest in really noticing or listening to the child when it is about feelings, vulnerabilities, or anything else that is not gratifying for the parent). It can be quite confusing for children who may have a comfortable home, plenty of toys, lovely clothes, and even lots of other interesting experiences, like vacations, yet who are rarely, if ever, heard or listened to—their emotional and internal worlds are completely underindulged.

EFFECT ON THE CHILD

Children in an over- and underindulged situation are confused. There can be some guilt that emanates from this because, on one level, their lives look "cool" and interesting, as there is often a wealth of stuff, but, on another level, there is little time or awareness from their parents. When I have worked with clients who experienced this pattern of over- and underindulgence as a child, more than once, they have said that they would have traded in the material stuff for an emotionally available parent. Children often receive the message from their parents that their material needs are being met, so asking for anything more is hubris, "You have everything a kid could want; what else do you want?" Children may not understand or be able to articulate that they have other needs— and will often just participate in the superficial stuff and needs that are being met but miss out on the critical period of developing an emotional vocabulary and an intrinsic value system.

HOW DOES THIS PLAY OUT INTO ADULTHOOD?

There may be a tendency for people to over- and underindulge themselves in adulthood. This may play out as seeking solace in superficial pursuits, such as shopping or acquiring expensive items, but not attending to their own emotional and internal needs. The echoes of guilt and confusion that may accompany this pattern may also surface as disappointment and frustration—a pattern that may be carried into adult relationships or a pattern of falling into relationships with people who provide well materially but not emotionally. Over- and underindulgence can also be a setup for their own narcissism in adulthood, because they were taught to regulate through external stimuli rather than internal modulation.

Mini-Me

In some cases, narcissistic parents will have an obsessive zeal for their children. They are typically not interested in the day-to-day work of parenting (diapers, homework, tantrums, coordinating the minutiae of a child's life), but they are the masters of the grand gesture—gifts, adventures, trips, Instagram posts. In addition, grandiose narcissists view the child as an extension of themselves, so they appear to tirelessly campaign for their child, advocating for the child with the soccer coach, greasing the skids to get the child into a particular college or private school, or getting the child connected with people associated with a family business—not for the sake of the child per se (although it may look like that to the world) but rather because they as parents want to ensure that they look good to the world, that they maintain the family brand, that their child shows the world their "greatness." Throughout this process, there is little attention paid to the child's inner or emotional world; these parents do not really "see" the child—they puppeteer the child. The child, in essence, becomes a grandiose "accessory."

EFFECT ON THE CHILD

Children of these kinds of grandiose narcissistic parents may spend their childhoods focused on achievement, as it is the only way to curry favor with the narcissistic parent. They also recognize that, if they do not go along with their parents' agenda for them, they will be rejected. It is conditional love at the most basic level.

HOW DOES THIS PLAY OUT INTO ADULTHOOD?

Well into adulthood, the children of these grandiose narcissists can remain puppets and seek validation from their domineering parents. If "mini-me" children try to carve their own niche in the world as an adult—for example, eschew the father's alma mater to choose a school that better suits their interests, avoid the family business because they would rather become an artist, or marry someone the parents do not feel is worthy of the family—then rejection is quite likely to follow. Adults who were raised in the "mini-me" scenario can often struggle with a sense of feeling imprisoned by guilt and familial expectations.

Can—or Should—You Maintain Contact as an Adult?

Many people are unwilling to "break up with" or "divorce" their parents. They value family, want their children to have grandparents, still want to be connected to other extended family or siblings, or maintain hope after years of abuse that things might turn around. In some cases, parents became disabled or ill with age, and their adult children feel a sense of responsibility for them. Because of the desire to preserve a family relationship, many of those I interviewed reported a tendency to continue to uphold the old patterns simply to stay in the relationship. They may be independent and well-put-together adults in their regular lives, but, around their parents they feel ineffectual and powerless. They still find themselves taking disproportionate and distorted ownership for what happened while they were children. There were risks to maintaining these relationships but also varied strategies for managing them (see box on page 220).

At the end of it all—as with all history—you cannot unring a bell, but you can think about it and behave differently. One story that stayed with me was that of a woman who had a brutally narcissistic and verbally abusive father. Throughout her childhood, he was prone to frequent and frightening rages, and he was cruel to her mother, who ultimately left him. As life went on, he lost most people, he no longer had a partner, and none of her siblings wanted anything to do with him. The woman I interviewed lived about an hour away from him. She said that he remained a difficult, critical, and cold but, ultimately, sad and pitiful man. Approximately every two weeks, she went to see him; she would check on him and ensure that he had groceries and other basic items that he needed. She would privately set a timer on her phone when she arrived. She found that about ninety minutes was as long as he could last before he became toxic and when the timer went off, she would leave before that happened.

When asked why she kept going to see him, she admitted that they didn't really talk about anything. Sometimes they just sat next to each other and watched TV. She said, "He didn't deserve to see me. I could have walked away from him forever with no guilt—he hurt all of us. But I recognized that I did not go there for him—I went there for me. The person I am *is* empathic. The person I am *is* kind, and I was not going to leave an old man with no one seeing him for the rest of his life. In trying to reject him, I was worried I would lose myself and, to retain my authenticity, I kept visiting him. But, to retain my sanity, I would set an alarm and get out of there before it got too toxic. I could not spend the rest of my life being angry that he was an asshole, because then I would keep living in that resentment and it would feel like he was still abusing me. I have no expectations from him to be caring or kind or respectful. I just don't want a sad old man to die alone. He doesn't really feel like a father."

Her story stayed with me because it represented the hybrid that is possible if people can let go of their expectations, remain true to themselves, and find a middle ground that doesn't leave them feeling victimized on an ongoing basis. It's just one story. I heard just as many that involved people walking away from toxic parents forever—and they were thriving and happy because they no longer had to face those situations. And I heard many stories from people who just kept taking the abuse and felt helpless to change it.

How to Navigate a Relationship With a Narcissistic Parent— and Protect Yourself

- Do not engage with the toxic parent except in the most superficial way; stick to simple topics such as the weather (the gray rock strategy).

- Do not engage when the toxic parent triggers you (purposely or not).

- Accept that the parent will not change.

- Protect your own partner. You may continue to engage with your toxic parents, but your partner may not want to witness or experience your parent's behavior.

- Do not invite parents to significant events that you know they will ruin or make about themselves (weddings, christenings, birthday parties, holidays). And, if you must invite them, assign someone to be a "handler" to manage them so you do not need to.

- Engage in minimal contact—minimize phone calls, physical contact, and text messaging.

- Remove toxic parents from your social media feeds.

Does Having a Toxic Parent Affect Your Own Parenting?

Many people reported that the moment when they recognized that having toxic and narcissistic parents impacted their own parenting was chilling, and it wound up being a real call to arms. Everyone I interviewed was deeply committed to not repeating the errors of their parents. Nearly all of them talked about how important it was for them to be clear and honest with their children—and to never gaslight them or question their reality.

In so many cases, the history of having toxic parents made them vulnerable to poor relationship choices as adults. This subsequently impacted their own children, because those toxic partners became toxic coparents. To be better parents, they committed to working on themselves and remaining aware of the impact their own poor relationship choices were having on their children.

Some acknowledged having children as a way to be loved unconditionally or finally create a functional relationship, while others noted that they did not have children because they did not feel as though they were up to the psychological challenges of being a parent, or that, after a lifetime of taking care of a parent, they did not want to take on the responsibility of taking care of a child.

I refuse to believe that having a narcissistic, sociopathic, psychopathic, or invalidating parent is a permanent destiny. I have worked directly with and observed people who endured these situations emerge with empathy and grace intact. Their adult struggles were more around self-doubt, second-guessing, and personal invalidation. I have also observed people who were crushed by these situations and find it nearly impossible to connect with their emotional worlds, other people, and a sense of safety in the world. They may even find themselves lashing out at others, as their parents lashed out at them. Your own inborn temperament can have an impact on how well you weather this storm—certain temperaments are more protective against the onslaught of abusive parents.

Perhaps the simplest shift is in language. Many people who have survived narcissistic parents think of themselves as victims and write themselves off as people who will never be able to be fully emotionally available to others. I disagree. The better word is "survivor." That simple shift in vocabulary from "victim" to "survivor" may arm you with enough strength to recognize that what happened with your parents happened *to* you—and you are not responsible for it. Nor do you need to replicate those patterns with your own children. What happened is a heavy load to carry—you can give yourself permission to put it down. The ultimate goal is then to elevate the term from "survivor" to "thriver."

The Other Parent

Pity children who have two narcissistic or toxic parents (and it happens quite often), because it can be harrowing. In some ways, the children become de facto parents for themselves, quickly learning to have to take care of things for themselves and to chronically walk on eggshells. In the absence of any advocate within the home, some children may have the good fortune to have a benevolent grandparent, godparent, aunt, uncle, or other adult stakeholder. Children from the double-narcissist-parent household have a steep mountain to climb: The attachment issues raised by this situation can set them up for a range of mental health issues in adulthood. If a child is raised by a single parent, and that parent is a narcissist, it can also have the same impact as having two narcissistic parents, because there is nowhere to receive empathy, assurance, consistency, or safety.

However, in most cases, the toxic parent is a solo act. It can be the mother or father (or stepmother or stepfather). This dynamic can be doubly painful. Not only are the children suffering from the impact of having a toxic parent and all of the fallout that accompanies that, but, also, they may be witnessing how badly the toxic parent treats the other parent. In some cases, the nontoxic parent is the one who really "saves" the children, by creating an attachment with them, caring for them, and loving them, but that nontoxic parent may also be distracted by the demands of managing the toxic spouse (because he or she will be enduring his or her own form of toxic abuse).

Parenting can then go down in one of two ways. In one way, non-narcissistic parents will attempt to protect or advocate for the child as well as they can and will be present with the child whenever possible. In these cases, it can be frustrating for the child, who deeply craves and values the time with this loving parent and will often come to resent the toxic parent for making all of their lives so miserable. The child may also become resentful and confused about why the loving parent sticks around for the abuse or doesn't end it. In the other way, the non-narcissistic parent, who means well, is so paralyzed by the toxic partner that he or she is not able to be there for the child as regularly as is needed. The toxic partner, in some ways, becomes like a louder, more problematic child that the other parent needs to deal with—with mealtimes, vacations, and day-to-day life catering to the toxic parent. In such cases, there can be deep resentment that the nontoxic parent cannot stop giving all of himself or herself to appeasing and taking care of the toxic parent.

The relationship with the other parent into adulthood can become quite complex for the children of narcissists, peppered with love and protection but also ongoing resentment—resentment about not advocating for them, for keeping them in the toxic situation, for not offering them better explanations when they were children, so they did not blame themselves for their toxic parent's treatment of them. The damage of a toxic parent on a family system is far-reaching and impacts not only the relationship between the child and the toxic parent, but also the relationships amongst all other family members.

When parents divorce and there is shared custody between a toxic, narcissistic parent and a non-narcissistic parent, it can be extremely challenging. Odds are that the divorce was contentious, and the custody battle arduous, and the time with the toxic parent in the absence of the healthier parent can become quite taxing for a child. Without the protection of the other parent, the toxic parent may become even more abusive or rageful, or may force children quickly into a new blended family (because narcissists are not good at being alone, they will often quickly jump into new relationships). The fallout of messy custody agreements and growing up in two homes that are run by very different sets of rules, is highly destabilizing for a child and fosters a sense of instability well into adulthood.

The Aftermath of Having a Narcissistic Parent

Not all narcissistic parents are created alike. Some are publicly indulgent and do not respect boundaries well—they are overly invested and involved in their children's lives (at least superficially), are controlling, and can be critical when the children do not behave the way they want them to. Some are completely disengaged, and the children are viewed, at best, as a nuisance, and it can even be worse, with parents' being verbally abusive when the children are not exactly as they want them to be. Narcissism, and the toxic symptomatology associated with it, is literally the *opposite* of the characteristics that make for a good parent. Ultimately, narcissistic and toxic parents miss the boat on providing their children with a sense of autonomy, self-efficacy, self-regulation, connection, attachment, safety, security, and unconditional love and regard.

Children who experience this type of parenting often carry a challenging legacy of varied patterns, including self-doubt, guilt, self-devaluation, poor frustration tolerance, and a tendency to try to appease other people, as well as a greater likelihood of choosing partners who tend to be narcissistic and toxic themselves.

A Chip Off the Old Block

The fact is that narcissistic and toxic parents can and do have children who go on to become narcissistic and toxic adults. If you reflect on Chapter 5, "How (Not) to Raise a Narcissist," you'll remember that ingredients such as not mirroring the child, providing only conditional love, modeling entitlement and other bad behavior, allowing the child to get caught up in the parent's grandiosity, and providing the child with inconsistent attention are the handiwork of a narcissistic or toxic parent. As a result, narcissists beget narcissists. In some ways, it makes sense: The children do not have an opportunity to learn about their emotional world; they learn they are valued only for superficial qualities and achievements, they are loved conditionally, and they are tremendously insecure.

Here's the rub: Odds are, if you are a toxic person or a narcissist, you are not reading this book. However, throughout the years as I have worked in this area, I have received countless emails from people and worked with numerous clients who come clean and say, "I am a narcissist, I am cold, I am calculating, I lack empathy, and I want to be a better person." They will describe their childhood at the hand of a cold, distant, and toxic parent (mother, father, or both) and will, as an adult, reflect on the damage it has brought to them and their close relationships. Those close to them often view this statement as a manipulation (and it may be), but, when I hear that clinically, I inform them that self-reflection and insight are important first steps (if a narcissist is not willing to acknowledge his or her patterns, then you are sunk and nothing can be done) and that it will be an arduous journey. It can be difficult to watch, because their narcissism is a challenging if not impossible boulder to move. Although they are committed to changing, under conditions of stress, loss, and/or insecurity, their typical patterns often kick in.

This, then, is the tragic legacy of narcissistic and toxic parenting: It often generates a new generation of narcissists—a new generation hobbled by insecurity, with behavior that harms themselves or other people. As this trend bucks up in our culture, and our world at large, this isn't just about larger-than-life politicians and reality TV stars sharing their shameless antics—this is about psychological damage to an entire generation and to those who may come into close contact with them.

Takeaways: Toxic Parents

Everyone I interviewed offered up advice they wish they had received or taken earlier. They shared guidance that they were living by and that they felt had significantly improved their lives:

- Trust yourself and do not second-guess yourself.
- Find a good therapist who understands narcissism.
- Establish and maintain boundaries and be aware that you will be more vulnerable to toxic people than people who may not have had toxic parents.
- Be judicious about whom you allow into your life.
- Learn to take care of yourself, because your parents did not adequately take care of you.
- Don't take the words or actions of the narcissistic parent personally.
- Distance yourself.

- If you are a young person, find a trusted, safe, and supportive adult who may be able to provide some insight.
- There is a painful recognition that you become an "orphan" if you make this mental switch of letting your parent(s) go—get the help you need to work through this.
- Read books and obtain knowledge.
- Maintain healthy friendships, as those may become a key source of self-esteem.
- Remember, this is not your fault.

There is no right strategy, but you can master this situation, you are not forever defined by it, and this becomes an opportunity to parent yourself in a way that you never were parented. The following strategies can help:

1. **Recognize that your parent is not going to change.** You are no longer eight years old and waiting for your parent(s) to get it right. As an adult, you may still be repeating that cycle, getting frustrated that your parents do not listen to you, or that they criticize you, or invalidate you—it's who they are. If you are going to keep your parents around, then adjust your perception and acknowledge that they will never change, especially as they age. With older age, your parent may become even more brittle and angry, so be prepared. Remember the concept of Radical Acceptance raised in the previous chapter. This is how it is, stop fighting it, fully accept it, and proceed accordingly.

2. **Manage your expectations.** It's the mantra for dealing with any toxic or narcissistic people. If you decide to keep them in your life, ratchet down your expectations. That doesn't mean you will never get disappointed or hurt, but hopefully you will not be blindsided, which can feel worse. Some of this is about acceptance. Many people struggle with the ideal balancing act with perhaps having to accept that their parents did the best they could, given their circumstances, but that does not mean they have to endure their parents' ongoing invalidating behavior. It's okay to practice acceptance, even compassionate acceptance, but simultaneously avoid engaging with them and maintain realistic expectations.

3. **Set boundaries.** It can be difficult to do this, but it is the only way to survive a toxic relationship with a parent. It may require a range of methods—time limits on phone calls, hours he or she can call you, having your parent (or yourself) stay in a hotel during visits, and having certain topics you do not discuss. It can also be more difficult, meaning you have to make difficult decisions, such as not having toxic parents attend certain events because you know they may mar the event. If you are a parent, you may also need to set those boundaries for your toxic parent's time and access to your children.

4. **Get therapy.** There is no real way around this. Through good work with a good therapist, you can address the patterns you experienced and devise strategies to ensure that these patterns do not keep repeating in other relationships in your adult life, as well as address patterns such as self-doubt, anxiety, and self-devaluation.

5. **Be mindful of how these patterns are impacting your life presently.** In many ways, having a toxic parent means that you have to be deeply tuned into yourself, mindful, and aware when selecting a partner. Many people with toxic and narcissistic parents almost reflexively choose an abusive partner and write off more loving and empathic partners as "boring." It can be the fight of your lifetime to let go of those old scripts and avoid choosing an avatar of your toxic parent as your new partner. You may also be more vulnerable to sticking it out with an abusive supervisor or boss or a dismissive and callous friend.

6. **Engage in self-preservation.** Do not bring up certain topics with your parents; do not make them privy to sensitive or important events in your life, especially if you know you are still vulnerable to their criticism. Stop looking for their approval—it hasn't come yet, and it won't come now.

7. **Build in buffer zones around the times you need to see your parents.** If you have a lunch date with them, take a moment before you go into the restaurant or their house to engage in some self-talk and remind yourself to manage your expectations, but also build some time in on the back end, because, no matter how

well you *do* manage your expectations, they will still manage to get under your skin. Take a moment, breathe, let it go, and get on with your day.

8. **Keep your family drama off social media.** I was recently shown a particularly toxic interaction a family had about what appeared to be a narcissistic parent, in which various adult children were parroting that their father was "dead to them." Followers on social media actually thought the old man was dead—and, when it was found out to be dramatic histrionics, the entire thread looked tacky. It is passive-aggressive to air family drama on social media. The narcissistic parent won't get it or will launch an even more toxic counterattack. In addition, it is, at best, uncomfortable for anyone who may be following your posts, and may be uncomfortable for other family members who were not involved in the social media tantrum.

Chapter 8

The Narcissist at Work

The tyrant is a child of Pride
Who drinks from his sickening cup
Recklessness and vanity,
Until from his high crest headlong
He plummets to the dust of hope.

—SOPHOCLES

"What the fuck is this???" The shouting was loud enough to be heard twenty cubicles away. "I didn't realize that incompetence was our new qualification for this job!" (A folder of papers is thrown on the floor, a pen is hurled to the ground, a chair is kicked). "Who does this? I told you I don't care that your team leader is dealing with a sick kid—not my fucking problem—you're making me look like a chump. Where the fuck is Ryan? What do you mean he went to get my coffee? I expect everyone to stay in place and be available when I need them. Stop sniveling. Oh, poor little baby, are you crying? Take that stuff, get out of here, and don't plan on seeing the inside of your house until it gets done and it gets done right! I will not have anyone make me look bad outside of here. Got it?"

Perhaps you have not witnessed anything quite this bad, or maybe you have witnessed worse. For reasons already described, narcissism in the workplace is on the rise. Not only do we incentivize it, but we are also scared of it. What makes it worse is that people who are entitled and/or narcissistic are able to don two faces at work: a charming one to clients or higher levels of management or administration and a cruel and bullying one to equals, competitors, or subordinates.

A relatively robust literature has popped up, indicating that many leaders—presidents, CEOs, prime ministers, emperors, kings, dictators, senators, mayors, and many other types of leaders—are more likely to be narcissistic than the rest of the population. In some ways, it doesn't add up. Why put the entitled people without empathy in charge of the entire enterprise when they are less likely to be concerned with the well-being of the individuals in the system? Those leaders who got there through birthright (an emperor or a king) may have been raised with such privilege that entitlement is a given. The rest had to keep fighting until they got there.

It may not be you who has the toxic boss. You may have a partner, family member, or friend who is enduring a toxic boss—and you keep hearing about it or watching the person close to you suffer. This can be so difficult because you may feel helpless and, at times, frustrated. Even though it is not your toxic workplace situation, it is still taking a toll on you. Or the toxic leader may not be someone you work for, but it may be someone who is a leader in the country, state, or town in which you live—and the media coverage of his or her leadership can be difficult to hear about, which results in that same sense of helplessness. Toxic leadership hurts more people than just those who are unfortunate enough to work directly for these people. Sadly, it is a trend that is not likely to go away anytime soon. Until people truly understand why they fall under the sway of these leaders, and until we stop rewarding them—whether they are elected, appointed, corporate, or any other form of institutional leaders—for their bad behavior and incivility, this is a trend that is likely to grow in the years to come.

One question that arises is where the line tips from a "tough" boss or leader to a "toxic" one. Tough bosses may be perfectionistic, exacting, and demanding, and these demands may be so unreasonable that such leaders and bosses are termed toxic. However, from my perspective, the tip-over into toxic territory really comes down to abuse and antagonism. Does the leader's conduct induce fear? Is the leader unempathic to the needs of the workforce, the clients, and others who interface with the organization?

Are communications characterized by humiliation, degradation, insults, or contempt? Does the leader demonstrate rage or other dysregulated displays of emotion in response to frustration or disappointment? Does the leader undermine employees within the organization, or otherwise abuse, exploit, or manipulate them? There are "tough" bosses out there who are able to maintain high standards while also having empathy, maintaining fairness, demonstrating appropriate emotional reactions, and ensuring employees and stakeholders feel safe and heard. Toxic leadership is about the process of leadership, and their conduct as leaders and as human beings. As you can imagine, narcissists are over-represented in the ranks of toxic leaders, bosses, and co-workers.

In this chapter we'll explore why toxic leaders can draw people in, the harm they cause to everyone, and why they appear to be on the rise. Sometimes the toxic person in your workplace isn't your boss—it may be your colleague or someone you supervise—and we'll take a look at that, too. You may have felt pressured to take a job you needed or may not have the option of leaving until you find another position, so I'll arm you with strategies for surviving a toxic workplace.

The Tyrant's Appeal

Interestingly, one might think that toxic leaders would be vilified or would send people running to find a new job, but Jean Lipman-Blumen, a professor of public policy, talks about their magnetism in her book *The Allure of Toxic Leaders*. Interestingly, she notes that not only are people not repelled by a toxic leader, but they may actually be drawn to them in some cases. There have been too many successful tyrants in our world, so somehow their approach works. But why?

Her description of what comprises toxic leaders is pretty much identical to what makes for narcissists, toxic people, and even psychopaths:

- Lack of integrity.
- Tendency to lie (especially lying to fortify their grandiose visions for the world or the company).
- Grandiose ambitions that they believe are bigger and more important than any individual human being within the organization.

- Arrogance and fostering a culture that rewards corruption and backstabbing as employees attempt to curry favor with them (it's almost as though the employees in these settings are like children trying to win the love of an unavailable and self-absorbed parent).
- Chronic intimidation, demoralization, and marginalization of others within the organization so that everyone is walking on eggshells and wondering when they will have to face the leader's wrath (or the wrath of one of his or her minions).
- Violation of the basic human rights of employees.
- Disproportionate and very personal criticism (rather than con-structive feedback) of employees.
- Undermining potential competitors, such as people who could become their successors, so they can hold tight to their power with no heir apparent anywhere nearby.

Toxic leaders tend to have an inner retinue of enablers and yes-men who do their bidding and protect them. Some of these hangers-on are hoping for a big payout, or for the crumbs and perceived power they experience by being in proximity to a toxic leader. Some just get "grandi-osity by proxy" by being close to a powerful person. Some may be family members who are somewhat shielded from the toxic burn due to their historical ties to the leader. And some are just as toxic and are earning their chops by learning from the master. They represent a new generation of toxic leaders who are being "mentored" in the finer points of narcis-sistic leadership. The sycophants who tend to hang around toxic leaders are the ones who take the blame when things go wrong and allow the toxic boss to take all the credit when things go right. They are the ones who are fired, let go, publicly shamed, or even imprisoned when things go south, leaving the toxic leader protected in many circumstances. It's a gamble to work for a tyrannical and narcissistic leader—you may end up in jail as a fall guy or you may wind up getting the keys to the kingdom (at least temporarily).

Another way that toxic leaders are "successful" is that, like all toxic people, they are able to exploit the vulnerabilities of their employees. In this way, they are similar to cult leaders because they exploit very human needs. Lipman-Blumen notes that toxic leaders play on common human needs, such as the need for authority, for security, to feel special, and for belongingness, as well as playing on the fear of ostracism and the fear of powerlessness. In some ways, those who gravitate to authoritarianism (and this can happen for any number of reasons, including having had highly authoritarian parents—especially fathers—or a desire for a sense of control and order) are more vulnerable to being drawn to highly authoritarian leaders. In much of the world, children are raised to obedience, and this propensity to obedience is putty in an authoritarian leader's hands and capitalizes on the need and admiration for authority many people maintain.

Toxic leaders are masterful at playing upon fear and, as such, can create complex and punitive policies that are framed as fostering safety and security but really are overkill. However, these policies give the toxic leader even more moral authority. Toxic leaders can facilitate a need for specialness and a need for belonging by bringing special perks into the workplace—this could be ultramodern and beautiful physical surroundings, lavish parties, bonus trips and other incentives, fully stocked lunchrooms, and other "goodies" that may not exist in other workplaces. There may even be inspirational speeches and rallies in which the toxic leader gets up on a stage or speaks through a large series of monitors and tells people they are the chosen and are part of a special organization. They foster a sense of specialness, which is seductive enough to eclipse any doubts about their despotism.

All of this plays off that fear of being ostracized. People do not want to be left out, and, if they were to speak against the toxic leader, there would be a strong likelihood that they would be put out, fired, or publicly called out. Many people in these environments are afraid to speak out. Thus, they may have the sense that perhaps they are the only ones who feel this way and that they are being "overly sensitive" to the toxic leadership. *Toxic leadership situations leave people feeling powerless*—powerless to remove the leader, powerless to correct the situation, powerless to have their voice heard. Many leave these kinds of jobs out of sheer psychological exhaustion or trauma or just plain disgust. But many endure because they cannot conceive of an alternative, or they get stuck because the job may pay so much more than other comparable jobs, or because they have other factors that keep them stuck, such as a retirement plan or other financial payouts, or because they truly believe that, if they stick it out one more quarter, one more year, things will get figured out. They believe that they can outlast the leader.

At times of insecurity—cultural or economic insecurity, wartime, times when there is the threat of war—toxic leaders flourish. Their greatest strength is to take insecurity and use it to their advantage. And, if it is not presently a time of insecurity, they will create it through workplace turmoil, frequent shifts in other leadership or management, or simply through their behavior. In addition, toxic leaders are masterful at "internecine warfare"—basically, they turn people against one another in the workplace. They polarize people, ensure that factions are created, and use employees against employees to maintain that sense of insecurity and hold on to their toxic pulpit.

As noted earlier, one of the traits that often clouds us to the dangers of an approaching narcissist is charisma—and charisma is a trait that is viewed as being important in a leader. A paper published by Jasmine Vergauwe, a researcher in the Department of Developmental Personality and Social Psychology at Ghent University, and her colleagues actually indicates that there is such a thing as too much charisma. They found a charisma "sweet spot" in the midrange; too little charisma was not rated well, but neither was too much. They believe that leaders with moderate levels of charisma are good at developing innovative strategies and at carrying them out (people with higher levels of charisma tend to come up short on the execution of strategies). Interestingly, these researchers found that leaders in their study believed that more charisma is better and overestimated the value of this trait. We also make the mistake of conflating charisma and capability, as well as charisma and leadership, and we make this mistake both in personal and work relationships.

#Everyonegetshurt by Toxic Leaders

In the wake of the #metoo and Time's Up movements, while I was emboldened to witness women speaking out against harassment in the workplace, these movements are disproportionately focused on the experiences of women from higher socioeconomic backgrounds or with more power in the workplace. This runs the danger of missing the majority of women who are regularly harassed and who have little recourse because they cannot survive without a job and are concerned about retribution. Workplace harassment is far more likely to happen to women in lower-wage jobs, such as in the food, beverage, hospitality, retail, and manufacturing industries, which account for nearly 40 percent of the jobs in which sexual harassment charges are made (Center for American Progress, 2018). But I was also concerned about the fact that the #metoo movement was missing something else. The conversation became so sexualized that no one was willing to mention the latest "N-word," narcissism. As I read story after story, this was about toxic leadership and exploitation and incivility and the normalization of entitled behavior in the workplace and just about everywhere else in the world. Abuse in the workplace affects both women and men. Sexual harassment is an important and deeply painful element of workplace abuse, but there is also the abuse people regularly suffer at the hands of a toxic and narcissistic supervisor who is a bully. Because we view many of the qualities of narcissism as being increasingly synonymous with leadership, perhaps a secondary #metoo campaign needs to expand to anyone—woman or man—who has been damaged by working for a toxic, narcissistic boss or supervisor.

Research examining the underpinnings of sexual harassment struggles to balance how much stems from our toxic culture and how much stems from the personality of the perpetrators. John Pryor, a professor of psychology at Illinois State University, has spent thirty years researching why men sexually harass, and his research has revealed that the three characteristics most consistently observed in harassers are a lack of empathy, belief in traditional gender roles, and a tendency toward dominance and authoritarianism. Not surprisingly, these are traits that provide the infrastructure of narcissism and entitlement. When those traits are placed in a context in which there is little consequence for the harassers' behaviors and they can perpetrate these deeds with impunity, then their behavior is, in essence, rewarded and will be likely to persist. Because narcissists have little insight, they are also highly unlikely to be self-reflective on the impact of their behavior not only on the other person, but also on the organization at large. The bottom line? Harassers don't care whom they hurt and, without real consequences, they will keep doing it. Never expect self-policing from a toxic leader.

People who work under the color of authority—whether because of their job title or the perception that they can wield power—have a tremendous advantage. Researchers at the Stanford University School of Business observed that the presence of a person who is perceived to be powerful can result in shifts in neurotransmitter levels, particularly serotonin. That shift can manifest as a slight distracted paralysis when faced with the "authority figure," during which a person feels unable to respond, engage, or react. Under such circumstances, many people may just do what they are told to do, and either do not question it or feel powerless to change it even if they want to (many people will think about an hour later, "Darn it, I wish I had said this" or, "I wish I had said that"—that missed opportunity is a by-product of becoming "paralyzed" or perhaps "mesmerized" in the face of an authority figure). This becomes a very dangerous setup when the person in power is also toxic or narcissistic, because it can sustain his or her bad behavior and diminish the likelihood that people will speak out against the abuse or the toxic leader. Interestingly, having power also affects neurotransmitter levels and brain function in a person who perceives he or she has the power, and work by multiple researchers finds an association between power or the perception of having power with increases in dopamine and enhanced executive functioning, as well as an enhanced sense of well-being.

Why Are Toxic Leaders Tolerated?

Many people find themselves scratching their heads as to why toxic behavior in the workplace is allowed to persist. Why doesn't anyone call these people out for their behavior? There have been numerous explanations put forward for this (each explanation more unsatisfying than the one before it). People are often unwilling to listen to the complaints made about someone, particularly a powerful someone who may have a reputation for excellence (profitability, major awards, professional achievements), because it would sully their image of that person. Powerful people are often quite valuable to an institution, a company, or a government, and others hold the blind hope that a complaint is a one-off (in many cases, it is a 1,000-off) that will disappear if they make the reporting process difficult enough. Institutions ranging from major corporations to universities to the UN have all been criticized for labyrinthine employee harassment and abuse reporting procedures (all the better to discourage already exhausted survivors of the abuse). The perpetrators often rely on their reputations and credentials to protect them. People are genuinely surprised when people with prestigious degrees and credentials, or prominent families, or important job titles finally get formally called out. These people with credentials are often protected for years, with the result that many more people are victimized. People find it hard to believe that a business leader who went to an Ivy League university would be capable of domestic violence or would be an abusive parent. That disbelief can lead their victims into the shadows, feeling silenced in their ability to seek out help, because they are afraid that no one will believe their allegations (and their fear is often borne out).

Their rationalization, and the rationalization of other stakeholders within the company or institution, is that the narcissistic leader may be generating "results," and the leader himself or herself may acknowledge that his or her style is "hard-driving" but that it is designed to generate said "results." It often reflects the hazing ritual or militaristic approach that characterizes so many industries, as though those whose spirit isn't broken by an abusive leader somehow represent the best workers. This stance of "hazing" is a rationalization applied to these leadership situations, and anyone who balks at them can be called out as weak or not well suited to a given profession. Once again, the toxic leader holds his or her power.

In addition, the colleagues or other people familiar with these abusers and harassers will often not heed the complaints because they themselves did not experience any harassment or abuse or witness any, so they do not want to believe it (which is a ridiculous disbelief). If a predatory narcissist preys only on young women, the odds that he would sexually abuse a male colleague at an equal level are very low (though he may still be a difficult overseer for male subordinates). *The Los Angeles Times* reported on the scandal of a former dean of the University of Southern California's medical school who had been living a double life of drug abuse and cavorting with sex workers, while serving as the highly valued and highly paid head of the medical school, and yet the institution stalled in its response, despite multiple complaints from other physicians, staff, and other individuals affiliated with the medical school. USC also supported a student health center physician who has now been accused by hundreds of women of sexually abusing them during gynecological exams. Multiple coworkers came forth and attempted to file complaints and encouraged frightened patients to do so. The university turned a blind eye for more than a decade. In both cases, the education, credentials, and fund-raising prowess of the individuals in question protected them. Institutions, when painted into a corner, issue anemic statements rationalizing their glacial attempts to take action. While all of us can appreciate due diligence, more lives are being destroyed by the toxic abuse of these authority figures while the clock is ticking. Sadly, in many of these cases, it is less about due diligence and more about "We hope this will go away," and the risk of this happening may be pronounced at universities, where the revolving door of students often means that students will graduate and leave, and the institutional memory can then fade.

Research by psychology professors and researchers Jonathan Kunstman at Miami University of Ohio and Jon Maner at Northwestern University reveals that powerful men actually overestimate the sexual interest that others have in them and, as such, behave in accordance with those misperceptions. Because they have power, their misperception almost becomes a problem with reality testing. These guys actually believe their own hype and skewed truth and assume everyone else is on board. When you lack empathy and are deeply entitled, you think everyone wants to bang you. It's a slippery slope. These powerful men truly believe that, if they propositioned someone, their target would gladly yield to the joy of sex with them.

Narcissistic and toxic leaders are also masterful at squeezing out dissenting voices. They will fire them or remove them, when possible, or make life so miserable or uncomfortable that they leave. Over time, this results in a workplace in which most people, especially those who are closest to the leader, are chronic yes-men and sycophants and, in that way, the toxic leader is able to maintain a distorted and almost delusional sense that everyone is in agreement with him or her. Narcissistic leaders are often genuinely surprised when there is vocal disagreement, largely because they have become so accustomed to hearing voices of agreement. This is actually a universal trend with narcissists—they tend to surround themselves with voices that agree with them and silence those that do not. Because of their greater likelihood of having wealth or power, they are able to attract subservient lackeys who will keep pumping them up. In this way, toxic leaders end up with workplaces full of toxic colleagues and toxic or brainwashed employees, with everyone joining the delusional chorus of voices that exist to support the regime of the narcissistic leader. Thus, when big companies fail, while there are obviously market forces at play, it is also likely that they hit a critical mass of toxicity: toxic leaders throwing tantrums about not getting big enough bonuses, C-suite-level folks engaged in all types of lies, and the rank and file living in fear or simply blindly following the cult-like demands of the environment and both wittingly and unwittingly becoming participants in the toxic community. It's like a house being eaten from the inside out by termites and rodents. One day, it does all come crashing down to the ground. It is for this reason that silently assuming that toxic leadership and narcissistic bosses are the new normal could actually hurt business as a whole, as well as quality of life for most of us.

Sometimes they are tolerated because they overcompensate by providing higher compensation than is typically observed in an industry, or offer incentives and perks that are not typically observed. This largesse can buy loyalty. No one wants to kill the golden goose, even when he or she is rageful, arrogant, toxic, and cruel. It becomes a Faustian bargain, and may diminish the likelihood of people seeking out recourse against a toxic boss if the financial and material benefits are so enticing.

Toxic bosses do not change and are hard to displace. Even middle-level toxic managers are masterful at massaging the egos at the top of the corporate or leadership ladder and treating the employees under them horribly. That means it can be difficult to get recourse from higher-level leaders. They may actually view the toxic midlevel leaders in the organizations benevolently, because they are treated well by them. (In fact, this is how, in so many instances, a foolish CEO, university president, or community leader gets in front of a group looking simply flustered about substantiated charges of an abusive person in their organization—because the leader was treated well by that person and so could not imagine that the person would abuse someone else.)

Which Came First, the Narcissism or the Leader?

Power, narcissism, incivility, entitlement, and toxic relationships are all spokes of the same wheel. Narcissistic and toxic people are often more drawn to being leaders, which raises a chicken-egg issue: Perhaps narcissistic traits are chosen for leadership, or perhaps being a leader results in more narcissism. Is narcissism a precondition for leadership in our current era of entitlement and toxicity? Or has it always been a quality that is more likely to be observed in a leader?

When we reflect on what we know about narcissism developmentally, it is more likely that the narcissistic personality style predated the leadership position and the quest for power and not vice versa (in layperson's terms: They were always jerks). University of California, Berkeley psychology professor Dacher Keltner's research on power supports the idea that power is associated with impulsivity, less adherence to social codes, and less awareness or even caring about one's effect on other people. In essence, power is associated with a lack of empathy and the presence of entitlement and carelessness (which logically extends the argument that power and narcissism go hand in hand). In an article in the *Harvard Business Review*, Keltner argues that power actually would corrupt anyone—and that we would all become vulnerable to these behavior patterns if we got power (he terms this "the banality of the abuses of power"). He has tested this using laboratory experiments and findings that are echoed by other infamous social psychology experiments, such as Philip Zimbardo's Prison Experiment. The Stanford Prison Experiment was conducted by Stanford psychology professor Philip Zimbardo in which Stanford students were randomly assigned to either be "guards" or "prisoners" in an attempt to understand whether sadistic behavior by prison guards is dispositional (simply who they are) or situational (created by the situation). In a short period of time, the guards took on their role and began brutalizing the prisoners, and the experiment was actually terminated early because the situation deteriorated so quickly. The Stanford Prison Experiment and Keltner's research both support this idea of "the banality of the abuses of power"—or that any of us would become abusive tyrants if given enough power.

Both of those researchers suggest that power corrupts, but my read on it is that power corrupts the corruptible. Most people who are not corruptible probably do not reach for leadership in the first place. Two of the best and most brilliant academics I know, who are world renowned for their work, never left their faculty positions for the climb through academic administration to higher-paid jobs as deans, provosts, or presidents. They are vaunted by their colleagues and respected by everyone for their integrity and their scholarship. They are also deeply empathic, respectful, and kind men. When I turned to them for mentorship and asked them why they never reached upward for a leadership position, they smiled and basically said, "Who needs the headache? I love my students, I love my research, and the money isn't worth the hassle." I found it fascinating that, even when offered such options, they didn't take them. Power is not equally appealing to everyone. Obviously, not all leaders are toxic, and, in fact, most are not, but the people who do assiduously pursue leadership and the power that goes with it are more likely to possess narcissistic traits than the rank and file who often derive meaning and purpose from their work.

In real life, the people who get power are the people who seek power, and the people who seek power are more likely to possess the patterns associated with narcissism. Thus, the odds that your boss will lack empathy and be entitled are higher than they are for a random person.

Narcissistic and toxic bosses can often hide behind a veneer of a company's excellence, whether that is profit; a charitable foundation that does good around the world; acclaimed films, writing, or artwork; or just a great brand. If there is any connection between people and work they have created that could actually leave others feeling good—films, art, charities—then it can easily mask their toxicity to the rest of the world. Toxic bosses also impact the culture of a company. With a sufficiently tyrannical leader at the helm of a company, it is simply a matter of time before that company's, institution's, or organization's culture shifts—and begins embodying the toxic traits of its leadership. The echoes left by narcissistic leadership can ring for many, many years. Increasingly, corporate entities are swift to distance themselves from toxic behaviors that may make shareholders nervous, but years of damage may occur to employees working for that individual before the public failure that leads to the person's dethroning.

Moral Cleansing Theory: Why It Fails with Narcissistic Bosses

Some believe that not all bosses who yell or inappropriately criticize are narcissists or difficult people. A study conducted in China by Zhenyu Liao, a professor at the Olin School of Business at Washington University, and his colleagues and published in the *Harvard Business Review* focuses on "moral cleansing theory." This theory posits that people try

241

to balance moral actions and immoral actions, and, if someone behaves in an immoral way (for example, screaming at work), then he or she will engage in behaviors to offset that "inappropriate" behavior to restore his or her moral image. Interestingly, these authors found that, after leaders behaved badly and felt guilty about this behavior, they would then engage in supportive behaviors to "morally cleanse" themselves. This is a great finding, except the authors did not determine whether the leaders were narcissistic or otherwise toxic.

The rub in this study is it assumes that, in order to engage in this "moral cleansing" and be a nice boss after dressing down staff, the leaders had morally aware or morally sensitive dispositions. That's a big assumption. More important, these authors also noted that leaders who scored low in moral attentiveness (for example, narcissistic or toxic leaders) did not make amends or offer support to their employees afterward (they just screamed or bullied and never tried to make it right). Given that most American companies do not use "morality" as a gauge for hiring leaders or promoting employees, the whole moral cleansing theory is not going to help most people. In addition, how long would you want to stay on this carousel—even if you had a boss who was willing to engage in any form of "moral cleansing?" Boss yells, boss feels morally bad, boss apologizes. Or boss yells, never really apologies but is extra nice (or offers up an anemic incentive like a pizza party) to compensate, and then, down the line, the boss yells again. If you are lucky, you get a morally aware and apologetic boss but, after a while, it starts to feel like any abusive relationship, and the apologies (or the pizza parties) will not offset your discomfort (and may make you tense about even seeing your boss or going to work, because you know what is coming).

Your Narcissistic Coworkers

While many people struggle with narcissistic and toxic bosses because they can wield power, do not underestimate the impact of a toxic coworker. In some ways, this can be even more profound, because you may have more regular contact with your coworkers, and because they may be in direct competition with you, their narcissistic machinations and manipulations may actually be more damaging to your career. It is not unusual for them to take more credit for work than is deserved, to monitor your behavior so they can use it against you, to gain your trust and then share those confidences down the road, to behave in a passive-aggressive manner, to violate boundaries with you or other coworkers (or engage in inappropriate relationships to advance their career), to create toxic alliances that can contribute to divisive workplaces, and to issue false accusations that negatively impact your reputation in the workplace.

Odds are that your narcissistic colleagues are narcissistic across the board and difficult at home, with friends, and with others in the workplace. However, they can be Machiavellian to the core and may be masterful at playing up to supervisors and company or institutional leaders, colleagues who will support them, and clients. It is here that their charm and charisma often leave them looking better than the colleagues they are harassing, a dynamic that merely adds insult to injury.

It is not unusual for people to feel blindsided by a narcissistic coworker. They may actually find themselves drawn in by toxic colleagues, and then, down the line, find out that some office gossip that was shared during a happy hour under the presumption that it was just "office chat" comes back to bite them. In more than a few cases, the toxic colleagues seem to outlast everyone, and it may very well be that, in the name of self-preservation, other people leave the workplace instead of enduring the toxic coworker. The long-term "commitment" of the toxic worker may seem like loyalty to folks higher up the command chain but, to anyone in the know, that kind of turnover should get further scrutiny. Many fellow workers may feel that it is not worth it to take on the fight and may quietly find a new job.

In addition, narcissistic employees can be very expensive for organizations. They are more likely to litigate and file grievances, and, as such, the organization may actually do more to appease the toxic employee than a deserving one, simply in the name of risk management and to avoid more problems. In this way, many organizations may find themselves hobbled by a critical mass of narcissistic employees (because everyone else leaves), and this, coupled with narcissistic leadership, can wind up eating an organization from the inside out.

A toxic coworker can insert significant stress into your work life, and we know that workplace stress is a form of stress that takes a significant toll on your health. Management and organizational researchers Joel Goh, Jeffrey Pfeffer, and Stefanos Zenios examined the impacts of poor management on health and on the basis of their data concluded that over 120,000 deaths per year and between 5-8 percent of health care costs may be related to workplace management.

Caitlin Demsky, an assistant professor of management at Oakland University, and her colleagues have reported on the association between insomnia and difficult workplaces. Their work suggests that we get caught in obsessive loops of thinking about our toxic workplace, which can make falling asleep and staying asleep difficult. Anyone who has ever had toxic coworkers knows what it is like to lie awake at two in the morning and get stuck in thinking about it, stewing over it, and feeling helpless in the face of it. We spend a significant proportion of our waking hours at work and, sadly, if it is a difficult job or toxic workplace, it can encroach upon the hours we have at home with family or friends, or even while we sleep.

If a toxic coworker has been there longer than you have and may very well be the last (wo)man standing, pay attention to that; the turnover may have occurred for a reason. When you do have toxic colleagues, it is essential that you dot your i's and cross your t's, because these people are often like hawks, monitoring the landscape for any transgressions or slips that they can use to their advantage. Boundaries and documentation are your best defense against toxic coworkers. It is also critical that you keep detailed notes and files on your contribution to product, sales, and other outcomes in the workplace—don't be surprised if your coworker blithely takes credit for your work. That documentation can be invaluable if there is a need to substantiate your work in the face of his or her claims.

Why Did You Take the Job in the First Place?

Obviously, sometimes you take a job because it may be difficult to find a job in your chosen profession, or because you need to pay the bills. At times of economic downturn, beggars can't be choosers. In some cases, you entered a sane workplace, but then, over time, due to retirements or changes in leadership, the toxic balance shifted, and the workplace you are now in looks quite different than the one you began in. However, when there is a choice, why do people wind up in jobs with toxic coworkers, narcissistic bosses, and toxic cultures? When postmortems are conducted with people who are leaving the painful battlefield of a job in which they had a particularly toxic boss, one question that arises is, "Why did you take the job?" Many people recollect feeling that their boss was unsettling very early on, even during the interview phase, or that they had heard from others in their industry that this person was difficult or even dangerous to work with.

The cognitive error that gets many people stuck is the idea that they will be the exception to the rule. The perception is, "Now that I know what he is about, I will be able to handle this." It is a bit irrational to believe that dozens of employees before you had been abused, criticized, or otherwise degraded by this person and that, for some reason, you would be the one to emerge unscathed. When reviewing the stories of particularly traumatizing bosses in the news of late, the recurring theme we can see is, "If I can just break into this company [or industry] and endure this toxic boss, then I will be able to sail on my own." For example, if a toxic boss disproportionately harasses and abuses female employees, a male employee may avoid the worst of the abuse, but, ultimately, toxic bosses create toxic workspaces, and survivor guilt can also plague those in situations in which coworkers were horribly treated. The one rule of thumb to remember with toxic people, including toxic and narcissistic bosses, is that you are not going to be the exception, and the toll of enduring or observing the abuse may not be worth it in the long run. There are no exceptions when it comes to narcissism. Everyone gets hurt; the question is how you face it down. During the interview phase, the three Cs of narcissism rear their head: confidence, charisma, and charm. We want to believe that this smooth, charismatic future boss we are meeting is the real thing, but those ten minutes of charm during an interview may be the last time you see that trait during your professional career with the person. Before taking a job, do your due diligence to the degree possible. Dig deep and try to get offline data on the real deal in that workplace. You may not always be able to get it, but it is worth an attempt.

The financial costs are also likely to be quite high. There are no statistics on the cost of narcissistic bosses in terms of productivity, but we can speculate that the cost of toxic behavior in the workplace results in healthcare costs, lost dollars due to disability or inefficiency that results from working with toxic coworkers and bosses, lawsuits resulting from pursuing damages against toxic coworkers and bosses, and other impacts of the toxic workers and bosses on clients, consumers, and the public at large. Toxic people themselves also tend to pursue frivolous and costly lawsuits against coworkers and employers and anyone else they perceive has wronged them, which can inflate insurance premiums for everyone from healthcare providers to drivers. The headlines of late have shown in no uncertain terms how costly narcissistic behavior can be in the workplace. Perhaps companies should simply build in a "narcissism tax" to draw from when their narcissistic leaders finally get caught.

It's Not Fair

No, it probably is not. Working with toxic bosses and narcissistic leaders can be even more taxing because it feels so unfair. Your work may be far better than that of a colleague, and yet your more politically well-connected colleague who has won over the difficult boss keeps getting raises and awards. You may be the brains behind a new concept or idea that your toxic boss then takes credit for. You may work on a team and find that one or two toxic colleagues have hijacked the team and are fostering uncivil discourse and derailing the efforts of the team while continuing to profit. When things are unjust, it feels awful, and this dynamic can be multiplied at work where the rules of fairness and logic are believed to apply—if you do better work, you expect to get recognized.

We have established throughout this book that relationships in any form with a narcissist feel unfair and unjust. It can be soul-sapping to observe a toxic colleague get raises, bonuses, and recognition. It can be demoralizing to witness an abusive boss be honored by the world at large and get bigger compensation year after year. It can be disgusting to watch a boss, leader, or colleague who is harassing and abusing subordinate employees get away with it. The lack of justice, sanctions, or consequences for toxic colleagues and leaders can sway your faith in life and take a toll on your mental and physical health. There is something to be learned from this. Narcissistic leaders often demand blind loyalty, despite behaving badly. Interestingly, Tianjiao Qiu, a professor of marketing at California State University Long Beach, and her colleagues reported that task and team performance improve when managers treat the team members fairly in their interpersonal interactions with them. Basically, treating employees fairly is better for everyone—employees, the organization, and leadership. Nonetheless, waiting for fairness, equity, and justice with a toxic leader is likely to yield nothing more than demoralization.

Takeaways: Toxic Bosses and Colleagues

Since toxic bosses or supervisors are not going to change, waiting around thinking that today is the day that they will give you credit for your work, mentor you, or foster your career is like waiting for a bus that is never going to arrive. Manage your expectations and recognize that they will not change or improve their behavior and, in fact, you can expect the opposite. The following strategies will help you to survive a toxic work environment:

1. **Document the hell out of the behavior.** Hopefully by reading thus far, you know the red flags, the signs, the definitions, and the landscape of narcissism. It is a good practice when you start in a job to make folders and start saving emails and then, as things evolve, especially if your boss is invalidating, dodgy, abusive, dishonest, or otherwise makes you uncomfortable, definitely save everything (and, if legally permissible, keep a copy of your documentation on your personal computer or device; otherwise generate hard copies and store them carefully). Take screenshots of text messages and save those as well. HR and supervisors really cannot do much without documentation, since you cannot just say, "He [or she] was mean to me" or, "He [or she] lied to me" and hope for much support. It is amazing how much narcissists put into writing that is damning—the key is to save it all.

2. **Avoid meeting with narcissistic bosses or coworkers alone.** Narcissistic, toxic, and entitled people often prefer phone conversations and one-on-one meetings, because they work better for bullying, and it is much harder to get proof of this behavior when you are alone with them (states including California have laws that prevent recording people without their permission, and such recordings typically become inadmissible without consent). In addition, they tend to be very inconsistent, saying one thing and then denying it later (workplace gaslighting), so getting something in writing is essential. Ask to have someone else present at meetings whenever possible. If that is not possible,

then ensure that you send a clearly written memo right after the meeting reiterating the key points of the meeting (ideally with the read receipts feature turned on). Even if they deny their words down the road, you have set some form of paper trail. Other than unavoidable chance encounters in places such as elevators (if you can, hop out and take the stairs), restrooms, or parking lots, do not take meetings alone or in non-workspaces, such as bars, hotel rooms, restaurants, or their homes. Even if an administrative person is taking minutes at a meeting that is not being recorded, ensure that you keep your own notes as well (it is possible that the notetaker may be part of the machine that is attempting to protect the toxic leader or has been instructed to take notes in a way to shield the leader from rebuke).

3. **Don't engage with them.** Many times, they dig their own grave through their conduct. When we try to engage and argue with them, their tendency to gaslight, project, and downright lie can often leave us wanting to defend ourselves. Pretend you are in a deposition, offer short answers, stick to the facts, and then let them be the ones who throw the tantrums. It's frustrating to feel you cannot share your reality, but it is a waste of breath because they won't listen anyhow.

4. **Be your own best advocate.** The difficult fact about working with entitled or narcissistic people is that they forward their own cause to the detriment of others—the classic "throwing other people under the bus." This puts you in a position of having to be your own advocate, letting supervisors or others at your workplace know about your achievements, contributions, and other good work (it is not unusual for a narcissistic or entitled coworker or supervisor to take credit for your work or downplay it, so make sure you get credit in any way you can, but also let others know of your contribution). This can be difficult for people who are humble by nature, but it may be better than losing your job or opportunity for advancement.

5. **Keep your social media clean.** The pent-up frustration of working with a narcissist can culminate in a desire to let the world

know about your tribulations. Narcissistic people will run with that and get you in the doghouse with HR very quickly, or they will engage with you. Even if the narcissistic person is not privy to your postings, it still becomes a public record and can hurt you down the road if the challenges at work get worse and place you in a position of having to defend your posts, rather than keeping the focus on the narcissistic boss or colleague. Posting on social media may also be in violation of certain company policies.

6. **Try to turn work off at times.** Toxic colleagues or bosses can infect your entire life. These situations can preoccupy you when you are with family and friends, on the weekends, or when you are on vacation. It can be difficult to avoid ruminating about it. If that happens, then they win, because you are still mentally at work and in conflict with them. Trust me, they are not spending their downtime thinking about you. This may mean ensuring that you are well fed, get decent sleep, and find ways of escape (ideally in places or situations that do not allow for cell phones or devices or emails in which reminders of the workplace exist). And, most important, avoid looking at your device in the hour before bedtime—reading a petty email at that time can keep you up half the night and leave you even more depleted the next day.

7. **Focus on what they do and not what they say.** Toxic bosses can be quite charming—that is part of how they advanced up the ranks. They will use their charm on you, so, when they make promises or fluff you up, it can be easy to forget the actual actions they have engaged in. As with all human beings, judge them by their actions and not by their words. If your toxic boss makes a big promise or feeds you lots of nice compliments, it doesn't mean a thing if it is at odds with his or her abusive behavior or is not followed up with real action. Do not allow yourself to be fooled.

8. **Craft an escape plan.** The odds are that a toxic leader or supervisor will outlast you. Start slowly crafting an escape plan. Quietly explore new career options (but be careful not to share them, because, if your impending escape gets back to your toxic boss, he or she may think you are disloyal and either turn your remaining

time on the job into a living hell or sabotage your attempt to seek new employment). Focus on building your portfolio at your present job and find allies who may vouch for you, and the hope of possibly escaping may make each day with that narcissistic boss a little more bearable.

9. **Avoid "social meetings."** While social meetings at trade shows, conventions, during work travel, or even while in town may seem like an essential form of networking in certain industries, they can be lethal with toxic bosses. These may include solo drinks meetings, meetings in hotel rooms or other private spaces, or casual meals or drinks while on business travel with toxic bosses. These settings are fertile ground for inappropriate requests or comments, and, sadly, the way the system is constructed, other stakeholders will often blame or call into question the motives of the person who joined the toxic boss for the meeting. The kind of favor you will curry with a toxic boss under these conditions is not likely to do you any favors and may even be more likely to raise problems for you.

10. **Listen to coworkers to determine if others are having similar experiences.** Lipman-Blumen's work suggests that, under conditions of toxic leadership, employees may actually band together and become stronger as a group. Be cautious, as it may be unclear if everyone can be trusted. Finding allies can help you cope, and the strength in numbers may also lead you as a group to develop your own venture, support one another's ideas, or at least give you the strength to get out.

11. **Don't get tempted or tricked by superficial manipulations.** While an in-house gym, ping-pong tables, free cappuccinos, or lavish tropical corporate retreats may be tempting, they are not sufficient in the long term to make a toxic boss worth it. Toxic institutions and bosses can buy devotion and loyalty by "spoiling" their employees, sometimes even through better compensation. Perhaps every soul has a price—be clear on yours, but also be clear on the toll. Would it be better to work for less money, perks, or prestige to work in a setting in which you are not abused?

12. **Bring compassion into the workplace.** Cultivate leaders who are compassionate. Sadly, in our culture, too many people view kindness and compassion as weaknesses, especially in men. But business or strategic acumen does not require narcissism or psychopathy to succeed. A compassionate and collaborative leader can draw the most out of his or her colleagues and employees, leaving them feeling supported, committed to the institution, and willing to go the extra mile out of commitment rather than fear.

13. **Don't let your boss's or colleague's insecurity becomes yours.** Remember that toxic leaders are at their core insecure, competitive, antagonistic, and driven by power and self—*not* by the well-being of the company, institution, or country they are running. It can be easy to let their insecurity and incivility get under your skin, but don't lose your passion because of their poison.

14. **Manage your expectations.** Toxic bosses are never going to mentor you or build up your career. They may throw you opportunities here and there, but that is largely because those opportunities do not matter to them and doing so allows them to keep you under their control (it's like someone giving you a cheap gift and you feeling grateful or beholden). It can be easy to get tricked by the crumbs that toxic bosses throw but, like all narcissists, at their core, they are pretty immovable, so be careful that you do not waste your career waiting for a moment of recognition or advancement that may never come. Many people believe that their years of devotion to a toxic boss will be rewarded; more often than not, you will wind up going down with the ship or be forgotten once the boss moves on to greener pastures. Prepare for that.

15. **Take care of your health.** Workplace stress often takes a larger toll on our health than other forms of stress. Your job has implications for your family, financial health, and insurance, and is the place where you may spend the bulk of your waking hours. Toxic bosses and workplaces can take a toll on your mental and physical health, sometimes with long-term consequences. If you cannot remove yourself from the situation quickly, attempt to

bring in some form of self-preservation, including therapy/counseling, talking with supportive friends, exercise, hobbies, and time with family.

16. **Pull ego and childish assumptions about a "just world" out of it.** Many times, people continue to suffer at the hands of a toxic boss because the situation is "unjust," and they want to stay long enough to ensure that it turns out fair. They can spend years of sleepless nights reflecting on how unfair it all is and plotting dramatic revenge fantasies. People often stick it out in these situations to get "what is due to them" or because they feel they were not properly treated in the past. They weren't, and it feels awful, but wasting years ruminating about it doesn't make sense. Give up assumptions of fairness and find your authentic path out of the situation. Life is not fair—saving yourself is.

17. **Be prepared for the fight of your life.** If you decide to take legal action against a toxic boss or institution, be prepared for the fight of your lifetime. In most cases, the ruling will not go in your favor. The nature of human resources, the types of documentation required, and the burden of proof mean that you may not get your day in court or the remedy you're hoping for. While we do sometimes read cases of people who get large payouts from toxic workplace situations, this is not the norm, and, for every payout there are thousands of people who endured these situations, tried to get reparations or damages, and wound up destroyed by the process. Toxic bosses are better liars than you and are more protected by the institution. Simply look at the myriad #metoo cases and other workplace harassment cases out there. It often took dozens if not hundreds of accusers to generate one of those cases and, even then, although there was a trial in the court of public opinion, savvy lawyers and publicists mean that true reparation may never happen. If you pursue litigation, keep your expectations realistic.

18. **Don't be a passive enabler.** Toxic leaders get away with their behavior because no one calls them out on it. You may not be able to call out all toxic leaders but, when the appropriate opportunity

places itself in front of you, there are things you can do, and these can range from appropriately expressing an opinion in a meeting to asking for greater civility in the proceedings (especially if you are empowered to do so by dint of your position within an organization). Silence gives bullies power. This doesn't mean that the toxic leader's behavior will change, but it can create a shift in the culture and empower the voices of others.

19. **Maintain your integrity.** When you are working with scoundrels, it is easy to start slipping down their ethically slimy slope. Don't. Stick to your values, even when you may be mocked or minimized for doing so. Ethically marginal workplaces can result in making lots of rationalizations, especially if you are making more money than expected or are receiving other perks. Check in with yourself and "keep it real." Lots of people in Bernie Madoff's organization thought that the operation was aboveboard and tried to rationalize the returns—we know how that ended.

Chapter 9

The Other Narcissists in Your Life
(Siblings, Friends, In-Laws)

All happy families are alike;
each unhappy family is unhappy in its own way.

—TOLSTOY

Her brother turned a blind eye to the chronic verbal abuse their parents heaped on them. Even as children, she knew that his excellence at baseball and other sports saved him. Her father rarely respected women, he treated her mother horribly, and her mother was so beaten down by their marriage that she never advocated for her children. Her brother went on to succeed in sports and in school, went to a top university, and then had a successful career. As far as her father was concerned, her brother delivered and delivered big. Every year, her brother would make a magnanimous gesture of a beach vacation for everyone at his large home on the coast—he picked up the bills for the tickets, the food, all of it. It was an atrocious experience. Her brother's entitled behavior was embarrassing for all to witness: He was still the four-year-old kid playing show-and-tell—"Look at my new car, look at my wife, look at my boat." Her brother's lack of empathy, his criticism, his entitlement—it was her father, part two. She felt angry; she wanted a relationship with her sibling, but his narcissism made it all but impossible. No one else was able to see it clearly either. Her mother walked on eggshells around her brother, her father was proud of him, and because her brother was so "generous," no one wanted to call out the "golden goose." Her biggest concern was that distancing herself from her brother meant having to distance herself from her entire family. Her own children loved their grandma and these annual beach retreats and their lavish holidays together.

* * *

"She's busy. Her job requires lots of travel. She just got married. She just had a baby. That's why she is so short with me. That's why it feels judgmental. That's why she never checks in with me." Jessica found herself making endless excuses for her friend, Molly. Molly was that coolly confident friend who came from a hypercool family, who was perfectly put together, whose family's wealth meant she did not have to go through the four-roommates-and-a-bus-pass phase of life. There was a clipped tone to her, but Jessica assumed that was confidence and the hurried patina of success. It was a one-way friendship. Molly often picked up the bill at the best restaurants and even paid for their vacations— and, if you could just get past her snobbishness, her entitlement, and her cold efficiency, there were moments with her that felt genuine and sweet. Molly had been a fixture in her life since college, and Jessica loved having someone in her life with a shared history and inside jokes. Then the bottom fell out. In the same month, Jessica's mother was diagnosed with cancer, Jessica found out that her boyfriend had been cheating on her, and her job gave her a layoff notice. She believed that, after years of listening to Molly's tales about boyfriends, business headaches, and family stuff that she could cry on her shoulder. Molly listened, looking distractedly at her phone, then gave her a big hug and said, "It's all going to be okay." Jessica then took that as permission to keep going to her "friend" and would text and call her, just feeling helpless and needing more reassurance. Apparently, Molly's ability to help a friend was a one-time deal, because she then sent her a text message saying, "I'm not a shrink. Figure it out. I'm so busy—I have a lot of stuff going on with the kids and life. Once you have it all figured out, hit me up—maybe we can do drinks or get our nails done...."

* * *

Mariana's daughter-in-law was from a different world than hers, but Mariana had two sons and looked forward to the day when one of them would be married, so she would finally have a "daughter." Mariana had anticipated being friends with her future daughter-in-law, passing down cherished family jewelry to her, and expanding the family in a meaningful and connected way. Her potential daughter-in-law always seemed a little cold, a little distant, but she assumed she was just shy, and she went to tremendous lengths to ensure that she felt welcome. One day, when telling her son about his aunt's illness, his son's girlfriend just looked at her phone and said, "Can we go? I have a lot to do." After her son proposed and a wedding date was set, Mariana was very careful to again ensure that her son's fiancée felt free to plan the wedding she wanted, and careful not to step on her toes. The few emails Mariana sent to her went unanswered, and once, when she called, her son's fiancée quickly passed the phone to her son. Mariana received an invitation in the mail with little consultation about what the wedding day would look like, or even what her son wanted from his parents that day. Mariana became frustrated and confused about how to connect with her almost daughter-in-law. When she finally sat down with her son and asked how she could do a better job of reaching out to his soon-to-be wife, her son looked at her oddly, and said, "Isn't she great? Everyone loves her!" Over time, Mariana and her son became more distant, as his wife was not interested in building a relationship with his family. The one time they did take a vacation together (they put Mariana in a coach seat, while they flew in the first-class cabin), Mariana was aghast by her daughter-in-law's entitled behavior and barely recognized her son. For Mariana, disliking her daughter-in-law was uncomfortable, but losing her son felt devastating.

* * *

There are so many other relationships in our lives beyond the seemingly bigger ticket relationships of parents, children, and partners. These include siblings, friends, and in-laws. These are all important relationships, but we do not always choose them. All of the usual standards and systems for understanding narcissism and toxic relationships apply. But each of these relationships brings unique challenges. In this chapter, we'll unpack the difficult terrain of toxic sibling relationships, the immense disappointment of unreliable narcissistic friends, the necessary boundaries for toxic in-laws, and even the random encounters with entitled strangers who can ruin your day and have an effect on your mental health. For each of these relationships, I'll provide you with a set of strategies for navigating the person's behavior and taking care of yourself.

Siblings

It can be poignant to look through an old family album, seeing yourself and a sibling seated in a bathtub together, in your pajamas at a holiday gathering, or one lovingly admiring the new baby sibling when he or she first comes home. Siblings can be our first friend, first playmate, and first confidant. They can also be our first bully. Our first tyrant. Our first abuser.

They may be the only shared historians we have other than our parents and the only people who may be able to understand what life was like during our childhood. While some siblings are best friends, others can be estranged. When the differences between siblings emerge, it can also become quite clear that, other than being siblings, you have absolutely nothing in common, and that you would be deeply unlikely to choose each other for your lives. Some siblings maintain ties that could never be cut, and others would be willing to throw (and have thrown) their siblings under the bus.

A toxic sibling can present some particular challenges. Depending on your family, you may be forced into circumstances in which you have to see him or her with some regularity, and holidays, weddings, and other major family events can be sullied by this person. Siblings also impact our development and can shape our personalities, especially an older sibling who has been there since the beginning of our life. If a sibling has been competitive, cruel, abusive, or bullying, this can have an impact on us later in life, as strong as a toxic parent's influence. In addition, a toxic sibling may also engage in behaviors that can bring harsh judgment on all members of a family, making childhood and even adulthood a complex minefield.

Feeling Betrayed

For some individuals, what may be remembered as a closeness during childhood tends to come apart at the seams during adulthood. There can be a sense of betrayal when an adult sibling is no longer close or a friend or confidant. Maybe you don't trust your brother, or you feel judged by your sister. You may find out that a sibling has been "two-faced"—behaving

257

one way in front of you and then saying terrible things about you to others when you are not around. Your brother may actually violate boundaries within a romantic relationship you may have, or your sister may have manipulated a parent for her own financial gain. I have worked with several people who said they felt "robbed" because they did not have a close relationship with an adult sibling. However, we are all shaped by numerous forces: parents, peers, education, and society. Even though they were raised in the same home, siblings can all have different experiences of childhood. In addition, two siblings may have very different temperaments or inborn constitutions. You may, in fact, realize that your sibling was always hypersensitive, a trait that became more pronounced and more abrasive with time.

It's Not Fair!

Another difficult issue that may arise is when one sibling suffers more at the hands of a toxic parent than another (e.g., the golden child vs. the scapegoat). This may happen for a number of reasons: Parents may divorce and a toxic parent may no longer be present in the same way for children from the same family, parents may treat children of different genders differently, and children may be differentially valued based on the types of interests and skills they have. A toxic father who loves sports may consistently validate an athletic child while demeaning another. If there is a significant age spread, it is also quite possible that demands in a toxic parent's life may shift and result in different treatment of siblings. This can contribute to a sense of alienation and isolation within the family, as a sibling who may have experienced less hurt due to a toxic parent may also not understand what another sibling endured or may even maintain a relationship with the toxic parent that is loving and very different than what other siblings in the family have. In blended families, toxic stepparents may scapegoat their stepchildren while treating their own children quite differently or vice versa. The complex dynamics of families mean that siblings may experience rather different childhoods.

Competition and Comparison

Siblings can be competitive. After all, there was a time in your life when you were competing for your parents' affection, toys, and the better room. When that starts to trickle into adulthood, and there are one or more toxic siblings involved, good-natured ribbing can turn into something a bit more sinister. Mean-spirited barbs, insults, or even smack talk amongst family members can take a toll. A toxic sibling can bring a family system to its knees and find you stuck in petty arguments that feel more like twelve-year-olds arguing than adults.

Research on sibling rivalry and conflict suggests that they are present in the majority of sibling relationships. Research by Helgola Ross and Joel Milgram, researchers at the University of Cincinnati, suggests that sibling rivalry often has its roots in childhood and is facilitated by the adults in the children's world. Their work traces some of this rivalry to both overt comparison—comparing siblings in an obvious manner, and this can be either positive or negative—and covert comparison, by which one sibling observes another receiving preferential treatment. Interestingly, Ross and Milgram found sibling rivalry to be more often initiated by a brother, and that it typically reflected a competition for parents' attention, recognition, or love, or for power or position within the family system. These patterns may start young, but they can persist into adulthood and be significantly magnified when one or more siblings within a family system are narcissistic.

Obviously, family and sibling relationships are incredibly nuanced and can reflect a lifetime of perceived slights or worse. Money is a variable that can exacerbate these dynamics in adulthood and reflect a point of intersection between toxic parents and difficult siblings. Toxic parents often use money (or the promise of money) as a means of control. In addition, siblings, particularly difficult siblings, can keep rather detailed balance sheets in their heads (or can keep actual balance sheets!). If one sibling had a lavish wedding paid for by the parents, and another sibling did not elect to get married, the unmarried sibling may demand the cash value of the wedding (or law school or a grandchild's college fund—you get the idea). In toxic families, a key dynamic is feeling "owed" something—"Mom and Dad owe me because you got more from them"—and it is often a rallying call in these relationships. That sense of obligation and feeling that something is due can create more tension between siblings as time goes on.

Takeaways: Toxic Siblings

1. **Follow the usual rules of narcissistic relationships.** All of the usual rules for dealing with toxic and narcissistic people apply when dealing with siblings: Don't take the bait, manage expectations, maintain boundaries, and recognize that they will likely not change much. Those rules don't change because there is a family relationship. They may be harder to enforce, because you have such a long history with this person, and maybe there was a time in your life when you were closer and you keep hoping to return to that. Remember, hope can be a dangerous emotion when dealing with a toxic person and, if your sibling is a narcissist, you are never going to have that close, idealistic relationship again. You may also feel torn because of allegiances to other family members, and it may be difficult to have one set of boundaries for your toxic sibling and another set for other family members with whom you maintain closer ties.

2. **Maintain the family relationships that matter to you.** You may have a perfectly fine relationship with other siblings, your parents, or extended family members. Don't get dragged down into the mud with your toxic sibling(s). Set boundaries and enforce those boundaries, even if it means you find times outside of family gatherings to cultivate healthy relationships with other family members.

3. **Don't ask people in the family to take sides.** Toxic siblings will often attempt to polarize the family and ask people to take sides. Do not ask people to make that choice; find a way to carve out a relationship with a family member who may want to attempt to stay close to both of you. If your other family members take sides against you at the behest of your toxic sibling, then that speaks volumes about them.

4. **Be prepared for strong feelings of grief and struggles around letting go.** There can be strong feelings of resentment, anger, grief, and loss when you feel that you have "lost" a sibling because you have to distance yourself. Seeking out therapy can help with

this. Consider whether you are putting energy into fighting for this relationship merely because this person is your sibling. The relationship is not likely to change, and you may be better off cultivating relationships that are healthy.

5. **Give up on the idea of "fairness."** You aren't five years old and fighting over a toy—you are an adult, and nowhere is it written that siblings share things evenly. You may end up taking on the lion's share of caregiving for aging parents, your toxic sibling may successfully co-opt family wills and trusts, your toxic sibling's children may receive more from your parents. Distance from this toxic dynamic may be all of the fairness you can hope for; don't fight empty battles that will make you sick over time.

Friends

Friends are an incredibly under-studied type of relationship, and yet they are so important to us. Unlike with family, relationships with friends are by choice and, as such, there can be a different kind of responsibility here. While many relationships in our lives are just "givens" (such as those with parents, siblings, cousins), relationships with people, such as our friends and partners, happen because we *choose* them. But, unlike with partners, the rules are different—friends don't require monogamy, and the boundaries are drawn differently. Many people will say that their friendships are often the most robust, hardy, and unconditional spaces in their lives and are built to withstand the years in a very different way than other relationships. They are typically less fraught with family drama and societal expectations and roles. Many people will report that friendships have been their salvation at difficult times and have shaped who they have become, and that friends have been safe people with whom to spend holidays. (And many is the person who will say, "I would rather live with or travel with my best friend than with my spouse!")

That said, friendships can also be a painful source of conflict. We rarely think about "breaking up" with a friend—we typically don't have a formal, sit-down, "We need to talk" situation with a friend. When friendships end, it is often a quiet and gradual ending—and over time, they are gone. Sometimes two people simply outgrow each other. They may also end because of changes in lifestyles (one person has kids, one does not), geographic shifts, or shifts in interests. Or maybe, as you get older, a friendship starts to feel one-sided, and you don't want to invest your time and energy in a relationship that has grown imbalanced, toxic, or unfulfilling (you are always there for a friend in crisis but, when you really need that person, he or she is MIA). These are the friends who regularly flake on you, choose a new boyfriend or girlfriend over the friendship, quickly replace you with friends they view as being of higher status, or just dismissively treat you as a convenience who is available when they want someone to spend time with. Problematic communication patterns; dysfunctional patterns such as passive aggression, betrayal, or competition; or even gaslighting can occur within the context of a friendship—and, since many friendships can and do outlast romantic relationships, these patterns can be deeply entrenched after many years.

Friendships can also be limiting, and we do outgrow them. When we meet a person at an earlier developmental stage (such as when we're in high school or college), we may still have a ways to go in our own growth, and a friend who may have been perfectly fine at that earlier phase of life may not be able to grow along with us. When the demands of life become more real and pressing, or when the competitive elements of life are writ large (such as who gets a better job, who has more financial resources, who has a better spouse), then the toxic elements of a friend may emerge. That said, friendships often do not require the same care and feeding as other relationships; two friends can find themselves having lost touch for a year and then pick up a conversation as if nothing happened. In that way, friendships can also be quite resilient—more resilient than most of our relationships.

The manifestations of toxic friends are similar to those of other toxic relationships—and so are the rules. Their toxic stuff may present itself through snarky comments, a lack of empathy, being unavailable when you need them (even when you are consistently available to them), inconsistency, or competitiveness. They may become jealous when you succeed but still expect you to be their cheerleader. Many people report that a toxic friend can be like a weight on a balloon—the friendship is fine if you are down at the same level as them but, if you succeed, then the friendship starts to fray.

While it may not be as potent as with a romantic partner, toxic friendships can still leave a person reeling with self-doubt, a loss of confidence, or a sense of insecurity. Because we often have more than one friend, these effects may be watered down, but they can be powerful, especially if it is a longstanding friendship. In fact, these dynamics may have been in place and have kept you off balance for many years. Keeping a toxic friend around can set you up to maintain other toxic relationships. Friendships may date from childhood or adolescence, and the tone and pattern set there may reproduce the invalidating dynamics of your family. Toxic friends may actually keep you around because you provide an audience for them, provide validation, and elevate them. It is not unusual for a toxic friend or even a group of toxic friends to scapegoat a more vulnerable member of the group—and this can negatively impact the self-esteem and mental health of the scapegoated friend. These dynamics may have been laid down years before and, out of familiarity, nostalgia, and comfort, many people simply stay in them. The same fears that plague anyone in a narcissistic or toxic relationship—fear of being alone, fear of being ostracized, fear of having to meet new friends—can stymie people in toxic friendships and leave them to keep enduring the abuse by the friend.

Why Do We Choose Toxic Friends?

What do you do when your friend is toxic or narcissistic? In much the same way that people can fall for narcissistic partners, it can be easy to fall in with narcissistic friends. They may be charming, charismatic, and confident. You may meet them at a vulnerable time or at a time when you are lonely (when you move to a new city, when you start a new job, when you start college, when you are a new parent at your child's school). Because time with a friend may be less concentrated, you may not notice the patterns as readily or they may not affect you as acutely. The potency of a friend's narcissism may not be as impactful, because you have other friends; it doesn't always have the lightning bolt effect of a narcissistic partner or parent or boss, with whom the stakes are higher.

The Stress Test

Stress can elevate the dynamic of a toxic or narcissistic friendship. A friendship may just be going along, but then something happens—for instance, your friend may get married and reveal herself to be a tyrannical bride—and you see the patterns grow larger. Or your friend may actually envy something you have, like a new job that brings some exciting new opportunities or a new boyfriend or girlfriend, and then his or her narcissistic character shines through. There may also be the situation in which your friend has told you, "I will be there for you no matter what you need," but, once you actually try to turn to this person at a time of need, he or she becomes resentful and unavailable. Often, because friendships tend to be more relaxed spaces, it can take some time for these patterns to emerge, and then it is easy to write excuses for the friends ("Well, gosh. We usually have so much fun; this must be a fluke."). It usually isn't a fluke—judge the friendship on the basis of how it behaves when things are difficult, not on how it rolls during happy hour. Or learn to consume the friendship differently, and recognize that some friendships have enough bandwidth only for happy hour, while others can go deep.

Social Media Drama

The modern age of social media can also make toxic friendships a perilous space. Even at the age of forty, it can hurt to be left off of a birthday party invitation—and seeing that your friend had a party and did not invite you because he or she was angry about something petty can sting. Toxic friends often issue passive-aggressive comments on social media as a way of collecting validation and punishing the transgressor without ever directly communicating about it ("Don't you hate when a friend comes home from vacation and doesn't call you back right away? #findingmytruefriendsFriday!").

Moving On From the Memories

Friendships can be some of the most important relationships in our lives, as well as some of the most resilient. However, they can also be complicated. The stakes can be higher than we think, and, if a friendship has lasted a long time, there can be a tendency to throw bad money after good—just as with other toxic relationships. We may want to hold on to the memories of childhood, high school, college, or other special experiences we have shared with a friend. They may be permanently memorialized in photos of a wedding, a child's christening, a vacation, or other family events. But toxic is toxic and, many times, people will endure toxic friends' abuse and manipulation for old times' sake. Walking away from a friendship can feel like losing a part of yourself or ripping a page out of a scrapbook, but nostalgia is not enough of a rationale for maintaining an unhealthy relationship of any kind.

Takeaways: Toxic Friends

1. **Maintain boundaries.** Know your narcissistic friend's limitations and construct boundaries appropriately. Don't keep wasting hope and getting hurt in the same way repeatedly. If the friend is part of a larger group of friends, you may be able to maintain boundaries with the toxic friend and remain a part of the larger group. If, however, the toxic friend draws alliances, polarizes the group, or engages in other problematic behaviors, don't fall for it. Protect yourself and follow the usual toxic-person rules: Maintain boundaries and have realistic expectations.

2. **End the friendship if you need to.** Remind yourself that friendships can and do end and that, when it was enjoyable, you enjoyed it, but that the relationship or the other person did not have the staying power to grow with you or grew in a different direction. It happens. Sticking around for old times' sake is not good for you. Healthy friendships can withstand changes in direction; as a rule, toxic ones cannot.

3. **Monitor social media.** Pay attention to how the friend uses social media and how it affects you. Sometimes a toxic friend may use social media in a way that can feel hurtful (posting from events from which you are deliberately excluded, posting passive-aggressive barbs, or putting up validation-seeking posts that make you uncomfortable). You can silence those posts or rethink whether the friendship is a healthy space for you.

4. **Reflect on why you are maintaining this friendship.** Just as with any toxic relationship, people maintain toxic friendships out of self-doubt, insecurity, fear of meeting new friends, fear of being ostracized from a group of friends, and nostalgia. Be aware of your motivations. A friendship should be a place of growth, not

insecurity. Hanging out with a toxic friend can reinforce your narratives of being not enough or can simply normalize invalidating behavior—patterns that can presage unhealthy choices in other relationships. Be careful how you engage with a narcissistic friend.

In-Laws

These are the family members you didn't bargain for, and they can be parents-in-law, siblings-in-law, and the entire extended family of the person you married, or someone that another family member married. You have little choice in these people, and you often lack the historical roadmap to make sense of the players. These are complicated relationships because in-laws come to you via a person you actually may have a healthy relationship with, such as your son's wife or your husband, but that person's family is unhealthy. That means walking a more delicate line, because you may be attempting to protect your family member while trying to endure toxic in-laws. It is a challenging psychological balancing act.

In the most classic telling of the tale, a person has a toxic mother-in-law, a timeless cultural trope. The meddling mother-in-law thinks you are not good enough for her daughter or son and violates boundaries left and right, with little regard for how you feel. But, as you have figured out by now, toxic is toxic, and in-law relationships can be a bit of a minefield, since these people may matter dearly to someone you love dearly (but then it turns out that they are actually narcissistic and difficult). Or, if you are fortunate, your partner may recognize that his or her parent is not an easy person, which can make the entire enterprise much easier. However, you may need to play by the rules of the person you married, or of the family member who is the bridge to these in-laws.

In-laws generally come into our lives when we are older, because they are acquired via marriage or via the marriage of other family members. Managing difficult in-laws means not only self-preservation but also preserving yourself in a way that protects the person who brought the in-laws into your life. Your spouse, your child, or your sibling may already have a way of dealing with the in-laws, and you may need to find your own stride or boundaries with them.

Relationships with in-laws may or may not be important. Other than the occasional family wedding, a sister's toxic mother-in-law may be irrelevant to you. In contrast, your toxic son-in-law may be very problematic if you live with him. In some cases, a toxic mother-in-law who lives far away with little contact may have little impact, while a toxic and entitled father-in-law who comes to your house regularly can have a significant effect on your life. As with many narcissistic relationships, it tends to be what we call a "dose-response" relationship—the more you are exposed to, the more you are affected.

When managing toxic or narcissistic in-laws, the usual toxic-relationship rules apply. However, you may need to manage these more delicately, in a way that is simultaneously self-preserving and does not step on the toes of the relationship your in-law has with his or her child or your own child. Boundaries, managing expectations, and remaining realistic are the classic tools that matter here as well. Communication is also an essential tool, because you may need to be clear and realistic but kind with your spouse about his or her parent, so as to more peaceably manage years of family events, parenting, and other issues that may be influenced by a toxic parent-in-law. Over time, children may be involved, and these may be your grandchildren. Having a framework for how to manage toxic in-laws of any kind may allow you to safeguard the relationships you hope to have with the next generation of children in your family. If your spouse is not able to work with you to safeguard your marriage in the face of toxic in-laws, then you may need to take a long, difficult look at your marriage. Moments like that can involve what feel like impossible choices. It could be as simple as a partner's agreeing to have the family stay in a hotel during a visit rather than in the same house as a mother-in-law who is a twenty-four-hour harasser.

If you yourself have toxic family members and are married, keep in mind that they are about to become someone else's in-laws. To that end, calmly prepare your partner for it, allow him or her to develop his or her own relationship with your family, but also validate any troubling patterns that you have already been observing for a lifetime. Toxic people get their power when there are no other witnesses to acknowledge your experience—if you draw together with a partner or other family members, the damage wrought by toxic in-laws can be managed.

Takeaways: Toxic In-Laws

1. **Apply the usual toxic-relationship-management rules.** As always, the usual rules apply: self-preservation, managing expectations, setting boundaries, and being realistic about what is (and is not) possible for that person.

2. **Communicate clearly to preserve the relationships that matter.** Communicate clearly with your partner or child or whoever is the bringer of the toxic in-laws, so you can retain existing healthy relationships with the healthy people around you and not allow the toxic person or people to undermine them.

3. **Mentally prepare before visits.** Ensure that you mentally prepare yourself before events at which the toxic in-laws may be present, so you do not feel blindsided or overwhelmed. Do not maintain unrealistic hopes that this time it will be different. Be cordial and gracefully exit any conversation before it becomes hostile, antagonistic, or abusive.

4. **Respect existing boundaries and relationships.** Respect the rhythms that your spouse, child, or other family members may have with the in-laws, and perhaps let them do their own thing, without getting drawn into their challenging rhythms and situations.

The Toxic Person You Don't Know

All of us, even the luckiest of people who do not have a parent, partner, boss, friend, sibling, or any other family member or acquaintance who is toxic or is a narcissist, do cross paths with these difficult folks on a regular basis. They are the myriad toxic strangers we encounter. And, in fact, this book began with those people: the "Don't you know who I am?"-ers. These can fall into one of two categories: the ones you experience vicariously (meaning that you watch them engage in their toxic behaviors, but the behaviors are not targeted at you) and the ones you experience directly (meaning that you find yourself mired in an unpleasant interaction with them).

It can be uncomfortable but also gruesomely entertaining to watch someone throw a DYKWIA tantrum in a public place. If anything, our discomfort comes from watching another person's having to endure the childish tantrum and abuse of a toxic person in a public place. It can be quite stressful to watch someone else be screamed at or bullied. It's never clear whether we should intervene or just turn away to avoid even more conflict.

When you are caught in a direct interaction with a toxic stranger, it is highly unpleasant. These interactions can take several forms: For example, you may ask people to politely turn down their music because it is disrupting your family, or to repark their car to open up a tight parking space, or to stop vaping near your children, or may ask a neighbor to remove trash from his or her lawn. You appropriately ask something. And then the person goes berserk—obscenities usually start the tirade; at the extreme, weapons are pulled out, or people try to run others over with their car. Then it becomes quite clear they have little power over anyone else in their lives, so they enact their toxic will by saying, "Why should I have to move?" or, "Fuck you, I will listen to my music the way I want" or, "Stay the hell out of my business." These stories can have deeply tragic endings, with shooting deaths over parking spaces and injuries over an airplane seat. These interactions can agitate you, make you anxious, put you in danger, leave you depleted, or even incite you to behave as badly as they do. At the core of these interactions is the perpetrators' pathological insecurity, entitlement, and powerlessness. These situations are increasingly making the world a more dangerous place in every way. They may be the by-product of a growing resentment in a world that is increasingly inequitable, and in which traditional assumptions of privilege are being shifted and tested. Regardless, the behavior is unacceptable.

Obviously, there are myriad other relationships out there: with aunts, uncles, grandparents, cousins, stepsiblings, community members, neighbors, and people on your social media feed. The patterns are the same across those situations and so too are the strategies and takeaways—maintain boundaries, set realistic expectations, and engage in self-reflection, self-protection, and self-preservation. Give up any assumptions of fairness or justice. Toxic, narcissistic, and difficult people are everywhere, and you do not need to reinvent the wheel every time. Learn to detect the behavior and set boundaries and expectations early. The simplest takeaway of all? Don't engage. If a person were clearly ill and coughing everywhere and not covering his or her mouth, you would move away from that person. It's the same thing: Consider toxic outbursts to be the psychological equivalent of an infectious germ you do not want to catch. You are not these people's therapist, and the compassionate gesture is to walk away, rather than to further incite whatever pain within them results in blind attacks against the world and the people in it.

Chapter 10

The Narcissist You Raised

Children begin by loving their parents; as they grow older
they judge them; sometimes they forgive them.

—OSCAR WILDE

This may be the most painful issue of all. Spouses can be managed or divorced. We can even distance ourselves from parents and siblings. We can always quit a job.

But our children?

Not so easy to quit.

The challenge here is that it is clear that narcissism may be more made than born, so, if you are a parent of a narcissistic, psychopathic, or otherwise high-conflict, difficult, antagonistic, or toxic person, there will be self-blame, and there may even be accusations from the world at large. The "recipe" for narcissism is not a simple one, and while parenting and early family environments have a lot to do with it, that is not all of it. All of this may be little consolation, however, if you are dealing with anger, invalidation, and abuse targeted at you by a narcissistic child.

You may have even read the "How (Not) to Raise a Narcissist" chapter and recognized some of your own parenting patterns. Many parents will look back and realize that perhaps they did "spoil" their children, or try to win them over in the wake of a divorce, or overspent to compensate for lean financial years in the marriage, or had to work long hours to keep the family financially afloat, or were not sufficiently present for any number of reasons, or spent too much time and focus on purchasing them things or ensuring they had the best tutors and coaches rather than simply being parents to them, or in some cases, will finally own up to abusive behavior. Some parents will self-reflect that they may not have been that perfect mirror or that something impacted the period of attachment. It may even be that you take stock and say, "I did foster my child's sense of entitlement." You may recognize that if you did have financial success, you lavished it on your children, and that may have helped in creating a monster. You may have just wanted to give them a good start, but the superficial focus on grades and achievement may have impacted them. It is not difficult in the current world order to be more concerned with what your children *do* rather than who they really *are*, especially their inner world.

Or maybe not. You may have done your very best and done quite well. You may have been present, worked yourself to the bone to ensure opportunities for your children, and been loving and consistent and still have a narcissistic or toxic adult child. As noted in the earlier chapter on raising a narcissist, there appears to be a constitutional or temperamental element at play that can get shaped by how the child interacts with the world, and how the world interacts with the child. You may have even noticed it during the early years, and his or her early temperament may have been in contrast to that of any siblings. Those early constitutional factors may have emerged as that little kid who never did well with frustration and disappointment, and who is now a grown-up who does not do well with frustration and disappointment; or the child who just could not be soothed and could not be taught to soothe himself or herself; or the child who HAD to be the center of attention to a fault. In most cases, there was also another parent involved. This isn't the blame game—the end product of your child reflects both parents' or caregivers' inputs (or absences) and something your child was born with; no one has to take the full burden on his or her shoulders. The combination of factors is complex and nuanced. Things may have happened that continue to devastate you and your adult child because you could not keep your child safe (for example, your child was abused by someone else), and perhaps, by the time you intervened, the trauma could not be undone.

In most ways, it doesn't matter, because you cannot unring a bell. The toxic and narcissistic adult child can be a tremendous source of heartbreak and conflict. In this chapter, we'll tackle the challenge of separating from your own adult child, the accompanying feelings of guilt, and how to approach inheritance, estate, and financial issues. We'll also address how to handle a difficult, high-conflict adolescent and consider strategies for navigating this complex relationship.

Letting Go of Your Own Child: The Painful Journey

Many parents maintain the idealized and hopeful vision that their adult child will be their friend and their ally, and that the hard work of parenting will pay off in the opportunity to watch their child blossom as an adult and to share that growth with them. When an adult child remains unempathic, entitled, rejecting, cold, manipulative, and abusive, it can be devastating. Parents dealing with narcissistic or toxic adult children will often witness their tantrums much as they did when the children were younger. But it's much more difficult to enact a time-out when they are thirty-three instead of three. Parents who have toxic adult children will often get into enormous showdowns and feel powerless, because they can no longer use the same discipline they once used at a younger age.

Of all the relationship reconfigurations, quitting or distancing from a child may be the most difficult. In most cases, when a parent met a child, it was love at first sight. Your baby and your child needed you more than anyone would ever need you. It can be difficult to let go of that image and recollection of a rapt infant or toddler in exchange for the vitriolic attacks of a narcissistic adult child. Most people with toxic adult children I interviewed reported that the difficult patterns had kicked in by the early teens and adolescence and never abated. The parents held on with the logical hope that adolescence would pass, and a more sane, levelheaded, and kind adult would emerge. Many parents reported that, when that didn't happen, and the patterns of entitlement, invalidation, rage, resentment, and disaffection intensified, they felt devastation and confusion.

In one situation I encountered, a mother who was divorced (the father of her child was not very present in the child's life after early to middle childhood) made every possible sacrifice for her daughter to have an excellent education, and then, when her daughter had an early lucky break in her career, the mother helped her manage her career (and, at her daughter's request, the mother even left her own career to ensure that her daughter was supported as the daughter took advantage of the opportunity she had been given). They collaborated on projects, each of them doing half the work, and, when one of their collaborative projects finally succeeded, the daughter cut her mother out of the project and the earnings.

As her star rose, the daughter became more and more dismissive of her mother, often yelling at her, criticizing her, and taking credit for all of her mother's contributions, and, when the daughter's lucky break did not continue, she became even more rageful at her mother. By now, the mother had been away from her own original career for too long and was now dependent on the bits of work her daughter would toss her way. Her daughter rarely inquired about her well-being, talked only about herself, and continually raged at her mother as her early success faded. The mother became deeply depressed and could not understand why her daughter was so angry with her all the time, why she would be so cold, clipped, rejecting, and unkind. Sadly, the mother spent her days and nights just waiting for a thank-you or some other show of gratitude. The daughter would engage in the same abusive patterns on a regular basis. Her mother could not bring herself to distance herself from her daughter, as she had built too much of her life around her, and simply because she loved her daughter. Because the mother was so sure that someday her daughter would thank her, and then, at that moment, she would be able to feel resolved and let go, she stuck it out, and is still sticking it out, waiting for the apology that never came—and likely never will. Meanwhile, her difficult daughter is growing older, less successful, and more resentful, and the mother's health is starting to fail secondary to older age and a lifetime of stress.

Protecting Your Health and Your Wealth

As parents and children age, these dynamics can become incredibly complex. The parents may now find themselves walking on eggshells around their children. Parents in these situations are concerned about what will happen to them as they get older, and they begin to recognize that their children will likely not be the ones to sign up for the job of helping them as they age. There may even be fears of being placed in a facility or in other settings that they may not want to be in because their narcissistic children cannot be bothered, or fears that the adult children will continue to take advantage of them as they age and view them more as an ATM than as a human being. In addition, wills, trusts, and probate can magnify these dynamics. Narcissistic children may engage in all sorts of machinations to ensure that they get their share of a family estate (or more than their share). This can result in painful and difficult conversations. If there is any wealth to distribute, parents in this situation may feel as though they are nothing more than a punching bag and lottery ticket for their children. Toxic children will often feel as though their parents owe them something due to the disappointments of their childhood, and that they are collecting on some kind of debt. It is also not unusual for narcissistic and otherwise toxic children to voice their opinion that parents have a lifelong obligation (typically financial) to children throughout their lives for bringing them into the world.

One important pattern to note is that, as pointed out earlier, these interpersonally difficult and conflictual patterns may be embedded in some other form of more severe mental illness or patterns—for example, borderline personality disorder, complex PTSD, or dual diagnosis (such as substance abuse and some other major mental illness). Interpersonal dysregulation is not unusual in these psychiatric patterns and, as such, may delimit adult children's ability to remain gainfully employed or sustain an adult relationship. Their difficult patterns may be less about narcissism and more about another mental illness that may require you to consider how you can ensure some level of support for them through establishment of a trust or other form of supervised financial oversight. It may be difficult to think like this if you are enduring abuse at the hands of your adult child, but understanding the pattern, and finding a way of coping that will help you feel at ease, is essential.

Guilt and Grief

Parents of toxic adult children often harbor guilt because they believe they had something to do with the narcissistic adult who has emerged. Even when parents openly acknowledge their personal "shortcomings" to children, or regrets they harbor from how they parented, it can be met with disdain or rejection from toxic children who simply have no empathy. Interestingly, despite the high levels of resentment adult narcissistic children may maintain toward their parents, they usually do not take the step of simply distancing themselves from their parents and, when the parents, in a last show of self-preservation, attempt to distance themselves from abusive adult children, the adult children will become quite enraged, as though they are frustrated at losing their punching bag.

Once again, I am pretty confident that relatively few of the people reading this book are raging narcissists themselves, so it is unlikely that there are lots of really abusive parents out there reading this. Frankly, if the nature of your relationship with your child during his or her childhood was genuinely abusive, then perhaps your child is distancing himself or herself as a means of protection, and it is not fair to label him or her as "unfairly difficult." Only you know your story, and, if you are deeply honest with yourself, then you will understand if this label is accurate or not. If abuse occurred during your child's upbringing, and you, as a parent, did little to prevent it or address it, then any anger or distance from your child may be your child's maintaining a boundary to preserve his or her safety. However, in the absence of that kind of history, there are rarely any winners when someone chooses to endure the vitriol and anger of a toxic adult child. If your child's narrative is that you did not do right by him or her, then that is your child's reality. Defending yourself is a waste of energy and time, and the more important work to do may be on grieving and letting go.

Toxic Adolescence—It May Be Temporary

Finally, don't get ahead of yourself. Nearly all adolescents behave in a manner that, at some point, feels toxic, contemptuous, and rejecting of their parents—they may cop an attitude, behave in a deeply entitled manner, say hurtful things, show virtually no empathy, and criticize and resent you at every turn. This may simply be the adolescent practice of "shitting the nest" (an individuation process whereby children make the parent-child relationship so unpleasant that it becomes easier to leave). It can be pointless to engage them. Parents may just need to endure a white-knuckle approach until their children's early twenties before they indict them for being toxic or narcissistic. In one study conducted over four years, researchers found that over time, adolescents whose conscientiousness increased, and whose negative emotional styles and responding (also termed neuroticism) decreased, reported a decrease in symptoms of narcissistic personality disorder. Increases in conscientiousness and drops in neuroticism are often what happens with maturation and acceptance of adult responsibilities—suggesting that your narcissistic adolescent's personality may shift as he or she matures, and basically grows out of a largely narcissistic personality style (Dowgwillo, Pincus, & Lenzenweger, 2019). This relative instability of narcissistic personality disorder patterns in adolescence is a reason that we do not issue this diagnosis before adulthood.

If difficult and cruel adolescents remain stuck and become toxic and narcissistic adults, they will be less likely to grow out of it, and it may be time to become more concerned. If it is a genuinely narcissistic pattern, it will generalize, and you will not be the only target of their verbal assaults. Your adult child may also be struggling with maintaining close relationships, friendships, and education or employment—and, as such, there may not be much you can do to safeguard yourself from his or her antagonism. There is an additional frustration in adolescence, because as a parent, when your child turns eighteen, you are no longer in a position to "require" mental health services, and can only strongly recommend them. And the content of their mental health sessions remains confidential, so you may not be privy to their progress. Many parents report feeling quite helpless at this stage, because they want to secure services and help for their children, but are limited in their ability to do so.

As with all narcissistic relationships, hope springs eternal. As your child traverses adulthood and may pass through varied rites of passage—graduating from higher education or entering the military, starting a job or establishing a career, getting married, having children—you may maintain the expectation that an empathic and non-entitled adult will emerge. The tribulations of being a "grown-up" may straighten him or her out, but they may not. Be prepared for the fact that your adult narcissistic child may not want you along for the ride or, if you are invited along, it will be a bumpy and abusive one. It can be difficult to recognize that perhaps the main job of a parent is to raise an independent adult, not necessarily an adult who is nice to you. But, if you set the boundary, then maintain it. Do not try to win over a difficult adult child with money or other favors. It will not work, and it is likely to leave you feeling even more helpless and resentful that the child took your largesse and still is beating you over the head with it.

It is beyond the scope of this book to address more dangerous issues, such as elder abuse, which can take the forms of physical, psychological, and financial abuse. In such cases, which are often perpetrated by toxic adult children, the involvement of appropriate state authorities, law enforcement, and legal counsel is necessary. If you believe that an older adult with whom you are acquainted may be experiencing financial or other forms of abuse at the hands of an adult child, consult online resources (that will vary based on region) to guide you in helping that person.

Takeaways: Toxic Children

1. **Engage in self-preservation.** If you are dealing with a toxic child who is chronically abusive, entitled, manipulative, and harsh, then it may be time to step away, take stock, and address your expectations for this relationship. If the patterns never shift, then at least recalibrate your expectations. Remaining in your child's life as nothing more than a punching bag will take a toll on you. Self-preservation is a right, and one that you have the option of enacting, even with your own child.

2. **Consider therapy with your adult child.** Even though adult children are not likely to change, and you cannot change your past or their narrative, consider therapy together to discuss these issues. If therapy is simply a rehashing of old hurts and reveals that they cannot lay down their grievances, it may be a painful wakeup call to let go of the relationship. However, it is also possible that, with the guidance of a therapist, you may be able to work through conflicts of the present and past and work on rebuilding a relationship.

3. **Plan realistically for your future.** If indeed adult children are narcissists or their behavior is toxic, they will not be likely to sign up to help you in the event of illness or other health issues that may impact you later in life. Plan accordingly and maintain realistic expectations. Do not foolishly invest in hope and then have to face a potentially tragic situation with the absence of a safety net and necessary supports if your health fades as you age.

4. **Maintain boundaries.** It is not your job to be the repository of their abuse. If they have unfixable grudges and grievances, then stop listening to the same tirade. It is possible that there are some conversations that you will still be able to have with them but, when the conversation shifts to the usual grievances, create distance and step away. Do not engage in the same conversation repeatedly and expect a different response.

5. **Walk the tightrope for other family members.** Understand that you may have limited access to other important people, such as grandchildren, or that your access to them may be used as a weapon. Many people endure toxic adult children because they want to see their delightful grandchildren or to protect the grandchildren from their toxic parent. It may require managing expectations and being realistic about the limitations of your relationship with your child in order to have time with your grandchild or other family members and be aware that your child may use that access as a way to punish you.

6. **Seek out mental health services.** When the realization arrives that a child is narcissistic and is not going to change, it is not uncommon for a parent to experience a sense of grief, as well as symptoms or episodes of depression and/or anxiety. You may also experience stress-related symptoms—both psychological and physical. Talking it out with a mental health professional and getting some perspective can be critical for maintaining your mental and physical health. This work may also allow you to manage expectations in a realistic way, which can be particularly challenging when it is your child—a person with whom you have had a variegated relationship, and for whom you may still feel very responsible.

7. **Get your finances in shape.** Meet with your financial advisor and attorney and be realistic about your financial picture. Parents of adult narcissistic children can become ATMs, with their entitled child thinking little of asking for money at every turn in the road. Parents may maintain the hope that, if they help their children financially, they will "win over" the children. You are

more likely to drain your bank account before you get through to your adult child. Ensure that you have set aside enough money for yourself, for your future, and for other dependents whom you want to provide for and be prudent and careful—your adult child is unlikely to pay you back, so plan accordingly. Also, ensure that your financial ducks are in a row with regard to wills and trusts. You may have the experience of having a child who is toxic but having other children or family members who have been present and loving. The toxic or entitled adult child is likely to contest or subvert a will or trust. Ensure that all documents are prepared as clearly and tightly as possible, so, upon the passing of you and your spouse, probate can unfold as smoothly as possible. If, for no other reason, do it to protect your other children and the intentions of your estate planning.

Part Three

STAYING SANE IN A NARCISSISTIC WORLD

*...Nothing momentous comes in this world
unless it comes on the shoulders of kindness.*

—BARBARA KINGSOLVER

Chapter 11

A Simple Survival Guide

To hold our tongues when everyone is gossiping, to smile without
hostility at people and institutions, to compensate for the shortage of
love in the world with more love in small, private matters;
to be more faithful in our work, to show greater patience, to forgo
the cheap revenge obtainable from mockery and criticism:
all these are things we can do.

—HESSE

How do you interact with a toxic narcissist? How do you navigate a narcissistic world? It's like the old riddle about the porcupine: "How do you hug a porcupine? Very carefully." Whether the narcissistic, toxic, or entitled person is a spouse, partner, friend, mother, father, other family member, neighbor, boss, or coworker, many of the ground rules remain the same. Always remember: These people are deeply insecure, they feel chronically threatened by the world and engage in grandiose or contemptuous shenanigans in response, they are more concerned with appearances than with anything of substance, they cannot regulate or manage their feelings (especially frustration or bruises to their ego), they are hypersensitive to anything that smacks of criticism, and they lack empathy. Armed with that framework, you will be better able to manage the beast. The prior chapters have provided pointed guidance and tips for how to manage a range of relationships in your life.

Some of the easiest techniques involve avoiding certain statements. Talking with a narcissist is a lot like walking through a minefield; every step and statement requires tremendous deliberation. If you want to avoid unending conflict, avoid pointing out their shortcomings, defending yourself, or asking them to take accountability for their behavior.

It all comes down to the goal of this book: Since there is literally nothing we can do about a narcissistic and toxic world, narcissistic and toxic institutions, and narcissistic and toxic people, the goal is to teach you how to *protect yourself from toxic people and toxic situations*. I want to help you avoid these relationships in the first place, be realistic about them if you are stuck in them and maintain the boundaries you need to stay healthy and sane in the face of them.

This book is meant to push back against the naïve assertion that narcissistic or toxic people will change in any substantial manner, that there will be that moment of enlightenment—the "aha" moment when they "get it," apologize for all of the hurt they've caused, and finally start getting it right, and everyone lives happily ever after. *With narcissists, there is no happily ever after.* It is my hope that, after you finish this book, you stop waiting for the happy ending that will never come and write a different and more realistic one. The prevailing societal narratives—fairy-tale romances, forgiveness, second chances, fame, fortune, and fantasy—place people at chronic risk of being swallowed up by toxic people. *You will not be the one to tame the toxic narcissist.* Stop getting mired in that narrative.

The Charlie Brown of It All

Anyone of a certain age will always remember the story of Charlie Brown and the football. Lucy (the toxic and invalidating friend) repeatedly asks the empathic and yearning Charlie Brown to play football, and she invariably pulls the football away as he goes in for the kick, leading him to fall flat on his back. Each time, he approaches it thinking it will be different—and each and every time, she pulls the ball away.

A relationship with a toxic person leaves you feeling like Charlie Brown. You keep going in, thinking that this time it will be different, that this time Lucy will not pull the ball. The first time she did it, it was time for him to be cautious; the second time she did it, it was time to never play ball again. That eternal hope that it will change is what keeps these relationships going (and keeps the Charlie Browns of the world repeatedly falling on their backs).

Throughout the book, takeaways have been issued for how to manage the varied narcissists in your life. The broad strokes are always similar: manage expectations, maintain boundaries, shore up your other supports, recognize that they will not change, take care of yourself, don't engage, and get mental health assistance. Expect the football to be pulled away. That means you may protect yourself from some of the disappointment when the ball does get pulled away, or, better yet, don't play ball with them at all. Doing all these things can take a seemingly uncontrollable soul-sapping situation and transform it into something still exhausting but, at least, predictable.

These rules also apply when dealing with the world in general. When politicians make foolish, polarizing, nasty, and divisive comments, recognize that they won't stop. When your Instagram feed leaves you feeling empty, limit your time with it. When you start feeling down because you are tired of witnessing entitled temper tantrums, frightening road rage, or more reports of cruelty in the world perpetrated by tyrants, narcissists, psychopaths, and other abusive, hostile, and antagonistic people, consider therapy to vent some of those feelings, but give up the idea that you can fix the world. The shifts in the world have normalized and legitimized narcissism, entitlement, and incivility and have given narcissists a sense of new power in the world. They feel emboldened to behave this way because the world appears to be cheering them on or, at least, giving them a *very* large platform. Increasingly, they also own the platforms, so they also control the message and our collective reality.

Closing the Gate

Some of this can be hard to swallow. In most of the Western world, there is the sense that everything can turn out fair and that we are the masters of our destiny. Sadly, when we bring narcissists and toxic people into the situation, it is not always that way. Some people get dealt a bum hand and have one or more narcissistic parents or toxic caregivers. Other people get dealt a bum hand and have narcissistic siblings. There are no choices in these cases. But you *can choose* to think differently about it, reflect on this dynamic, and not allow it to define you.

Once you attract one narcissist into your life, you start attracting more—it's like ants at a picnic. Once you start making accommodations for narcissists, always appeasing them, reassuring them, validating them, compromising for them, and succumbing to their reality, you become accustomed to these patterns and are not only less likely to recoil when you meet a narcissist, but also more likely to make accommodations for *more* narcissists. Many people (especially those with narcissistic or toxic parents) become masterful at being chameleons, chronically taking the temperature of the room and accommodating themselves to the bad behavior around them, providing more narcissistic supply, validating everyone, and caregiving because they have been doing that since childhood.

Your patterns *can* be broken. It just requires you to be willing to identify them and do things in a different way. These patterns are readily apparent; change can be as simple as attempting to stop being a "pleaser," listening to your inner voice, and distancing yourself from people with whom you do not grow, who throw you off balance, who are controlling, who are abusive in any way, and who are willing to throw you under the bus. Too many people believe that a worthwhile or exciting relationship is one in which they are forever trying to prove themselves. This pattern is a relic of having that unpleasable parent or maintaining the inner narrative that you are not enough. *Everyone is enough.* More than enough.

Once the narcissists are in your life, you will one day lift your head and find out that there are lots of them, and cleaning house can take some time. It may mean making new friends. There is also the phenomenon of "trickle-down narcissism"—once you start spending enough time with enough toxic people, you run the risk of losing some of your own empathy, simply because you aren't ever being given any. Empathy is like a language; if you don't hear it or speak it enough, it seemingly loses its utility. It is not enough to identify the toxic people around you; you must also start distancing yourself physically or psychologically (or both) so you can grow to your full potential and stop questioning yourself. Create the necessary boundaries and start closing the gate. And, when you see a toxic narcissist headed your way, lock the deadbolt. The following strategies will help you close the gate and protect yourself.

Stay Connected

Meaningful close relationships matter. Social connections in your community matter. It's that simple. The "technification" of the modern world means that we are starting to believe that we can all make it alone. Armed with a phone, Siri or Alexa, GPS, social media, and Postmates, we are sure that we have direction, companionship, and food. "What else do I need?" you may ask. Don't be so sure. A virtual relationship may be the equivalent of artificial sweetener—it tastes sweet but is not the real thing and, in the long run, may not be good for us.

A review by Julianne Holt-Lunstad (2010), a researcher at Brigham Young University, suggests that better quality and more connected social relationships can increase the likelihood of survival by 50 percent, and that lack of social connection may be as harmful to our health as risk factors including obesity, physical inactivity, and smoking more than half a pack a day. We are getting lonelier, so, even though we have the means to contact anyone in the world in our pocket at all times, 20 to 40 percent of older adults experience frequent loneliness (Perissinotto et al., 2012).

While some studies have reported that our social networks have declined 30 percent since 1985, cell phones and social media are actually not turning us into isolated cyborgs (Hampton et al., 2011). Our devices in combination with *real* relationships may represent the best balance. Secure and committed intimate relationships are actually good for the heart—people in such relationships have a lower risk of heart disease, and those who have conflictual relationships (something that is much more likely to happen with a narcissistic partner) have a higher risk of heart disease (a *true* broken heart) (Smith et al., 2017).

What does any of this have to do with the narcissism and toxic entitlement of our world? Lots. We are feeling more isolated in part because the world is feeling like a meaner place, and people are believing that they are having social connection when, instead, they are witnessing a social media feed. Loneliness and bad relationships are taking a toll on our health and subsequently taking years off of our lives. This isn't just about someone's being an asshole or having a vapid Instagram feed—this is about real life and health.

Sadly, and at one level, I get it; psychologists who address relationship difficulties focus on techniques including communication and enhancing relationship quality, as well as on emotional adjustment. In many cases, that is a noble endeavor that requires a fair shake. Here is the challenge: None of that works with narcissistic people, whether they are your parent, partner, boss, or friend. Anyone who has attempted to communicate with a narcissistic or entitled person knows that you come out of it more frustrated than when you went in. You may try multiple therapists who keep giving you the same prescription to work on listening and communication, and you know that handy therapeutic trick will not work in these cases. If a narcissist is meant to be an important source of social connection for you, you may be coming up short. Instead of trying to work on your communication with a narcissist, focus on developing meaningful connections with kind, compassionate, and empathic people. And keep the communication with the narcissist to a minimum.

Instead of Offering Forgiveness, Learn to Let Go

Forgiveness is narcissistic people's dream. They love it because they benefit from it tremendously. Forgiveness is a thorny issue in research, therapy, and spiritual counseling. By and large, we consider it to be a good thing—the problem is that it is a very powerful tool, and it is often misused and misconstrued. Forgiveness is considered divine, a virtue, and believed to be an antidote to resentment. However, when dealing with toxic people and with narcissists, a slightly more holistic and critical view may be needed.

The definition of "forgiveness" is "to cease to feel resentment against (an offender)" (Merriam-Webster, 2018). To cease to feel resentment means that you have let go of the resentment. Far too many people say they have forgiven someone even when the resentment remains. Because forgiveness is viewed as such a virtue, people want to get there, but, if the resentment persists, then it may be an empty victory. If you say you have forgiven someone, but you still resent him or her, then what do you have? Forgiveness is an active process, and the motivation to forgive and let go of resentment is required.

Forgiveness can be confusing because it gets heaped in with other processes, including condoning behavior, excusing behavior, pardoning behavior, and forgetting behavior (Toussaint et al., 2015). These are actually different processes, and the different processes that are subsumed under forgiveness become even more complicated when we start thinking about how to manage the varied toxic people in our lives.

The pressure to forgive comes from all kinds of sources: friends, family, society at large, daytime television shows, spiritual teachings, most major world religions, even books at the drugstore checkout counter. All extol the benefits of forgiveness. The literature on forgiveness is also quite compelling, and literature reviews have highlighted work that suggests that forgiveness facilitates psychological healing, improves mood, improves health, restores a sense of power, and may even have larger world benefits, such as reconciliation and resolution of conflicts between groups (Enright and Fitzgibbons, 2015).

Because of this pressure and compelling evidence, many people rush their process of forgiveness ("Hurry up and forgive!"). And, even when forgivers are aware that all they are doing is attempting to stop the feeling of resentment, the forgive-ee may take the forgiveness to represent absolution. In the wrong hands, forgiveness can be interpreted as, "We're good, wonderful, so let's go back to how things have been." Let's return to the key premises of toxic people and narcissism as a whole: lack of empathy, lack of insight, entitlement, inability to learn from past behavior or consequences—not exactly fertile ground for people who have been forgiven to learn from their behavior or even understand what it is they did wrong. In fact, narcissists are likely to believe they have a right to that forgiveness with little regard for the pain they have caused or a change in their behavior. It can be difficult to forgive, especially if the transgression is particularly hurtful, such as infidelity, stealing money or resources, a hurtful lie, harming someone's career or job, or emotional or physical abuse. And, if the person who has been forgiven turns around and *does it again*, it can be devastating for the person who provided the forgiveness.

Narcissists may sometimes feel guilt when they behave badly, but, by and large, they feel sheepish and ashamed at getting caught, and they feel the inconvenience of getting caught. They are more likely to feel shame, which then propels them into more bad behavior. Sociopaths and psychopaths don't even experience guilt or remorse, so forgiveness for them is pointless; they don't care either way. Unfortunately, since narcissists rarely are self-reflective, forgiveness does not often result in behavioral change—they typically just do what they want and clean up the messes later. Your forgiveness just becomes part of their cleaning up their mess.

Over the years in my work with survivors of toxic relationships, and with those who choose to remain in relationships or other situations with narcissists—whether a spouse, a parent, a best friend, an employer, a child, or a sister—I've learned that forgiveness is a personal process. People should not feel that there is a time frame, nor should they feel it is required to forgive another person. In general, people are uncomfortable with conflict, so they rarely call toxic people out on their bad behavior. As a result, many narcissistic, antagonistic, and otherwise toxic people are able to behave badly in an unchecked manner for a very long time. This can often happen because people do keep forgiving them. Everyone is a forgiveness cheerleader these days and will encourage other people to forgive repeat offenders such as narcissists. That drive to "keep the peace" means that the toxic person keeps getting forgiveness and Get Out of Jail Free cards and is never made to be accountable for his or her behavior.

It is essential to draw a distinction between forgiveness and letting go, because they are somewhat different processes. Demanding forgiveness or requiring people to stop resenting is a tall order. But helping them release the resentment, teaching them that they are not responsible for the bad behavior of a parent or a spouse or a boss, allowing them to accept that they deserve something better, and creating a psychological distance that feels safe—that is letting go. In the societal rush to forgive, the person impacted often does not have the opportunity to engage in step one, which is letting go. Letting go empowers you and also allows you to stop living in the toxic relationship space. By letting go, through distance and stepping back and setting boundaries and taking care of yourself, you can move forward. Whether that someday culminates in forgiveness is a personal journey. Letting go is often the most some people can get to, and that is just fine. You are not likely to forgive someone if you know he or she is going to behave badly again, but you may be willing to let it go if that means you can just walk away from it. Letting go doesn't mean you have to embrace the person, pick up where you left off, or let him or her off the hook; it is really the equivalent of taking a heavy load off your back and laying it down—of not carrying the burden of another person's bad behavior.

These processes can be made all the more difficult when people around you are insisting that you forgive so everyone can just get on with their lives. I have worked with numerous individuals who have been told that they are being cruel, or mean, or un-Christian by not forgiving an abusive narcissist who abused them. Narcissists' behavior is kept in place by the groupthink or status quo of the people around them and, if the system is prone to forgive and forget, then everyone in that group is going to expect you to jump on that train too. In some ways this can feel like being revictimized, as though you are as toxic as your abuser because you won't just hurry up and heal. I have termed this process "gaslighting by proxy." Keep in mind that this is the selfish need of the stakeholders around the narcissist (who may have had a hand in creating the narcissist) to not have to face the situation for what it is, or who are simply relieved that someone else is taking the abuse, and they want you to remain in your role as proverbial punching bag. They may be trying to avoid a change to their lifestyle and social structure and are fine with your being a sacrificial lamb in the name of that status quo.

The misinterpretations around forgiveness mean that many people believe that letting go of resentment means that they also must go back to life as usual with the transgressor. Absolutely not. Desmond Tutu, an advocate of forgiveness, actually suggested a better balance when he said, "Forgiving is not forgetting; it's actually remembering—remembering and not using your right to hit back. It's a second chance for a new beginning. And the remembering part is particularly important. Especially if you don't want to repeat what happened." Yes. The remembering part is important, because, as we have seen, we cannot always let the difficult and narcissistic people in our lives go completely—it may be an elderly parent we still feel a humane desire to help or a boss in a job we have to keep. It may be an unkind sister or a spouse with whom the decision to remain in the relationship feels necessary. So, yes, the remembering part is important. The letting go is the first step on this train, and perhaps some people never get to full forgiveness but, by creating a safe space within themselves, they may be able to create the distance and space to protect themselves.

However, even forgiveness may not be the end of the line. Tutu went on to say, "Once you have been able to forgive, the final step is to either renew or release the relationship you have with the one who has harmed you. Indeed, even if you never speak to the person again, even if you never see them again, even if they are dead, they live on in ways that affect your life profoundly."

Perhaps the most painful part of toxic relationships is that they can haunt you for a lifetime. Even after having therapy, reading, learning, growing, and being surrounded by loving forces and doing things you love, the scars remain. The angry voice of a parent echoes forth from childhood into your adulthood. The unending insults and accusations of a controlling and narcissistic partner, the mocking tones of a toxic group of friends, the insults and professional damage incurred from a psychopathic boss all stick around. For many clients I have worked with, and in the myriad narratives I have heard about these relationships, the self-doubt remains for years. People experience physical health issues secondary to stress that lingers long after the relationship dissipates, and the inability to trust can haunt them for decades. The echoes and shadows cast by a toxic relationship are long—and all of this can make forgiveness a complex process.

Do not put yourself on a forgiveness schedule. Instead make the decisions that accelerate *your* healing. If you do forgive a narcissist, do so with eyes wide open: He or she may transgress again. That means that your forgiveness, if you chose to offer it, was not a gift to the narcissist but rather a gift to yourself. It may bring an end to the damaging process of ruminating about what someone did to you—and again, letting go is the first step in that journey.

Stop Defending Yourself

We defend ourselves to provide a rationale for our behavior to other people. It rarely works. If you actually did do something wrong, defending yourself serves as a rationalization when, often, the other person wants an apology. Thus, if you actually did do something wrong, then apologize. If you did not do anything wrong, then why are you defending yourself? The difficulty with narcissistic and toxic people is that they are always accusing people of all kinds of transgressions, small and large. Because they rely largely on projection as a defense and will often project their shortcomings and sins onto other people, people who have to deal with toxic people find themselves endlessly defending themselves. When faced with a narcissist's accusations or criticisms, it is tempting to pull out text messages and emails and a slew of documents to "prove" your case. In addition, it can be tempting to show toxic narcissists the "error of their ways" by trying to school them, teach them, and perhaps even communicate with them about how you feel. Here's the rub: They do not care. While the standard mental health advice is to communicate, it is a pointless exercise with a narcissist, who will not listen, not care, and likely not change.

The smallest things set them on edge. Remember, narcissists and toxic people in general are *hypersensitive*. So the small things often set them off. If you introduce yourself to someone before they do, if you don't buy the correct brand of toothpaste, if you don't call them by the correct title, they experience these oversights as massive insults. You may find yourself tiptoeing around the minefields they create, and that tension can make you more likely to say the "wrong" thing. There is no point in defending yourself—you will never get it right. It's a catch-22: If you do it wrong, they will get angry; if you do it their way and they don't want it that way that day, they will get angry. If you try to defend yourself and say, "But this is what you asked for," they will not listen, or they will contradict you. Relationships with narcissistic or toxic people are chronic catch-22s or double binds—you can't win. It's easier to not play, definitely easier to not defend, and absolutely easier to not personalize it.

Narcissists also have a tendency to hold on to grievances and air them repeatedly. They must keep little vaults where they place all of the times they believe that someone has wronged them, so they can pull them out. This means that, the longer you are in a relationship with a narcissist, the more grievances pile up. When you do get into an argument with narcissistic or toxic people, they will march out the things you did wrong months or even years ago. When they pull out their various grievances, ignore them, or nod politely, but definitely do not defend yourself. Odds are, they won't be listening anyhow.

Your best technique can be simply termed "psychological minimalism." You can forestall the frustrating practice of defending yourself by just sticking to the facts. Don't give long explanations, don't give them facts they are going to ignore, don't give them more information than they need, don't share your feelings and, obviously, don't defend yourself. It is easy to descend into a texting abyss with them and waste an entire day sending increasingly long and angry texts. Stick to "yes," "no," "okay," and "thank you." It is tempting to want to make your case but save your energy for things that matter.

Stop Handing Over Your Kindness

This guidance is going to be paradoxical, and I may seem to be contradicting myself toward the end of this chapter. Bear with me.

Think of your kindness or compassion as a fragile antique vase that is worth a lot of money. You would not give that fragile antique vase to a three-year-old to hold, would you? And your rationale would be that the vase is expensive, and that the small child would not be able to manage it. He or she would be likely to drop it and break it and not really be able to appreciate how valuable it is. To prevent this from happening, you would not give the child the priceless vase to hold in the first place.

Use that framework to understand your kindness. If you hand over your kindness and compassion to a careless narcissist, it will be dropped and broken. It is valuable and important, and if it is repeatedly dropped, it will break. The existing narrative often teaches good, kind people that, if they expend enough goodness, enough kindness, or enough compassion, they can turn someone around. They can rescue a dark-hearted person from the darkness. It doesn't work that way with narcissists. They will take that kindness and drop it on the floor, and, while one can say, "That's okay, it can be replaced, kindness exists in a bottomless well," kindness is, after all, not a "thing." That raises the larger question of how many times you can be hurt before you break. How many times can your kindness be denigrated, rejected, and abused before you start losing your sense of self?

That is not to say that you should put away that kindness. Use it, and use it often, but with worthy recipients. Sadly, we give significantly more of our kindness away to the people who disregard it, misuse it, or denigrate it than to the people who deserve it. Treat your kindness as a resource that brings health to your life and the lives of deserving recipients. Narcissists, psychopaths, high-conflict people, antagonistic individuals, difficult people, and anyone engaging in otherwise toxic behavior cannot be rescued, and it is not your job to do so. Distribute your kindness judiciously and, when the narcissist abuses it, don't be surprised. It's time to shift the equation upside down. Stop giving 90 percent of the best of you to the most toxic people, reserving only 10 percent for those who are good and compassionate. Flip the math; give the 90 percent to the reciprocal and healthy relationships and the 10 percent to the narcissists with whom you are forced to interact. Never be deliberately cruel to anyone, narcissistic or not, but stop handing over the best of yourself and your time to the people who cannot engage in a reciprocal and respectful relationship. The best course of action is to simply be kind to everyone, but do not wait for it to be reciprocated with a narcissistic recipient.

Manage Them

Ironically, despite how manipulated we feel by narcissists, it is so easy to manage them! In fact, it is like taking candy from a baby.

Think about the singular air they breathe: validation.

So validate them. Insincerely and briefly. But validate them. It doesn't cost you anything but maybe a moment of discomfort.

We cannot cut all of these people out of our lives. If you do need to interact with them—perhaps the toxic coworker, or the difficult aunt during the holidays, or the narcissistic sister you will see at a family wedding—you need a game plan. Maintain distance and boundaries when possible but, if you do need to interact, give them what they need. Validate them. By now you know what matters to them—it may be their appearance, their accomplishment, their clothing, their family, their many stories about themselves. Whatever it is, validate it.

Then get out of there.

These little bursts can help manage the situation. The narcissists are often too self-focused to sense the inauthenticity. But then do not tangle with them any further. If they try to joust with you (backhanded insults, pissing contests), don't engage. By not engaging, you may frustrate them even more, but you keep yourself clean and, in some ways, empowered.

The formula is simple for managing them: validate, smile, don't engage, and exit gracefully. It is deeply empowering to take away their power. Many people will push back against this guidance, saying, "But then I am not being authentic" or simply that it feels awful to validate them. Maintaining a relationship with someone narcissistic does mean pawning off a part of your authenticity. In an ideal world, you would not need to engage but, if you do, you want to make it as seamless and nonconflictual as possible. It is better for your mental and physical health to avoid unnecessary conflict.

Start Gatekeeping and Boundary Keeping

My goal for this book is to help people engage in gatekeeping—to not allow the narcissistic, the difficult, the controlling, and the cruel in the door in the first place. Once they get in and do their damage, it can exact a tremendous toll on people. The habit of letting them in is hard to break, and, once you have one narcissist in your life, odds are you will have more.

Gatekeeping works in two ways: one, not letting them into your life; and two, once they are in your life, creating distance and boundaries to manage the situation. Let's term these "gatekeeping" and "boundary keeping" respectively.

When we break down the various relationships in life, there are a few pathways to consider:

1. *The people you do not get to choose because you're related to them:* These include mothers, fathers, sisters, brothers, stepparents, stepsiblings, half siblings, aunts, uncles, cousins, grandparents, and in-laws. Gatekeeping would not work here because you did not really choose them, but boundary-keeping would.

2. *The people you do not get to choose because they are part of a larger system:* For example, you may choose a job or a school, but you may not choose your fellow students or colleagues. Again, this is where boundary keeping plays a role.

3. *The people you do choose:* These include intimate partners and friends. In these cases, gatekeeping can really work and work well. However, if your gatekeeping doesn't work, then boundary-keeping is a necessity to ensure that you are not subjected to abuse.

4. *Jobs you choose and the people who may be hiring you:* You can actually do homework on these people, and you can also trust your experience of them. If they come off as glib, dismissive, or just generally unpleasant in the interview, it isn't going to get better, and, if the intel on these people reveals them to be toxic or difficult bosses, then you are not going to be the exception. It becomes a case of gatekeeping.

We often miss the opportunities for gatekeeping, not just because we do not have a choice, but because we are not paying attention. A lifetime of other narcissistic relationships can make us vulnerable to miss the cues. Indoctrination into societal myths that "love can cure all" can leave us believing we can rescue an unempathic or contemptuous person with our compassion. Boundary keeping requires flexing very different muscles and can be exhausting over the months and years, but can still be less exhausting than arguing, defending, and sparring with a narcissistic person.

Practice Self-love

Ironically, the greatest antidote to narcissism is self-love, self-compassion, or self-valuation. The word "narcissism" derives from the ancient myth of Narcissus, who ultimately suffered and died from the torment of being enraptured by his own reflection (Narcissus's reflection in the water may have been one of the first famous selfies!). However, narcissism is often erroneously labeled "self-love." As we have established, narcissism is, in essence, the opposite of self-love; it may, in fact, be a form of self-loathing, pathological insecurity, and hollow self-aggrandizement. But, even for the rest of us—the non-narcissists, the nontoxic, the rank-and-file regular folk—the self-love part does not come naturally. Something about our culture results in the opposite of self-love or self-valuation. It could be argued, in line with the research on materialism and consumerism, that self-love means that we will not consume. If we love ourselves, and are internally secure, then we don't need different hair or thinner hips or more stuff—we would be content and sustained by our love for ourselves, a secure sense of self, and healthier relationships. Self-love or, at least, self-comfort feels like an impossible goal to reach because, in a capitalist and consumerist economy, insecurity sells. To add insult to injury, buying new things or transforming ourselves is pitched as self-love ("Don't you deserve a new handbag [or car, vacation, candy bar, shoes]?").

There are numerous reasons that the narcissistic have, in essence, overtaken our lives, leadership, and psyches in so many pernicious ways. But one of the most fundamental is that many of us never learned the concept of loving or even liking ourselves. We are self-effacing to a fault, we believe we are not good enough, and that message can come from numerous sources, including our families, our society, our media, and our advertisers. One of the *best* interventions we have to protect us in the toxic landscape of people is self-love, self-compassion, and a secure sense of self, and the constant reminder that all of us are good enough, whether or not we get an A, or drive a new car, or are overweight or underweight, or are depressed, or have a job that doesn't pay much. All of us are more than good enough. It is a mantra that should be recited every morning in every school—a different sort of pledge of allegiance.

A shift in enhancing authentic self-love in our world is essential. First, it is a critical prevention tool. When we value and love ourselves, we also advocate for ourselves and trust our judgment when we feel that something or someone is unhealthy for us. People who engage in self-love and accurate self-appraisal do not equate hoop jumping with love. Kids who feel secure may be less likely to succumb to high-risk behaviors or be less likely to bully and intimidate other children. Second, it gives us the power to walk away. When we love and value ourselves, we do not stay at the table with people who chronically devalue us. We may need to show up to work with them, we may need to share our holiday tables with them, we may need to listen to their rants on airplanes and at soccer games but, when we value ourselves we do not engage with them, we do not fall for their party line, their hype, their manipulations and projections, and we are able to draw psychological boundaries in our minds and just not let them in. Self-love is a sort of psychological "condom" that protects us from the toxic stuff around us and gives us the strength to walk away from it, close the door before it even gets in, and remain serene and strong in the presence of it. Self-love is not about being a doormat and putting up with it; it's about learning to safeguard yourself and to stop hoping they will change, and about just distancing yourself and valuing yourself. Self-love is, in essence, a sort of reverse kryptonite— and, when you are in possession of it, it often entirely disarms the toxic people around you. Narcissistic people are always looking for a fight, and they are also prone to boredom. If you don't provide validation and don't provide them an outlet for their rage and insecurity, they lose interest. The best way to eliminate their impact from your life? Don't give them the fight and disengage.

Because self-love is not built into our culture, most people need to work on it. In that case, self-love is like a muscle that needs to be developed. How do we do this?

DEVELOP FRIENDSHIPS AND RELATIONSHIPS
WITH PEOPLE WHO VALUE YOU FOR YOU

These are the people who value you not for what you can get them, or because you make them look good, or because you improve their status, or because you endure their BS, or because you take care of them. They value you for you. That means giving up old patterns. It means to stop choosing people you feel you need to chase or because they are exciting. To stop choosing people who leave you feeling like you are not enough because that is an old familiar feeling. To come clean with yourself and recognize that you have been poisoned by a status-conscious world or invalidating messages from childhood, and that you have stuck it out with someone not because he or she is a good person, but because he or she is successful or powerful or wealthy or privileged or criticizes you like Mom and Dad did. We have all done it, but you can undo it by being honest and reflecting on how you are treated. Pay attention to how people make you feel.

DO THINGS YOU LOVE

If you are fortunate, you love your job, but many people do not get to be paid for doing the job they love, and it is not always realistic for that to happen. It would be great to live in that world, but we don't—and most of us do not have access to trust funds or independent wealth. For those of us who don't, we can take on that hobby, join a group of people who do that thing we love (a hiking group or a band or local choir), volunteer, travel on the cheap, or find whatever it is we love and develop it. When we have that sense of efficacy, which is a belief in our ability to success-fully do something (and, ideally, we enjoy it), it goes a long way toward helping us love and value ourselves. Clocking into a job you hate, going home to a partner who invalidates you, spending family time with people who undermine you, and tuning in to a media pitching poison and polar-ization are surefire ways to *not* love yourself. Switch up your paradigm. What do you want to remember as the curtain starts to drop? That you endured a lifetime of toxic people and toxic situations, or that you took back your life and authentically made it your own?

<u>WORK AT IT</u>

Sadly, yes, self-love, self-compassion, and self-valuation are effortful. On most days, we will snap back to our usual self-devaluation, our tendency to make excuses for people who treat us badly, our belief that we do not deserve any better. Many people get the implicit message throughout their lives that they do not deserve better. And, for that reason, people stay in abusive situations and invalidating relationships of all kinds. The people who tell you or imply that you do not deserve better are the ones who are clipping your wings and keeping you from flying away. Their insecurity means that they use criticism as a way of elevating themselves or sinking the dreams of others, so those people can't leave them.

Don't Get Into the Mud With Them

This is difficult. When people want to fight dirty, the temptation is to sink lower with them. For reasons of ego and of reciprocity, we have a tendency to meet people where they are, even when it is low. When someone accuses us, we defend ourselves; when someone insults us, we are tempted to insult them too; when someone swings a proverbial punch, we want to get them right back. This can be *magnified* when the attacks are public, such as on social media, in other public forums, or at family gatherings.

Not getting into the mud means not getting into pissing contests with Facebook trolls, internet idiots, Twitter bullies, or other sad people who get a rise out of posting despicable sentiments in the hope that other people will engage with them. Nearly all internet trolls are narcissists, sociopaths, psychopaths, difficult, uncivil, or toxic in other ways. Don't descend into their mud puddles. Over time, if people stop giving oxygen to their fires, they will retreat back into their caves.

If the trolling really spins out of control, with a genuine threat to your reputation or livelihood, then the assistance of legal counsel and cease-and-desist orders may be necessary. But if it is merely a "he said/she said" situation or another kind of smear campaign that is much smaller in scope, hold your head high and be reminded of how important it is to not engage with these people. Narcissists tend to have brass knuckles on their soul—don't take the fight. In addition, as already noted, they become frustrated when people will not fight with them; they actually become galvanized by arguing. Take away their power, and do not give them the satisfaction. It will be better for your health if you avoid the conflict.

LESS IS MORE

In communicating with narcissists, less is more. Far more. They tend to be able to manipulate communication, gaslight, or just argue you to death if you give them too much to work with. Your best approach is often to treat communication the way you would with an interrogator—keep it brief, spare, sparse, and simple. An easy rule of thumb: Never start a comment to narcissists with the word "but." If you start a sentence with "but," you are likely defending yourself or contradicting them. An argument with them is not worth it. Disengagement in every way is the only way these relationships work—and keeping communication simple and brief is an easy way to achieve that.

Hold On Tight to Your Own Reality

This is actually more difficult than holding on to your own hat on a blustery day. It's clear that individual narcissists gaslight other people and doubt their reality. Gaslighting is a classical element of the narcissistic personality style. The fact is also that *the world is a place that gaslights us*—that questions how we feel, that second-guesses us, that implores us to give second chances to other people who have wronged us ("Give him a chance—it's just boys being boys," or, "That wasn't a racist statement," or, "Women need to stop being so sensitive"). That's actually a mindfuck, because it is one thing if a person doubts your reality, but when the entire world is in on it—it can be very difficult to hold on to your point of view.

Remember that privilege is a societal manifestation of narcissism—the idea that some people are entitled to better treatment and more of everything. We are living in polarized, politically charged times, in which all forms of social media appear to hold the rights on reality. When the world is permitted to gaslight us, then we are more vulnerable to individual gaslighting, and then we are more vulnerable to allowing narcissists into our lives and letting them stay in our lives. Racism, sexism, classism, heterosexism, ableism, ageism, and all other isms are all forms of gaslighting—to doubt and defame the reality of others, to leave them second-guessing themselves, and by so doing holding on to the power.

We can take back that power by checking in with ourselves on our reality. If something feels invalidating, dehumanizing, or disconnected, take a long, critical look at it. Don't make excuses for it. Step back gently and take a moment to touch base with yourself about your reality. Gaslighting works because it makes us feel like our reality is questionable. Certainly, all of us can listen to other points of view; we do not always need to yield to them. A "kumbaya" world of all of us finding middle ground with people who doubt our reality is nonsense. The ultimate way to respect yourself is to respect your reality and to value empathy, compassion, respect, reciprocity, and kindness from others. I have plenty of friends who have markedly different opinions from me, but we share those differences with respect and never doubt the reality of the other. It is possible. But it means valuing yourself first. Once differences descend into a personal attack, it's no longer about sharing opinions; it's abuse. And that means it's time to go.

Don't Make It Personal

This is the hardest guidance of all to follow, because it sure as hell *feels* personal. When someone is insulting you, it's personal. When someone is cheating on you or lying to you, it's personal. When someone is yelling at you, it's personal. When someone is invalidating you, it's personal. However, if we spool back to the original issue, remind yourself that people who do this are *deeply* insecure and lack insight. That is the core of this behavior. It's not an excuse—it's a framework. Their insecurity turns them into tantrum-throwing selfish children all the time. They are angry at the world, they are envious of other people, they feel the world owes them something, they are afraid of being alone, they feel like they deserve fame and fortune, and they are chronically frustrated. This is all happening inside them, and they can't stand this uncomfortable feeling, so they take it out on everyone else. There is an old adage that states: *Hurt people hurt people.* It can be hard to get your head around the idea that it is not you, and it is not personal.

When you take their behavior personally, when you buy their hype that you are not enough, then you are internalizing their emptiness, you are making their fears and their insecurity your own, and you are empowering their words. The closer you are to narcissists, the more you have to endure their abuse, invalidation, and contempt. Whenever possible, don't take it personally. At some level, they mistreat everyone, unless they stand to gain from them. So it's not personal—it's who they are. Find other people who know them. They either are narcissists too (so they don't get it) or have been through what you have with this person. Learn from that. If it were personal, they would not be doing it to everyone else too. By making it less personal, you can create more distance and learn to become impervious to it, which is the best way to stay sane. Interestingly, narcissists tend to save their harshest words and strongest punches for the people who are most vulnerable to them or closest to them (such as spouses, children, and parents), so keep in mind that, if you are close to a toxic person, you are getting the worst of it.

In an increasingly narcissistic world, it can be easy to take the many cruel things happening in the world and make them personal, such as policies and sentiments about racial groups, social class, gender, LGBTQ groups, immigrants, and religious groups. These sentiments may reflect a group of which you are a part, people you care about, or issues you work for. At some level, taking them personally may help invigorate your fight, but choose your battles. If you make the battle too personal, you may exhaust yourself. Find that balance—and I acknowledge this isn't easy. The more personal you make it, the less able you will be to cope with narcissism at either the individual or societal level. Recognize that narcissists are equal-opportunity offenders—they are generally mad at the world.

Retain Your Sense of Humor

Narcissists are so formulaic that it starts to feel like a clown in a circus or a gag in a cartoon—the joke always plays out the same way. Because they are formulaic, and, once you can see their behavior as such, you can laugh at it. Many of my clients report that, once the formula is cracked, they will smile or laugh to themselves at how the same pattern is followed every time. Narcissists don't even try to shift up their game; they just do the same things every time. In that way, narcissists are basically human "knock-knock" jokes—ridiculous, immature, predictable, and funny only when you are drunk or stoned.

I am asking you to laugh through your tears. Because the hurt of these relationships is real. However, once you see it for the pattern it is, it can feel less personal. You can have your personal chuckle and leave before the punch line. When the ridiculous world leader gets caught with his foot in his mouth (again), when the celebrity is found cheating on his or her wife (or husband) with someone thirty years younger, when the Instagram celebrity gets caught in a "Don't you know who I am?" moment on an airplane, when the reality star goes on a rant and is caught on video, when the ludicrous person starts screaming at people in a parking lot for not getting out of his or her way, just laugh. They trail their insecurity, behaving foolishly and narcissistically, everywhere they go. Think of them as rodeo clowns and court jesters put into the world for your amusement and entertainment. And then just laugh loudly and let their behavior go instead of letting it get you down. These patterns are not going to change; we have incentivized them, so you can only shake your head and hope that not too many people get hurt.

Find Meaning and Purpose

Viktor Frankl wrote, "Those who have a 'why' to live, can bear with almost any 'how.'" If you have endured or are still enduring narcissistic relationships, you are managing one hell of a *how*. A relationship with a narcissist can often sap you of your authentic sense of self, of any sense of meaning and purpose outside of yourself. A friend of mine termed it "being worn down to a nub." You feel as though you cannot think of higher-order issues, such as your own goals or dreams (often because they were minimized, mocked, trivialized, and devalued, or simply because you are exhausted). Setting a boundary or walking away from the narcissists in your life can and should be translated into an enactment not only of your goals and possibility, but also to give yourself permission to reflect on the meaning and purpose in your life. For so long, when you have to manage a life around a narcissist, at best, you are surviving, but you are often not thriving. You are getting through the days and trying to dodge bullets and insults and make sense of the inconsistent patterns. Frankl also speaks to how we can find meaning in suffering, and evolve through it. Nobody should intentionally seek out suffering, but once it finds you (perhaps in the form of an invalidating and antagonistic relationship), extract some meaning from the suffering, and evolve into a better you.

Once you devote part of yourself to meaning and purpose—through creativity, work, volunteering, spirituality, or simply loving the people around you—you'll be on a fast track to regenerating yourself and healing from the damage wrought by a relationship with a narcissist. A primary struggle for narcissistic people is that they do not devote themselves to the pursuit of meaning and purpose; do not let that devalue this process for yourself.

Take Care of Yourself

I loathe the concept of "self-care"—it's highly subjective, and many people are too busy or broke to achieve it. Self-care often takes in territory such as meditation, massages, baking bread, or binge-watching TV, as a moment when you take care of you but, if you are not careful, it can feel forced and like one more thing you feel that you are "supposed" to do! That said, self-care sometimes means engaging in daily practices or other rituals that pull you out of the typical toxic spheres in which so many people face invalidation or hostility and allow you to replenish. Think of it as a detoxification of sorts and, whether that means putting down the social media for a period of time before bedtime, or calling a friend who is uplifting during the daily commute, or giving yourself permission to stay home on a Saturday night and watch a guilty pleasure instead of succumbing to the fear of missing out (FOMO), it's a time when you do not fall into the rabbit hole of consumption, competition, and posturing and you just take care of yourself for a fleeting moment. A little of this every so often may fortify you and inoculate you for when you are faced with toxic circumstances.

Get Therapy

Many times, people who are trying to navigate narcissistic people and situations need a sounding board. The experience of chronic invalidation that accompanies any relationship with a narcissist can impact mental health in myriad ways, ranging from anxiety, sadness, and confusion to post-traumatic stress symptoms, in cases of more profound abuse and trauma. It is essential to have access to mental health services that allow you to address these symptoms, learn coping tools, understand the patterns that may keep you stuck when relating to narcissistic people, and receive some education on these patterns. Sometimes just a few sessions can be very useful and allow you to recalibrate. However, sadly, therapy is not a resource that is readily accessible to many people for reasons of money, insurance, access, stigma, and sometimes even fear. There are websites that can provide information about affordable and accessible resources. The Substance Abuse and Mental Health Services Administration (SAMHSA), a federal agency that addresses mental health services, provides a mental health locator service in the US. There are clinics that will take clients on a sliding scale. Your insurance may also pay for a certain number of therapy sessions. If there is a university near you that trains students in therapy, you can get therapy with a trainee for a very low cost (these trainees are closely supervised by more senior clinicians). Group therapy is another option and, for far less money than individual therapy, you can not only get the expertise of an experienced therapist, but also hear the experiences of other people who have endured similar circumstances and relationships.

Ensure that you choose a therapist with whom you feel comfortable—not all of us are created alike, and not every therapist is a perfect fit. It's okay to switch if you do not feel comfortable. In addition, not all therapists are well versed in the territory of high-conflict difficult relationships and in patterns such as narcissism. You may need to ask around to find someone who understands the specifics of these issues. Overall, therapy can be an invaluable resource to address mental health concerns, the confusion brought about by narcissistic relationships, the fallout from managing the feelings, and the ongoing sense of insecurity that these relationships leave behind.

Tend to Your Own Garden

We cannot fight all of this. No individual or, frankly, even a relatively well-organized group of individuals is going to push back against the existing structure of a narcissistic world. The bad guys are winning, but that doesn't mean that all is lost. The tendency is to believe that, if you have to deal with dirty fighters, you have to become a dirty fighter yourself. And, as these toxic patterns of antagonism, meanness, bullying, combative language, and societal narcissism overtake the world, it is easy for everyone to get pulled into the psychological gutter.

One of the hardest things to do, but one of the best, is to transcend it. Don't get in the mud. Let the toxic folks stay down in their native habitat of entitled, contemptuous, and superficial swamps, and simply don't engage. But then all of us need to go one step further: We need to ensure that we *do good* in our spaces. That may mean raising empathic children, being nicer to one another, practicing civility in all of our spaces, no longer looking for a fight, and trying to understand the perspective of other people. It means doing good work that feels meaningful to us, and not just a chase to get the nicest car, biggest house, and most expensive purse. It means that we stop living solely in pursuit of an Instagrammable lifestyle and instead live an authentic one.

There are so many small ways each of us can do this each day. Don't flip someone off on the highway. Don't get into a shouting match over a parking spot. Be kind to the cashier at the store and ask about the person's day. Leave a nice note for a neighbor who moved your package out of the way of the sprinkler. Send a thank-you card. Call a friend out of the blue for no other reason than to check on how he or she is doing. Buy a child's Girl Scout cookies or soccer-supporting candy (and then, if you don't want it, perhaps give it to someone else who may appreciate it). Smile at a stranger. Give up your seat on the subway to someone weighed down with bags. Offer your place in line to the person who has only one item. Offer to lift someone's bag. Don't roll your eyes at the parent who boards a flight with a child; instead, offer to help put away the person's luggage. Be warm to the person who is checking you in at a hotel. Don't yell at a clerk who can't answer your question as quickly as you want. When a service worker is less than graceful with you, ponder whether something difficult may have happened to the person that day, and yet he or she still had to come to work. Step out of yourself and find the small ways to share some empathy and spread it around a world that is populated by parking lot fights, racist vitriol, entitled shoppers, and "Don't you know who I am?" around every corner.

In doing this, each of us can create our own personal "gardens" of empathy, compassion, and authenticity. Push the toxic behaviors, situations, and people out of them—in essence, weed your garden; otherwise, they will kill everything you plant! My favorite writer, Barbara Kingsolver, wrote in her masterpiece *The Poisonwood Bible* of "making something right in at least one tiny corner of the vast house of wrongs." Stop worrying about the lives of the toxic people around you, stop trying to compete with them, and stop defending yourself in the face of them. Live your life fully and authentically. I hold firmly to the conviction that there are more kind and good people than toxic and difficult people out there; however, because the toxic people suck most of the oxygen out of the world, command the airwaves, infuse us with their insecurities, and run our countries and large corporations and other institutions, all of us spend too much of our time adjusting ourselves to "the vast house of wrongs." If, instead, each of us would just focus on tending our own gardens and keeping our side of the street clean, then perhaps—just perhaps—these scattered good garden patches may start to interlink to form something bigger and good—a larger space that becomes a sanctuary from the toxic people you now know how to outmaneuver. If you are going to give out second chances, give them to the people who deserve them. Stop wasting them on the narcissists.

* * *

Hopefully, this survival guide has better enabled you to close the gate and keep the toxic narcissists out of your life—or, at least, out of your heart. When you work on developing meaningful relationships and staying connected to the people who deserve your kindness, it becomes easier to manage or even laugh at the narcissists. Remember, your biggest weapons against them are self-love, self-valuation, and an accurate understanding of who you are, and part of this means acknowledging to yourself that you are enough.

Chapter 12

The Big Picture

Civilization is a hopeless race to discover remedies
for the evils it produces.

—ROUSSEAU

Are we in trouble?

Yes.

Up until now, we have considered narcissism and entitlement and general interpersonal toxicity as issues related to an *individual* (narcissistic husband, entitled sister, toxic boss, narcissistic mother, toxic best friend, narcissistic ex-girlfriend). We have discussed strategies for identifying this *person* and managing this *person*. If a person can be narcissistic, can a system be narcissistic, entitled, or toxic? Can a workplace be? A school? A country? A civilization?

Yes.

The central thesis of this book hovers around the fact that spending time with a narcissistic, entitled, toxic person is not good for us. It leaves us feeling full of self-doubt, unsettled, anxious, depressed, and confused. We feel "not enough" and start spending our time chasing scraps of validation from narcissistic people who notice us only when we are useful to them.

It's a bit of a reciprocal relationship: Societies that lack empathy and are entitled, superficial, and grandiose are likely to house more narcissistic and entitled people. However, societies that are narcissistic and entitled are also more likely to foster conditions that reinforce and value narcissistic and entitled patterns. It winds up being a one-two punch—narcissistic societies may be causing damage because they contain narcissistic people, but it is possible that narcissism in the society at large is also the issue. Narcissistic societies give platforms to antagonism, dehumanization, invalidation, and polarization. These systems also devalue intrinsic and relational factors. Factors may include:

- Deregulated financial systems that are rewarded for their inequitable business practices
- Media platforms that celebrate polarizing discussions
- News that disproportionately features divisive rhetoric
- A celebration of materialism and consumerism
- Measuring success by wealth and consumption rather than happiness or well-being
- Maintenance of existing oppressions that do not provide adequate protections for vulnerable citizens
- Trivializing vulnerability and expression of emotion in men or branding it as weakness

When we live in such societies, do we lose our true north? Is living under such conditions the equivalent of breathing polluted air? Even if we are not participating in the incivility, the invalidation, and the societal narcissism, are we inevitably being affected by it? Even if you do not have a narcissistic person in your life, perhaps all of us are in a relationship with a narcissistic culture.

Are we simply getting used to it?

Our Habituation to Narcissism

Habituation, as mentioned earlier, is the adjustment to a condition, even if it is unpleasant, so it does not affect us as strongly anymore—we just stop responding to a stimulus because we adjust to it. After a while, we may stop noticing the cacophony of traffic outside a bedroom window or a smell in the air. We adjust. That is not necessarily a good thing, because that ongoing exposure to noise is actually not good for us in the long term, and the smell may actually be an irritant that may damage our health.

311

I was recently asked by someone hopeful, who had been deeply hurt in a narcissistic relationship, "Hey, now, with all of these narcissistic leaders and all of this narcissistic bad behavior, it's drawing attention to it, right? Now people are mad, and it will change, right?" No. If anything, all of the bad behavior is giving permission to it and emboldening it, and we are noticing it less. When this kind of behavior is not called out by society, and is instead rewarded by it, or simply ignored or accepted, then it is more likely to creep into our families, personal lives, and professional lives. We have become a world of narcissists and people who have become masterful at enduring narcissism. Because our words rarely result in any change, we may, as a world, be simply feeling helpless.

But are we habituating to the bad behavior of presidents, prime ministers, cabinet members, CEOs, studio heads, television personalities, professional athletes, celebrity chefs, and reality TV celebrities? Are we so accustomed to it that we no longer notice it and then run the risk of treating it as normal? There appears to be "outrage fatigue." People cannot swivel their head quickly enough to take note of the most recent disturbing scandal, whether it is misappropriated tax dollars, racist utterances by the celebrity du jour, another slate of sexual harassment accusations, a road-rage shooting, an airplane assault, or the abuse of low-wage workers. Even if outrage is issued, the bad behavior gets replaced by another transgressor and another transgression. We can't keep track. At some level, we are getting used to it. Once we become accustomed to it, the danger is that, either we accept it, or it becomes endemic.

We are in the era of "trickle-down narcissism." Just as it can affect us in an individual relationship, it can happen societally. When we hit a critical mass of narcissism as a normalized pattern in leadership, communities, commerce, legal systems, schools, and universities, then it will trickle down. The people at the top of our hierarchies set the tone and remain the noisiest influencers. Their behavior trickles down to us and guides our expectations for our own behavior and the behavior of other people—most unfortunately, our children. When this becomes the new normal, it starts to make sense why we "talk ourselves into" narcissistic relationships and give them a free pass, and perhaps even become less loving and more selfish ourselves. That's the real tragedy of trickle-down narcissism. How much of the best part of our selves do we lose in this new world order?

The Well-Being Vortex

According to the Gallup-Sharecare Well-Being Index, "the world's largest data set on well-being," 2017 was the worst year for well-being that has been documented. Interestingly, it was worse than the period after the recession in 2008. That implies that perhaps the drops in well-being are not solely the economy—something else is happening. According to the data, in the period after the recession (2009), numerous regions of the country did evidence a drop in well-being; however, these drops were linked largely to financial concerns. This is consistent with other polls tracking happiness, which have been showing a steady downturn for the past few decades. The decrease in well-being in 2017 suggests that the discontent and the diminished well-being that's being observed now may be more linked to psychological issues: emotional factors, sadness, discontent with jobs, discontent with relationships. Even more notable is that every single demographic group exhibited a drop in well-being in 2017 *except* for wealthy white men (privilege is protective).

What the Gallup-Sharecare poll does not get at is the *why*. Obviously, numerous hypotheses have been forwarded, including shifts in leadership in the US and around the world, disproportionate wealth distribution, the greater polarization between the red and blue and the left and right on issues including guns, immigration, race relations, gender equality, healthcare, and religion. Money continues to concern Americans, but in a very specific way. The concern is obviously about a livable wage and consistency of employment but also about future uncertainty, magnified by concerns about healthcare costs, occupational stability, and planning for old age (and, with more and more narcissists out there, it is less likely that family members will serve as caregiving safety nets for one another).

Epidemiologists Richard Wilkinson and Kate Pickett write in their book, *The Inner Level,* that societies characterized by greater income inequality evince higher levels of psychological dysfunction, as manifested by higher levels of stress, anxiety, mood disorders, and addiction. They also present analyses that reveal associations between income inequality and what they term "self-enhancement bias," which is, in essence, grandiosity. So this trend of narcissism isn't just about parenting and biology, it's about economic equality as well.

We are also living in a time of what has been termed "diseases of despair" (Case and Deaton, 2015). Suicide rates have risen 30 percent in over half of the states in America (CDC, 2018), 116 people per day died of opioid overdoses in 2016 (HHS, 2016), and 57 percent of adults with a mental illness did not receive mental health care (MHA, 2018). Drug overdoses are now the leading cause of death in adults under age fifty. While there is no way to empirically divine this, I remain convinced that a primary driver of this despair is the societal slippage into more and more narcissism and incivility. Everything in our world fosters insecurity, and conditions of insecurity give a home-field advantage to the narcissistic and toxic amongst us. The economy grows stronger, and yet we despair more. When vulnerability is viewed as weakness, emotions are viewed with contempt, insecurity is preyed upon by consumerism, and lack of empathy is praised as efficiency, then despair will spread like wildfire. Despair is not addressed by money, or stuff, or status. It is addressed by feeling whole, purposeful, meaningful, and loved.

Loneliness and Love

There are other trends afoot. Loneliness has been highlighted as a "public health issue." Vivek Murthy, the US surgeon general, notes in the *Harvard Business Review* that "we live in the most technologically connected age in the history of civilization, yet rates of loneliness have doubled since the 1980s." So, at a time when we can connect with a virtual human being at any time, night or day, we are feeling alienated. Murthy cites the physiological dangers of loneliness, which is a major contributor to stress, which, in turn, is associated with greater inflammation throughout the body and increases the risk of earlier mortality and heart disease, diabetes, joint disease, depression, and obesity. There are multiple explanations for loneliness, including migration patterns leading to families' living away from one another, longer work hours, telecommuting and gig employment, and lower rates of marriage. However, given the epidemic of narcissism, entitlement, and toxic relationships, perhaps the world at large has stopped incentivizing human relationships. Interestingly, research indicates that people who are characterized as being more materialistic (meaning that they endorse greater valuation of material possessions, and a greater focus on acquiring possessions) experience more loneliness (Pieters, 2013). Apparently, a cool new gadget or fancy new shoes aren't adequate replacements for a human relationship.

While we know we are supposed to value intrinsic outcomes such as happy relationships, and most of us actually do, there is an overall societal disdain for vulnerability, gratitude, slowing down to be with others, and empathy. When the narcissists started running the show, they were not going to value emotional states and qualities that they did not possess (empathy), and, instead, placed a higher value on those that they did (superficiality, vanity, validation, and entitlement). In this way, genuine gratitude went out of style, and individualized celebration such as selfies came into style. Human relationships are less valued if the prevailing power structures do not value them. It is also more profitable to "sell" cures for health, disease, diabetes, and depression than it is to teach people to also draw upon the "no-cost" solutions, such as cultivation of closeness, empathy, and human relationships. Mental health services are essential; however, the focus on "get better quick" schemes instead of on developing existing strengths misses a major opportunity for health and well-being for many people.

Sexual intimacy, a key part of close relationships, has also lost some of its value as an element of the human experience that draws people closer. We have commodified sex and sexuality in every way. In addition, powerful men often conflate sex and power—and, in fact, power makes the world their sexual playground, a commodity that can be acquired by coercion, money, and/or force. In the months when I was writing this book, the "incel" movement received mainstream attention due to the tragic events in Toronto whereby a man drove a van onto a busy city sidewalk, subsequently killing multiple people and pledging his support both of the "incel rebellion" and of a past perpetrator of a mass shooting ("incel" is a hybrid word that means "involuntarily celibate"). Incels often present with the patterns of covert narcissism or sociopathy: They have a brooding, angry, entitled rage at a world that withholds sex from them. In this "incelistic" view, women are commodities who deliver sex with little expectation of reciprocity or connection, and the incels maintain expectations that men have a right to a certain type of woman who has status by dint of her appearance or age. Incelism tends to generalize beyond just a disdain for women and reflects a general contempt for the world at large. While this incel movement mercifully is rather isolated, its tenets of sexual entitlement, devaluation, and dehumanization of women, wrapped up in the sullen brooding and petulant rage of socially stunted men, have pervaded a global worldview of sex. Sexual exploitation accounts for 66 percent of global profits from human trafficking (ILO, 2017) and an epidemic of rape is being observed in numerous cultures worldwide.

When the leader of one of the largest developed countries in the world brags about commodification of women, and we elevate male banter about sex by the numbers (more is better), narcissism and entitlement have effectively sucked the intimacy out of intimacy. Sex has become increasingly transactional, whether via pornography or "seeking arrangement" websites, and it's only a matter of time before virtual reality (VR) and artificial intelligence (AI)-enhanced robots become the purveyors of sex for people who do not have the appetite for intimacy or empathy. Recent research by Emily Cross and her colleagues at the University of Auckland in New Zealand homes in on this idea of "hostile sexism" (the belief that women want to control men in relationships, turning relationships into power struggles rather than spaces of intimacy, and the fear held by men that they will lose power as women gain more economic and social equality). These researchers reported that men who are "hostile sexists" believe that they have less control in a relationship, which can underlie a greater likelihood of aggressive responses to regain power in a relationship. While the authors did not examine narcissism in these relationships, constructs such as hostile sexism are likely to be congruent with narcissistic patterns and speak to yet another mechanism whereby narcissistic relationships can be unhealthy or downright dangerous.

In a world in which AI is resulting in machine models of computerized therapists and friends, the AI people may be onto something. As empathy becomes a hollower and less valued quality, and programming capacities expand, perhaps an AI robot will still be able to summon up more consistent empathy than a narcissist. Brave new world indeed....

The Era of Incivility

We are all getting a little touchier. While people who are narcissistic, entitled, or toxic have very short fuses and a propensity to overreact to frustration, disappointment, or even a sideways glance, none of us is immune to overreacting. Emily Yoffe, in an article on Slate, notes, "It seems we live in a culture devoted to retribution on the behalf of the thin-skinned." Truth.

The most thin-skinned tend to be the petty character-disordered folks, but, as the world becomes more toxic, all of us become more likely to fall prey to pettiness. Jonathan Haidt's work on evolutionary psychology beautifully captures this yin-yang of human nature. He describes humans as possessing both gratitude and vengeance, which promote sociality and interdependence but also eagle-eyed awareness. He has noted that our propensity for gratitude allows us to grow our social networks and develop alliances, while our propensity for vengeance is designed to ensure that we do not get taken advantage of. Social judgments tend to be automatic, and we are masterful at writing the justifications after the fact (Bargh, 2007). Anyone who studies human behaviors has noticed that the world has become more hostile on a broader level. Incivility is being observed at 35,000 feet, in the lines at Disneyland, at children's birthday parties, at Monday-morning meetings, on the freeway, and on social media platforms of all kinds. Being an asshole is now normative.

A tone gets set. And, even though we may bristle at it, we also adapt to it. That is the wonder of human beings—they adapt to climates, conditions, and situations and slowly adapt to a new normal. As a species, we have traversed tens of thousands of years of evolution, systematically developing systems that foster survival and jettisoning vestigial systems that are no longer needed. Evolution is slow, but adaptation can be rapid. We humans were not even using telephones a hundred years ago, and now many in the world are reliant on communications unthinkable a century ago. We adapt. Adaptation can obviously be a wonderful thing—it allows us to grow, experience new circumstances, and to weather difficult experiences.

However, we are adapting to a new world order—a world order too often characterized by incivility. Internet trolls. Road rage. "Don't you know who I am?"–ing. Angry tweets. World leaders mocking dissenting voices. The past few years in the US have seen an uptick in hostile speech, and no group is immune. People are vilified on the basis of race, gender, sexual orientation, income, nationality, religion, disability, age, political leanings, and geographic area of residence. Because this behavior is also being demonstrated by people holding leadership positions, it emboldens such views and words on a global level. We are in an era in which uncensored and thoughtless comments about other groups are being conflated with courage and truth telling. And this is seeping into the collective consciousness of the country and the world. We have lost our appetite for meaningful and respectful debate. As we parrot the toxic debates that unfold around us, typically spearheaded by toxic, self-interested people whose voices tend to ring out louder than others', we amplify their narcissistic, cruel, and toxic rhetoric in our own lives.

Once again, social media, the internet, and search engines, such as Google, and their varied algorithms (and now the loss of net neutrality), mean that we are all at risk of hearing only our worldviews repeated to us, with little opportunity to hear a tempered and thoughtful version of other points of view. Because the folks making the most noise in these spaces tend to wear toxic and narcissistic hats, we are becoming less practiced in the ability to endure different points of view and are climbing into ideological silos. On the national news level, the incivility festers. One example of this was manifested in the wake of the late Senator John McCain's progressing illness. A member of the White House staff joked about his impending death. Kelly Sadler, a White House aide, allegedly dismissed McCain's opposing view on a White House nomination by stating, "He's dying anyway." The White House, instead of coming out against the impropriety of the statement, in true narcissistic fashion, focused on figuring out where the leak was coming from. This sets a tone of deflection of blame, and it is a tone mirrored by misbehaving eight-year-olds, entitled adolescents, disaffected college students, and disgruntled employees. It shifts the society. When this is considered appropriate conduct in leadership circles, we are in trouble. The narcissists, the toxic folks, and the deeply entitled are running the asylum.

Here is where empathy may actually not be doing us any favors, because empathy can result in people's becoming emotional sponges. And, just as a baby smiles when smiled at (mimicry is the seed of empathy in a child), we get testy when people are testy with us. The most empathic in our midst suffer more greatly, because they try to hear others, heal others, and soak up the pain and poison of other people. As the world becomes more difficult, and we hear more yelling, hostile anger, criticisms, and insults from the White House, the halls of Parliament, boardrooms, community meetings, and classrooms, we start mimicking that tone. Our empathic sponges soak it all up. The critical mass of people who do not behave in accordance with traditionally valued patterns, such as reciprocity, compassion, respect, and mutuality, means that the tribal rules of order have shifted, and all of us are going to get a bit more vengeful, testier, and less reciprocal. How many times will you give of yourself until you expect something in return?

There is a pettiness to toxic people and narcissists, and this contributes to the epidemic of incivility. It often falls under the rubric of hypersensitivity. Take an example that arose back in 2017. Louise Linton, the wife of Treasury Secretary Steven Mnuchin, posted on Instagram during a trip she took to Fort Knox (an irony not lost on anyone) to view the solar eclipse. She posted "Great #daytrip to #Kentucky" and then proceeded to list via hashtag the designer labels she was wearing (poor optics for a state experiencing as much poverty as Kentucky). An ordinary citizen then responded, "Glad we could pay for your little getaway #deplorable." Given that Linton is the wife of a very wealthy man who also holds tremendous power, the sensible play would have been to simply ignore any comments by the proletariat. But, instead, she turned it into a personal Waterloo, responding, "Aw!!! Did you think this was a personal trip?! Adorable! Do you think the US govt paid for our honeymoon or personal travel?! Lololol. Have you given more to the economy than me and my husband? Either as an individual earner in taxes OR in self-sacrifice to your country? I'm pretty sure we paid more taxes toward our day 'trip' than you did. Pretty sure the amount we sacrifice per year is a lot more than you'd be willing to sacrifice if the choice was yours." And then, with the narcissistic cherry on top, she accompanied her posts with emojis of a curled bicep and a face blowing a kiss.

Okay.

In essence, narcissists and toxic people want to be vulgar and brag about their "amazing" lives and remain arrogant, entitled, and generally boorish. But they don't want to be called out on it (e.g. the 2019 college admissions scandal). And, when they are called out, the outrage is rapid and unrelenting. While this interchange played out on a public stage, anyone who has endured a toxic exchange, whether in person or in a technological space, recognizes that toxic people tend to be twitchy, petty, and hyperreactive. One would have to wonder why a woman with endless resources and access would have to tangle with an ordinary person she has never met. It's how these people are, and, in this case, high-paid publicists and damage-control teams sweep in and school folks like Linton on how to play nice. She will not change, but the minions manning the battle stations in the Treasury Department will ensure that they tighten the trigger switch.

The balance between wanting to get along with others and protecting ourselves is one of the most exquisitely difficult to achieve. Nobody wants to be a sucker, but most of us don't want to be tyrants. We actually do want to get along, but we do not want to be played. Jonathan Haidt and other evolutionary and social psychology researchers suggest that once we get angry or frustrated, we will take on our vengeful position and become defensive. As we live in a more anger-inducing and frustration-inducing world, we are more likely to hold our vengeful and prosecutorial stance. Under these conditions, all we can do is become a little more masterful at extending olive branches, meeting people halfway, changing our tone, and owning our part. That's not to say that the other people will meet us halfway, or even 1 percent of the way, but we can aspire to live in a way that mirrors the kind of world we want to live in.

Ego is usually our biggest enemy. When we are wedded to our ego, it gets in the way because we try to protect our ego. We take the fight because "it is not right" that someone gets away with something. Says who? Life is inherently unjust, unfair, and inequitable. We wrote systems of justice, punishment, and reparation to address the very fact that life is unfair. Crimes may sometimes get punished, but there is no larger system in place to ensure that the daily injustices will get addressed, because it is not possible. The more you protect your ego, the more likely you are to perceive threat. If you can get your ego out of the way, you may not be as likely to see these slights as such pronounced threats. But, admittedly, that is a tall order, especially for people who are narcissistic. The narcissists will always be jousting at windmills, demanding that life be fair *for them* (keep in mind, justice, and fairness for others rarely keep them up at night).

How Does All of This Make Us Feel?

Not good. The range of reactions is wide, and the research and my personal observations as a clinician have all revealed that the reactions to the stress of a polarized and invalidating culture and narcissistic relationships can include:

- Depression
- Anxiety
- Sleep problems
- Changes in appetite
- Rumination
- Self-doubt
- Alcohol and drug use
- Emotional eating
- Shopping and other spending
- Social isolation
- Anhedonia (losing pleasure in activities or pursuits that once gave a person pleasure)
- Irritability
- Anger
- Chronic frustration
- Suicidal thoughts
- Loss of confidence in decision-making abilities
- Loss of self-esteem
- Loss of identity
- Confusion
- Lack of concentration
- Distractibility
- Hypervigilance (being over-attuned to the surrounding environment and overreacting to triggers in the environment)
- Hyperarousal (being on edge and experiencing arousal symptoms such as racing heart, shortness of breath, anxiety, difficulty concentrating)
- Grief

Physiologically, we can observe stress responses associated with increased inflammation, diminished immune function, muscle tension, exacerbation of physical pain, and indirect physiological pathways, including poorer self-care (worse diet, not exercising, not taking medications), feeling apathetic, and lack of follow-up with doctors' appointments or recommendations. Being overly focused on pleasing the narcissist in your life results in less time for you to take care of you (narcissists are very time consuming—it is a never-ending job to please an unpleasable person). These patterns can leave us feeling devalued, and that devaluation can manifest as poorer self-care.

Some of the more intense revelations about this were observed in the aftermath of the 2016 presidential election, when divisiveness along party and ideological lines was endorsed as a significant source of stress for many people, especially in the workplace. In an American Psychological Association survey addressing some of the psychological fallout following the election, 25 percent of respondents reported feeling stressed secondary to political debates in the workplace, with nearly half indicating that the divisiveness and negative impact of the political discussions in the workplace had negative impacts, including reduced productivity, increased workplace hostility, and more negative views of their coworkers. In every election, some people lose and do not get their candidate elected—it is the nature of the beast—but something switched this time. The discussions became more ideological and took on third-rail topics such as race, gender, sexual orientation, social class, and immigration—the issues that feel personal. Multiple vectors came together this time, not only the qualitative elements of this particular election but also the multiple inputs of 24/7 news sources through cell phones and social media, as well as subterfuge in the form of the deliberate placement of misinformation. The information (and misinformation) never stopped. Many of these conversations had a hostile and dismissive tenor. Spirited political discussions, even when there is dissent, are not necessarily unhealthy. But, in this case, an ad hominem and personal nature had sprung up: a meanness in the conversations, a dismissiveness, and a loss of compassion. This has been an important shift in tectonic plates contributing to an overall toxicity in the world (or perhaps it is a reaction to the increased toxicity of the world). As more of these types of interactions grow antagonistic, they are clearly taking a toll on Americans in the workplace.

The prevailing lack of empathy leaves us feeling unheard and devalued, the entitlement activates us and, as Haidt suggests, our natural drives for both gratitude and vengeance can get triggered, and we become more hypersensitive. Narcissists' chronic validation seeking exhausts us; their gaslighting confuses us; their rage scares us. Each one of their patterns has a deeply negative effect on the people around them.

One phenomenon that has received more attention of late is something labeled complex PTSD, or C-PTSD. The diagnosis or symptomatology of typical PTSD is reserved for people who have experienced a clearly defined trauma (assault, combat, accident, natural disaster, kidnapping, sexual violence, observing a loved one experience a trauma). C-PTSD is applied when a person has experienced long-term, chronic trauma, such as chronic abuse during childhood or long-term domestic violence or other intrafamilial abuse. People who have experienced C-PTSD cannot easily escape their circumstances for a variety of reasons, which fosters a sense of helplessness and hopelessness. In people with C-PTSD, we can observe emotional dysregulation, rumination, and constantly thinking about the abuse (to the degree that they are distracted from life, work, school), becoming preoccupied with thoughts of revenge or justice against their perpetrator, becoming socially isolated and struggling with trust, and a general sense of hopelessness. This pattern of C-PTSD is not unusual in people who have had to maintain long-term relationships with narcissists and other high-conflict toxic people—and this can include narcissistic parents, partners, siblings, colleagues, and bosses. C-PTSD is not considered a diagnosis per se but is a pattern of symptoms that are somewhat distinct from traditional PTSD and feel like an obsessive, anxious, and self-negating pattern that accompanies years of enduring invalidation, dehumanization, and emotional manipulation.

Being in the purview of the narcissistic, the entitled, the toxic, the uncivil—whether it is a person, an organization, an institution, or a society—is stressful. Many of the reactions listed above are typical reactions to stress, which a mountain of literature has shown is *not* good for our health. The behaviors and words associated with narcissism, entitlement, and toxic situations are like secondhand smoke. It doesn't matter if you don't smoke—being around it can make you very sick. The narcissists have created a world that often caters to their needs (even if they don't perceive it that way); it's more like a world where the secondhand smoke can make you sicker than if you were the smoker.

Global Narcissism

Personality characteristics are both universal and contextual. A trait that may be valued in one culture (extraversion) may not be valued in another. For example, being extraverted as a white man in the US is a positive attribute, a pattern that often results in material gain and valuation by others socially and is associated with a variety of good things, including happiness. As such, those who are extraverted are rewarded, and it becomes a "good" trait. On the other hand, in a culture such as India, an extraverted woman, especially a woman from a lower socioeconomic position, would not be valued for extraversion, may be viewed as impertinent and inappropriate, and may face social approbation or alienation—or even violence—by dint of possessing the trait. The trait of extraversion and other personality traits, such as agreeableness, openness, conscientiousness, and neuroticism, have been shown to exist globally and present similarly. What is often different is how the trait is valued.

Narcissism as a pattern is deeply embedded in many cultures and is typically a function of gender, social class, or both. In numerous cultures, men can and do behave with impunity and are inculcated with the belief that empathy for others is completely unnecessary as long as they are fulfilling a social role, such as being a provider. This can culminate in epidemics of violence against women that remain unaddressed around the world. In addition, the almost blind pursuit of "Western" success via financial and material success is a true north in many developing economies, particularly those that once experienced the scourges of colonialism. As globalization and migration patterns expose all of us to a diversity of social ways of being and relating, long-standing relationship structures are being viewed differently. People from regions characterized by long-standing male-dominated hierarchies may now be exposed to and aspire to more balanced reciprocal and mutual connections within their close relationships—and established cultural patterns make this less likely because the existing patterns are so entrenched. Perhaps this means a global call to compassion, empathy, and loving relationships. In many male-dominated hierarchical cultures, narcissism is not even labeled as such. It is often simply accepted as "how things are." One positive element of the increasing globalization of communication and information is that people are learning that narcissistic, unempathic, controlling, and invalidating patterns are not healthy. In addition, entrenched patterns that can often differentially value dismissiveness, power, and control (such as machismo in Latinx cultures) can be culturally validated but experienced as antagonistic and invalidating by those on the receiving end.

And narcissism may actually hurt our planet. Just as narcissists show no empathy to other people, to their neighborhoods, or to their communities, they are also not particularly empathic to their environments or the planet itself. Even with all of the mounting data on climate change, the impact of fossil fuels, the pollution of our oceans, the deleterious impacts of plastic, and industrial pollution, corporations and governments (and their toxic leadership) often ignore the evidence base and the data and focus on the self-serving pursuit of profit. Planets don't give second chances. And, just as climate change is deleteriously impacting vulnerable species, children's health, and ocean health, the response of narcissistic leadership is the same to the planet as it is to other people: aloof indifference and lack of empathy. This isn't just about broken hearts, cheating spouses, and invalidating parents; this is also about the health of our planet, our species, and all living things. The toxic, narcissistic, and blind rhetoric of profiteers and politicians is literally poisoning our world, because land and other species need empathy too. Future research may unpack this phenomenon further. For now, at least the rest of us can recycle, vote, be responsible consumers, and do our best to safeguard our planet from narcissism.

As the world becomes deeply interconnected through social media and globalized media, and the mentality of "winner take all" leads global business, narcissism is likely to be validated as a desirable trait worldwide. While numerous societies, especially those with cultures of privilege on the basis of gender, caste, religion, or race, already have enduring systems that reward and cultivate narcissism, this is an evolving issue that has received very little formal study. Sadly, global acceptance of narcissism is an old story that sustains.

Chapter 13

The Aftermath

Extraordinary people survive under the most terrible circumstances and they become more extraordinary because of it.

—ROBERTSON DAVIES

My goal for this book was to give people the framework for why this is happening, why it is getting worse, and the damage it is causing—to let people know that they are not "going crazy," that this is a real phenomenon. To educate people about the nuances of narcissism and human toxicity and how they infect us and affect us. To teach people how to prevent these patterns from doing even more damage to themselves by stopping narratives of being not enough, to parent better, to shore up their boundaries, to avoid toxic people in the first place, to stop handing out second chances so cavalierly, to replace the toxic voices with new ones that are self-affirming and authentic, to give the best of themselves to the people who are validating and loving, and to stop giving themselves over to the narcissists in the futile hope that "today I will win them over." To teach people to tend their own gardens and to start a quiet movement of wise warriors who stop getting in the mud with narcissists, who stop engaging with them, who stop acting surprised when the narcissist shows no shred of empathy, who learn the fine art of indifference and save their vulnerability for the people who can safeguard it.

326

"Narcissists' Rights"

I have been criticized for some of my approaches and assertions. I regularly receive hate mail and vitriolic attacks via social media, telling me I am unprofessional or cruel or unfair for labeling narcissists or people engaging in antagonistic or conflictual behaviors "toxic." People have expressed their concern that I am not being "fair" to the narcissists by labeling them "toxic" and not trying to understand their side of the story. Some have expressed their concern that it is damning to label narcissists and toxic people in general as unchanging, as though it eliminates all hope. I frequently receive emails from self-proclaimed narcissists, sociopaths, and psychopaths, telling me I am deeply unfair and that they are misunderstood. They provide me with rationalizations for their lack of empathy, including profoundly abusive childhoods. They rationalize their vindictiveness and their need to control their partners. They justify retribution toward people who left them. My inbox has become a frightening place and a crucible for the society at large.

Many therapists don't like using the damning N-word. They avoid calling clients out as narcissistic, instead describing them as having anxious attachments and high conflict or being emotionally restrictive and poorly regulated, all in an effort to try to avoid the label. I am fine with that. There is no need for a label—it's convenient to have a term without having to say "unempathic, entitled, grandiose, arrogant, superficial," etc. every time. But, in the absence of a label, there remains a need for clarity. It is *crucial* that we educate people and forestall more heartache in people who are stuck in relationships with narcissists. The label is irrelevant—the person can be called narcissistic or difficult or antagonistic or high conflict or Cluster B or anything else that is descriptive. But, in the zeal to avoid a label, there is a risk of leaving a person on the receiving end of these patterns confused, lost, and frustrated. These clients often get critiqued by well-meaning therapists who question them on whether they are the reason for the communication problems or if they are being clear enough or honest enough in their communication. This can actually leave people afraid of ever seeking out mental health services again, and, frankly, in some cases, can leave them retraumatized by having their relational reality again questioned, but, this time, by a therapist. These clients are already struggling with a feeling of being not enough—therapy should not be a place where this is reinforced.

I could not have understood narcissism and related patterns if I did not also work with clients with a wide range of interpersonally toxic patterns, including narcissism. I regularly work clinically with people who are very narcissistic and manifest numerous toxic patterns, ranging from deep entitlement to lying, to cheating, to antagonism, to hypocrisy, to stalking, to poorly regulated moods, to just good old-fashioned meanness. To my interactions with them I bring empathy and compassion, and I listen to their backstories (some of which are quite difficult and painful) and remind them that they are not defined by the bad things that have happened to them. I also call them out on their proverbial shit: I tell them when they are being an asshole, that lying does not feel good to other people, that they are not entitled to special treatment, that being a predator is not okay. We practice empathy and putting themselves in the mind and heart of the other. I understand where these patterns come from and, from having worked with these clients closely for months and years, feel compassion, kindness, and connection with them.

But if I encountered someone like them in my own life, would I want to embark on a close, deep relationship with them? Probably not.

I would not want them as my partner or sibling, as my parent or coworker. Because, no matter how deep we go, no matter how well they do in our session, they have hair-trigger tempers and hypersensitivities that require that every single word be carefully chosen. Their tendency to react quickly and badly in most situations means that they say hurtful things to those who are close to them (including me), and they insult, yell, and otherwise invalidate and dehumanize their partners, family members, coworkers, and employees. They behave badly in restaurants and in places of business and criticize and bark at waitstaff, valet parkers, receptionists, or any other person unfortunate enough to have to serve them or work for them. They walk around making "Don't you know who I am?" pronouncements and engaging in their entitled mantras and are grandiose when they get their way and sullen when they don't. Sometimes, in moments of clarity, they own it. They tell me how shallow they know they are, that their lives are empty, that they actually struggle with caring about other people's feelings, and all of that means life doesn't feel good. Especially as they get older. I teach them to accept, on some level, that it is who they are and recognize that they may never have the empathic and intimate bandwidth they need. We work on the big-ticket relationships, like being a better parent or partner. We make some small gains, and that may be enough for them and their families.

If people want to write off my approach as unkind, so be it—it is not intended to be. I have seen too much good come from giving people the narcissist's playbook and helping them understand what is happening to them, instead of their blaming themselves and wondering what more they could do. I teach people that to endure abuse is never okay. And that, no matter how horrifying someone's backstory is, it does not give him or her carte blanche to turn another person into a punching bag. I am always heartened to see that any group has advocates, and glad to see that the narcissists and other high-conflict personalities have advocates as well.

The Danger Is Real

The burgeoning trend of narcissism, entitlement, incivility, grandstanding, and bad behavior is bad for all of us, because even those of us who are well-intentioned, warm, kind, and humane people run the risk of experiencing something I term "infectious narcissism." If you spend enough time with a narcissist, you may take on some of his or her characteristics. Narcissistic and toxic people tend to be emotional vampires—they suck the love, hope, positive emotion, aspirations, and humanity out of people. The risk then becomes that you will become more like them (in the traditional telling of the vampire story, if a vampire bites you, then you become one too). At some level, simply to coexist with a narcissist requires a person to slowly start pruning and trimming his or her emotional world. You may not intend to become less empathic or colder and more distant, but that may be a defense or a form of self-protection that occurs when you are living under conditions of narcissistic abuse and emotional starvation. It is a pattern also often observed in individuals who have experienced trauma; after the trauma, they become more and more socially isolated. As the world increasingly normalizes and rewards narcissism, there are more people who may become cold, distant, and unempathic, and we are more likely to be exposed to them. As that happens, we may actually start losing some of the best parts of ourselves if we decide to keep narcissists in our lives. Even if we lower expectations and keep them at arm's length, they are still a toxic and difficult presence in our world, and over time, that will make us sick and hamper our growth.

The menace of narcissism and toxic people is real—and it is dangerous. In *The Washington Post* on July 2, 2018, Petula Dvorak laid out what many in the field of psychology already knew: In the endless search for the profile of a "mass killer" (the person who murders three or more people he or she typically does not know in a single event or brief period of time), the disdain for women is always a prominent characteristic. But it is more overarching than that. By and large, mass killers are dispossessed, disillusioned, contemptuous, and disdainful, and they feel that life has passed them by, that life owes them something (massive entitlement), and they use social media and other forms of internet contact as a weapon to stalk, harass, troll, and otherwise bring misery to other people (typically women). They assume that there are intimacies and a closeness that do not exist with people they've just met, and they twist a person's kindness into sexual interest (because they themselves do not express kindness to others without an agenda). They feel wronged by the world and spend years ruminating about their revenge. By definition, this fits the archetype of the covert narcissist or sociopath. On the face of it, there is not a lot of "there" there. They are *not* charming, charismatic, or successful. They typically cannot get the girl.

Sadly, our legal, judicial, and school systems are not set up to manage the threats leveled by narcissistic and toxic people until it is too late. Our systems are designed for punishment, not prevention. As Dvorak laid out in her article, the signs are often there for years before massive crimes are perpetrated. Our systems are not designed to do much, even when these patterns are identified, even when those targeted by these folks say, "This is dangerous; please do something." Many women reported that their biggest mistake was allowing these people near them in the first place; their kindness was misinterpreted, and the covert narcissist used the foot-in-the-door technique to get in. One woman was stalked for years after merely accepting a man with these characteristics as a Facebook friend. That man went on to perpetrate a mass shooting at a DC-area newspaper.

This goes well beyond the narcissistic mother who criticizes you at Sunday dinner, the narcissistic boyfriend who keeps texting his ex-girlfriends, the toxic friend who is never there for you when you are going through a difficult time, or the toxic boss who takes credit for your work. *This phenomenon of toxicity and narcissism is fostering patterns that are downright dangerous.* It's manifesting as an uptick in hate groups, which have been growing steadily over the past few decades as documented by monitoring groups such as the Southern Poverty Law Center, and actively promoting more and more violence toward anyone who is not like the people in them. And, each day that we incentivize and reward incivility, entitlement, and grandiosity and disincentivize human emotion, human connection, warmth, and kindness, we are digging ourselves into a darker and more dangerous place. As we live in a world in which increasing numbers of people believe they are owed something, who think nothing of yammering, "Don't you know who I am?" there will be increasing numbers with hair-trigger tempers or dark, ruminating souls who are dangerous.

Can We Prevent It?

If we could prevent narcissism, I would be out of a job. And I would be thrilled.

As with most human behavior, we can shape it to an extent. Human behavior can be quite simple: According to B.F. Skinner and Edward Thorndike, the key behavioral theorists in our field, a behavior that is rewarded is repeated. Obviously, it does get a bit more complicated, but, at the core of it, that's about it. Children may work harder on spelling tests if they get a gold star; employees may work harder if they get a bonus.

To prevent narcissism on a larger scale would mean preventing the insecurity that grows and fosters narcissism. That would mean training parents to nurture a sense of security and of being enough in their children, for parents to be present, mindful, and loving with their children, and to teach them empathy, compassion, and kindness; it would mean that schools stop focusing solely on standardized tests, math, GPAs, and college admissions and teach empathy, authenticity, and critical thought about media and technology; and that all of us model civility, kindness, and warmth. For parents, society, and the world at large, it would mean teaching boys and men not just that vulnerability and communication of feelings are acceptable but that being vulnerable and communicating actually make them stronger than not doing so. All of that would be a great place to start—and it is not going to happen. Parenting doesn't require a license, and as such, lots of people who have kids simply do not have the requisite skill sets to parent them. Parenting well is hard work—physically and psychologically—and many people are not up to it. It's not just about putting three meals on the table and providing a bed—it is far more than that. Even the parents who are well intentioned (especially in such economically uncertain and difficult times) are too often more concerned with their children's financial and occupational security than with their character or mental health or well-being. As noted previously, narcissism is typically a mash-up of an inborn sensitivity with an insecure or inconsistent early environment. Teaching parents to get it right would be a start, but we do not have the mechanisms to do this. We return children to abusive environments repeatedly, hoping the situation will get better, but, by then, the damage is done.

The short answer is that, if people can love and be loved and if children and adults can learn to accurately appraise their abilities, strengths, and weaknesses, and to develop a solid core sense of self, that is the antidote and a way to prevent these cycles. But those lessons need to start early, and since most parents are plagued by their own lack of self-love and feeling of not being enough, the cycles easily get replicated. We tend to sneer at the "softness" of the message of self-love and self-compassion, and children learn early that love needs to be "earned." Few people have received messages of unconditional and genuine love—and, if these messages finally do arrive in their adult lives, they are not able to accept them and integrate them.

By the time these patterns settle in adulthood, it starts to be too late. But, if someone doesn't care, then all of the behavioral shaping in the world may not matter. I do also believe that another key prevention tool would be to destigmatize resources such as psychotherapy, to make them more available to everyone. However, the other shifts that are needed—away from consumerism, materialism, political polarization, and the veneration of wealth—are less likely to happen. Those are the conditions under which these patterns of narcissism, toxicity, incivility, entitlement, and antagonism proliferate, and if those don't change, narcissism is here to stay.

That's Just How They Are

During the recent spate of harassment scandals, turmoil in the American political system and other world governments, poorly behaved people in positions of power, and celebrity scandals on a regular basis, the prevailing discourse has been "That's just how he [or she] is." As though bad behavior is excusable on those grounds. "He screams a lot—that's just how he is." "He keeps grabbing women or is just really handsy—that's just how he is." "She says inappropriate things at work—that's just how she is." "She says stuff that people might think is racist—that's just how she is." "He has a short temper—that's just how he is." "She never asks me how I am doing—that's just how she is." "He can be really interpersonally abrupt—that's just how he is." "He never comes home for dinner on time or listens to how the children are doing—that's just how he is." "He posts such gross stuff on social media and likes the bikini pictures of eighteen-year-old girls—that's just how he is."

At some level, it is true. That *is* just how these people are. And perhaps, to be in these situations or in these relationships with narcissists, you simply have to resign yourself to "That's just how they are" and either accept it or get out. However, this sort of resigned acceptance does not address the weed at its roots and raises the likelihood that the toxic patterns will continue. Narcissists get away with it because, by believing "That's just how they are," we do not call out and address the behavior. Their actions are often rationalized: She had a cruel father, he is a brilliant businessman, he keeps winning Oscars, her mother neglected her, he is a genius, she gives so much money to the community. The rationalization of "That's just how they are," with explanations for that behavior or the extolling of "virtues" of the person vis-à-vis achievement or success, is often how they get away with this behavior. If they are writing big donation checks, then who cares if they are verbally abusing their employees? Outdated rationalizations based on concepts such as "the old boys' club" or "locker room talk" or even culture are trotted out as ways to understand people who behave in negating, invalidating, and dehumanizing ways.

With narcissists, people often hang in there with the hope that someday will be better. No matter how much you endure, you may end up more likely to have post-traumatic stress than a promotion. It is more likely that, once that deadline passes, there will be something else. And, after the exceptions don't work out, or you have endured more abuse at the hands of these narcissistic, entitled, and toxic people, then there are psychological scars to work through. Giving up hope is no easy matter. "That's just how they are" becomes a brutal echo that can ring through a lifetime—and the hopes attached to it rarely materialize.

Over time, people become so expert at letting narcissists off the hook that they start to learn to let everyone off the hook. It is in this way that the narcissistic and toxic person can just blaze a trail of destruction that can culminate in an arrest, an investigation, or some other publicly messy business, with lots of people wringing their hands, wondering how it got so bad. There is no mystery. It was always this bad. People just got so good at looking the other way, constructing excuses, issuing apologies, and hoping things would get better that, once the circumstances hit critical mass, the mess just blew up. Anytime I hear a saga of a studio boss, CEO, politician, or celebrity who blows up, I never think, "How surprising." I simply wonder what took so long.

"The Line"

There is that day. A moment. Maybe you have already experienced it. The day when you look across the table, at the phone, at the email...and you finally see it. The line finally gets crossed, and you will never unsee it.

Something happens. Maybe you got therapy. Maybe a friend pointed something out. Maybe you read a book. Maybe the person crossed a moral line or a legal line. You finally recognize that you are dealing with a narcissist or some other form of toxic person. And then you wonder what to do about it. In many ways, "the line" is your rock bottom. It's no different than what we witness in addiction—there is that moment, that personal rock bottom, and only when people hit it do they start mounting a battle against that monkey on their back.

This can take a *long* time—in some cases, forty to fifty years. If you are fortunate, it may take only a few months or less than a year (you are reading this book, so we can ensure that it does not take that long next time).

Many of the people I have interviewed and with whom I have worked clinically have indicated that they could have and would have endured the narcissist's abuse indefinitely had they not hit "the line" or rock bottom. However, the day the narcissist started criticizing something precious—for example, their children or other people or situations that were important to them—was the day that the *line got crossed* and they finally recognized what they were dealing with. Interestingly, victims of narcissistic abuse often lose the gumption to advocate for themselves but still tirelessly attempt to protect or defend people around them, especially vulnerable or important people such as children or family members. This may in part be because people who endure narcissistic abuse are often quite empathic, full of second chances and compassionate views on people, which sadly translates into being a long-term punching bag for a narcissist but also translates into a propensity for caregiving and protecting the people they love.

For others, it took a specific behavior. Their toxic or narcissistic person may have insulted their appearance, called them stupid, embarrassed them in front of their family, or isolated them from friends, and they put up with it. But the day they cheated on them with someone else, for some reason, that was their line. It was one behavior that was a no-fly zone that pushed them over that line. Many behaviors have been cited as "the" behavior that resulted in their moment of awareness or "quitting," and these have ranged from cheating to financial misbehavior to physical abuse to insulting a family member. Interestingly, one person's no-fly behavior may have little relevance for another person, but it took that one thing. That's "the line."

Information is also a key variable in becoming "woke" to narcissism. Given how narcissistic the world has become, it is not surprising that all of us are becoming accustomed to it. If you spend enough time with narcissistic and toxic people, you adjust to them and fall into the "That's just how they are" of it all. With enough time, it can be easy to believe that being devalued, invalidated, dehumanized, scapegoated, and abused are normal ways of relating. For some people, a workplace that is supportive or a trusted mentor at school can be the wake-up call—that "Whoa, there are other ways for people to be treated" moment. In addition, reading, watching videos, or having other sources of information can often provide validation and allow people to rub their eyes for a minute and really see clearly what is happening around them. Interestingly, narcissism tends to reflect lifelong engagement: People with narcissistic, entitled, cold, or invalidating families and parents tend to fall into those relationships in adulthood and fall in love with narcissists who maintain the familiar pattern of invalidation, work for and tolerate narcissistic bosses, and endure narcissistic friendships (we explored this a bit in Chapter 7, "The Narcissist Who Raised You"). Many people have revealed that their "line" got crossed when another person finally treated them with respect and the contrast opened their eyes. I have worked with *many* survivors of narcissistic families and relationships who, when given consistent empathy for the first time, looked at it questioningly in the early days and then, once they grew accustomed to it, ate it up hungrily after a lifetime of invalidation. There is nothing more wonderful than watching another human being finally receive deserved empathy and compassion and subsequently blossoming into his or her full potential. Getting to your "line" is a very personal process. Accurate information, awareness, compassion, kindness, and respect can help expedite it.

Close the Floodgates

Many times, people have asked me, "What is your hope or dream for this work?" My highest-level dream would be to stop people from getting into these relationships in the first place. Sadly, even after a person gets out of a narcissistic relationship, it leaves scars—and these scars can run very deep. The inner voice that keeps telling you that you are not enough, long after you leave these relationships, is one of the deepest. These relationships may also leave you with a lifetime of self-doubt, difficulty making decisions, and second-guessing. In addition, if you have to coparent with a narcissist, it can be a lifelong challenge of painful and expensive custody battles, followed by a lifetime of families' being polarized and split by the bad behavior of the narcissistic parent. So the best strategy is prevention, to not enter into the relationship in the first place.

As noted earlier, there are generally two types of narcissistic relationships: those that are "involuntary" (family, siblings, coworkers) and those that are "voluntary" (spouses, other partners, friends). Obviously, in the case of the involuntary relationships, the best you can do is *choose* to maintain watertight boundaries, distance, and, if needed, no contact. It's in the voluntary ones that you have an opportunity to do something—to close those floodgates before it is too late. We spend more effort teaching people how to buy a car than how to choose a life partner. And, once people make that bad choice, we expect them to stick it out. It's time we started teaching our children and young people (even if they don't want to hear it) how to understand themselves before embarking on a lifelong commitment that can have treacherous consequences.

Pink Flags

These are the subtle signs; they are often so subtle that, more often than not, we rationalize them, minimize them, or even criticize ourselves for letting them affect us. Some examples of pink flags include too many photoshopped social media images; one too many social media photographs of their dinner plates or cocktails; a frenzy of activity when they are on a trip or out to dinner to ensure it all gets documented, tagged, and shared; a bit of oversensitivity in the face of an innocuous comment and a tendency to get a bit "snippy" with a waiter or a retail clerk; a distractibility when other people are talking; being overconcerned about superficial details; paying the check for other people, then reminding them later about it.

One of the most noteworthy pink flags is how a person drives. Do they cut people off? Lay their hands on the horn and honk for far longer than needed? Speed up when they sense someone wants to change lanes? Drive erratically? Scream at, gesture at, or threaten other drivers? Stop their car in traffic to get out of their car to berate another driver? Rarely come to a complete stop at a stop sign? Park where they should not park? (e.g., a space reserved for drivers with disabled placards). Erratic and entitled drivers are dangerous, and likely lack empathy because they do not concern themselves with the safety of others on the road. (I spend many hours driving through Los Angeles traffic wondering about the mental state of the myriad dangerous drivers on the road....)

These patterns are pink flags, because any one of these patterns in isolation is annoying, petty, and perhaps indicative of insecurity, but may not be a full-fledged red flag that narcissism lurks around the corner. However, when they are a pattern and are consistent, pay attention. These "pink flags" may be a signal to remain aware of whether lack of empathy, entitlement, grandiosity, and validation seeking are present as well. And may provide an early glimpse of darker and more toxic days to come.

Family Patterns

People who grew up in narcissistic family systems are often much more likely to fall for the tricks of the narcissist, as I discussed in Chapter 7. The old scripts people bring from their families ("I'm not good enough") can set up a person to believe that it is not exciting, or it is not love unless he or she has that old family feeling of not being good enough (yes, it is twisted but true). It is for this reason that it is important for people who have narcissistic family systems, who emerge into adulthood not feeling good enough, to do some of the inner work they need to do before throwing their hat into the ring with a flashy partner. Odds are, with the broken compass that people take out of a narcissistic family, their choice will be to choose the antagonistic partner who keeps invalidating them. Both of their parents invalidated them, so perhaps love equals invalidation. In addition, narcissistic or depleted family systems also leave people feeling as though they do not deserve better or that they are lucky to even find someone to pay attention to them in the first place, and they may just choose a partner (even when it doesn't feel good) because they do not believe anyone else will ever come around. Women, in particular, are vulnerable to this dynamic; they are sometimes told to grab the first person who comes around because they will not do better. Then, because narcissists are so controlling, they will often rob the woman of any financial freedom, placing a person in this relationship in a form of double jeopardy—stuck in an abusive relationship with a narcissist with no means of escape. The rookie mistake most people make in narcissistic relationships is thinking that they will change this person. They hope that someday it will be better. As soon as you recognize patterns of entitlement and invalidation or notice that someone is a little too charming or a little too glib, or love-bombs you a little too much, get out. Fast. These relationships also tend to move too fast—people get married too fast, move in too fast, have children too fast. This puts narcissistic partners at an advantage, because the relationship becomes entrenched and more difficult to leave—they then imprison their source of narcissistic supply. The practical plus the psychological chains that bind make it difficult to see these patterns for what they are.

Interestingly, people from overly happy families may also fall into a trap. Because of a tendency to see everything through "happy glasses," they are in the other group that also often falls for narcissistic and toxic partners. People who believe in "happily ever after" because they saw it during childhood may believe they can "rescue" the misunderstood and tragic narcissist and also fall for the charm and charisma of it all, because why not? Don't fairy tales come true? In addition, people from happy homes have lots of hopes and an endless bag of second chances, and they really do subscribe to the *Beauty and the Beast* fantasy of "If I love him enough, he will become a sweet, compassionate angel." In some ways, never having seen anything malevolent during their childhood and seeing their parents' happy marriage mean that they are somewhat disbelieving when their story goes south. Maybe the sweet spot is just enough family dysfunction to keep you from being naïve, but not so much that you are vulnerable to falling for the familiar abuse of a narcissist.

You Are Enough

The main pushback I hear is, "My story will be different." "My guy is grumpy because he is so important/busy/has tons of responsibility at work [or because he is misunderstood or because he had a tough childhood]." "She deserves to be at the front of the line because her time is so valuable." The excuse-making starts early and then, much like a person might get pulled into a cult, people start believing the delusion that they slowly bought into. I am quite confident that, as one person, I am not going to change the prevailing Zeitgeist that celebrates "bad boys" and "sexy unhinged passionate demanding girls." I am not going to be able to shift the narrative so that people celebrate and embrace the somewhat self-effacing, kind, compassionate man over the rich guy with swagger and a big ego and bankroll. When the wedding is more show and the relationship is less substance, when Instagram reveres couples who look good and live big, when people are still holding out for grandiose fairy tales with predatory princes and helpless princesses, the supply of people who will fall for the charming, glib narcissist, who believe they will be the one to rescue the misunderstood tyrant, to outsmart the villain, to find the inner teddy bear in the fearsome beast, will be endless.

I obviously cannot stop narcissistic, toxic, and abusive people from having children, nor can I stem the tide of entitlement in our world, to slow the demands of consumerism and the reverence of materialism. All of these patterns—"If I own enough, then I am enough"—contribute to the condition of insecurity that not only fosters the prevalence of narcissism but also makes people vulnerable to it. *The bottom line is addressing insecurity—to help people feel whole,* to help them feel as though they are enough (I know I've said this before, but it bears repeating). Perhaps schools should spend less time having children memorizing capital cities of countries or preparing for spelling bees or learning differential equations and spend more time having children learn to be critical thinkers, recognizing the manipulations of advertisers and their own worth—whether they make lots of money or not, whether their parents tell them or not, whether they conform to what the people around them want them to be or not. The bulk of neurosis originates from that gap between people's true self and the self they construct to please the demands of their parents and the world. Perhaps we need to focus on making that gap as small as possible, to teach people to validate themselves instead of posting edited images and putting out desperate calls to the outside world, begging others, *"Please tell me I am enough."* Perhaps doing these things can stem the tide of people's sacrificing themselves on the altar of narcissism. However, as has been the case since time immemorial, young people believe they know better, and so another generation may make the same errors, except that as narcissism becomes more virulent, the stakes become higher.

For now, I can only offer up this book as a manual for managing narcissism once you are in it and making sense of all of it with the hope that you do not get too hurt by it. Give narcissists enough time and they will hurt you—it's what they do—intentionally or not. And, by now, you have encountered several narcissists, and I promise you that you will encounter several more, whether at dinner tonight, at work tomorrow, at Thanksgiving dinner, in line at the market, or on your next first date.

Don't Expect Justice

The main challenge of walking away from narcissistic relationships is that, even when you walk away from the situation and the person, you still live in it. You obsess over it. You think about it. You can't let it go. You think that, by forgiving, things will work out, but they won't. The rumination about how a narcissist gets away with it all—thinking about the cheating husband, the insulting wife, the invalidating mother, the never-pleased father, the toxically competitive sister, the demanding friend, the ex-part-ner who moves on two days after you split up—can get stuck in your head. It becomes impossible to let it go because it isn't fair. People hold out because they hope the karmic scales will be set straight. They obsess, ruminate, and obsess some more because they want it to be set right.

Most of all, they want *justice*.

The quest for justice is what brings down most people who are strug-gling in the face of abuse from any narcissist. The seemingly utter injustice of being gaslighted, dehumanized, invalidated, second-guessed, lied to, manipulated, devalued, and criticized, and watching the perpetrator of this behavior feel no negative feelings and experience little consequence can feel insurmountable. So many people who have been hurt by nar-cissists say, "I could get past this if I could see them face some kind of retribution." They probably won't. Because, even if someone points it out to the narcissists, they either do not care or do not get it. And, because they are so slick, they often get away with it. There are no laws against narcissistic behavior.

Our systems reward manipulators, entitled people, and bullies. You will stand back and watch a deceitful coworker get promoted, or a patho-logical CEO get a $20 million bonus, or a tyrant get elected or appointed to an important leadership position. You will witness the partner who cheated on you quickly find a new partner, or your abusive father create a new family with a new partner and new children, or a mean-spirited and vindictive friend find a nice person to marry.

Their lack of empathy means that they do not really feel much emotional consequence from their wrongdoing. They are also quick to blame other people for their misfortunes. If things do go south for them, they will blame everyone around them, from "backstabbing" friends to "ungrateful" family members to a "biased" media, for making them look bad. Rarely will they take responsibility, and, if a public apology is called for, the one they offer will be anemic and disingenuous at best. It is far more likely that they will blame you or others for any misdeeds than take responsibility or ownership, or even offer an apology.

People who have been hurt by narcissists hope and pray for that day of reckoning—the day when it does all come crashing around the ears of the narcissists, the day that they finally come back on hands and knees, *begging* for forgiveness and clearly and honestly owning up to everything they did wrong. Typically, when they ask for forgiveness and attempt to take ownership it is to save face, rather than an authentic apology per se. And you will be waiting a long time for that day of redemption.

This can lead to the mistake we have discussed of wanting to defend yourself, explain yourself, and call them out on their bullshit. There is no point; they never listened to you before, and they will not listen now—and they will out-defend, outmaneuver, and outplay you. By the end of it all, you will be more exhausted and disgusted than before you attempted to defend yourself. So many people spend hours and hours composing eloquent emails and letters and texts and other messages to narcissistic parents and partners, siblings and friends, elegantly laying out their case, sharing their hurts, trying to get them to take responsibility or, at least, see their side of the situation. Save the paper and the time. They won't get it, and, if they *do* read your message, they will come back at you with a cruel denial of your experience. People hope these messages will be met with enlightenment and clarity, but that almost never happens.

The time wasted obsessing about what narcissists got away with is time wasted. It means you are still in the relationship. They didn't really win; they are still stuck being them. It is easy to get caught up in the idea that winning means that they got the nice house, or the custody setup they wanted, or the new wife, or the bulk of the inheritance, or the promotion, or simply not having to take responsibility for their conduct. Ultimately, though, they are in possession of impoverished inner worlds, with few deep relationships. That's not a win. A primary focus of my clinical practice is to work with clients who have endured difficult, narcissistic relationships and are looking to get their lives back. This issue of justice is our biggest stumbling block. With the plaintive hurt of a child, many people are unable to fully get their head around the idea that the unfairness of the situation may not be rectified, and that karma does not appear to apply where narcissists are concerned. The healing happens the day you recognize that this isn't about justice or fairness; it's about self-preservation and peace.

If you no longer have to deal with them, then you have won. If you have found a way to keep your distance, then you have won. If you do not have to listen to their verbal abuse and invalidation, then you have won. If you keep obsessing about whether or not they get "punished," then you are still wasting mental energy on them. In most cases, by the time the bad things happen to them, you will have moved on, feeling nothing other than perhaps pity.

Life is not fair. Life is not just. And, if you are coming to this insight only as an adult, consider yourself lucky. More often than we would like, bad things happen to good people and good things happen to bad ones. There is no karmic abacus in the sky ensuring that the metaphysical accounting books all get balanced out in the end. Some people win the lottery, and some people's houses burn down on the day they learn their mother has cancer.

The best way to get any sense of justice in these situations is to remove yourself as a source of narcissistic supply, to remove yourself as a punching bag, and to not react to their baiting or succumb to their manipulations. Their shock and destabilization at not getting the satisfaction of your hurt feelings, of your chronically defending yourself, of your arguments will be prize enough for you. *In fact, the best narcissist repellant out there may not be yelling or screaming or revenge but simply indifference.* You win when you *stop* giving the best of yourself to the narcissist and *start* giving it to worthy recipients. You win when you commit to self-preservation rather than waging a futile battle against their denials and projections.

If you can let go of a sense of injustice, you *will* heal from narcissistic abuse. Life is not fair, and, instead of forgiving, just let go (as you learned in Chapter 11), and the first step to letting go is to recognize that it isn't fair, and that the true win is to take back your life and to pity those who are still jousting with narcissists or waiting for them to change.

That may be justice enough.

The Crystal Ball

The questions that plague so many people about whether to leave a narcissistic relationship are, "What happens next? What if I am wrong? What if this is as good as it gets?" They wish they had a crystal ball to see what will happen in the future—whether they stay in the relationship or leave.

One of my podcast listeners answered the question of staying or going more eloquently than I could. She was responding via letter to another listener's question. The woman who wrote the letter had stayed in a marriage with a narcissist for ten years and was responding to a listener who wondered what her own life would be like if she stayed in her marriage for another ten years. The woman who wrote the letter had no relationship to the listener; she just wanted to share her story in the hope that it could save the listener some heartache. This is the letter she sent. Pay attention to the lessons of others. She was gracious enough to allow me to share it.

What you see now is what you will see ten years from now, only you'll see it much more clearly. What you feel now is what you will feel ten years from now, only amplified. The crushing loneliness. His disdain for everything you love and believe in. The awareness that nothing you do will ever be enough to earn his respect. The deep longing for kindness and intimacy. The anxiety, the fear, the sheer terror you feel when you disappoint or inconvenience him.

You will get smaller and smaller and be less and less yourself to make room for him, but that will never be enough. He will always be angry, he won't ever consider your feelings or perspective, he will turn every argument around on you. You will hide from him when you cry, because he will mock you and accuse you of trying to manipulate him.

He will go to therapy with you but he won't engage. He'll be surly and difficult and forget appointments or start working late and soon you'll just give up. He might turn the therapist's attention away from the acute issues of your relationship or convince the therapist that the issue is really your mental problems. At the very least he'll probably learn some psychological buzzwords and accuse you of "gaslighting" him.

If you have children, he will see them as inconveniences that need to be handled by someone else (you). He'll be outraged when expected to put in a small fraction of the effort you expend caring for them. You will rely on friends and family when you need help caring for them. He will be offended by this.

And through all this he will occasionally tell you how much he loves and appreciates you, and that will make you feel slightly unsettled because it's the opposite of what his actions communicate. You won't be able to identify why it unnerves you, though, so you'll just try to ignore it.

You will think, "Every relationship has its ups and downs." You will tell yourself you can't expect one person to meet all of your emotional needs. You will tell yourself that you must make your own happiness and not rely on him. So you will forgive him and focus on bettering yourself.

You will cultivate your friendships and explore new hobbies. You'll spend time with your beautiful children.

And you will be dying inside. You will dread being around him and resent him when he's away. You have no idea how you'd survive without him, if you were to leave, but you know for sure that if you stay barely surviving is all you can hope to do.

That is what your life will be like if you stay with this man. Make no mistake about it—there will never be FEWER red flags. All the ways he hurts you now, he will continue to do that and more. It may be difficult to walk away now, but trust me, it won't get easier.

Chapter 14

The Modern Happily Ever After

I am not what happened to me, I am what I choose to become.

—JUNG

Can there be any happy endings where narcissistic, psychopathic, or other toxic relationships are concerned? I actually think there can be. The greatest challenge about happy endings in real adult life is that they rarely look like the ones we crafted when we were young. Our younger narratives tend to be quite formulaic: falling in love, weddings, picket fences, babies, vacations, nice home, family dinners, and growing old with someone. Obviously, these are not the same for everyone, but our narratives typically reflect family values, societal expectations, cultural traditions, and media messages.

Toxic relationships can puncture those narratives, and, if our stories do not resemble the gold standards dictated by society, it can be devastating. People who come from narcissistic families may feel as though they missed out on having a parent as a supporter in adulthood; people who have married narcissistic partners may find themselves mired in a nightmare of emotional abuse; people who have narcissistic bosses may watch a career they worked hard for disappear. Few people write stories of their lives that build in disappointment.

In my many years of doing this work, I have found that survivors of all kinds of toxic relationships can and do have happy endings—the endings just do not look like the survivors thought they would. People may lose a big house in a divorce, but their small apartment where no one invalidates them feels like paradise. They may have envisioned a future of holidays with family but letting go of the toxic Thanksgivings means that they now spend holidays volunteering or hiking or traveling or having potluck dinners with friends.

People fall in love again. Some of the happiest endings meant that, for the first time, people who survived relationships with narcissists held out for someone who respected them and showed them empathy. It was a new feeling, and they would tell me that sometimes it would take years before they could fully accept the reality of a partner who didn't control them, criticize them, lie to them, or ignore them. These love stories are poignant, and the narcissistic abuse survivor would often say, "Before learning about narcissism and toxic relationships, I would have never once even looked at a person like this, but I learned to regard myself as enough. I learned what was important in a relationship, and whole, healthy love followed."

Open the Gate for Good People

I have witnessed people leave narcissistic groups of friends by whom they had been mistreated for decades, fearful of being alone if they stepped away, and, once they were able to walk away from their invalidating friends, those former friends were replaced by new groups of friends and a full and joyful life. You are bigger than this; you can revise the "You are not enough" voice that still resonates, and you can reparent yourself. You can look at the entitled shenanigans of the "Don't you know who I am?"-ers and realize that you do not give a damn about who they are and that you *know* who you are.

As noted before, when you leave the door open and allow one narcissist in, or you already have one in your life, before you know it, you are surrounded. I tell people that you need to learn to be the doorman to your own soul, and only allow in guests you actually want in your life. It goes back to habituation and your increased tolerance for the bad behavior—you become less skilled at detecting it. It works the other way too. *As people engage in a "toxic dump" and distance themselves from the toxic, antagonistic, abusive, hurtful, and narcissistic people in their world, they find that now there is room for new, empathic, compassionate, respectful, and good people, and, once one comes in, more follow.* People who are able to walk away and distance themselves from narcissists become more discerning, and the new group of friends may also be accompanied by new, healthy job opportunities and life opportunities. Being with healthy, empathic people fills us up and starts quieting those voices that say, "You are not enough." You stop walking on eggshells. Slowly, more affirming voices replace the negative ones. This can also be accompanied by greater self-care; you may be more likely to exercise or do new things you hadn't tried (salsa dancing, wakeboarding, and Moroccan cooking were some of the ones I heard), because you value yourself. Where there were once narcissistic voices silencing you, now there are encouraging voices, helping you become your best version of yourself.

Celebrate Your Scars

Writer and artist Kahlil Gibran wrote: "Out of suffering have emerged the strongest souls; the most massive characters are seared with scars." Don't hide those scars; they are beautiful parts of you. Just like laugh lines show that we've smiled, your psychological bruises show you that you have survived. You may become more patient, not only with the world but also with yourself, immersed in the gratitude of distance from the toxic abuse. You may actually pursue the aspirations you had shelved for so long because you kept hearing the old voices telling you that you would fail. You may appreciate simple, elegant moments with a transcendent awareness—a sunset, a rainy day, a shooting star—because you are no longer polluting your mind, obsessing about the hurts you are enduring or have endured, or distracted and worried about being criticized or saying the wrong thing.

The poet Rumi wrote: "The wound is the place where the Light enters you." Having spent so much of my career working with survivors of these relationships, these ancient words ring true nearly 800 years later. It is through these scars, heartaches, and hurts, and the courage to push back against them, where the light did enter people, and I have watched brave men and women start careers, pursue dreams, fall in love, make art, write books, pursue degrees, and make peace with themselves and their histories.

A Global Neighborhood of Goodness and Love

The inimitable Mr. Rogers has been memorialized in a 2018 documentary called *Won't You Be My Neighbor?* (I grew up in the 1970s, and he was a part of my after-school routine.) In this documentary, he says: "Let's take the gauntlet and make goodness attractive in this so-called next millennium. That's the real job that we have. I am not talking about Pollyannaish stuff; I am talking about down-to-earth actual goodness. People caring for each other in a myriad of ways, rather than people knocking each other off all of the time…. What changes the world, the only thing that ever changes the world, is when somebody gets the idea that love can abound and can be shared." In the new world of reality TV, polarized news coverage, and toxic media debates, Mr. Rogers would sound like a heretic. We have fallen far away from the Mr. Rogers idealism of my childhood. I never imagined we would fall this far, this quickly. But perhaps we can reawaken his vision of a global neighborhood, of fostering love and empathy. Tending those gardens. Finding meaning. Cultivating purpose. However, also becoming savvier, keeping our eyes wide open, and being gatekeepers for ourselves, to keep the invalidating voices at bay. When possible, not allowing toxic people entry in the first place. Replacing our insecure inner voices with self-affirming ones.

Yes, the world is becoming increasingly toxic and uncivil and mean, but learn to look at it with doubt and even bemusement. Don't let the global epidemic of insecurity infect you. Inoculate yourself. Receive your social media feed as entertainment and not as a yardstick for self-worth. Be wise to the machinations of advertisers: Remember, your insecurity is their profit. Find some common ground with other people, instead of living in polarization. Practice kindness. Choose your friends and romances with care. Every life story can be a miracle or a tragedy—it just depends on how you write it and how you read it. These days, anyone who is surviving with his or her empathy unbroken, heart intact, integrity in place, compassion replete, and sense of humor in place is nothing short of heroic.

Transitioning from Survival to Growth

While the words survival and survivor carry within them a strength, resilience, and resolve, they also imply a singular focus. When people are survivors, all of their resources go into getting through an experience alive or intact. When survival is a short-term endeavor, it can simply be about getting enough food, shelter, and water until the situation resolves. However, when we start considering long-term survival, it's a different conversation. It means all resources go simply into staying alive for years—whether literally gathering essential needs, or just getting through the day. It's about grinding through a routine in an unquestioning manner, so you can get through another hour. Survival is about endurance.

Growth is a different animal. Growth is about evolution, moving forward, testing your own limits, taking risks, integrating new parts of yourself, trying new things, perhaps failing, and then trying again. It's about moving forward and, in essence, expanding your wingspan. Growth often requires that other basic needs are being met—it's hard to think about growth when you are trying to survive. Survival is tunnel vision. Growth is scanning the horizon. Survival is keeping your head down and avoiding threats. Growth is raising your head high and taking on challenges.

So much of the narcissistic abuse literature is about survival. Even my second book was subtitled "*Surviving* a Relationship with a Narcissist." Staying in narcissistic relationships and enduring narcissistic relationships are definitely about survival. It's about putting your head down; it's about avoiding abuse; it's about decoding confusing behavior and feelings; it's about being invalidated and still getting up and pushing through another day.

My hope for this book is that you go beyond just survival. It is meant to give you the tools to also start making this about growth. The one good thing about survival is that it reminds you that you have the grit, the fortitude, and the courage to have kept yourself going, even under atrocious circumstances. Many of us living in this difficult and narcissistic world are surviving, still being kind to strangers, even when more and more of them are being unkind to us. We are still maintaining hope for the world, even in the midst of toxic discourse and incivility. I would argue that, if we can maintain that hope, that's not just survival—it's thriving. Heed the wise words of Maya Angelou: "Surviving is important. Thriving is elegant."

Even if you have narcissists in your life, it is my hope that you can start lifting your head, scanning the horizon, recognizing that you were strong for identifying these patterns, and finding ways to cope with them, all while recognizing that you are not defined by these toxic patterns and relationships. For years, your goals may have been vilified, your hopes trivialized, and your feelings denied. Growth means dusting off those goals, launching those hopes, and expressing those feelings. Growth means wresting away your reality from the distortions of the narcissist. Growth means taking risks, and not being afraid of the narcissist's mockery and contempt. You *can* stop listening to the words and voices of the narcissists around you, even if you cannot actually walk away from them. Growth means psychologically silencing the narcissists, the toxic people, the entitled, the uncivil, and the cruel. We may hear with our ears, but we listen with our souls. Listen to yours. The narcissists aren't going anywhere, but we cannot let them keep us down.

You have survived, but that's not the last stop on this odyssey. The real destination is self-realization, self-actualization, and growth. The choice to embark on the final leg of that journey lies with you.

New Beginnings

Time is your friend. So is forgiveness. This is *not* so for the narcissist—but it is for you. Understand why you made these choices, accept that you cannot control who your parents or family members are, and exercise your freedom to think differently about the situation. Take back your life. The narrative may have taken turns you didn't expect or understand. Amy Tan wrote: "That is the nature of endings, it seems. They never end. When all the missing pieces of your life are found, put together with glue of memory and reason, there are more pieces to be found."

You can walk away or distance yourself from these situations with compassion. Ultimately, that is the part of the story that many narcissists missed out on, and may have been what landed them in their emotionally impoverished spaces. To the degree you can, when you walk away from them, do so quietly, peacefully, and kindly. There is no place for deliberate cruelty in anyone's lives, no matter how badly we are hurt. There is no need to hurl insults, or even provide a laundry list of all of the pain you endured. Compassion does not mean sticking it out for more abuse, but rather to honor your authenticity, recognize their limitations, minimize the hurt, and silently, in your heart, hope they can find their way. Barbara

Kingsolver once wrote, "In a world as wrong as this one, all we can do is make things as right as we can." Don't throw hurt after hurt. Your self-preservation and compassion will heal you, and be one more piece of civility in a world that desperately needs it.

Walking away from a narcissist can overwhelm you with a complicated mix of grief and relief. Anytime we walk away from someone, grief is a normal reaction, and it can sometimes lead to self-doubt. When someone dies, that grief may be doubt about whether we said everything we wanted or regret about missed opportunities. When you walk away from narcissists, they are still alive, and the confusion rendered by grief can often propel you back to them. It is difficult to grieve the living. After the grief, if you give it a moment, comes the relief. For a long time, their angry and negating voices will remain in your head, but, over time, they will fade. The relief can come simultaneously quickly and slowly, and, one day, you exhale. One day, you begin to feel as though you are enough and worthy of love, respect, compassion, and kindness. The ultimate goal is to recognize that there is divinity within each of us, and there is also a vulnerable child. You may be full of self-loathing but protect that child and unleash that divinity. The painful life lessons garnered from these relationships can shape you and befuddle you but also can leave you stronger than you ever imagined—with so many more stories yet to come.

> *...Hope*
> *Smiles from the threshold of the year to come,*
> *Whispering 'It will be happier.'*

—TENNYSON

It is my sincerest wish that all those who have lost themselves in the chasm of narcissism no longer yoke their hope to their narcissistic or toxic relationship but to themselves. You are the one sure thing in your life. My sincerest wish is that hope does smile on you and whisper, then shout, "It will be happier."

Bibliography

Ackerman, R.A., Witt, E.A., Donnella, M.B., Trzesniewski, K.H., Robins, R.W., and Kashy, D.A. (2010). "What Does the Narcissistic Personality Inventory Really Measure?" *Assessment, 18* (1): 67–87.

Ainsworth, M.D.S., Blehar, M., Waters, E., and Wall, S. (1978). *Patterns of Attachment: A Psychological Study of the Strange Situation.* Hillsdale, NJ: Erlbaum.

American Psychiatric Association (2000). *Diagnostic and Statistical Manual of Mental Disorders IV.* American Psychiatric Publishing, Inc.

American Psychiatric Association (2013). *Diagnostic and Statistical Manual of Mental Disorders, fifth edition.* American Psychiatric Publishing, Inc.

American Psychological Association, Boys and Men Guidelines Group. (2018). *APA guidelines for psychological practice with boys and men.* Retrieved from http://www.apa.org/about/policy/psychological-practice-boys-men-guidelines.pdf

American Psychological Association (2017). Stress in America: 2016 Report.

Bandura, A. (1977). *Social learning theory.* Englewood Cliffs, NJ: Prentice Hall.

Bargh, J.A., ed. (2007). *Frontiers of Social Psychology. Social Psychology and the Unconscious: The Automaticity of Higher Mental Processes.* New York: Psychology Press, 173–217.

Baughman, H.M., Dearing, S., Giammarco, E., and Vernon, P.A. (2012). "Relationships between bullying behaviours and the Dark Triad: A study with adults." *Personality and Individual Differences 52* (2012): 571–575.

Baumeister, R.F. (1999). *Evil: Inside Human Violence and Cruelty.* Holt Books.

Baumeister, R.F., Heatherton, T.F., and Tice, D.M. (1993). "When ego threats lead to self-regulation failure: negative consequences of high self-esteem." *Journal of Personality and Social Psychology 64* (1): 141–156.

Baumeister, R. F., and Leary, M.R. (1995). "The need to belong: Desire for interpersonal attachments as a fundamental human motivation." *Psychological Bulletin 117* (3): 497–529.

Black, M.C., Basile, K.C., Breiding, M.J., Smith, S.G., Walters, M.L., Merrick, M.T., Chen, J., and Stevens, M.R. 2010 Summary Report. USDHHS Center for Injury Prevention.

Bowlby, J. (1988). *A Secure Base*. New York: Basic Books, 1988.

Bowlby, J. (1979). *The Making and Breaking of Affectional Bonds*. London: Tavistock.

Campbell, W.K., and Miller, J.D. (2013). "Narcissistic personality disorder and the five-factor model delineating narcissistic personality disorder, grandiose narcissism, and vulnerable narcissism." In Widiger, T, and Costa, P.T. (Eds). *Personality Disorders and the Five-Factor Model of Personality.* 3rd edition. Washington DC: American Psychological Association.

Carlson, S.M., Shoda, Y., Ayduk, O., Aber, J.L., Sethi, A., Wilson, N., Peake, P.K., and Mischel, W. (2018). "Cohort Effects in Children's Delay of Gratification." *Developmental Psychology.* 54 (8): 1395-1407.

Case, A., and Deaton, A. (2015). "Rising midlife morbidity and mortality, US whites." *Proceedings of the National Academy of Sciences* 112 (49): 15,078–15,083.

Center for American Progress (2018). "Gender Matters: Women Disproportionately Report Sexual Harassment in Male-Dominated Industries." (Article posted August 6, 2018)

Cheek, J.M., Hendin, H.M., and Wink, P.M. (2013). "An expanded version of the hypersensitive narcissism scale (The maladaptive covert narcissism scale)." Paper presented at the Association for Research in Personality, Charlotte, NC.

Chetty, R., Grusky, D., Hell, M., Hendren, N., & Narang, J. (2017).

"The Fading American Dream: Trends in Absolute Income Mobility Since 1940," *Science,* 356(6336): 398-406.

Cleckley, H.M. (1941). *The Mask of Sanity: An Attempt to Reinterpret the So-called Psychopathic Personality*. St. Louis: The C.V. Mosby Company.

Cooper, A.M., and Ronningstam, E. (1992). "Narcissistic personality disorder." *Review of Psychiatry* 11, 80–97.

Cross, E. J., Overall, N. C., Low, R. S. T., & McNulty, J. K. (2018). "An interdependence account of sexism and power: Men's hostile sexism, biased perceptions of low power, and relationship aggression." *Journal of Personality and Social Psychology.* https://doi-org.mimas.calstatela.edu/10.1037/pspi0000167 .supp (Supplemental).

De Veirman, M., Hudders, L., and Cauberghe, V. (2017). "Effect of exposure to peers' luxuriously looking Instagram accounts on state self-esteem." Presented at the European Happiness Days—Happiness Economics Conference.

Bibliography

Demsky, C.A., Fritz, C., Hammer, L.B., and Black, A.B. (2018). "Workplace Incivility and Employee Sleep: The Role of Rumination and Recovery Experiences." *Journal of Occupational Health Psychology.* 19 (2): 195-205.

Department of Health and Human Services (2017). "Mortality in the United States." 2016 NCHS Data Brief No. 293.

Dhawan, N., Kunik, M.E., Oldham, J., and Coverdale, J. (2010) "Prevalence and treatment of narcissistic personality disorder in the community: A systematic review." *Comprehensive Psychiatry* 51 (4): 333–339.

Dimaggio, G. and Attinà, G. (2012). "Metacognitive Interpersonal Therapy for Narcissistic Personality Disorder and Associated Perfectionism." *Journal of Clinical Psychology* 68 (8), 922-934.

Dinwiddie, S. (2015). "Psychopathy versus sociopathy." *Psychiatric Annals* 45 (4): 165–166.

Dowgwillo, E.A., Pincus, A.L., and Lenzenweger, M.F. (2019). "A parallel process latent growth model of narcissistic personality disorder symptoms and normal personality traits." *Personality Disorders: Theory, Research, and Treatment* 10 (3), 257-266.

Durvasula, R.S. (2015). *Should I Stay or Should I Go: Surviving a Relationship with a Narcissist.* Post Hill Press.

Dutton, K. (2013). *The Wisdom of Psychopaths: What Saints, Spies, and Serial Killers Can Teach Us About Success.* Farrar, Straus and Giroux.

Dvorak, P. (July 2, 2018). "Tormented and traumatized: Rage toward women fuels women mass shooters." *The Washington Post.*

Enright, R.D. and Fitzgibbons, R.P. (2015). *Forgiveness therapy: An empirical guide for resolving anger and restoring hope.* Washington, DC: American Psychological Association.

Fanti, K.A., Demetriou, A.G., and Hawa, V.V. (2012). "A longitudinal study of cyberbullying: Examining risk and protective factors." *European Journal of Developmental Psychology* 9 (2): 168–181.

Frances, A. (2017). *Twilight of American Sanity: A Psychiatrist Analyzes the Age of Trump.* William Morrow and Sons.

Freud, S. (1914). *On Narcissism: An Introduction,* standard edition.

Fromm, E. (1964). *The Heart of Man.* Lantern Books.

Gallup-Sharecare Well Being Index (2018).

Gebauer, J.E., Sedikides, C., Verplanken, B., and Maio, G.R. (2012). "Communal narcissism." *Journal of Personality and Social Psychology* 103 (5): 854–878.

Greenwood, D., Long, C.R., and Dal Cin, S. (2013). "Fame and the social self: The need to belong, narcissism and relatedness predict the appeal of fame." *Personality and Individual Differences* 55 (5): 490-495.

Haidt, J. (2006). *The Happiness Hypothesis: Finding Modern Truth in Ancient Wisdom*. Basic Books.

Hampton, K.N., Goulet, L.S., Rainie, L., and Purcell, K. (2011). "Social networking sites and our lives: How people's trust, personal relationships, and civic and political involvement are connected to their use of social networking sites and other technologies." Internet and American Life Project, Pew Research Center.

Hare, R., and Babiak, P. (2006). *Snakes in Suits*. New York: Harper Collins.

Hazan, C., and Shaver, P. (1987). "Romantic love conceptualized as an attachment process." *Journal of Personality and Social Psychology* 52 (3): 511–524.

Hendin, H., and Cheek, J. (1997). "Assessing hypersensitive narcissism: A re-examination of Murray's Narcissism Scale." *Journal of Research in Personality* 31: 588–599.

Hickman, S., Watson, P., and Morris, R. (1996). "Optimism, pessimism, and the complexity of narcissism." *Personality and Individual Differences* 20: 521–525.

Holt-Lunstad, J., Smith, T.B., and Layton, J.B. (2010). "Social Relationships and Mortality Risk: A Meta-analytic Review." *PLOS Medicine* 7 (7).

Holtzman, N.S., Vazire, S., and Mehl, M.R. (2010). "Sounds like a Narcissist: Behavioral Manifestations of Narcissism in Everyday Life." *Journal of Research in Personality* 44 (4): 478–484.

House J.S., Landis, K.R., and Umberson, D. (1988). "Social relationships and health." *Science* 241: 540–545.

Institute for Policy Studies (2017). "Billionaire Bonanza: The Forbes 400 and the Rest of Us."

International Labor Organization (2017). *Global Estimates of Modern Slavery: Forced Labour and Forced Marriage.*

Jauk, E., Weigle, E., Lehmann, K., Benedek, M., and Neubauer, A.C. (2017). "The Relationship between Grandiose and Vulnerable (Hypersensitive) Narcissism." *Frontiers in Psychology* 8: 1,600.

Jordan, J.J., Sommers, R., Bloom, P., and Rand, D.G. (2017). "Why do we hate hypocrites? Evidence for a Theory of False Signaling." *Psychological Science* 28 (3): 356–368.

Judge, T.A., Livingston, B.A., and Hurst, C. (2011). "Do nice guys—and gals—really finish last? The joint effects of sex and agreeableness on income." *Journal of Personality and Social Psychology* 102 (2): 390–407.

Kahneman, D. and Deaton, A. (2010). "High income improves evaluation of life but not emotional well-being." *Proceedings of the National Academy of Sciences* 107 (38): 16,489–16,493.

Kasser, T. and Ryan, R. (1996). "Further Examining the American Dream: Differential Correlates of Intrinsic and Extrinsic Goals." *Personality and Social Psychology Bulletin* 22 (3): 280–287.

Keltner, D. (October 2016). "Don't let power corrupt you." *Harvard Business Review.*

Keltner, D. (2016). *The Power Paradox: How we gain and lose influence.* Penguin.

Keltner, D., Gruenfeld, D.H., and Anderson, C. (2000). "Power, approach, and inhibition." Research Paper Series, Stanford University School of Business.

Kernberg, O.F. (1985). *Borderline Conditions and Pathological Narcissism.* Rowman and Littlefield.

Kernberg, O.F. (1993). *Severe Personality Disorders: Psychotherapeutic Strategies.* Yale University Press.

Kiecolt-Glaser, J. (2018). "Marriage, divorce and the immune system." *American Psychologist* 73 (9): 1,098–1,108.

Kim, J.W. and Chock, T. (2016). "Personality Traits and Psychological Motivations Predicting Selfie Posting Behaviors on Social Networking Sites." *Telematics and Informatics* 34 (5): 560-571.

Kohut, H. (1971). *The Analysis of the Self: A Systematic Approach to the Psychoanalytic Treatment of Narcissistic Personality Disorders.* University of Chicago Press.

Kunstman, J.W. and Maner, J.K. (2011). "Sexual overperception: power, mating motives, and biases in social judgment." *Journal of Personality and Social Psychology* 100 (2): 282–294.

Lasch, C. (1978). *The Culture of Narcissism: American Life in an Age of Diminishing Expectations.* New York: W.W. Norton and Co.

Liao, Z., Yam, K.C., Johnson, R.E, Liu, W., and Song, Z. (2018). "Cleansing My Abuse: A Reparative Response Model of Perpetrating Abusive Supervisor Behavior." *Journal of Applied Psychology* 103 (9): 1039-1056.

Linehan, M.M. (1993). *Cognitive-Behavioral Therapy of Borderline Personality Disorder.* Guilford Press.

Lipman-Blumen, J. (2006). *The Allure of Toxic Leaders.* Oxford University Press.

357

Lowen, A. (2004). *Narcissism: Denial of the True Self.* Simon and Schuster.

MacArthur Foundation Reports on Digital Media and Learning (2008). "Living and Learning With New Media: Summary of Findings from the Digital Youth Project."

Maslow, A.H. (1943). "A theory of human motivation." *Psychological Review 50* (4), 370–396.

McConnell, A.R., and Brown, C. M. (2010). "Dissonance averted: Self- concept organization moderates the effect of hypocrisy on attitude change." *Journal of Experimental Social Psychology* 46 (2): 361–366.

McLelland, D.C. (1987). *Human Motivation.* Cambridge University Press.

Mental Health America (2018). "The State of Mental Health in America."

Michl, P., Meindl, T., Meister, F., Born, C., Engel, R.R., Reiser, M. and Henning-Fast, K. (2014). "Neurobiological underpinnings of shame and guilt: a pilot fMRI study." *Social Cognition and Affective Neuroscience* 9 (2): 150–157.

Miller, J.D. and Maples, J.L. et al. (2015). "Narcissism and United States' culture: The view from home and around the world." *Personality Processes and Individual Differences* 109 (6), 1068-1089.

Millon, T. and Davis, R. (2011). *Disorders of Personality: Introducing a DSM/ICD Spectrum from Normal to Abnormal,* third ed. Wiley.

Lazarus, D. (August 25, 2017). "Mnuchin's wife isn't the only one defining herself through the brands she posts." *Los Angeles Times* (August 25, 2017).

McCrae, R.R., and John, O.P. (1992). "An introduction to the five-factor model and its applications." *Journal of Personality* 60 (2): 175-215.

Murthy, V. (September, 2017). "Work and the loneliness epidemic: Reducing isolation at work is good for business." *Harvard Business Review.*

Paulhus, D.L. (2001). "Normal narcissism: Two minimalist accounts." *Psychological Inquiry.* 12, 228-229.

Paulhus, D.L. and Williams, K. (2002). "The Dark Triad of Personality: Narcissism, Machiavellianism and Psychopathy." *Journal of Research in Personality* 36 (6): 556–563.

Pemment, J. (2013). "Psychopathy versus sociopathy: Why the distinction has become crucial." *Aggression and Violent Behavior* 18 (5): 458-461.

Perissinotto, C.M., Stijacic, C.I., Covinsky, K.E. (1993). "Loneliness in older persons: A predictor of functional decline and death." *Archives of Internal Medicine* 172 (14): 1,078–1,083.

Bibliography

Pieters, R. (2013). "Bidirectional Dynamics of Materialism and Loneliness: Not Just a Vicious Cycle." *Journal of Consumer Research* 40 (4): 615–631.

Piff, P.K., Kraus, M.W., Côté, S., Cheng, B.H., and Keltner, D. (2010). "Having less, giving more: The influence of social class on prosocial behavior." *Interpersonal Relationships and Group Processes* 99 (5): 771–784.

Piff, P.K. and Moskowitz, J.P. (2018). "Wealth, poverty, and happiness: Social class is differentially associated with positive emotions." *Emotion* 18 (6): 902–905.

Piff, P.K., Stancato, D.M., Côté, S., Mendoza-Denton, R., and Keltner, D. (2012). "Higher social class predicts increased unethical behavior." *Proceedings of the National Academy of Sciences* 109 (11): 4,086–4,091.

Pryor, J.B. (1987). "Sexual harassment proclivities in men." *Sex Roles* 17 (5–6): 269–290.

Qiu, T., Qualls, W., Bohlmann, J. and Rupp, D. E. (2009), "The Effect of Interactional Fairness on the Performance of Cross-Functional Product Development Teams: A Multilevel Mediated Model." *Journal of Product Innovation Management*, 26: 173-187. doi:10.1111/j.1540-5885.2009.00344.x.

Raskin, R.N., and Hall, C.S. (1979). "A Narcissistic Personality Inventory." *Psychological Reports* 45 (2): 590.

Raskin, R.N. and Terry, H. (1988). "A principal components analysis of the Narcissistic Personality Inventory and further evidence of its construct validity." *Journal of Personality and Social Psychology* 54 (5): 890–902.

Rideout, V., Foehr, U., and Roberts, D. (2010). "Generation M2: Media in the lives of 8- to 18-year-olds." Kaiser Family Foundation Study. http://www.kff.org/entmedia/8010.cfm.

Roberts, B.W., Edmonts, G., and Grijalva, E. (2010). "It Is Developmental Me, Not Generation Me: Developmental Changes Are More Important Than Generational Changes in Narcissism—Commentary on Trzesniewski and Donnellan." *Perspectives in Psychological Science* 5 (1), 97–102.

Rogers, C. (1995). *On Becoming a Person: A Therapist's View of Psychotherapy.* Houghton, Mifflin, Harcourt.

Rogoza, R. and Fatfouta, R. (2018). "Normal and pathological communal narcissism, in relation to personality traits and values." *Personality and Individual Differences* 138. https://doi.org/10.1016/j.paid.2018.03.039.

Ross, H.G. and Milgram, J.I. (1982). "Important variable in adult sibling relationships: A qualitative study." In Lamb, M.E. and Sutton-Smith, B., eds. *Sibling Relationships: Their Nature and Significance Across the Lifespan,* 225–349. New Jersey: Erlbaum.

Sapolsky, R. *Behave: The Biology of Humans at Our Best and Worst*. New York: Penguin Books.

Schriber, R.A., Chung, J.M., Sorenson, K.S., and Robins, R. (2016). "Dispositional Contempt: A First Look at the Contemptuous Person." *Journal of Personality and Social Psychology* 113 (2). 280-309.

Sherman, R. (2017). *Uneasy Street: The Anxieties of Affluence*. Princeton University Press.

Skinner BF. *About Behaviorism*. New York: Alfred A Knopf; 1974.

Smiler, A. (2012). *Challenging Casanova*. Jossey Bass.

Smith, A., & In Cannan, E. (1922). *An inquiry into the nature and causes of the wealth of nations*. London: Methuen.

Smith, T.W. and Baucom, B.R.W. (2017). "Intimate relationships, individual adjustment, and coronary heart disease: Implications of overlapping associations in psychosocial risk." *American Psychologist* 72 (6): 578–589.

Spengler, M., Brunner, M., Damian, R.I., Ludtke, O., Martin, R., and Roberts, B.W. (2015). "Student characteristics and behaviors at age 12 predict occupational success 40 years later over and above childhood IQ and parental socioeconomic status." *Journal of Personality and Social Psychology* 51 (9): 1,329–1,340.

Stanton, S.C.E., Selcuk, E., Farrell, A.K., Slatcher, R.B., & Ong, A. (2019). "Perceived partner responsiveness, daily negative affect reactivity, and all-cause mortality: A 20-year longitudinal study." *Psychosomatic Medicine*. 81, 7-15.

Stein, J. (May 2013). "The 'Me' Generation." *Time*.

Stinson, F.S., Dawson, D.A., Goldstein, R.B., Chou, S.P., Huang, B., Smith, S.M., Ruan, W.J., Pulay, A.J., Saha, T.D., Pickering, R.P., and Grant, B.F. (2008). "Prevalence, correlates, disability, and comorbidity of DSM-IV narcissistic personality disorder: results from the wave 2 national epidemiologic survey on alcohol and related conditions." *The Journal of Clinical Psychiatry* 69 (7): 1033–1045.

Stone DM, Simon TR, Fowler KA, Kegler, S.R, Yuan, K., Holland, K.M., Ivey-Stephenson, A.Z., & Crosby, A.E. (2018). "Vital Signs: Trends in State Suicide Rates—United States, 1999–2016 and Circumstances Contributing to Suicide—27 States, 2015." *MMWR Morbidity and Mortality Weekly Report*. 67:617–624.

Stout, M. (2006). *The Sociopath Next Door*. Harmony Books.

Thorndike, E. L. (1927). "The law of effect." *The American Journal of Psychology*, 39, 212–222.

Toussaint, L.L., Worthington, E.L., and Williams, D.R., eds. (2015). *Forgiveness and Health: Scientific Evidence and Theories Relating Forgiveness to Better Health.* Springer.

Vater, A., Ritter, K., Strunz, S., Ronningstam, E.F., Renneberg, B., and Roepke, S. (2014). "Stability of narcissistic personality disorder: Tracking categorical and dimensional rating systems over a two-year period." *Personality Disorders* 5 (3): 305–313.

Vergauwe, J., Wille, B., Hofmans, J., Kaiser, R.B., and De Fruyt, F.D. (2018). "The Double-Edged Sword of Leader Charisma: Understanding the Curvilinear Relationship Between Charismatic Personality and Leader Effectiveness." *Journal of Personality and Social Psychology* 114 (1): 110–130.

Vogel, E.A., Rose, J.P., Roberts, LR., and Eckles, K. (2014). "Social comparison, social media, and self-esteem." *Psychology of Popular Media Culture* 3 (4): 206–222.

Wilkinson, R.G., & Pickett, K. (2019). *The Inner Level: How More Equal Societies Reduce Stress, Restore Sanity and Improve Everyone's Well-Being.* New York: Penguin.

World Health Organization (1992). *The ICD-10 Classification of Mental and Behavioural Disorders: Clinical Descriptions and Diagnostic Guidelines.* Geneva: World Health Organization.

Yoffe, E. (October 2017). "Well, Excuuuuuse Meee!: Why humans are so quick to take offense, and what that means for the presidential campaign." *Slate.* https://slate.com/technology/2008/10/why-humans-are-so-quick-to-take-offense-and-what-that-means-for-the-presidential-campaign.html.

Acknowledgments

Books are group ventures, even when there is only one author's name on the cover. I feel fortunate that there is a long list of people to thank and recognize. As always, thank you to my publisher, Post Hill Press, and Anthony Ziccardi, who remained mindful of some of the backdrop to my life as I wrote this book and was far more patient than the average publisher would be. Thank you, Anthony, for your solicitude as the book unfolded. My gratitude to everyone at Post Hill Press, particularly Maddie Sturgeon and Seane Thomas, for ten revisions of the cover, patience with edits, and the back and forth-ing that gives birth to a book. As always, to Lara Asher, editor, lady of letters, and friend extraordinaire, thanks for seeing the story in the thickets of my words and with exquisite patience making them louder and stronger.

To all my clients who entrust me with their stories, thank you. I recognize the strength it takes to render yourself vulnerable to another human being—and you are willing to go there. To people who shared their stories and experiences to be included in this book, thank you for your willingness to pay it forward through the lessons you have learned. To every person who has endured abusive relationships, I hope to fight for you throughout my career, and I commend your bravery. We can all work together to shift the paradigm from victim to survivor and ultimately to thriver....

Kelly Ebeling, this book literally would not have been possible without you. You went above and beyond the call of duty and redefined "grit" and commitment. Thank you for being a sounding board, a jack-of-all-trades, a human hard drive and filing cabinet, and dynamic in every way—this project would have gone upside down without you. To Irene Hernandez, your social media prowess and natural curiosity and devotion to mental health awareness are the only reasons anyone is ever going to know about this book. On days I want to quit, your strength of character is a beacon to me. To my other graduate and undergraduate students—your graciousness with my delays on your thesis projects has not gone unnoticed, but I see that you are more independent researchers now, and I am proud to mentor you!

Dr. Pamela Harmell, behind every good shrink is a better shrink. You skirted that clinically elegant line of keeping me real while keeping it real. Thank you for shepherding me through the minefields of my inner world.

To the University of Johannesburg and particularly Dr. Jace Pillay, thank you for welcoming me into your midst, and hopefully we can discuss these issues more fully throughout South Africa. To my colleagues at the American Psychological Association, the APA Minority Fellowship Program, the Women's Programs Office, the Office on Socioeconomic Status, and my other academic colleagues around the country, particularly Keyona King-Tsikata, Shari Miles-Cohen, and Andrew Austin-Dailey (and everyone from the MFP advisory board), thank you for encouraging me and giving voice to my work—I would have never pushed myself without your encouragement. To the Leadership Institute for Women in Psychology of the APA, thank you for making me say out loud 11 years ago that I would write a book, and for supporting me as I reached my third. Thank you to the National Institutes of Health for funding my research on personality disorders, and to Dr. Perry Halkitis for my opportunities as a consulting editor for the journal Behavioral Medicine. Dr. Tim Kasser, thanks for the gift of your time and for jumping on the phone with me and further illuminating your work on materialism and consumerism—your work is an inspiration!

Bill Costanzo and Silvia Saige, and Frank Prather, thanks for sitting in dusty bail-bonds offices and basements, talking about relationships and developing *Sexual Disorientation.* Those recording sessions are some of the most engaging moments of my week (and people around Los Angeles now think I am running afoul of the law on a weekly basis). To everyone at MedCircle who brought a huge audience to this work on narcissism, especially Kyle, Brigid, and Doug, thank you for working tirelessly to push back on the stigma of mental illness, while still having the difficult conversations. To my colleagues at TONE Networks who have been empowering women and providing a platform for women to better understand these themes in their relationships—Gemma, Paula, Val, and Sheri—thanks for the constant reminder of the power of the sisterhood. To the ladies of Campowerment, you allowed this work to have a voice before anyone else. Thank you for reminding women of their strength. To Rob Portil and his team at TEDx Sedona, thank you for giving me a platform for delivering a TEDx talk that is in essence a summary of this work. To Debra Newell, I am grateful for our time together to better understand the back story of your story, and to Kathleen Shelton for bringing us together.

I am grateful to have been a faculty member at California State University, Los Angeles for the past twenty years. My students and classrooms have often been a place where some of the purest insights have been realized based on their questions and their willingness to share their stories. A special thank-you to Drs. Pamela Regan, Diane Lewis, and Olajide Bamishigbin for your gentle smiling faces when I needed to be reminded that my old bones would endure the long days of academia.

To my friends all over the country who manage to stay in touch, even though I take your calls only on the freeway—thanks for asking me about my next flight of fancy and sharing the journeys of motherhood and life (yes—that's you—Jill, Mona, Lisa, Christine, Kara, Eric M., Eric B., Kathianne, Hitomi, Kieran, Jenifer, Emily, Stephanie). I love all of you dearly. To Manju Reddy, you have been a mentor and a friend—our work in India remains a beacon of hope to me. Dr. Kaveri Subrahmanyam, thanks for being a patient and wise coteacher in India and Los Angeles. Sabena Sarma, you truly taught me the art of the deal. I got one house and a lifelong friend. Thank you for making a long-held dream come true and closing two escrows while I finished a book.

Ellen Rakieten, I probably learned more about these issues from talking with you on a variety of balconies around Los Angeles than from any of my research. Perhaps walking through the fires together was all the lesson either of us needed. I adore you and I can't imagine getting through the days without you. Anytime I wanted to hang up my penchant for love, you knocked me in the head and reminded me that not everyone is unkind. And yes, it is cold in the winter.

Charlie, you are a coparent extraordinaire, a dear friend, a true Renaissance man, and a father who reminded our girls to be simultaneously strong and kind. You keep me honest as a mother, scholar, and clinician. I am glad the kids got your humor and my erudition—the other way would not have been as fun.

To John and Elizabeth Wearn. Thank you for your son; he is an angel. Elizabeth, the six days I got with you are a gift that I treasure. John, your cheeky smile and loving heart in the midst of loss remind me to do the same.

Mom, there are no words. You tacitly taught me through my lifetime what I ended up writing about: strength, grace, resilience, and always about mothering. Dad, thanks for asking about the books, even though I know they are not quite your style. It took me a while, but I think you are proud.

And, to the myriad generations of women in my family who went before me and did not have my opportunities, every time I get to enact a dream, I invoke your name.

To my sister, Padma, my only hero, I live in awe of you most days and, on the other days, you just make me laugh. You allow me to be a humorist more than a cynic in my writing. Your son, Tanner, represents all that is good in the world, and, Joe, you are a reminder that men can be simultaneously strong and vulnerable.

Richard, you were the final chapter that tamed the cynic in me. Just when I was going to give up, you showed up. You trail light into a room. You remind me of the myriad ways that love can heal and that there can be second acts, and, through your patient love, every hurt disappeared. Thank you for telling me to write, for making sure I ate, for embracing my writing weekends, for reminding me to write just another page on the days I wanted to quit, for subsisting on cereal and austerity during the lean months, for enduring my long absences, and for agreeing to grow a life with me. I love you.

Always, to my daughters. Maya, as the book finished, you moved 5,000 miles and eight time zones away. I didn't understand courage until you did that. I hope that someday you are able to see the brave and brilliant soul that you are. Shanti, you are a galaxy unto yourself—an artist, a poet, a songbird, and a sweet spirit who believes people are good. You are my monument to hope. The two of you put up with an empty refrigerator, too much takeout, a noisy apartment, and my five a.m. writing sessions. Please always pursue your dreams, no matter how messy and inconvenient they are. When you do fall in love, do it from a place of courage and not fear. I can only promise you forever a soft place to land. Being your mother is the greatest gift and treasure I could know. I love you.

About the Author

Dr. Ramani S. Durvasula (Dr. Ramani) is a licensed clinical psychologist in private practice in Santa Monica and Sherman Oaks, California, and professor of psychology at California State University, Los Angeles, where she was named Outstanding Professor in 2012. She is also a visiting professor at the University of Johannesburg.

She is the author of the modern relationship survival manual *Should I Stay or Should I Go? Surviving a Relationship with a Narcissist.* She is also the author of *You Are WHY You Eat: Change Your Food Attitude, Change Your Life,* as well as of numerous peer-reviewed journal articles, book chapters, and conference papers.

After receiving her B.S. in psychology from the University of Connecticut, she went on to complete her M.A. and Ph.D. degrees in clinical psychology from UCLA. She completed her clinical training at the UCLA Neuropsychiatric Institute (Semel Institute).

Dr. Ramani has been featured on series on Oxygen, Bravo, the Lifetime Movie Network, National Geographic, the History Channel, Discovery Science, and Investigation Discovery, as well as in documentary films on health. She has been an expert commentator on nearly every major television network, as well as on radio, in print, and in internet media. She has been an invited speaker at SxSW and at TEDx and is a featured expert for MedCircle and TONE Networks.

She is also involved in national governance in the field of psychology and has served as the chair of the Committee on Socioeconomic Status at the American Psychological Association and the Committee on Psychology and AIDS, as well as vice chair of the Committee on Women and Psychology, and she is presently chair of the STAY training advisory committee of the Minority Fellowship Program of the American Psychological Association. She is also an Associate Editor of the journal *Behavioral Medicine*.

Dr. Ramani recognizes that the normalization of narcissism has changed the landscape of love, relationships, family, career, education, and society, and provides keen insights on how to survive in the climate of narcissism, entitlement, interpersonal toxicity, and incivility. As a South Asian woman and daughter of immigrants, she also brings a nuanced understanding of issues around immigration, assimilation, cultural tugs-of-war, and the role of cultural expectations on our experiences of mental health and mental illness. Dr. Ramani brings a unique expertise and an authentic voice as a professor, clinician, researcher, author, media commentator, and mother of two daughters. She lives in Los Angeles, California.